PREPARING A NATION?

THE NEW DEAL IN THE VILLAGES OF PAPUA NEW GUINEA

BRAD UNDERHILL

ANU PRESS

PACIFIC SERIES

ANU PRESS

Published by ANU Press
The Australian National University
Canberra ACT 2600, Australia
Email: anupress@anu.edu.au

Available to download for free at press.anu.edu.au

ISBN (print): 9781760466619
ISBN (online): 9781760466626

WorldCat (print): 1451077786
WorldCat (online): 1451078087

DOI: 10.22459/PN.2024

This title is published under a Creative Commons Attribution-NonCommercial-NoDerivatives 4.0 International (CC BY-NC-ND 4.0) licence.

The full licence terms are available at creativecommons.org/licenses/by-nc-nd/4.0/legalcode

Cover design and layout by ANU Press. Cover photograph: 'Weighing and selling copra, 1948', NAA, A1200, L9904, item 11861723.

This book is published under the aegis of the Pacific editorial board of ANU Press.

This edition © 2024 ANU Press

Contents

List of Figures	vii
List of Tables	ix
List of Maps	xi
Acknowledgements	xiii
Acronyms	xv
Preface	xvii
Introduction	1

Part One: Australian Postwar Ambition for the Territory of Papua New Guinea

1. The Impetus for the 'New Deal for Papua New Guinea': Australia's Response to a Unique Postwar Colonial Circumstance	31
2. Provisional Administration: 'We Stopped Them Putting the Clock Back'	53
3. Administering the 'New Deal' from the Extreme Centre	81
4. The Australian Objective: Understanding the Hasluck Development Pyramid	101

Part Two: Indigenous Influence: Local Conditions and Autonomous Actions

CASE STUDY: CHIMBU

5. Chimbu: Australia's New Deal Problem?	133
6. Highland Labour Scheme: Indigenous Opportunity or Government Solution?	155

CASE STUDY: MILNE BAY
7. Milne Bay: The Emergence of Indigenous Autonomy   175
8. Indigenous Advancement: Only on the Colonialist's Terms   193

CASE STUDY: MAPRIK
9. Sepik: 'If You See a European, Don't Call Him Masta'   215
10. Village Rice Development: Co-opting Indigenous Enterprise 233

CASE STUDY: NEW HANOVER
11. New Hanover: Colonial Control and Indigenous
    Sociopolitical Agency   257
12. Cooperatives and the Hasluck Pyramid at Work in the
    Villages of New Hanover   277

CONCLUSION
13. The 'New Deal' Assessed: Just Rhetoric or the Basis
    for Independence?   307
Bibliography   321

List of Figures

Figure 0.1: Sir Paul Hasluck, Minister of Territories, 1951–63.   4

Figure 1.1: Minister for External Territories Edward John Ward.   33

Figure 1.2: John Curtin and Mrs Elsie Curtin with General Sir Thomas Blamey in 1944.   45

Figure 2.1: Colonel JK Murray.   59

Figure 2.2: Paul Hasluck attending a meeting of the Hanuabada Local Government Council, Port Moresby.   75

Figure 3.1: Commonwealth Bank in Papua New Guinea, Minister for Territories, Paul Hasluck on an official party visit to a village in the Highlands, 1955.   82

Figure 3.2: Percy Spender, New External Territories Minister, December 1949.   84

Figure 3.3: Paul Hasluck at a village in the Highlands in 1955.   88

Figure 3.4: Rachel and Donald Cleland (right and second right) with Governor-General William Slim in 1959.   91

Figure 3.5: The administrator, Donald Cleland, breakfasting outside house 'Kiap' Fatmilak, New Ireland, in 1954.   92

Figure 3.6: Territories Department, 1952.   96

Figure 4.1: Paul Hasluck on an official 1955 visit to the Territory Administration, Port Moresby.   102

Figure 4.2: Hasluck Development Pyramid.   108

Figure 4.3: On 7 April 1961, Paul Hasluck opened the Madang General Hospital. The guard of honour was made up of hospital orderlies and infant child and maternal health nurses.   112

Figure 4.4: An example of the harsh environment patrol officers dealt with in the early postwar period of 'pacification'.   114

Figure 4.5: Teacher trainees assembled on the playing field of Popondetta, Educational Centre, 1955.   118

Figure 4.6: Paul Hasluck at the official opening of the Legislative Council in November 1951. 123

Figure 5.1: Women bringing food to the Chimbu Police Post in the early days of its establishment in 1937. The post can be seen in the background. 138

Figure 5.2: Villagers in Goroka deriving a cash income from their natural timber stands. 145

Figure 7.1: The District Office at Samarai in 1958, the administrative headquarters for the Milne Bay district, Papua and New Guinea. 179

Figure 7.2: According to the caption (1950), 'at Kwato Mission, the girls are taught dress-making and laundering'. 183

Figure 7.3: Interior of the joinery works and factory of the Milne Bay Development Company, 1952. 185

Figure 8.1: Caption reads as follows (1952): 'Village election, one of the Wagawaga headman strikes a triangle to indicate that the poll is open'. 198

Figure 8.2: Alice Wedega talking with girl guides in 1958. 208

Figure 9.1: Mahuru Rarua-Rarua in 1959 addressing the Papua and New Guinea Legislative Council. 221

Figure 10.1: Clearing land for dry rice in 1952 in the Sepik District. 235

Figure 11.1: Sister Clematia and Mr McGuigan watching the unloading of a barge in 1947 on New Hanover. 261

Figure 11.2: Anelaua Leprosarium staff, including priest, European sisters, New Guinean sisters and lay brother, 1947. 262

Figure 11.3: Taskul station seen from the Officer's house in 1947. 263

Figure 11.4: Weighing and selling copra, 1948. 272

Figure 12.1: Husking coconuts for copra. 280

Figure 12.2: CJ Miller, Registrar of Co-operative Societies, Territory of Papua New Guinea (TPNG), speaking at the 1951 Congress of Queensland Co-operatives. 282

Figure 12.3: United Nations Mission members with Mr Henry Ramon, Secretary of the New Ireland Native Societies Association, at the cooperative headquarters in Kavieng, 1959. 292

List of Tables

Table 2.1: Australian grants (for the year ending 30 June). 57
Table 2.2: The effect of the war on public servants, 19 June 1945. 60
Table 2.3: Selection criteria for attachment to Colonial Office. 65
Table 2.4: Cooperatives: Primary organisations (year ending 31 March). 69
Table 2.5: Establishment of local government councils, 1950–54. 78
Table 2.6: Expansion of local government councils, 1951–63. 78
Table 3.1: Australian grants (for the year ending 30 June). 95
Table 3.2: Public service, Auxiliary Division and administrative patrols. 98
Table 4.1: Public service, 1961–64. 111
Table 4.2: Extension of government influence. 113
Table 4.3: Agricultural extension officers. 117
Table 5.1: Northern Chimbu: Population land density. 141
Table 5.2: Administration control or influence in the Central Highlands, 1949–54. 146
Table 5.3: Age group and marital status. 150
Table 5.4: Number of workers employed in the Highlands, 1951–52. 151
Table 5.5: 1957 absentee labour statistics, Central Census Division. 152
Table 8.1: 1952 Ealeba Council budget. 202
Table 8.2: 1956 Ealeba Council budget. 204
Table 9.1: 1957 Sepik rural progress societies. 224
Table 10.1: 1952 milling unit. 238
Table 10.2: Agricultural extension officers, Maprik subdistrict, 1950–63. 241
Table 10.3: 1958 Maprik subdistrict rural progress societies. 244
Table 10.4: Supari RPS peanut production. 247
Table 10.5: Albiges coffee tree planting. 248

Table 10.6: Yield per acre. 250
Table 11.1: Price of copra: Papua–New Guinea, 1925–48. 273
Table 12.1: New Ireland cooperative societies, 1955–61. 285
Table 12.2: 1960 New Hanover cooperative societies. 286
Table 12.3: World copra price (Pacific Coast), 1948–59. 286
Table 12.4: New Ireland District copra rejection rates, October 1954–57. 291
Table 12.5: Whole-of-government effort on New Hanover, 1958. 293
Table 12.6: Percentage of cooperative staff positions filled, 1955–61. 294
Table 12.7: Cooperative staff, 1955–61. 295
Table 12.8: New Ireland District extension staff: 1954–58. 295
Table 12.9: 1959 estimated religious breakdown of New Hanover population. 297
Table 12.10: Inland vs coastal income, Lavongai census division, 1961. 301
Table 12.11: 1961 Lavongai census division. 302
Table 13.1: Comparison of postwar development: 1946/47–1963/64. 312
Table 13.2: Comparison of education facilities for the year 1963. 314
Table 13.3: Comparative change in public health facilities, 1947–63. 315

List of Maps

Map 0.1: Map of Papua New Guinea highlighting the four regions studied.	9
Map 2.1: Papua New Guinea, Territory of Papua and New Guinea, 1949.	54
Map 5.1: Chimbu Province.	134
Map 7.1: Milne Bay.	175
Map 8.1: Milne Bay.	194
Map 9.1: East Sepik Province.	216
Map 9.2: Detailed map of East Sepik province.	227
Map 11.1: The Bismarck Archipelago.	258

Acknowledgements

The bulk of this thesis was written on the lands of the Wurundjeri people of the Kulin Nation. I pay my respects to their elders, past and present. Sovereignty was never ceded.

I have been most fortunate to have a long and close relationship with the Centre for Contemporary History at Deakin University as a student, teacher and research assistant. I have found all the historians at the centre supportive, friendly, interested and generous with their time. Their generous collegiality has been a wonderful representation of the possibilities of a supportive academic community. I would like to express my sincerest gratitude to Helen Gardner who has been my guide and role model throughout both my undergraduate and postgraduate studies. I have had the great pleasure of recently working on several research projects with her. Helen was the unit chair and lecturer in my first unit (AIH108—ironically, a unit I now teach) when I returned to study as a mature-aged student in 2013. I was nervous and felt completely out of place when I began my studies, but Helen immediately engaged my curiosity and opened my eyes to new ideas and concepts. Midway through this first trimester I saw Helen in an intense discussion with a student in a café on campus, clearly, they were both focused on some scholarly issue, and Helen had the full attention of the student. I envied this student and was determined to one day work closely with an academic such as Helen. These last six years have not disappointed! Helen, you are a compassionate and wise supervisor, but more importantly, you are a wonderful person. Thank you.

Likewise, Chris Waters has provided endless guidance, support, understanding, empathy and knowledge. David Lowe has not only provided advice on this project but is also generous in guiding early career researchers. For someone so busy I am always amazed when he is happy to drop everything to meet and discuss potential research projects. Jon Ritchie has been an enormous source of knowledge on all things Papua New

Guinea (PNG) and is always generous with his time and with sharing his unrivalled personal PNG network. Special thanks also to Dr Bart Ziino, to whom I spoke earnestly about research and the potential of further studies. Bart's enthusiasm provided me with the confidence to follow the somewhat frustrating, but immensely satisfying, path of historical research. Furthermore, he has become a mentor, work colleague and friend. Bart is a truly wonderful person and I have been fortunate to work closely with him on several projects. Carolyn Holbrook is always enthusiastic to learn about your project and has on many occasions provided advice and support on how to best move forward with research opportunities.

I am grateful for the archivists at the National Archives of Australia, the National Archives of Papua New Guinea and the National Library of Australia. While in Canberra on my research field trips, I had the wonderful opportunity of meeting and being advised by an expert of the postwar socioeconomic development of PNG, Dr Scott MacWilliam. His research and advice were critical to this project. Thank you, Scott.

I would like to thank my close friends and fellow early career researchers, Dr Anna Kent and Dr Deb Lee Talbot. They have been a constant support, our WhatsApp conversations and coffee catch-ups have sustained and entertained and advised me for many years. Thanks guys!

Thank you to my immediate and extended family. I proudly follow my Popa who also studied at university as a mature-aged student. And like him, I too worked at the kitchen table—he, studying at night with a young family in tow, myself the consequence of Covid and downsizing to a small apartment.

Thank you to my children, Lil and Gen. Some of my fondest memories include walking Daisy (dog) with Lil as she genuinely questioned me on my methods and theories, while Gen always kept me on my toes with her acerbic wit. Thank you, Steven, for your interest and for keeping Gen busy!

And to Kate, without whom this book would not have been possible. Your support and love for me is not quantifiable and I cannot thank you enough. When I started my university journey I was at a very low ebb, and it was you who encouraged and supported me throughout. It is you who have sacrificed weekends and evenings while I doggedly studied. It was you (and only you) who always believed in me. It was you who made this possible. Thank you.

Acronyms

AIB	Allied Intelligence Bureau
ALP	Australian Labor Party
ANGAU	Australian New Guinea Administrative Unit
ASOPA	Australian School of Pacific Administration
CHD	Central Highlands District
CMB	Copra Marketing Board
DASF	Department of Agriculture, Stock and Fisheries
DDSNA	Department of District Services and Native Affairs
DEA	Department of External Affairs
DET	Department of External Territories
DNA	Department of Native Affairs
DORCA	Directorate of Research and Civil Affairs
DOT	Department of Territories
EHD	Eastern Highland District
HLS	Highland Labour Scheme
KEA	Kwato Extension Associates
LGC	Local Government Council
LHQ	Army Land Force Headquarters
MBDC	Milne Bay Development Company
NAS	Native Authorities Section
NID	New Ireland District
NINSA	New Ireland Natives' Societies Association
RPS	Rural Progress Society
TNG	Territory of New Guinea

TP	Territory of Papua
TPNG	1945–1949: Territories of Papua or New Guinea
	Post-1949: Territory of Papua and New Guinea
UN	United Nations

Preface

When Brad Underhill came to me with his proposal for his PhD dissertation, I thought it an interesting idea but did not believe it was feasible. He wanted to understand both the formation of policy for the Territory of Papua and New Guinea (TPNG) in the postwar years—the New Deal—and the implementation of that policy on the ground through close case studies. It was the kind of project normally undertaken by scholars much further advanced in their career, for it required an extraordinary amount of archival and other research. Further, it was essentially two dissertations. The first section covered the Chifley Government's aims for their territories north of the Torres Strait in the postwar years and the implantation of the Menzies' Government vision through the 1950s and early 1960s. This section required an understanding of the Australian commitment to TPNG in terms of resources, and the influences on the mid-century policymakers who were excited by global theories of colonial development and by Fabianism in particular. It demanded long hours photographing in the National Archives of Australia and the careful management of a substantial set of research materials. It required, also, close examination of personal papers in the manuscript sections of other libraries. The second part of the thesis required a different set of skills. The reports of the patrol officers, the kiaps, are a crucial set of documents for any research into colonialism on the ground in Papua New Guinea. But the patrol reports are a complex archive both in terms of their management, for while they are digitised they are not always searchable, and of their analysis: they demand careful reading with an explicit methodology to discern both the 'government man on the ground' perspective, and Indigenous responses. Brad read these documents against the grain. In the process, he has shown that patrol officers were caught between Indigenous ambition and demands for economic and educational advancement and fear that this knowledge would diminish the coloniser and challenge their authority. To understand the motives and social organisation behind the local responses to the New

Deal policies, Brad tackled the anthropology and development studies relevant to each case study. And each region had its own contact history with mission and colonial literature. I agreed to his thesis plan while imagining that as with most theses, it would be refined and contained through the course of his research.

I was wrong. Brad never wavered from his initial proposal. Through the three years that he photographed and organised thousands of documents from the archives while tackling the mountain of literature relevant to Australian government policy and each case study, I learned never to underestimate him. His undergraduate studies had already revealed his talent, his capacity for clear thinking, his enormous work ethic and a shrewd sense of how best to utilise his considerable skills. His deep interest in economics granted him the Business School Graduate of the Year at Deakin University in 2016 and prepared him for the close examination of the economic policies, the cooperatives and the trading world of TPNG. He was the winner of the Vice Chancellor's Award for Arts and Education in 2018. He could think big but keep his eye on the detail. His first introduction to Papua New Guinea through an undergraduate course in decolonisation sealed his fate: he became enamoured of Australia's nearest neighbour that was clearly Australian history but in a distinct and largely unexplored register. In so doing, he joined the large number of honours and postgraduate scholars at Deakin University for whom Papua New Guinea offered a new and thrilling view of the history of Australia.

This book is the outcome of Brad's deep research and analysis. It is a mature and important assessment of Australia's postwar aims for the territories across the Torres Strait. If he had simply focused on government policies and key public servants such as Bill Forsyth, David Fenbury, John Black and their energetic minister Paul Hasluck—who brought a particular form of liberalism to his vision for TPNG—this would have been a worthy undertaking. The innovation comes in the second half of the book with Brad's close exploration of these policies on the ground in the subdistricts of Chimbu, Milne Bay, New Hanover and the Maprik District of the Sepik region. Here patrol officers worked alongside or locked heads with Papua New Guineans whose visions for their future did not always correspond with Australian policies. Henry Leki in Milne Bay, along with Alice Wedega, utilised church and Indigenous networks and war compensation to establish new businesses and forms of community. Pita Simogun and Augen, of Maprik in the Sepik, pressed ahead of Australian government policies to introduce cash cropping and then spread these ideas through local alliances. The energetic Singerau in New Hanover, thought to be a threat to government control, used New Deal policies for his own purposes. In this book, Brad brings together several tiers of government colonial control, with the politics of place and the specificity of local responses based on social organisation and colonial experiences. This combination of approaches grants a special insight into the perennial question of the decolonisation of Papua New Guinea: To what extent did the New Deal prepare TPNG for independence? Brad tackles this question in his last chapter, where he assesses the New Deal up until 1963 and beyond, after the Foot Report from the United Nations Visiting Mission of 1962 demanded the implementation of universal political representation and a much greater emphasis on education. I commend the reader to this important contribution to the history of Australia's policies on the territories across the Torres Strait and the light it sheds on the shared histories of Australia and Papua New Guinea.

Associate Professor Helen Gardner (Honorary)
Centre for Contemporary Histories
Deakin University

Introduction

On 4 July 1945, Labor's External Territories Minister Eddie Ward delivered a headline statement to the House of Representatives outlining the Australian task and strategy for the postwar development of the recently merged Australian Territory of Papua New Guinea (TPNG). Generally recognised as the 'New Deal for Papua and New Guinea', it was a policy statement that radically departed from prewar laissez-faire economics and was instead geared towards protecting and advancing its colonised peoples. The Minister described his 1945 speech as:

> a comprehensive program ... for the rehabilitation and development of the Territories having regard to the moral and material welfare of the native inhabitants and the strategic importance of the area to Australia.[1]

Ward intended to introduce regulations that would end the exploitation of Indigenous labour on European-owned plantations: 'to give the native an opportunity to advance in his own right and not merely to be an instrument for employment by non-native agriculturists or industrialists'.[2] While Ward's speech was more rhetorical than substantive in detail, it did provide a roadmap for the future development of TPNG, one accepted and built upon by the Menzies Liberal/Country governments of the 1950s and early 1960s.

The Australian colonial development strategy was based on a controlled gradual introduction of new socioeconomic and political ideas. It was implemented in a paternalistic manner which assumed limited space for innovative or autonomous Indigenous activity. Government officers, reporting to Port Moresby and following programs often designed in Canberra, were frequently at odds with local leaders who manipulated

---

1   Commonwealth (Australia), *Parliamentary Debates*, House of Representatives, 4 July 1945 (Edward Ward), 'The Papua-New Guinea Provisional Administration Bill: Second Reading'.
2   *Parliamentary Debates*, 4 July 1945 (Edward Ward).

or adjusted government programs to suit their local communities. Patrol officers (kiaps) played an essential role in the implementation of government development policies in the villages of the Territory. They were, as noted by ABC reporter Liam Fox, in a recent article, 'administrators, census takers, policemen, magistrates and gaolers'.[3] They were usually the first contact and most important conduit between the village and the Australian Government. The personal attitudes of the officers to the government development policies and their reactions to villager responses (or lack thereof) to the plans they implemented in the villages were crucial in understanding what had happened in these small communities. In the patrol reports, despite being bureaucratic and formulaic in layout, officers were often surprisingly candid in their personal views of individual villagers and the success or failure of government policies (and the reasons for them).

Papuan and New Guinean leaders such as Pita Simogun and Augen (Sepik), Henri Leki and Alice Wedega (Milne Bay) and Singerau (New Hanover) had returned to their villages following their experiences working for the church or police duty or military service in World War II with their own ideas for the development of their communities. They were not necessarily belligerent in opposition to their coloniser, but neither were they satisfied to be passive onlookers in the development of their subdistrict. However, the Australian response to these people suggests the maintenance of control was a priority over the rapid advancement of its colonised people. Similarly, young men from Chimbu returned home after working as government-sponsored plantation workers on the coast to challenge pre-existing norms the government wished to maintain as part of a control measure. While these returnees brought back new agricultural techniques, an enthusiasm for cash cropping and a demand for a money economy, their new knowledge represented a political threat to the administration's indirect rule. As such, they acted in a manner which directly suited themselves and their communities and which did not accord with Australian expectations, effectively undermining administration influence.

Australian development of TPNG was a project of the late colonial epoch, a period which favoured constructivist state power to advance its colonial peoples. The Australian attitude and direction as outlined in the 'New Deal' fits within this broader narrative of colonial re-evaluation. This research project spans the period 1945–63 and explains Indigenous reactions to

---

3   Liam Fox, 'Historical records of Australian patrol officers in Papua New Guinea documented online', *ABCNews*, 25 August 2016, accessed 14 August 2021, www.abc.net.au/news/2016-04-25/history-of-png-kiaps-documented-online/7356286.

Australian development, and how the colonial state, guided by trusteeship and security concerns, struggled to accommodate the emergence of Papuan and New Guinean autonomy. The first part focusses on the genesis and motivation for Australian postwar development plans for TPNG and the implementation of government policy. Part Two explores the 'New Deal' in the villages through four case studies: a cross-cultural analysis of the experience of local people and government officers to the implementation of Australian development plans.

In this way, when assessing the success or otherwise of 'New Deal' planning, the contribution of local people can be appropriately emphasised, placed at the centre of analysis and weighed against Australian hopes and efforts for the postwar development of its colony. These chapters provide an opportunity to articulate the varied responses of a diverse range of Indigenous communities to postwar development, and the Australian Government's response to challenges to its authority. Local demonstrations of political and socioeconomic independence did not always accord with Australian expectations. Therefore, this book examines both the intent of the colonial planners and how Papuans and New Guineans encountered, dealt with and understood the introduction of new socioeconomic programs. It contributes to the ongoing debate over how well Australia prepared TPNG for independence and contributes to the current historical discussion regarding Australia's imperial legacy. More broadly, it adds to the continuity or discontinuity debate of postwar government policy following the December 1949 change of government from the Chifley Labor Administration to the Menzies Liberal/Country governments.

While the Labor 'New Deal' provided the broad Australian intent, it was the long-term Liberal Territories Minister (Sir) Paul Hasluck who had the most pronounced impact on policy development and implementation strategy. He had a classical liberal belief in the rights of the individual and was also a gradualist by nature and wedded to Australia's trusteeship commitment for eventual Indigenous self-rule. Hasluck foresaw the Australian objective in TPNG as primarily ensuring a stable country to the north, and this meant building a sustainable public service, independent judiciary and competent political governance. Furthermore, in the villages where most people lived, he envisaged a strategy for the gradual improvement of the standard of living through the voluntary efforts of local people. Hasluck was not averse to using state power to encourage a particular version of individual and community autonomy. However, in terms of application, despite the appearance of positive and progressive development plans, the lived reality for local people was that the Australian Government often did not deliver on these aspirations. This was primarily due to inadequate staff and resources and poor planning on the ground, but also the government's tendency to prioritise colonial control over Indigenous autonomy in circumstances where subjugated people objected to or resisted the expected narrative of the compliant or Westernised 'native'.

Figure 0.1: Sir Paul Hasluck, Minister of Territories, 1951–63.
Source: National Archives of Australia (NAA), A1200, L16892, item 11163499.

INTRODUCTION

The dichotomy of these positions, of a liberal desire to free the individual from government regulation versus colonial control, fundamentally influenced both the effectiveness of government programs and the lived experience of Papuans and New Guineans. Just as Joseph Hodge, Associate Professor at West Virginia University, has questioned the motivation of the British in the late colonial period for their constructivist use of state power to prioritise the socioeconomic advancement of its colonised peoples, this book asks whether the Australian Government's postwar colonial development objective was to control and placate its subjugated people.[4] The case studies explore this dynamic, identifying circumstances where the government opted for control and acted to close down or isolate local groups not acting in accordance with its expectations. Government officials justified these actions by portraying the 'native' as intractable and ungovernable and promoted Australia as a benevolent coloniser or neighbour, one steeped in an evolutionary appeal to colonial wisdom. The resulting increased tension on the ground undermined government messaging and diminished efforts at improving the lived experience of local people. In summary, the broad outline of Australian colonial ambition in the postwar period espoused political and economic autonomy, yet this vision was undermined due to a lack of resources on the ground and anxiety over the autonomous actions of local people.

Historically, prior to World War II, along with expatriate development, Australian thinking had prioritised a security land barrier. Originally, this was due to a perceived German threat in the 1880s and later the rising naval power of Japan. This leads to the question: What changed in the strategic vision or motivation for the 'New Deal' and later colonial development programs? In simple terms, the aims remained similar but the targets for Australian action changed dramatically. In the short term, the 'New Deal' was designed to address geopolitical issues, protect the Indigenous population from a sudden influx of international capitalist activity, reverse the deplorable prewar neglect of the colony and finally provide a platform for the socioeconomic development of the territories. In the long term, as witnessed by political discourse and policy documents of the time, it was to create an independent nation-state ruled by Papuans and New Guineans, though this was a distant future with no clear timeline. During the 1940s and 50s, following the drafting of the 'New Deal', there were

---

4   Joseph M Hodge, *Triumph of the expert: Agrarian doctrines of development and the legacies of British Colonialism* (Athens: Ohio University Press, 2007), 180–81.

several planning documents written by Territory officials which expanded on the long-distant ambition of independence. These papers argued that for postwar development to be successful it must be for the mutual benefit of both Australia and Papua New Guineans. For instance, in 1947 John Black, Director of Policy Planning and Research in the provisional administration, wrote a directive to patrol officers which outlined the stark choice facing Australia in TPNG. Australia had to either choose to maintain a separation between European and Indigenous communities and face growing unrest, or both sides would have to work together in recognition of their mutual interest.[5] Black's words of warning were oft repeated over the years by others within the administration, including senior Territory official David Fenbury and Territories Minister Paul Hasluck. Fenbury argued the developers of TPNG policy must be cognisant of Australia's own strategic interest, that any realistic analysis could only conclude that Australia was committed to TPNG indefinitely unless forced out by superior foreign armed forces or by internal unrest. Therefore, the priority of the Australian Government had to be the satisfaction of the Indigenous population, an aspiration to manage affairs so that their continuing presence was regarded by the 'advancing Indigene' as essential to their continuing wellbeing.[6]

Hasluck sought to align TPNG development and eventual self-rule with Australian fears of a future failed state. To meet this objective, a nation-building strategy of universal development was employed, one which prioritised Indigenous socioeconomic welfare, but contained a control measure to limit the emergence of one Indigenous group at the expense of another. As will be explained in this book, Hasluck's approach can be best understood in conceptual terms as resembling a hierarchical pyramid, a demand-driven strategy aimed at stimulating Papuan and New Guinean needs and wants in the hope that it would lead to the ultimate attainment of self-government. This amalgamation of Australian intent for a stable and competent neighbour and trusteeship commitment for eventual Indigenous self-rule was a persistent message advocated by Hasluck during his 12-year reign as Territories Minister.[7]

---

5   John R Black, 'The aim of policy', Department of District Services and Native Affairs (DDSNA), 7 March 1947, pp. 1–2, Papers of John Black, MS8346/12/15, National Library of Australia (NLA).
6   David M Fenbury, 'Notes on native policy', Department of Native Affairs (DNA), 17 April 1956, pp. 2–10, Papers of David Maxwell Fenbury, MS6747/3/5, NLA.
7   Examples: August 1956 'Progress in New Guinea'; May 1958 'The legend of remote control'. Paul Hasluck, New Guinea speeches, articles and notes, M1775[2], National Archives of Australia (NAA); Paul Hasluck, *A time for building: Australian administration in Papua and New Guinea, 1951–1963* (Carlton: Melbourne University Press, 1976), 209–11.

This book combines analysis of Australian high-level policy with mid-level implementation and Papua and New Guinean response to Australian colonialism. The primary task of this project is to explore and explain policy decisions and execution strategies and then compare them with the experience of both local people and government officials on the ground in TPNG. In terms of structure, this book investigates the social and physical impact of Australian policies in the villages through four case studies in the administrative regions of Chimbu, Milne Bay, Maprik and New Hanover. These subdistricts provide an opportunity to contrast colonial intention with Indigenous experience. The research explicitly addresses how successful or not Australian colonial planners were in designing and implementing programs which would combine disparate people into an 'imagined community', one capable of becoming an independent nation-state.[8] Prior to this research, there has not been a comprehensive study of how postwar colonial development evolved from idea formation to impact in the villages. Studies have either focussed on aspects of postwar policy, development theory or individual case studies. Therefore, this book explains Australian development planning and how it was implemented, and then analyses the direct impact of government programs in several locations in the territories. There will be four cases from four subdistricts in four distinct regions.

Factors impacting the choice of subdistrict

One of the most important decisions regarding this project was the choice of locations for the case studies. Even today, given the geographic diversity of the nation, it is difficult to select representative regions in Papua New Guinea (PNG); this is further magnified in the postwar period as locations varied due to the impact of the war and the level of prewar European contact. The first major decision was whether to choose hamlets, villages or subdistricts as the representative demographic structure. Hamlet or clan groups (from two or three families up to several hundred) are the ubiquitous Indigenous common social structure of Papua New Guinea.[9] The difficulty of using a hamlet was the small sample size, which made them more susceptible to a diverse experience, or to an individual's actions, not reflective of the greater population. Villages became increasingly prevalent during

---

8   Benedict Anderson, *Imagined communities: Reflections on the origin and spread of nationalism* (London: Verso, 2006).
9   Brian Jinks, *New Guinea government: An introduction* (Sydney: Angus and Robertson, 1971), 8.

colonisation. John Barker, Professor of Anthropology at the University of British Columbia, has described how the village was the 'primary venue of [European] control', more concerned with a geographic location than 'the people living in it'.[10] On the other hand, a village provided a broader cross-section of a local community and was an important Indigenous social structure within the Territory Administration. So, in many ways, a village was an appropriate structural size. Eventually, subdistricts consisting of multiple villages were selected as the most suitable social structure for this study. There were several reasons for this. Firstly, these districts provided the opportunity to uncover and explain the personal appeal and political influence of Indigenous leaders such as Simogun, Augen, Leki and Singerau, who were active over a larger area, particularly in relation to the implementation of or opposition to government programs. Secondly, often the administration would encourage subdistrict-wide projects as part of the 'New Deal', for example when introducing cooperative societies. Finally, government officers generally patrolled a subdistrict, or multiple subdistricts, and therefore patrol reports were easily identifiable and provided a more accurate chronological study of a particular region.

The four subdistricts were chosen because of their geographic location and level of socioeconomic 'development' or prewar European contact. In terms of geographic location, an important 'New Deal' focus was socioeconomic opportunity in the villages. Therefore, these new programs were reliant on agroeconomics and subsequently the physical characteristics of the landform. The introduction of government development programs was also substantially affected by climatic diversity throughout the Territory; coastal areas have tropical climates of high temperatures, humidity and rainfall, whereas the Highlands often experience frosts and drought. Other geographic considerations included a balance of remote and high population centres, island and mainland experience, the physical and emotional impact of World War II, and locations in both the Territory of Papua (TP) and Territory of New Guinea (TNG). The level of socioeconomic development varied enormously. Most coastal areas and islands of the territories had some degree of contact with the colonial administration over the preceding 60 years. This usually meant coastal Papuans and New Guineans had experience working on plantations, perhaps some education and medical services, and physical infrastructure such as roads. However, people in

---

10   John Barker, 'Village inventions: Historical variations upon a regional theme in Uiaku, Papua New Guinea', *Oceania* 66 (1996): 213, doi.org/10.1002/j.1834-4461.1996.tb02552.x.

other locations, particularly the Highlands, had only recently had, or had yet to have, any contact with Europeans. These considerations substantially affected the rollout of government programs and the engagement of local people with postwar development.

The case studies: Chimbu, Milne Bay, Maprik and New Hanover

Map 0.1: Map of Papua New Guinea highlighting the four regions studied.

Note: Circles denote the location of the four case studies: Maprik (north-west mainland), Chimbu (central mainland), New Hanover (island to the north of the mainland) and Milne Bay (east mainland).

Source: Shutterstock.

The first case study is Chimbu which, in 1946, was a subdistrict of the Eastern Highland District (TNG). The subdistrict was remote from government control; the first official contact between Chimbu and Europeans had occurred only 12 years previously as part of the 1933 Taylor–Leahy exploratory expedition.[11] At the end of the war, government officers were charged with introducing large-scale agricultural development in an area with a harsh environment and limited arable land. Chimbu's estimated population of 200,000 people were not only coming to terms with new rules and new sources of power, but due to the prevailing geographic conditions, were also unable to fully participate in the Australian Government's development plans.[12]

The second case study, Milne Bay (Gehua patrol post), differs from Chimbu in terms of war experience, European contact and population size. Located at the eastern extremity of the mainland, and a subdistrict of Eastern District (TP), the region had a relatively long history of European–Indigenous relations (traders, miners, whalers and missionaries). An influential European presence, not matched in any of the other case studies, was the Kwato Mission, which fostered technical and general education in the hope of making Papuans economically self-sufficient but inoculated from potential Western temptations. A coastal subdistrict, by the commencement of the Pacific War, it had been under administrative control for 30 years and had a small population of just 16,092 people.[13] The area suffered significant war damage, including the destruction of plantations, timber, sago palms, village gardens and housing.

The third case study is the Maprik subdistrict, located inland from the Sepik District (TNG) headquarters, Wewak. During the colonial period, the Sepik District was one of the largest and most densely inhabited in the Territory.[14] The Maprik population was estimated at 40,925 with minimal European influence, as the subdistrict was cut off from the coast by a mountain range. During World War II, local people in the area were trapped by the savage military action of both the Australian and Japanese

---

11   Bill Gammage, *The sky travellers: Journeys in New Guinea 1938–1939* (Carlton: Melbourne University Press, 1998), Chapter 1.
12   Department of External Territories (DET), *Report to the General Assembly of the United Nations on the administration of the Territory of New Guinea: From 1st of July, 1949 to 30th June, 1950* (Canberra: Government Printer, 1950), 82.
13   DET, *Territory of Papua Annual report for the period 30th October, 1945 to 30th June, 1946* (Canberra: Government Printer, 1946), 15, 39.
14   DET, *Report to the General Assembly of the United Nations, 1950*, 82.

troops, which resulted in the total physical devastation of their surroundings. This meant officers were overwhelmed with the task of reconstruction, rehabilitation and war damage compensation in the early postwar period, a void filled by an entrepreneurial Indigenous leadership class.

The final case study is the Kavieng subdistrict (TNG), primarily the island of New Hanover, in the New Ireland District (NID). A large island with a small and isolated population of just over 6,000 people, New Hanover, unlike Milne Bay and Maprik, suffered limited damage during the war.[15] While the Japanese did not occupy the island, plantations were abandoned and many locals fought in the Allied Intelligence Bureau, returning from duties having witnessed the extraordinary wealth, power, and efficiency of external armed forces. And, as in the Sepik, they emerged as leaders and enablers on their own terms, determined to utilise the resources offered by the Australian Government to improve the living standards of their local community.

The case studies chosen are diverse in geographic location, population, war experience and European–Indigenous relations. These characteristics had a significant impact on the success or otherwise of Australian postwar development plans, factors which frustrated officers on the ground but were too often ignored by government planners in Port Moresby and Canberra.

Immersed in the archives

This book is based on extensive archival research across several government departments. While Australian colonial development policy planning had a consistent objective and intent during the first 20 years following World War II, it was produced in different arms of government. More specifically, the location of primary sources and distinctive bureaucratic styles were determined by three distinct periods. During World War II the army, more particularly the Directorate of Research and Civil Affairs (DORCA), was responsible for the bulk of the ideas for the 'New Deal'. Most of these records are held in the Melbourne and Canberra branches of the National Archives of Australia (NAA), while the personal papers of key personnel are held in the National Library of Australia (NLA). The second period

---

15   EM Holland, 'Leprosy in New Guinea', *International Journal of Leprosy* 4, no. 2 (1936): 171–76; Corbett Kimmorley, Report 4 of 47/48, p. 5, New Ireland District, Kavieng, 1946–48, National Archives of Papua New Guinea (PNGA).

can be defined as the postwar period up until the arrival of Paul Hasluck as Minister of Territories in April 1951. This period is marked by a basic disconnection between the Territory Administration and the Department of Territories (DOT). As such, many of the initiatives were generated out of subcommittees of the Territory Administration; records are held primarily in the PNG National Archives, Port Moresby. Fortunately, there are many planning records in the personal papers of members of these subcommittees held at the NLA. Once Hasluck was in charge, decisions were made almost exclusively by the department in Canberra; these records are held in the National Archives.

The second major source for this book was the patrol reports. In an important innovation, fundamentally expanding public access to the archives, the University of California (San Diego) recently digitised the patrol reports for this period. Although patrol reports were created by outsiders, and reflect the specific needs of their creators, they also constitute an important source of Papuan and New Guinean history. Written from a Eurocentric stance and expressing the opinion and ambitions of the patrol officers undertaking their duty, they often also reveal the reactions of local people to new policy ideas. These reports were complemented by other sources such as anthropological studies completed during this period, missionary diaries, church reports and other external reports, which expanded the picture of what was happening on the ground. These resources, particularly some anthropological studies or dissertations by social scientists, provided qualitative information which sometimes confirmed, and at other times led the researcher to question, the official records.

Crucially, these records provide an opportunity to first, locate new spaces for a previously marginalised group and second, yield evidence of Indigenous reaction to government action, both important research priorities for this book. However, as historian and anthropologist Professor Bronwen Douglas has warned in a carefully thought-out analysis of colonial texts, reliance on such documents is fraught with danger for the researcher. She wrote that colonial archives (such as patrol reports) are 'neither internally nor discursively homogeneous, but riddled with ambivalences, ambiguities, and dissonances of voice and genre which make them susceptible to informed colonisation and exploitation for ethnohistorical purposes'. In other words, patrol reports need to be reviewed critically, and reflexively, within what Douglas explains as 'an integrated critique of text, contexts, discourses, language, authorship and audience'.¹⁶ The written style, although formulaic, was in the first person, the officer an active participant in the report, their views and personal opinions part of the narrative. Patrol reports are an example of how the state maintained colonial control. They reveal the worst and best manifestations of records themselves and how minority bureaucracies could hold sway for so long over non–record–producing majority. As archival scholar Professor Jeanette Bastion has explained, colonial records (such as patrol reports) are explicit in their power and textual bias; they both appropriate as well as maintain authenticity, each of which speaks as much to the authority as to the malleability of written information.¹⁷

This was most evident when reading reports from different officers on the actions or attitudes of the same Indigenous leader or community. At times these officers would have diametrically opposed opinions and would freely express them, and while adhering to government policy, would direct their efforts at a local level in accordance with this opinion. So a confused picture of events emerged. This confusion is also an acknowledgement that hegemonic colonial rule is a fallacy, and instead, that the interaction between patrol officers and local people on the ground was unique to each circumstance. These different accounts—of patrol officers and other arms of the administration—created an opportunity to recognise this distinction and proactively search for traces of Indigenous autonomy.

The archival trail indicates patrol reports travelled up and down the Territory bureaucracy: from a remote patrol post to a subdistrict office or district headquarters, where further comments were made, until they reached the desk of the Director of the Department of Native Affairs (DNA), Port Moresby. These official exchanges within the Territory Administration, as well as between the Territory Administrator and the Minister for Territories, provide what Ann Stoler, Professor of Anthropology, describes 'as reference guides to administrative thinking'.¹⁸ The digital archive of the patrol reports has captured a significant, although not complete, record of these bureaucratic exchanges. Memos or commentary, usually from department heads or district officers, outlined a broader colonial strategy and often provided an interesting insight into the attitude and ambition of

---

16 Bronwen Douglas, 'Encounters with the enemy? Academic readings of missionary narratives on Melanesians', *Comparative Studies in Society and History* 70, no. 2 (2001): 42.
17 Jeanette A Bastian, 'Reading colonial records through an archival lens: The provenance of place, space and creation', *Archival Science* 6 (2006): 269, doi.org/10.1007/s10502-006-9019-1.
18 Ann L Stoler, 'Colonial archives and the arts of governance', *Archival Science* 2 (2002): 95, doi.org/10.1007/BF02435632.

the Territory Administration. This could include high-priority direction, and the reasons why a patrol officer had to urgently attend to a certain matter; it may be criticism directed at an officer for not meeting the goals of a district; or it may offer background information on an Indigenous leader gleaned from previous dealings with the administration. What was clear is that this communication flowed both ways and that the colonial administration was heavily reliant on these reports to maintain control, disseminate expectations and justify decisions.

Locating new historical spaces for previously marginalised subjects is an important ambition for this book. A contextual examination of documents such as census records and patrol reports revealed traces of Indigenous autonomy. As Bronwen Douglas points out, researchers must be alert to nuance, silences, the individual instances of 'culturally framed native agency' and, in my case, contradictions between a patrol officer's ethnocentric expectation and subsequent experience.[19] Reading carefully along the grains of these government documents revealed many examples of Indigenous agency, but also the haphazard, inconsistent and piecemeal introduction of the new socioeconomic programs. Of even more interest was the gradual evolution of attitudes and understandings by some officers to the roles they played in colonial projects. The archives expose a genuine emotional involvement of patrol officers and villagers—frustration and enthusiasm—in the administration of Papua New Guinea.

Interrogating the literature

There are two distinct historical literatures relevant to this book. Specific literature on development in TPNG and that of Ward and Hasluck and the assessment of their legacies. In addition to this historical work, multidisciplinary researchers from The Australian National University (ANU), along with other social scientists, have analysed and explained the impact of colonial development programs in the villages of TPNG.

The existing historical scholarship has focussed on aspects of postwar government programs, of their successes and failings, but not from the perspective of the rural village. Key texts such as Ian Downs's *Australian Trusteeship* (1980) provide a comprehensive explanation of how and why

---

19 Bronwen Douglas, 'Introduction: Fracturing boundaries of time and place in Melanesian anthropology', *Oceania* 66 (1996): 177–88, doi.org/10.1002/j.1834-4461.1996.tb02550.x.

policy was formed and the problems of implementation. Paul Hasluck's memoir of his time as minister, *A Time for Building* (1976), justifies in some depth the reasoning behind policy strategy. Others, such as historian Scott MacWilliam, explain why the Australian Government adopted a village-based strategy of development. Debate and widespread criticism have centred on the Australian policy of universal and gradualist development. This has been led by academics such as Brian Jinks, Allan Healy and Hank Nelson, who argue it left Papuan and New Guineans underprepared for self-government and with limited opportunity to impact the outcome. This book addresses this gap by explaining policy design and implementation and, crucially, placing local people at the centre of analysis where their contribution can be appropriately emphasised.

So how did Australian planners align modernisation and protection? A simple answer is that Australia was instrumental in the formation of the United Nations (UN) Trusteeship Council, which monitored the governance of most postwar colonial territories. Huntley Wright and Scott MacWilliam, who have both researched and written extensively on postwar colonial development in TPNG, agree that an Australian commitment to the UN trusteeship resolution was an important factor in their planning. However, Wright and MacWilliam's analysis is more particular to TPNG, for they argue that Territory officials developed policies to align with pre-existing social systems and rural households.[20] According to Wright, the defining nature of postwar colonial development doctrine was the distinction between spontaneous and intentional development. The first, described as immanent or laissez-faire development, is the unintentional process of 'progress' that unfolds outside the immediate control of the colonial state. The second is constructivist in intent, and plans to ameliorate the destructive tendencies of capitalist accumulation.[21] What is discussed in the literature of postwar TPNG is whether Australia's colonial intent to develop was constructivist or immanent in terms of the principles of trusteeship. This project adds to this debate, particularly regarding the village experience, weighing up problems of 'enforced' development, disappointment and colonial expectations for Indigenous behaviour, against evidence of autonomous and entrepreneurial Indigenous action which, ironically, was often stimulated by the constructivist plans of the government.

---

20   Scott MacWilliam, *Securing village life: Development in late colonial Papua New Guinea* (Canberra: ANU Press, 2013), 3, doi.org/10.22459/SVL.05.2013.
21   Huntley Wright, 'State practice and rural smallholder production: Late-colonialism and the agrarian doctrine in Papua New Guinea, 1942–1969' (PhD thesis, Massey University, 1999).

In terms of policy intent, Wright argues rationalism, not idealism, was at the root of postwar development planning for TPNG. In his 1999 thesis, 'State Practice and Rural Smallholder Production', Wright explains that justification for new postwar colonial development was generally premised on three characteristics: humanitarian intent, supposed pre-adaptiveness of some groups to previously non-capitalist social relations, or, at a minimum, the subsidising effect of capital accumulation on vulnerable and unsophisticated peoples. While Wright agrees with such explanations, he argues that pragmatism and political imperatives were also at play, inasmuch as the changing economic realities of postwar global capitalism, domestic security and Australian aspiration for full employment aligned with trusteeship ambition and Indigenous welfare.[22] This is further underlined by Wendy Timms, whose 1996 thesis takes up these debates, but from the perspective of the expatriate planters who were dealing with the repercussions of an administration policy which prioritised Indigenous smallholder agriculture.[23] This book expands upon these arguments by firstly, explaining in depth the government's policy ambition, and secondly, the experience on the ground for villagers and Territory officials during the implementation of new agricultural and economic concepts.

More concisely, the 'New Deal' focussed on agrarian development—unsurprising, according to Scott MacWilliam, given the prominence of agriculture to development thought in the late colonial period.[24] There are two reasons for this, and both align with the 'New Deal' intention. Firstly, according to Cowen and Shenton, agrarian development was designed to promote the retention of a population in the countryside, discourage the drift to the urban centre, and the creation of a landless proletariat.[25] Secondly, MacWilliam argues in his 2013 book, *Securing Village Life*, that colonial policymakers envisaged developing agricultural production as the basis not just for an improved output for export, but a direct improvement to Indigenous living standards. Fundamental to agricultural development in TPNG was the utilisation of household labour processes. In essence, households would grow cash crops, the state would market the product, income earned by the villagers would be spent on consumption, and

---

22 Wright, 'State practice', 113.
23 Wendy Timms, 'The post World War Two colonial project and Australian planters in Papua New Guinea: The search for relevance in the colonial twilight' (PhD thesis, The Australian National University, 1996), 70.
24 MacWilliam, *Securing village life*, 9.
25 Michael Cowen and Robert W Shenton, *Doctrines of development* (Routledge, 1996), iv.

INTRODUCTION

this would lift living standards, improve welfare and maintain the rural community.[26] In this way, trusteeship and the 'New Deal' are examples of twofold state power not just for preserving Indigenous attachment to land but ameliorating the effects of capitalist accumulation. This book explores MacWilliam's arguments on agriculture and smallholder development through four case studies, detailing the experience of local people from four distinct regions to the implementation of Australian plans, and how reality on the ground was influenced as much by government resources as the manipulation of programs by Indigenous leadership.

The origins of the 'New Deal' and early postwar period generally revolve around an interplay of humanitarianism, most prominently espoused in this context by DORCA officers; trusteeship ambitions advocated by the Department of External Affairs (DEA); general disinterest of the Minister of External Territories Eddie Ward; and the failure of the Territory Administration to implement, in a timely manner, an adequate bureaucratic structure to implement the promised reforms. The secondary literature debates the merits of Australian policies and performance regarding political, agricultural and economic planning. This book engages with these questions and brings the crucial dimension of Indigenous responses to colonial policies to the fore.

The ANU New Guinea Research Unit fostered interdisciplinary work on TPNG during the 1960s and 70s, publishing bulletins and monographs, which are an important resource for examining Australian postwar development policy in TPNG. For instance, Richard Shand and WF Straatman's *Transition from Subsistence* (Bulletin 54, 1974) and Sumer Singh's *Cooperatives in Papua New Guinea* (Bulletin 58, 1974) document the growth in the cash economy at the village level. Both are empirical studies of individual and community responses to new economic incentives and opportunities provided by government at an early stage of monetary development. The ANU Development Studies Centre also produced a series of monographs during this period, some of which focussed on TPNG. Diana Howlett, R Hide and Elspeth Young's *Chimbu: Issues in Development* (1976), is a comprehensive study of conditions in Chimbu at the end of Australian colonialism. Another example is David Fenbury's *Practice without Policy* (1978), which details the practical tasks and implementation of local government councils during the 1950s. Fenbury is a key figure in

---

26 MacWilliam, *Securing village life*, 9.

this research project, and alongside his personal papers, this monograph provides an indispensable account of the assumptions and mindset which informed Australian development planning in the postwar period.

There have been many anthropological, geographical and sociological studies/dissertations of village social systems in the territories, some of them covering the postwar period: all are a valuable resource for this project; for instance, the work of anthropologist Paula Brown and geographer Harold Brookfield on Chimbu land use and landholding patterns in the late 1950s and early 1960s.[27] Other important research includes Bryant Allen's dissertation on the adoption and diffusion of new development ideas in the Sepik District.[28] Anthropologist Dorothy Billings's work on New Hanover was crucial in understanding inter-island social dynamics, while another anthropologist, Cyril Belshaw, was commissioned to write a number of influential reports for the Australian Government on Indigenous entrepreneurial activity in the Milne Bay subdistrict in the early 1950s.[29] These works were crucial to understanding what was happening on the ground; in several cases, they include revealing interviews with local leaders who provided expansive reflections that contrasted sharply with official Australian records.

The 'New Deal' was designed by officers of DORCA, inspired by Fabian humanitarian intent and the liberal internationalist rhetoric of Labor's External Affairs Minister, Herbert Vere Evatt.[30] The 'New Deal' was, for all intents and purposes, a result of progressive Australian Labor Party (ALP) principles of social welfare and full employment. One of the arguments tested by this book was whether, given that postwar colonial development policies originated with the ALP, the intent of development remained consistent following the election of the Menzies Liberal Government in 1949, and remained so until the World Bank report of 1965. This new strategy, to improve the living standards of Papua New Guineans, mirrored British postwar principles of economic, social and cultural ideals

---

27 Paula Brown and Harold C Brookfield, *Struggle for land* (Melbourne: Oxford University Press, 1963).
28 Bryant Allen, 'Information flow and innovation diffusion in the East Sepik District, Papua New Guinea', (PhD thesis, The Australian National University, 1976).
29 Cyril Belshaw, *Economic development in South East Papua* (Port Moresby: Government Printer, 1950); Cyril Belshaw, 'In search of wealth: A study of the emergence of commercial operations in the Melanesian society of Southeastern Papua', *American Anthropologist* 57 (1955): 1–84.
30 The Fabian Society is Britain's oldest political think tank (founded in 1884). Fabians are a non-revolutionary, social progressive organisation that fight against inequality by means of evidence-based, rational argument. They argue that elite individuals were the beneficiaries of circumstance, of uneven distribution, and consequently should promote social good by helping those less well off.

for colonised peoples. In Australia, there were two major sources for new colonial development ideas: policy advisers to the Ministers of both External Territories (Ward) and External Affairs (Evatt). These government officers adhered to the innovative British ideas of development, steering a middle ground of increased control with a targeted form of intervention, encouragement, cooperation and advancement.[31] While most studies of postwar colonial development concentrate on links to Britain, and the Fabians in particular, the term itself, 'the New Deal', suggests a link to 'Rooseveltian' development thought and liberal internationalism. This historical work explores the deep roots of the term 'New Deal' in this colonial context and the political and economic policies which flowed from this crucial concept.

The literature on wartime administration is crucial to this book. Alan Powell's 2003 book, *The Third Force: ANGUA's New Guinea War, 1942–46*, focusses on the defence of PNG by the Australian Army and the story of the Territory's civil administration. Importantly, Powell provides an excellent summary of the exploitation, both prewar and during the war, of 'native labour'.[32] Graeme Sligo's 2013 book, *Backroom Boys*, documents the extraordinary rise to prominence of DORCA within the army apparatus during World War II, and in particular the political manoeuvrings of the brilliant, ambitious, but erratic directorate head, Alf Conlon. Sligo describes in detail the ability of Conlon to mould together a small elite group of talented academics to carry out research and produce papers and recommendations on colonial administration. Geoffrey Gray's 2012 edited collection, *Scholars at War*, explores this discourse further, each chapter dedicated to the key players in the directorate. Brian Jinks's 1975 thesis on the early postwar provisional administration explicitly describes how the dominance of DORCA academics over planning in the postwar period ensured the rejection of prewar paternalistic rule, and the appointment of an administrator (JK Murray) sympathetic to the army directorate's own approach. What these scholarly works all agree on is the influence of the British Colonial Office, and Fabianism in particular, as the intellectual origin of postwar colonial development.

---

31   John D Legge, *Australian colonial policy* (Sydney: Australian Institute of International Affairs, 1956), 187.
32   The commission was known as the Melrose Report. Mandated Territory of New Guinea, *Report of a commission appointed to inquire into the matter of native labour in the Territory: Majority report*, M2101 [1], NAA.

Two participants, former DORCA officers John Legge and WEH Stanner, later wrote about postwar colonial development in the Territory. Legge wrote in his 1956 book, *Australian Colonial Policy*, of the powerful psychological impact on the Papuan New Guineans of the Pacific War: destruction caused by hostilities, a bewildering change in overlords, demands of military service and devastated village economies. As Legge points out, it was hardly surprising that the war 'should leave a ferment in Papua and New Guinea', which also offered the 'Administration the opportunity of turning new aspirations into desirable channels'.[33] Stanner, a conservative, was, on the other hand, scathing of Murray's lack of direction, his poor management and his preference for ethics, humanism and ideology, rather than dealing with the reality of the circumstances facing the administration. In his 1953 book, *Transition in the South Pacific*, Stanner described the widespread acceptance within planning circles of postwar development as a vehicle for prioritising Indigenous advancement and was critical of the eventual form of development chosen.[34] Huntley Wright criticised this summation, arguing that as early as October 1943, DEA had completed detailed practical planning based on the 1940 British *Colonial Development and Welfare Act*.[35] This book takes up these debates and explores in great detail the ferment of ideas produced within the Territory during the provisional administration, and how some of these would become significant development programs during the Hasluck years.

While Hasluck is the central figure in this book, his ideological motivation concerning development is open to conjecture. He has been the subject of much historical analysis including two substantial biographies: Robert Porter's 1993 *A Political Biography* and Geoffrey Bolton's 2014 *A Life*. These books do not apportion significant space to Hasluck's TPNG period, but provide an important insight into Hasluck's personality, prodigious work capacity and eye for detail. Although Hasluck held the classical liberal belief of individualism, it was tempered by protective and ameliorative concern for the vulnerable or disadvantaged.[36] These traits are generally attributed to being the son of two dedicated Salvation Army officers, and are widely referred to in the Bolton and Porter books, but also in the edited collection,

---

33 Legge, *Australian colonial policy*, 186.
34 WEH Stanner, *The South Seas in transition* (Sydney: Australasian Publishing Company, 1953), 68, 92–93, 118.
35 Wright, 'State practice', 111.
36 Commonwealth (Australia), *Parliamentary Debates*, House of Representatives, 30 September 1959 (Paul Hasluck).

Paul Hasluck in Australian History: Civic Personality and Public Life (1999), and Hasluck's own reflection of his early years, *Mucking About* (1984).[37] Historian Judith Brett agrees Hasluck's form of liberalism is marked by his Salvation Army childhood (and later estrangement). She makes the interesting point that while it promoted a strong sense of duty, his parents' evangelism embarrassed him to such an extent that he rejected political grandstanding and limited himself to a politics of administration at the expense of connection with the very groups of people he aspired to assist.[38]

In terms of ideological motivation, it is a question of conjecture as to whether Hasluck was inspired by Fabianism, although as pointed out by MacWilliam, he did express admiration for some Fabians, particularly postwar British colonial secretary Arthur Creech Jones.[39] This book takes up an alternative line of argument for this meeting of minds, one which is inspired by Alexander Zevin's 2019 book detailing the history of the *Economist* magazine, *Liberalism at Large*, and in particular his description of a Liberal 'extreme centre'.[40] In terms of the main drivers of Australian policy in postwar TPNG, liberalism as an 'extreme centre' aligns with Alfred Deakin's 'ethical state', what Walter James categorised as 'a liberal polity where freedom was associated not solely with individualism, but with state intervention to assure conditions where a level of liberty could be meaningfully enjoyed by all'.[41] In that sense, this book explores how liberal moderates such as Hasluck were able to align classical liberal imperatives of individualism and reward for effort with the constructive hegemony of Fabianism and state developmentalism, one advocated by the original architects of Ward's 'New Deal'.

Paul Hasluck was the single most influential policymaker to contribute to the development of TPNG in the postwar period. In his memoir, *A Time for Building*, he presents the evolution of policy in candid detail, frequently

---

37 Paul Hasluck, *Mucking about*, 2nd ed. (Nedlands: University of Western Australia Press, 1994), 147; Robert Porter, *Paul Hasluck: A political biography* (Nedlands: University of Western Australia Press, 1993), 6–10; Anna Haebich, 'The formative years: Paul Hasluck and Aboriginal issues during the 1930s', in *Paul Hasluck in Australian history: Civic personality and public life*, ed. Tom Stannage, Kay Saunders and Richard Nile (St Lucia: University of Queensland Press, 1999), 95.
38 Judith Brett, 'Limited politics', in Stannage, Saunders and Nile, *Paul Hasluck in Australian history*, 192–94.
39 MacWilliam, *Securing village life*, 31.
40 Alexander Zevin, *Liberalism at large: The world according to the* Economist (London: Verso, 2019), 15, 166.
41 Walter James, *What were they thinking: 150 years of political thinking in Australia* (Sydney: University of New South Wales Press, 2010), 109.

quoting from minutes and memoranda. As a source of reference, it is of vital importance to this book, confirming his dedication to individualism and an economic system based around the Indigenous smallholder. A discussion paper by academics Tony Voutas, Brian Jinks, Allan Healy and Hank Nelson (among others), provides an alternative perspective, a counterweight to the Hasluck reflection, one which acknowledges his contribution but is critical of many aspects of his decision-making.[42] Regardless, Hasluck so dominated all aspects of policymaking during his period as Minister that it is difficult to overestimate the significance of his role and opinion on most subjects to do with postwar colonial development in the territories.

A recently published book from historian Nicholas Ferns, *Australia in the Age of International Development, 1945–1975*, provides an interesting and informative perspective of the influences shaping Hasluck's development ideas. While this book has focussed on internal debate and colonial practice in the Territory, Ferns provides an important analysis of how modernisation theory, which played such an important role in United States development practice, increasingly influenced Hasluck and Australian policymakers' plans for PNG. Ferns argues that a key assumption of policymakers throughout the Hasluck period was that once modernisation and development had commenced then it would become an irreversible process. He points out that Hasluck and his policymakers were shaped by a fervent belief in the unique situation of PNG as a development and colonial project, especially in relation to its 'primitive' nature, and how this informed their faith in replacing tradition with the positive effects of modern infrastructure (civil, political, technical).[43] Another important figure of this period was Ian Downs who, like Hasluck, wrote a detailed book on his experience in the territories during the postwar period. His 1980 book, *Australian Trusteeship*, is an extraordinarily detailed account of his experience as a patrol officer, district commissioner, coffee planter and politician.[44] It is a significant source of reference for academic literature written on postwar development in TPNG.[45]

---

42 Alan Ward, Tony Voutas and Brian Jinks, eds, *The Hasluck years: Some observations. The administration of Papua New Guinea, 1952–63* (Bundoora: Latrobe University, 1977).
43 Nicholas Ferns, *Australia in the age of international development, 1945–1975: Colonial and foreign aid policy in Papua New Guinea and Southeast Asia* (Cham: Palgrave Macmillan, 2020), 84–85, doi.org/10.1007/978-3-030-50228-7.
44 Ian Downs, *The Australian trusteeship: Papua New Guinea 1945–75* (Canberra: Australian Government Publishing Service, 1980).
45 Wright, 'State practice'; MacWilliam, *Securing village life*; Timms, 'The post World War Two colonial project'; John Connell, *Papua New Guinea: The struggle for development* (London: Routledge, 1997).

Agriculture is the primary category of analysis. Wendy Timms argues the most obvious difference between pre- and postwar policies was the increasing contribution to the production of tree crops for export by Indigenous Papua New Guineans.[46] In the main, the secondary literature describes Australian colonial practice as one of duality, preferencing Indigenous smallholder agricultural production to protect rural communities and improve living standards. MacWilliam, Wright, Timms and others explain that smallholder farming (instead of plantation or town-based industry) provided an opportunity to maintain existing rural social systems (also a control measure) while advancing Indigenous participation in the production of tree crops for export. This is further expanded by Kim Godbold in her thesis detailing the experience of agricultural officers in the late colonial period.[47] However, as critics including John Connell and Diana Howlett have argued, this commitment reduced the potential for a rapid transition to wage labour.[48] Regardless of the outcome of this policy, the intent of smallholder agriculture practice was analogous to 'New Deal' intent, to ameliorate the impact of capitalism and improve the living standards of Papua New Guineans. Both the Chifley Labor and Menzies Liberal/Country governments advocated, to some extent, the defence of small-scale ownership of agricultural holdings in preference to large-scale plantations. Ideologically, the basis for their arguments was different—Labor to protect the villager, Liberal to encourage individualism—but the result was the same. The four case studies of this book explore this debate, particularly the lack of government officers, which substantially affected the implementation of agricultural development policy.

Outline

This book is arranged into two parts. Part One consists of four chapters which explore and explain the Australian postwar ambition for TPNG, the rationale behind its development plans and the early provisional Territory Administration and later Hasluck years. It is a Eurocentric explanation of what the Australian Government 'intended' to do, the development tools

---

46 Timms, 'The post World War Two colonial project', 114.
47 Kim Godbold, 'Didiman: Australian Agricultural Extension Officers in the Territory of Papua and New Guinea, 1945–75' (PhD thesis, Queensland University of Technology, 2010).
48 Diana Howlett, R Hide and Elspeth Young, *Chimbu: Issues in development* (Canberra: Development Studies Centre, Monograph no. 4, The Australian National University, 1976); Connell, *Papua New Guinea*.

they planned on using and why they chose to use those tools. Part Two includes four case studies, each comprising two chapters. Each case study investigates and assesses the social and physical impact of Australian policies in the villages, the reaction of local people particularly regarding autonomous actions, and how the Australian Government reacted to conditions on the ground in relation to physical and sociopolitical challenges. The conclusion provides a summation of postwar colonial development from both the official and local viewpoint, assessing the performance of the Australian Government as outlined by Ward in 1945.

Part one: 'Australian Postwar Ambition for TPNG'

Chapter 1 covers the period from the early 1940s to October 1945. Beginning with Ward's July 1945 'New Deal' speech, this chapter explains the difficult circumstances Australia faced in attempting to introduce progressive colonial development programs to an undeveloped territory in the immediate aftermath of a world war and a decolonising world. It explores the general Australian attitude of the time towards TPNG, imperialism, development and reconstruction. A significant portion of this chapter is dedicated to the disparate views of key Australians associated with the future of TPNG, including Territory officers, expatriate settlers, army directorate academics, and officers in both External Territories (DET) and DEA. Given these complexities, the final section of this chapter explains the impetus behind the 'New Deal', how and why postwar colonial development plans were structured around smallholder agroeconomics, and Indigenous welfare.

Chapter 2 covers the period following the end of World War II until the appointment of Paul Hasluck as Territories Minister in April 1951. This chapter charts the early postwar years of the provisional administration and explains how the efforts of progressive Territory officers were able to maintain, to some degree, the impetus of the 'New Deal' in the face of resistance from many prewar officials and an inactive Territories Department in Canberra. It argues that many of the ideas which originated out of the provisional administration, particularly community development, would play a critical role in the Hasluck Administration of the 1950s and 60s. This chapter, and the one following, emphasise the importance of such programs which played out on the ground in the villages where local people often embraced them with enthusiasm.

Chapter 3 covers the 12-year period of Paul Hasluck as Territories Minister, 1951–63. It explains the philosophical underpinning of Hasluck's development beliefs, especially social trusteeship, assimilation and public administration. It explores his interventionist development program against the extremes of capitalism and the promotion of Indigenous welfare and social advancement. This chapter concludes with an examination of Hasluck's view on public administration and the structure of the Territory Administration, before describing how the lack of staff and structural issues in the bureaucracy hampered the implementation of policy.

Chapter 4 outlines the Australian objective for TPNG. It introduces the Hasluck Development Pyramid, a key research tool of this book, to explain how the government's 'demand-driven' development policy was expected to develop the needs and wants of local people and progressively prepare them for the ultimate attainment of self-government. This chapter introduces problems such as a lack of resources and staff that would later hamper the implementation of policy. It also makes clear how the government placed faith in Australian expertise at the expense of Indigenous knowledge and input, which would later prove a major failing, forcing the government to radically adjust and introduce new development programs. Therefore, while this chapter fixates on Hasluck and Australian planning and implementation of postwar development policy, it also encapsulates the disconnect between the coloniser and colonised.

Part two: 'Indigenous Influence: Local Conditions and Autonomous Actions'

The first case study (Chapters 5 and 6) is of the Chimbu subdistrict's postwar development experience, one profoundly shaped by regional characteristics and the demands of the Chimbu people. These chapters explain how government officials on the ground were unable to implement 'New Deal' plans for commercial agriculture due to a scarcity of arable land, high population density and a local population who demanded equality of opportunity to raise their living standards. In response, the government introduced the Highland Labour Scheme, which aimed to address short-term Territory-wide economic concerns (lack of plantation labour) but morphed into a temporary labour migration scheme in the hope of overcoming the inherent problems associated with the subdistrict. This case study provides the first example of how local factors were integral to development practice: the Chimbu postwar experience highlights the interdependent relationship between the aims of the Australian Administration, the regional characteristics on the ground and the autonomy of local people.

The second case study (Chapters 7 and 8) is of Milne Bay, one dominated by an Indigenous elite led by Henri Leki, who utilised proceeds from war compensation to establish socioeconomic enterprises of dynamism and vision. These chapters explore the genesis behind these activities and the response of the Territory Administration, more concerned with its inability to control events and local repercussions if these ventures should fail. It investigates how a colonised people were able to demonstrate a significant measure of Indigenous socioeconomic autonomy, and yet were forced to operate within the strictures of their colonial guardian. The final part of this case study explains how, in a rare example of a coordinated approach to community development, an agricultural officer (William Cottrell-Dormer) and local leader (Alice Wedega) successfully established Village Women and Agricultural Committees by melding together colonial ambition and Indigenous autonomy.

The third case study (Chapters 9 and 10) is of Maprik subdistrict located in the Sepik District. These two chapters describe how local people on the coast and the inland foothills of the Maprik subdistrict moved ahead of the administration in the introduction of cash cropping and economic opportunity. The genesis for these new ideas was Pita Simogun, who established a movement of dynamic Indigenous leadership, vision and energy, one which spread through inland diplomatic networks. In this case study we follow how Augen, a former police colleague, implemented Simogun's ideas in Maprik, inspiring villagers to work together and become independent. Later, Paul Hasluck, on a visit to Sepik, noted the expanding garden scheme and directed the establishment of a village rice scheme. This book explores this program, the administration and Indigenous responses, and the outcome of its implementation.

The final case study (Chapters 11 and 12) is of the postwar experience on New Hanover Island. These chapters describe a situation of contrasting and confused ambition between the people of New Hanover and the colonial administration. The government regarded the people of New Hanover as a dangerous and unsettled people, and this attitude informed much of the development programs for the island, one reflected by tension, of colonial control, development and repeated disappointment. Local leadership was headed by Singerau, a dynamic, forceful and entrepreneurial person who proactively manipulated government programs to benefit himself and his community. These chapters explore the administration's relationship with this dynamic leader as it evolved over the Hasluck era and the remarkable agency of the New Hanover people in the development programs. It assesses the growing failure of these programs in this subdistrict and points to the fine line that colonised people such as Singerau had to tread to stay within the boundaries of proper behaviour, an attitude true for all colonial administrations.

Conclusion: 'The "New Deal" Assessed: Just Rhetoric or the Basis for Independence?'

Chapter 13 provides a summation of postwar colonial development from both the official and local viewpoint. While it is important to recognise that Minister Ward's speech was broad in nature, it did provide a platform and an outline of plans for the postwar development of TPNG. On a macro level, an assessment can be made on the conditions in 1946 and at the end of the Hasluck period in 1963. For example, a claim of the number of local councils, cooperative societies, children in school and so on for a subdistrict reported in the 1965 World Bank report can be compared with 1945. A deeper analysis can look at where they are located, and how they have changed the lives of Indigenous people. By drilling down further, studying multiple patrol reports, annual reports and other extraneous sources, the 'real' effects can be understood on the ground. This chapter answers questions such as: Were the criticisms levelled at the Australian Administration warranted? How did they compare to the grand rhetoric of Ward in 1945? Were the failures understandable, or even in their control? Was the reality on the ground in the subdistricts dramatically different to the official reports? What is a fair assessment of Australian rule in TPNG from 1945 to 1965?

Part One: Australian Postwar Ambition for the Territory of Papua New Guinea

1

The Impetus for the 'New Deal for Papua New Guinea': Australia's Response to a Unique Postwar Colonial Circumstance

> This new bill is an earnest indication of a new deal for the dark races ... It means that we have decided that, although we shall proudly sustain the policy of a White Australia, we shall also, if we have subject races under us, eventually provide them with conditions comparable to our own.[1]
>
> Leslie Haylen (Labor member for Parkes)

A general summation of the historiography on Eddie Ward is that he was an uninterested Territories Minister who, nevertheless, was the catalyst for a shift in emphasis towards the needs of the Indigenous population of the Australian Territory of Papua New Guinea (TPNG).[2] The first TPNG

---

1 Commonwealth (Australia), *Parliamentary Debates*, House of Representatives, 18 July 1945 (Leslie Haylen).
2 The literature includes: John Connell, *Papua New Guinea: The struggle for development* (London: Routledge, 1997); Ian Downs, *The Australian trusteeship: Papua New Guinea 1945–75* (Canberra: Australian Government Publishing Service, 1980); Huntley Wright, 'State practice and rural smallholder production: Late-colonialism and the agrarian doctrine in Papua New Guinea, 1942–1969' (PhD thesis, Massey University, 1999); Brian Jinks, 'Policy, planning and administration in Papua New Guinea, 1942–1952: With special reference to the role of Colonel J.K. Murray' (PhD thesis, University of Sydney, 1975); Scott MacWilliam, *Securing village life: Development in late colonial Papua New Guinea* (Canberra: ANU Press, 2013), doi.org/10.22459/SVL.05.2013; Paul Hasluck, *A time for building: Australian administration in Papua and New Guinea, 1951–1963* (Carlton: Melbourne University Press, 1976); WEH

administrator, JK Murray, was more generous, describing Ward as not only approachable and a good listener, but a humanitarian in outlook and 'most responsible for basic policy for the entire post-war period'.[3] Ward's 'New Deal' was part of a larger Labor aim in the postwar Pacific, one informed by the efforts of Department of External Affairs (DEA) Minister HV Evatt, who proposed a compulsory system of trusteeship for monitoring colonial powers at the 1945 San Francisco Conference on International Organisation. These Labor policy platforms originated from the work of DEA government officers and the Army's Directorate of Research and Civil Affairs (DORCA). These efforts resulted in Australia posing as a defender of small nations in an international context, while domestically, Ward's 'New Deal' forthrightly promoted Papuan and New Guinean welfare and advancement at the expense of prewar expatriate capitalism.

Ward's opposition to the labour practices and the economic dominance of expatriate settlers was the basis of new Australian colonial policies. His changes transformed Indigenous experiences and ended capital accumulation among white traders and plantation owners. Ward's approach to colonial development was an amalgamation of two interrelated ideologies: labourism and populism. The core tenets of labourism date back to the Federation and the Australian settlement: White Australia, tariff protection, the Labor party, compulsory arbitration and strong unions. Labourism is associated with other opposition movements of the nineteenth century to the social relations of capitalism: Fabianism, the Chartist Movement and the ideas of William Cobbett.[4] To Ward, it was an approach for getting a 'fair deal', negating the demanding excesses of laissez-faire capitalism; populism is an attractive political style because, by its very nature, it breaks down ideas into simple digestible pieces.

Stanner, *The South Seas in transition* (Sydney: Australasian Publishing Company, 1953); John D Legge, *Australian colonial policy* (Sydney: Australian Institute of International Affairs, 1956); Wendy Timms, 'The post World War Two colonial project and Australian planters in Papua New Guinea: The search for relevance in the colonial twilight' (PhD thesis, The Australian National University, 1996).

3   JK Murray, 'In retrospect—Papua–New Guinea 1945–1949 and Territory of Papua and New Guinea 1949–1952', *Australian Journal of Politics and History* 14 (1968): 321, doi.org/10.1111/j.1467-8497.1968.tb00711.x.

4   Wright, 'State practice', 128–39.

Figure 1.1: Minister for External Territories Edward John Ward.
Source: National Archives of Australia (NAA), A1200, L21653, item 11257948.

For a politician of the far left such as Ward, populism was a way of utilising or incorporating social justice, equality, fellowship and cooperation with effective anti-elite and anti-capitalist rhetoric. It was, therefore, in many ways, a meeting of ideas with style. Ward and his key advisers were enamoured with Fabianism, which is reflected in the grand humanitarian rhetoric of the 'New Deal' speech. On the other hand, the speech and planning documents reveal a concerning lack of detail. Ward's later management of the Department of External Territories (DET) portfolio further underlines this. From 1946, Ward provided almost no policy direction, deliberately shutting himself off from the Territory Administration, and creating a policy vacuum that stifled further innovation.[5] Therefore, any analysis of the 'New Deal' must begin with the question: Was it merely a program of anti-capitalist ideas set within populist humanitarian rhetoric? Or was the 'New Deal' a genuine attempt to negate the harmful effects of capitalist accumulation and encroaching globalisation?

This chapter is predominantly concerned with explaining the difficult circumstances Australia faced in attempting to introduce a revolutionary new suite of development programs to an undeveloped territory in the immediate aftermath of a world war and a decolonising world. It is broken into three sections: the first analyses the Ward speech of 4 July 1945; the second explores the complex task facing Australian colonial administrators; and finally, the third examines the impetus behind Australia's postwar colonial development programs.

Ward and the 'New Deal'

In the postwar period, Fabianism became an intermediary force between capitalism, globalisation and imperial networks. Fabians were responsible for advocating new colonial development theories that mediated the excesses of capitalism. Ward's key advisers, academics working at DORCA, were, for the most part, Fabians and they provided most of the policy innovations for the 'New Deal'.[6] Ward was amenable to their radical new ideas for colonial development because he associated the programs most closely with labourism and desired an end to indentured labour. While short on detail, the 'New Deal' provided the space firstly, to check the advance of European-controlled labour relations, and secondly, to encourage state-sponsored Indigenous agriculture programs at the expense of plantation and trading capital.[7]

---

5   Jinks, 'Policy, planning and administration', 528.
6   For more details see: Geoffrey G Gray, Doug Munro and Christine Winter, eds, *Scholars at war: Australasian social scientists, 1939–1945* (Canberra: ANU Press, 2012), doi.org/10.22459/SW.01.2012; Graeme Sligo, *The backroom boys: Alfred Conlon and Army's Directorate of Research and Civil Affairs, 1942–1946* (Newport: Big Sky Publishing, 2013).
7   Wright, 'State practice', 127.

Given Ward's ideological convictions, conditions of labour, and particularly indentured labour, were of prime interest to the government. He had a reputation as a radical leftist and was particularly uncomfortable with being held responsible for a system of indentured labour which he regarded as akin to slavery.[8] It is unsurprising that his 'New Deal' speech emphasised the intention to introduce regulations which would end the exploitation of Indigenous labour on European-owned plantations: 'to give the native an opportunity to advance in his own right and not merely to be an instrument for employment by non-native agriculturists or industrialists'.[9] In fact, Indigenous labour dominated the substantive content of his speech: more than one-third of the 3,000 words explained the government's intention to abolish indentured labour 'as soon as practicable'.[10] Other radical changes to labour policy included the creation of a Department of Labour, and in the interim before indenture's eventual termination, 13 amendments were proposed to existing employment conditions, including an increase of the minimum wage to 15 shillings per month; improved rations; elimination of professional recruiters; government controls of labour recruits from any one location; reduced maximum work hours per week to 44; maximum employment contract period of one year, after which a worker must be returned to their village for a minimum of three months; minimum age of employment increased to 16; and provision for worker's compensation.[11]

The elimination of indentured labour was a direct response to concerns regarding labour demand and how it would continue to 'impose a serious strain on native social life'. At the December 1944 meeting of the Ministerial Sub-Committee on Australian Territories, it was noted that:

---

8   Report of Minister Ward's tour of Papua–New Guinea, 16/4-9/5/1944, Papers of Edward John Ward, MS2396/43A/2, National Library of Australia (NLA).
9   Commonwealth (Australia), *Parliamentary Debates*, House of Representatives, 4 July 1945 (Edward Ward), 'The Papua-New Guinea Provisional Administration Bill: Second Reading'.
10 *Parliamentary Debates*, 4 July 1945 (Edward Ward).
11 Wages prewar and during the war were 5 shillings per month. Ward proposed a minimum threefold increase and a government investigation into wage conditions (in 1947/48, the highest minimum for semi-skilled workers [drivers, for instance] was 70 shillings and skilled labourers [cabinet-makers or senior clerks] of 180 shillings per month. The anger felt by Papua and New Guineans working for the Australian New Guinea Administrative Unit (ANGAU) was described in a *Pacific Islands Monthly* article of September 1945: 'The natives are resentful because they cannot understand why the Government holds them under labour conscription, and why proposals to increase the basic wage rate from 5s. to 15s a month did not become operative immediately'. 'Native Troops Mutiny', *Pacific Islands Monthly*, 18 September 1945, Native Labour: 1945–51, B213 [3/2], National Archives of Australia (NAA). See also *Parliamentary Debates*, 4 July 1945 (Edward Ward).

resumption of development along the same [prewar] lines would leave little scope for a policy of developing a native peasant economy. There is good authority for the opinion that the latter form of [smallholder] development is more consonant with long-term native welfare than the permanent regulation of the native population to the status of wage labourers.[12]

Ward believed in an interventionist state, one where its primary role was to protect workers including small producers and consumers by regulating the industry.[13] Ward's sense of radicalism, of compensating for the negative consequences of primary capitalist accumulation, aligned with other interested parties (DORCA, missions) and provided the platform for postwar colonial development in TPNG. Prior to the Ward speech, TPNG had never been seriously considered a domestic issue in Australia, and therefore did not figure significantly in metropolitan postwar plans. Nevertheless, the 'New Deal' contained elements of the Australian Labor Party's (ALP) intent for full employment and reflected the party's international trusteeship welfare attitude. In December 1946, the Trust Agreement for New Guinea was approved by the UN General Assembly. Australia was designated as the sole administering authority of the Territory and could act as if it were an integral part of Australia.[14]

The complex task facing Australia's colonial rulers

The Australian Government was facing a congruence of complex issues when formulating postwar plans for TPNG. Firstly, at a geopolitical level, the postwar world would involve a radical reordering of the international political order: the Cold War and trenchant anti-imperial attitudes of the new world powers, the USA and the Soviet Union; the establishment of a new international peace and security organisation, the United Nations (UN); and particularly the creation of the trusteeship system, which was strongly advocated for by Australian External Affairs Minister, HV Evatt. Secondly, an amalgamation of the Territory services brought with

---

12   Minutes of Ministerial Sub-Committee on Australian Territories, 6 December 1944, Australia Internal External Territories Civil Administration 1944, A989 [1944/735/144/6], NAA.
13   Elwyn Spratt, *Eddie Ward: Firebrand of East Sydney* (Adelaide: Rigby, 1965), 3.
14   Michael Leifer, 'Australia, trusteeship and New Guinea', *Pacific Affairs* 36, no. 3 (1963): 251, doi.org/10.2307/2754350.

it a merging of substantially different attitudes to colonial administration, one which significantly affected the implementation of 'New Deal' plans. Thirdly, the lack of genuine interest in the territories as anything more than a security buffer meant that in the postwar period, the sudden move towards progressive direct action was hampered by the lack of adequate preparation on the ground in the villages. Fourthly, the physical and social impact of the Pacific War on TPNG and its subsequent influence on postwar colonial planning. Fifthly, the internal socioeconomic, political and physical characteristics of the Territory, which hampered any direct external action. Finally, dynamics within the Australian Government and between Ward's chosen advisers, DORCA and DET, stifled planning and future implementation of 'New Deal' ideas.

A significant influence on the Australian rule of TPNG was the UN trusteeship monitoring system advocated for by Evatt. The trusteeship and the international monitoring matched the internationalism of Evatt, and the broader Labor goals for development.[15] It aligned with other activities of the DEA during this period such as the January 1944 Australia–New Zealand pact (known as the ANZAC Agreement) and prominent advocacy for international liberalism (of which the trusteeship system is an excellent example).[16] Evatt was surrounded by a new elite, people such as William (Bill) Forsyth, Herbert Coombs, John Burton and Paul Hasluck, who brought a strong belief in liberal internationalism, trusteeship in colonial policy, and the central role of the state in nation-building.[17]

The ANZAC Agreement was the first international treaty signed by Australia without Britain being a co-signatory. Historian Chris Waters describes the ANZAC pact as an attempt by Australia to coopt power in the Pacific, 'a blueprint for Australian international policy in the region'.[18] Evatt, in his statement of 21 January 1944, felt:

---

15   David Lee, 'The Curtin and Chifley governments: Liberal internationalism and world organisation', in *Evatt to Evans: The Labor tradition in Australian foreign policy*, ed. David Lee and Christopher Waters (St Leonards: Allen and Unwin, 1997), 60; Wayne Reynolds, 'H.V. Evatt: The imperial connection and the quest for Australian security, 1941–1945' (PhD thesis, Newcastle University, 1985), 321; W Hudson, 'Australia and the New World Order: Evatt at San Francisco, 1945' (PhD thesis, The Australian National University, 1993), 31–34.
16   Department of External Territories (DET), 'Australian New Zealand Conference October 1944 colonial policy: Mandates', Australia Internal External Territories Civil Administration 1944, A989 [1944/735/144/6], NAA.
17   Christopher Waters, 'Creating a tradition: The foreign policy of the Curtin and Chifley governments', in Lee and Waters, *Evatt to Evans*, 36.
18   Waters, 'Creating a tradition', 38.

> the Conference is of the greatest value to the cause of the United Nations in the Pacific. The peoples of the United Nations will certainly look to the two great British democracies of the South Pacific to give a lead in the post-war period.[19]

In the aftermath of the Japanese air raids on Australia in 1942, the Commonwealth demanded a form of security barrier be maintained. At the same time, the DEA was mindful of international concerns regarding imperialism and the future of colonies. Social trusteeship was conceived as antithetical to prewar colonialism, as a method of eliminating the exploitation of colonised peoples by European powers. Evatt explained in a speech on 28 April 1943 at the Overseas Press club, New York, that peace and stability in the Pacific were reliant on taking:

> into account the legitimate aspirations of the peoples and if we provide a basis for economic development which will provide improving standards for all the peoples of the Pacific … no world or regional system of security, however, can be permanent unless it has an adequate basis in economic justice.[20]

British and Australian officials often disagreed over the terms of the colonial governance, particularly over Australia's insistence on a limited form of UN supervision. Australian postwar colonial planners were not fervently opposed to British thinking. Both envisaged Indigenous socioeconomic development: British via independent state-sponsored programs whereas Australia via social trusteeship. Evatt believed that Australia had to satisfy its own conscience about imperialism and argued for a form of international supervision for trustee states that clearly distinguished postwar trusteeship from prewar imperialism.[21] Evatt acknowledged that 'the lust for colonial areas is a constant threat to the security of the world and will no longer be tolerated by the public opinion of enlightened peoples'. However, by proceeding:

> on the basic principle that those countries whose historical development has placed them in control of colonial areas are to be regarded as occupying the position of trustees.[22]

---

19   Herbert Evatt, *Foreign policy of Australia: Speeches* (Sydney: Angus and Robertson, 1945), 155.
20   Evatt, *Foreign policy*, 114–16.
21   Wright, 'State practice', 92.
22   Evatt, *Foreign policy*, 117.

At the San Francisco conference, Evatt directed his key advisers on specific aspects of the UN Charter: Hasluck on international security, Burton on economic development and Forsyth on the trusteeship colonial requirements.[23] Waters explains that Evatt's actions in several arenas, beginning with the ANZAC pact and including forceful debates with the Great Powers (the United States of America, the United Kingdom, the Union of Socialist Soviet Republics, France and China) at San Francisco, had two aims.[24] Firstly, to garner an international reputation as a strong independent nation, but secondly, and far more significantly regarding TPNG, to implement its international program. Australian foreign affairs advisers, such as John Burton and Bill Forsyth, foresaw the principle of trusteeship as essential to the administration of TPNG, and the advance of welfare to Indigenous peoples throughout Southeast Asia. It also met Australia's strategic objective for the Territory as a security buffer against potential invasion. In other words, trusteeship could be used as a vehicle to deliver Australia's twin goals for its colonial Territory. These views aligned with, and were politically acceptable to, the Atlantic Charter and UN Charter: as trustees whose responsibility was to provide an administration focussed on socioeconomic advancement and political independence; and recognition that colonial powers should be held responsible for their actions to an international body.[25] As such, the ANZAC pact included a proposal for a South Seas Regional Commission, an in situ Pacific UN, to monitor and 'recommend a common policy for advancing the interests of all native peoples'.[26] During the early 1940s, Forsyth's development opinions on Asia and the Pacific were apparent from personal correspondence with (Sir) Frederic Eggleston, articles in the Australian Institute of International Affairs' bimonthly journal *The Austral–Asiatic Bulletin*, and in policy documents for the DEA.[27] Wright describes Forsyth as playing a similar role to British Labour politician (and Fabian) Arthur Creech Jones, both advocating for colonial policies that tied the provision of welfare and

---

23 Transcript of oral history, Papers of William Douglass Forsyth, MS5700/8/1/45, p. 85, NLA.
24 Gerry Simpson, 'The Great Powers, sovereign equality and the making of the United Nations Charter', *Australian Year Book of International Law* 21 (2000):133, doi.org/10.22145/aybil.21.8.
25 Waters, 'Creating a tradition', 39, 44; Evatt, *Foreign Policy,* 114–16.
26 Evatt, *Foreign policy,* 157.
27 Personal correspondence between Eggleston and Forsyth from the 1940s, available in Papers of William Douglass Forsyth, MS5700/13/6/3, NLA. For more details on *The Austral–Asiatic Bulletin* see: James Cotton, 'The Institute's seventieth volume: The journal, its origins and its engagement with foreign policy debate', *Australian Journal of International Affairs* 70, no. 5 (2016): 471–83, doi.org/10.1080/10357718.2016.1167836.

economic development. As such, colonial trusteeship became the medium through which postwar development was provisioned, attempting to balance the dual needs of Indigenous welfare and fiscal responsibility.

Prewar officers were often resistant to new postwar colonial ideas. Before the war, officers faced very different circumstances; in a sense, they were indoctrinated by ideas of racial superiority and the 'prehistoric' nature of Indigenous culture.[28] Many were dismissive of new egalitarian ideas for Indigenous welfare and economic development introduced by external academics. They had lived with hardship and faced practical difficulties; many believed the level of sociopolitical development was so low that even if new opportunities were provided Indigenous groups would not take advantage of them.[29] These beliefs had begun to be challenged with the entrance of new officers from the Australian School of Pacific Administration (ASOPA) who were educated in a more liberal outlook.[30] This division in racial attitudes between new and old officers caused much discontent within the postwar Territory Administration.[31]

In 1948, David Fenbury, at the time an ASOPA lecturer, delivered a presentation to new officers in which he argued there was a 'cultural lag typified by provincial or colonial society' in TPNG which was making a 'concerted effort to estrange those who have begun to develop in the direction of a civilised way of life'. He warned these prospective officers that many prewar officers, and the general expatriate community, wanted the Territory to revert to type, to the way things had always operated in the colonial period.[32] For his part, Ward regarded the planters as colonial capitalists and as such were the worst form of expatriate. Contempt ran both ways. Expatriates were scathing of not just the new direction of the Australian Government, but the administration during the war: the widespread confusion, lack of preparation and their summary treatment by the military.[33] In this environment, the European community became an effective opposition to the postwar administration, hampering efforts on the ground in TPNG while instigating political unrest

---

28 John R Black, 'Native administration', Papers of John Black, MS8346/12/10, NLA.
29 Jinks, 'Policy, planning and administration', 59.
30 A 1946 circular issued to officers noted that they were expected to keep themselves fully informed as to 'native thoughts and hopes'. Department of District Services and Native Affairs, 'Maintenance of Native Confidence', 1 November 1946, Papers of John Black, MS8346/11/2, NLA.
31 Jinks, 'Policy, planning and administration', 54.
32 David M Fenbury, 'ASOPA lecture notes 1948/49', Papers of David Maxwell Fenbury, MS6747/3/2, NLA.
33 DET, 'Inquiry into new administration and circumstances of army takeover in 1942', 24 November 1944, Civil Administration of Papua and New Guinea (Post War) Full Cabinet Decision of February 1944, A5954 [603/4], NAA.

in Canberra via links with various conservative politicians.³⁴ In May 1942 an advocacy group, the Pacific Territories Association, was formed. This group communicated vigorously on behalf of the expatriate planters with both the Australian press and politicians. A persistent theme was one of bitterness towards Australian bureaucrats who expatriates felt, unfairly, exercised final control over the territories without having to undergo the relative hardships of New Guinean life.³⁵

The overall effect of the war upon the Indigenous population was dramatic. It had a grave impact in many parts of the Territory, particularly New Guinea, which suffered on many fronts: major food shortages; deaths from bombs, bullets and disease; demand for indentured labour which decimated village social, political and economic systems; the emotional toll of fleeing battles; and wholesale destruction of villages.³⁶ There was a powerful psychological impact as Papua New Guineans were confronted with Western technical power. Apart from destruction caused by hostilities, there was a bewildering change in overlords with the advance and flight of the Japanese, and the demands of military service devastated village economies, accelerating the forces of social changes.³⁷ General Blamey wrote in February 1944 of the wholesale destruction of the Territory, that for 'all intents and purposes' commercial interests were non-operative.³⁸ Ian Downs described Port Moresby as a 'visible testimony to its own hardships'. A victim of Japanese bombing and Australian looting, it resembled an 'unkempt graveyard' as soldiers ripped away walls and flooring from empty houses to improve distant temporary camps.³⁹

Of considerable importance was the union of the Territory Administration in March 1942 under the auspices of the Australian New Guinea Administrative Unit (ANGAU). Firstly, because it overcame the longstanding opposition to the joint administration of the territories. Secondly, it was a unique opportunity to witness the effect of the massive incursion of virtually unlimited financial and human resources, and logistics support in spheres of communication, district administration and health services.⁴⁰

---

34   David M Fenbury, 'History of the Territory Administration', Papers of David Maxwell Fenbury, MS6747/3/3, NLA.
35   Jinks, 'Policy, planning and administration', 54, 63, 65, 92, 95.
36   DET, 'War damage compensation', Papers of Edward John Ward, MS2396/12/1071-1145, NLA.
37   Legge, *Australian colonial policy*, 186.
38   T Blamey to J Curtin, 4 February 1944, The situation of Australian colonies as at January 1944, A989 [1943/735/144/3], NAA, pp. 8–10.
39   Downs, *The Australian trusteeship*, 8.
40   'Functions and organisation of ANGAU', Pacific-Australian Territories–ANGAU, A989 [1944/655/22], NAA; DET, Report to Minister Ward, 'Public service staff at time of suspension of civil administration', Papers of Edward John Ward, MS2396/43A/5, NLA.

PREPARING A NATION?

However, ANGAU was a military operation: measures introduced were intended to promote military goals. They were in control of two territories devastated by war where normal civilian services such as public works, electricity and telephones were not in operation, or were converted for military use. As such, they prioritised organisational needs, especially the mobilisation of labour, the training of Indigenes for military service, and the provision of health services to increase labour supply. Regardless of its utilitarian motives, in terms of medical services, the impact of ANGAU was impressive. For example, for the year to September 1944, 84,617 people were treated in hospital while a further 68,332 were assisted during 523 patrols; the costs of drugs, rations and equipment alone exceeded the whole prewar Papuan budget by 35 per cent.[41] One area where ANGAU had a negative effect was the indentured labour policy. An investigation undertaken by Army Land Force Headquarters (LHQ) in 1944 was scathing of the treatment of Indigenous labourers. It described an environment where brutal overseers remained in charge despite clear indications that they were unfit to exercise authority. Army command was accused of wasting labour, and the investigation described many instances of corruption.[42]

The DET, established in 1941, was formerly a small part of the Prime Minister's Department, and under wartime conditions had few duties to perform.[43] The Department Secretary, James Halligan, was a long-term public servant who was not sympathetic to progressive, socially inclusive Indigenous economic systems but instead favoured large-scale enterprises and the re-establishment of plantations.[44] David Fenbury described him as 'quite ignorant of the special problems involved' in developing TPNG.[45] Regardless of criticism of the Secretary, as Scott MacWilliam points out, the department was too small and suffered from constant staff shortages: there was not the resources or time for detailed planning even if the desire existed.[46]

The Labor Government began preparations for a return to civilian rule in July 1943. On the recommendation of the DET, Professor George Paton and an officer from ANGAU, Major Nicholas Penglase, attended

---

41 Jinks, 'Policy, planning and administration', 100–4.
42 Stanner, *South Seas*, 80–81.
43 Spratt, *Eddie Ward*, 143–45; Connell, *Papua New Guinea*, 20.
44 Jinks, 'Policy, planning and administration', 271.
45 David M Fenbury, draft article to Pacific Islands Monthly under the Pseudonym 'Kiap', 1 September 1952, Papers of David Maxwell Fenbury, MS6747/3/1, NLA.
46 Skilled personnel shortages were a worldwide problem. MacWilliam, *Securing village life*, 42.

training in colonial administration in the US and Britain.[47] However, their forthcoming report was supplanted by the establishment of DORCA on 6 October 1943. Over the next two years, DORCA became almost the only source of advice to the Australian Government on the future of TPNG.[48] The director was Lieutenant Colonel Alf Conlon, regarded as somewhat of a visionary by his colleagues, and as an interfering dreamer by his opponents, more interested in theory than in practice. According to Julius Stone, his genius was in combining both. The activities and output of the army directorate divide opinion, but there is one point of consensus: Conlon enjoyed direct access to, and exerted a remarkable influence on, Prime Minister Curtin, Minister Ward and General Blamey. (Sir) Donald Cleland, in a personal diary report of a visit to LHQ Melbourne in July 1944, describes meeting and observing Conlon at work, noting his unusual work methods and eclectic manner. Interestingly, Cleland, in his role as ANGAU chief of staff, was also assessing the relationship between Conlon and Ward, describing it as an 'unknown factor', and praising Conlon's observation of Ward as 'difficult and unpredictable'.[49] This attitude hints at the tension which existed between DORCA and government/military officials involved in the territories, primarily due to the close relationship between the Minister and his key advisers at the directorate. Jinks explains that it was Conlon's unorthodoxy as much as his intellect that attracted these leaders to him. Simply, Curtin and Blamey were under great pressure, and to discuss broad-ranging policy with someone as unorthodox as Conlon provided some respite. Furthermore, Conlon was able to smooth communication issues between Blamey and Ward.[50]

By February 1944, the army directorate boasted an impressive array of anthropologists, economists, lawyers and other academics with expertise, described by Ian Downs, as 'probably unmatched for the variety of their skills in any Commonwealth department at that time'.[51] DORCA was regarded as a group of talented people who, with almost no operational responsibility and ample time for discussion, were able to construct a radical new postwar direction for TPNG. Critics, including prewar patrol officers, ANGAU officers and expatriate settlers, regarded the group as an impractical

---

47 Paton committee, 'Reconstruction of Papua and New Guinea', 9 July 1943, *Papers of Sir Donald Cleland*, MS9600/4/17, NLA.
48 Sligo, *Backroom boys*, 45–55.
49 Personal diary of Donald Cleland: visit on Land Force Headquarters, Melbourne, 9–27 July 1944, Papers of Sir Donald Cleland, MS9600/4/19, NLA.
50 Jinks, 'Policy, planning and administration', 124, 129.
51 Downs, *The Australian trusteeship*, 10–11.

talkfest which did not achieve any concrete results.[52] Understandably, the directorate's effort at institution-building alienated many people, but at a minimum created an atmosphere for urgent change. Anthropologist Lucy Mair regarded just the effort to prompt a change in philosophy as an accomplishment.[53] Despite Halligan's attempt to limit access to the Minister by these unorthodox academic thinkers, Ward was enamoured of them and effectively ignored his own bureaucracy. Murray regarded the army directorate as the major influence, the key component in the formulation of the 'New Deal'. Because Ward accepted the directorate proposals, it ensured the tacit approval of both Curtin and Chifley. It was not until Curtin's death in July 1945 and Blamey's resignation as Commander-in-Chief on 1 December 1945 that the influence of DORCA began to wane, and the department took control of planning and exercised full powers.[54]

Motivations for the 'New Deal'

Blamey to Curtin: The situation of Australian colonies as of January 1944

In February 1944, Commander-in-Chief (Australian Military Forces) General Thomas Blamey wrote a letter to Prime Minister Curtin outlining the situation in the Australian colonies. The letter was drafted by DORCA officers and as such is of much interest on several levels. Firstly, it provides an interesting insight into not only their attitude to colonial development theory, but also their willingness to advocate for new measures by pointing out the practical benefits for Australia. Secondly, these officers recognised the end of the Pacific War as a unique moment: a congruence of new attitudes to imperialism around the world, an awakening of interest by the Australian public to the plight of the Territory, and the unusual and specific form of military rule currently in place in TPNG that provided an opportunity to generate change. Thirdly, the letter spells out in specific terms what the policy planners felt were the appropriate steps forward: a roadmap to the 'New Deal'.

---

52 Jinks, 'Policy, planning and administration', 124–27.
53 Lucy Mair, *Australia in New Guinea* (London: Christophers, 1948), 203.
54 Jinks, 'Policy, planning and administration', 128–30.

1. THE IMPETUS FOR THE 'NEW DEAL FOR PAPUA NEW GUINEA'

Figure 1.2: John Curtin and Mrs Elsie Curtin with General Sir Thomas Blamey in 1944.
Source: NAA, M1218, 5, item 242650.

The proposals of the directorate were a revolutionary departure from prewar precedents of minimal Commonwealth interest, a lack of funds, Indigenous servitude and a dominant expatriate economy. Instead, the 'New Deal' placed Indigenous welfare and agency at the centre of proposed plans and increased Commonwealth funding, which reduced reliance on the expatriate economy. The memorandum advocated a dual policy of 'assisting to correct past abuses which have accompanied imperialism in the Pacific colonies' and providing for the defence of Australia. While the directorate had only been established for several months, the genesis for future colonial development planning of the unique opportunity available was clear. Blamey wrote of:

> generations of peace-time politics would probably never produce another comparable situation, in which the controls so often denied to or unobtainable by authority are actually in the hands of the present Government to a hitherto unparalleled degree … use policy on the highest moral level as a justified weapon of power politics to protect not only the future of the native peoples of the Pacific but

> the strategic security of Australia. It may be that we are confronted with one of those rare moments in history when morality coincides with expediency.[55]

Blamey wrote that an 'informed and forward-looking Australian policy' would not only correct past abuses but also control the powerful forces of commercialism operating in the colonies. The experience of the Pacific War had emphasised to all Australians the value of TPNG as a vital strategic buffer. Murray, regarded generally as an idealist, spoke of Australia's twin obligations to the Territory, firstly to prevent the invasion of the Commonwealth and secondly, 'to hold it, we must accept obligations regarding its people'.[56] This observation by Murray would be debated within the government (Canberra and Port Moresby) in the 20 years following the end of World War II, shaping Australian policy towards its northern colony and how development policy would be implemented.

The Japanese invasion of New Guinea in December 1941 reinforced in the minds of all Australians the strategic importance of the large island to the north. What makes Blamey's letter to Prime Minister Curtin particularly relevant is the framing of the new policies. Instead of arguing on purely humanitarian or even geopolitical grounds, the paper outlines the practical benefits to Australia of not just holding onto the Territory as a security barrier, but that the development of the islands was essential to future defence requirements. Blamey acknowledged that not every decision regarding the territories needs to be governed by military considerations. He reasoned:

> the quality and structure of economic development will largely determine the amount of resources available for improving and maintaining communications. It seems, therefore, that the basic strategic requirement is closely linked with total policy for the area, especially when it is remembered that there can be no real development unless the problem of native economic organisation, health and diet are taken up and solved.[57]

Blamey's letter provides an early indication of the future policy direction detailed in Ward's 'New Deal', of overcoming 'classical problems of colonies' such as:

---

55 T Blamey to J Curtin, 4 February 1944, pp. 4–8.
56 JK Murray, 'Talk by his Honor the Administrator', 7 June 1949, Papers of Edward John Ward, MS2396/12/792-889, NLA.
57 T Blamey to J Curtin, 4 February 1944, pp. 5–11.

malnutrition because of native ignorance and faulty diet; superstition and backward techniques; great economic poverty because of isolation; undeveloped resources and improper utilization of those resources which are possessed; exposure of native economic and social welfare to the impact of boom and depressions because of the domination of colonial productive activity by commercial interests, which themselves are subject to world economic cycles.

The letter argues that the challenges can be addressed at this unique moment. That the government should be open to 'accumulated experience of colonial problems in other parts of the world', continue the military's policy of employing technical research scientists, and utilise 'the matured experience and insight of selected individuals of its own former administrative staff for the accurate identification of conditions to be remedied'.[58]

As discussed earlier, Conlon was able to manoeuvre events in favour of the directorate primarily due to his close relationship with both Blamey and Ward. In fact, he was responsible for arranging meetings between them which influenced the Cabinet's approval for a subcommittee specifically focussed on postwar development in TPNG.[59] Apparent from the minutes of the Ministerial Sub-Committee on Australian Territories meetings was the influence of 'modern' colonial thought, a philosophy reflected in the 1940 British *Colonial Development and Welfare Act*. This Act enabled the British Government to approve schemes likely to promote the development of any colony regardless of potential benefits to the metropole. Conlon attended the first meeting held on 10 February 1944 as an adjunct to General Blamey. The subcommittee agreed that until the return of civil administration, DORCA would assume the major role in policy and planning.[60] Eight days later the subcommittee presented to the full Cabinet and warned 'that if the Territories are to be developed, the Commonwealth Government must make available much greater sums of money than have been provided for the areas in the past'.[61]

---

58 T Blamey to J Curtin, 4 February 1944, pp. 15–16.
59 Cabinet Agendum 597, 'Territories of Papua and New Guinea', 21 January 1944, Post War Reconstruction Australia, A989 [1944/735/144/3]; John Curtin, 'Instructions for subcommittee', 22 February 1944, Civil Administration of Papua and New Guinea (Post War), A5954 [603/4], NAA.
60 Downs, *The Australian trusteeship*, 11.
61 Cabinet Agendum No. 597, 'Funds for the Administration of Papua and New Guinea', 18 February 1944, Ministerial Sub-Committee, Reconstruction Policy and Post-War Planning, CP637/1 [44], NAA.

In the two years following the 10 February 1944 meeting, directorate staff studied conditions and wrote reports that directly influenced postwar development plans. Ian Hogbin, an anthropologist with vast field experience in Melanesia (particularly in the Solomon Islands), was directed to study labour conditions.[62] His recommendation was for labourers to be repatriated urgently, arguing that any new economic plan must ensure the stability of village life. Barrister and University of Queensland law lecturer Thomas Fry provided the legal advice to support the unification of the two territories.[63] His January 1945 report titled 'Relief and Rehabilitation in Australia's Territories in New Guinea' was a substantial and far-reaching document. Fry summed up the Ward–Conlon vision, with many of his recommendations included in Ward's speech of July 1945: control of economic development to protect village communities; increased Indigenous participation in justice and other duties of government; £20 million in war rehabilitation and reconstruction; and a considerable increase in annual grants.[64]

Another directorate initiative was the School of Civil Affairs, which was established on 9 January 1945. In his press release, Minister for Army Frank Forde directly associated the army with the directorate's humanitarian intentions, and explained how it would be 'similar in many respects to the British School in Civil Affairs at Wimbledon and the American School at Charlottesville'. Directorate links were further underlined as Forde promoted the quality of future school personnel who also happened to be prominent directorate officers: Stanner, Wedgewood and Hogbin.[65] An important assumption was that the military administration, having progressive views inculcated by the new school, would be able to institute sufficient reforms to make it impossible for the restored civil administration to revert to prewar policies.[66]

---

62   Jeremy Beckett and Geoffrey Gray, 'Hogbin, Herbert Ian Priestley (1904–1989)', *Australian Dictionary of Biography*, National Centre of Biography, The Australian National University, published first in hardcopy 2007, accessed online 21 December 2021 at: adb.anu.edu.au/biography/hogbin-herbert-ian-priestley-12644/text22783.

63   Thomas P Fry, 'Survey of legal systems of the Territories of Papua & New Guinea', 1946, A52/7 [349/95], NAA; Ian Carnell, 'Fry, Thomas Penberthy (1904–1952)', *Australian Dictionary of Biography*, National Centre of Biography, The Australian National University, published first in hardcopy 1996, accessed online 21 December 2021, at: adb.anu.edu.au/biography/fry-thomas-penberthy-10257/text18141.

64   Jinks, 'Policy, planning and administration', 132–33.

65   Department of The Army, Press statement, 26 February 1944, Army School of Administration, A989 [1944/735/144/6], NAA.

66   Jinks, 'Policy, planning and administration', 150–55.

1. THE IMPETUS FOR THE 'NEW DEAL FOR PAPUA NEW GUINEA'

The directorate promoted the idea of an inquiry into the devastation in TPNG. Conlon persuaded Ward to appoint JV Barry, in October 1944 as the commissioner/chairman of the war compensation inquiry.[67] Barry visited the territories in January 1945; however, the detailed field work was completed by directorate officer Ian Hogbin and ANGAU officer Jim Taylor.[68] The report, submitted in August 1945, made 21 recommendations, including the establishment of village councils, treasuries and nurseries, and cash compensation for death, injury, incapacity, deterioration of land, damage to property and destruction of possessions, food and livestock. The report reflected the intention of postwar planners to make a clean break with the prewar 'pay as you go' policy that was clearly spelt out in the British 1940 *Colonial Development and Welfare Act*. There was criticism among prewar officers and expatriate settlers who argued the financial compensation would ruin the Territory economy and render the villagers less dependent on manual labour as a source of cash income and therefore less reliant on Europeans.[69] The Barry Report was approved by the Cabinet on 17 December 1945. In October 1946 the Administrator advised the probable cost would exceed £9 million. The assessment and payment of compensation claims took up an inordinate amount of a field officers time from 1947. Every village visited provided an opportunity for every person to lodge a claim, no matter how small. As noted by Ian Downs, an officer during this period:

> there can be no doubt that payment of war damage compensation did a great deal to restore the confidence of the people in the civil government. In most cases, compensation was carefully assessed and paid in the manner intended.[70]

Of concern in the creation of postwar colonial development was the protection of colonised peoples from the undesirable effects of capitalist development, of becoming an impoverished landless people. Huntley Wright describes this as a form of 'social injury', most prevalent when the majority of the Indigenous population is employed by Europeans to work on their plantations.[71] Forsyth detailed in a DEA memorandum of

---

67 Press statement: '(Barry) Inquiry into new administration and circumstances of military takeover in 1942', 24 November 1944, Civil Administration of Papua and New Guinea (Post War), A5954 [603/4], NAA.
68 Jim Taylor was a prewar patrol officer, and sharply critical of the ANGAU labour practices. He was regarded as one of the few officers sympathetic to the Army Directorate's policies. Sligo, *Backroom boys*, 92.
69 Jinks, 'Policy, planning and administration', 214–17.
70 Downs, *The Australian trusteeship*, 41.
71 Wright, 'State practice', 91.

10 November 1943 how this should be avoided, insisting that government programs must 'be based on the broad principle that the interests of the natives are paramount and that nothing should be allowed to impinge on this principle'.[72] This sentiment was met with wide approval in the department, firstly attracting the attention of Paul Hasluck who ensured the paper was read by Minister Evatt, who immediately took up the idea.[73]

It was the separation of Indigenous people from their homes and their social systems that was of the greatest danger. By moving to the towns, or working on the plantations, the potential for a disenchanted proletariat with all the associated social dysfunction was greatly magnified. Therefore, an agrarian doctrine of development became the most appropriate vehicle for, on the one hand, the protection of Indigenous peoples from the risk of social dislocation emanating from laissez-faire capitalism, and on the other, a way of improving the diet and living standards of people living in the villages.[74] MacWilliam explains there were three key assumptions to delivering this policy. Firstly, that the colonial state was the central driver of bringing development to the village and improving the living standard of villagers. Secondly, to deny the introduction of any commercial operation which could potentially damage village life. Finally, that a strong economic base was regarded as the first step towards creating the political infrastructure for eventual self-government.[75]

A new beginning? The end of the Pacific War

The smooth transition envisaged by the army directorate was rendered impossible due to the sudden end of the war; their plans were based on the war continuing for a further 12 to 18 months. The Pacific War officially ended on 2 September 1945; civil administration in the Territory began in most parts on 25 October 1945. The sudden withdrawal of the military created enormous problems for the civil administration. It not only lifted the lid on simmering tensions between old rivalries in and out of the public

---

72 WD Forsyth, 'Notes on the rehabilitation and reconstruction of New Guinea, Papua and Nauru', 10 November 1943, CP637/1 [44], NAA.
73 Transcript of oral history, Papers of William Douglass Forsyth, MS5700/8/1/44, p. 76, NLA.
74 Forsyth, 'Notes on the rehabilitation'.
75 MacWilliam, *Securing village life*, 5–12.

1. THE IMPETUS FOR THE 'NEW DEAL FOR PAPUA NEW GUINEA'

service but magnified physical and service difficulties including minimal transport, shortages of food, stores and materials of all kinds and lack of accommodation and labour. Towns resembled army camps.[76]

One final act by Minister Ward, the immediate cancellation of labour contracts on 15 October 1945, was not only an example of his ideological passionate distaste of forced labour, but one of the last times he would have a direct influence on Territory matters despite being Minister for much of the next four years. The decision not only inflamed tensions in the territories, but hampered reconstruction, the reintroduction of civil administration and the commencement of postwar colonial development programs.[77] These issues are dealt with in the next chapter which primarily focusses on the Territory's provisional administration, 1945–49.

Ward's decision was a definitive statement to back up the intent of the 'New Deal'. According to Griffin, Nelson and Firth, 'Ward was as simple-minded in his attitude to colonial policy as the planters who opposed him'. He was not the socialist they supposed, but someone who 'thought of Papua New Guineans as primitive working men in need of protection'.[78] His speech of 4 July 1945 set in motion a raft of policy ideas that would radically reshape TPNG. As this chapter has outlined, there were myriad different people—planners, administrators, politicians, patrol officers and expatriates—who provided the conceptual framework for the postwar development of the territories. However, as the next chapter details, the early civil administration was left with minimal concrete plans; Territory officers were expected to design and implement development programs congruent with the conceptual fervour of Ward's 'New Deal'. In essence, this was to meet Australia's twin goals of strategic security and, on the ground in the territories, place Indigenous Papuan and New Guinean welfare at the forefront of all decision-making.

---

76   Jinks, 'Policy, planning and administration', 192–96.
77   Stanner, *South Seas*, 138–41; Legge, *Australian colonial policy*, 208.
78   James Griffin, Hank Nelson and Stewart Firth, *Papua New Guinea, a political history* (Richmond: Heinemann Educational Australia, 1979), 103.

2
Provisional Administration: 'We Stopped Them Putting the Clock Back'

> [The] provisional administration faced all the problems of the devastation, the disturbance of population, the disruption of civil rule and the loss of trained staff which had been caused by the war. In most parts of the country, it had to start again from scratch; in some parts it started from behind scratch because of the effects of the war. It had on its hands an initial job of re-construction and rehabilitation and the stabilizing of a population which had become unsettled by wartime experiences.
>
> Paul Hasluck, statement to the House of Representatives,
> 23 August 1960, p. 4[1]

The provisional administration was overwhelmed with the rehabilitation and reconstruction of the colony following the end of World War II (WWII). Despite the strain of these restorative efforts, there were significant efforts made in the Territory to plan for the future of the Territory of Papua New Guinea (TPNG). Following the 'New Deal' speech of July 1945 which outlined the Chifley Labor Government's overall strategy for TPNG, influence from planners within Australia waned and internal tensions within the Territory heightened. Some prewar conservative officers, now in positions of significant influence, were able to stifle the ideas and initiatives of those officers informed by the progressive ideas of DORCA: the principles

---

1 Paul Hasluck, *Australian policy in Papua and New Guinea: Statement in the House of Representatives* (Canberra: Government Printer, 1960), 4.

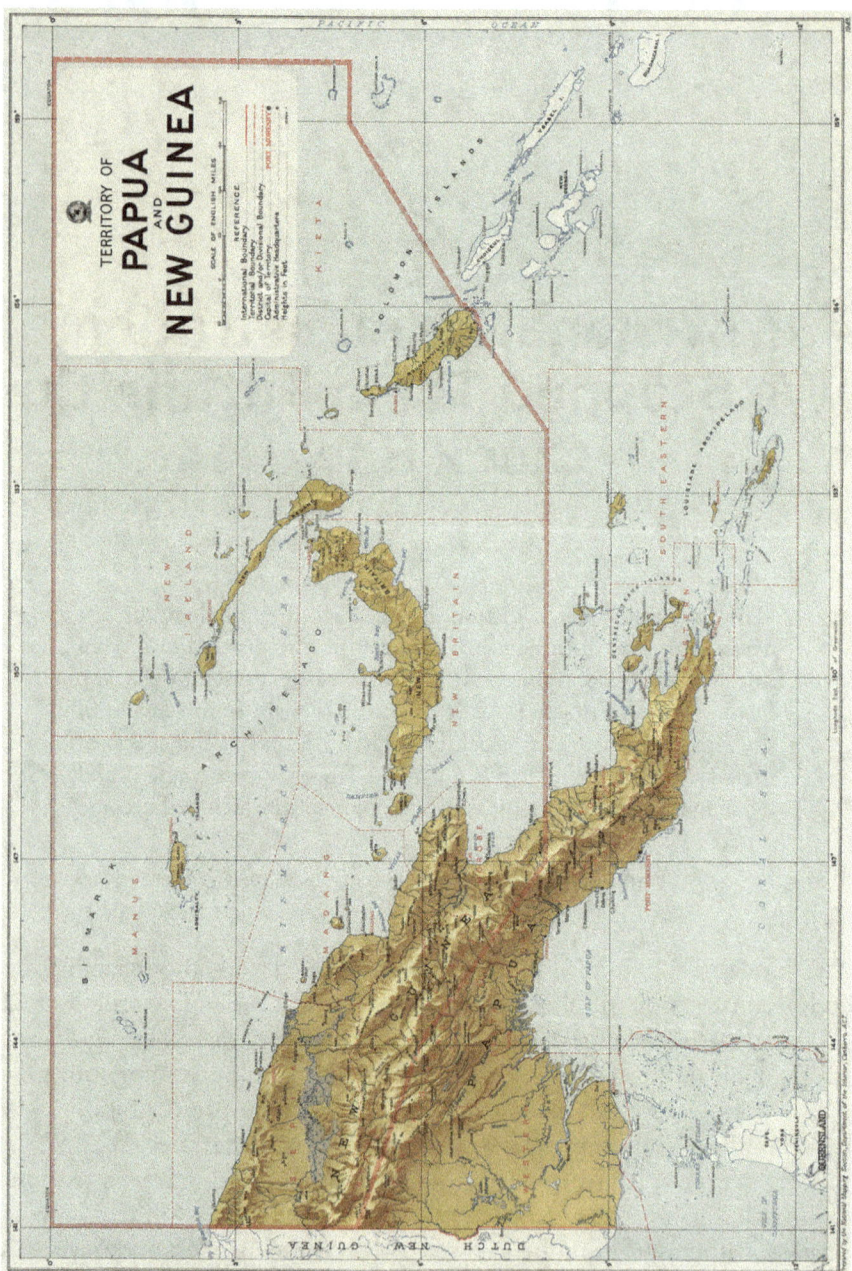

Map 2.1: Papua New Guinea, Territory of Papua and New Guinea, 1949.
Source: Australia National Mapping Section, Department of the Interior.

of trusteeship expressly aimed at ending the era of development primarily directed by European enterprise. This chapter charts the early postwar years of the provisional administration, and explains how the efforts of progressive Territory officers were able to 'stop them putting the clock back'.[2] These officers were inspired by the ideals expressed in both the 'New Deal' and the United Nations (UN) Charter, which promoted the welfare and advancement of Indigenous Papuans and New Guineans.[3] Therefore, in a sense, momentum for progressive change in TPNG came from two distinct arms of the Australian Government: officers within the Territory Administration and international efforts of the Department of External Affairs (DEA), particularly its Minister, Evatt, who played such a significant role in the establishment of the Trusteeship Council. This chapter is primarily concerned with events within the Territory, and how the impetus from the 'New Deal' evolved into community development schemes during this early postwar period, and how they would eventually play a critical role in the Hasluck administration of the 1950s and 60s.

This chapter is a chronological and necessarily Eurocentric explanation of what the Chifley Labor Government 'intended' to do, the development tools they planned on using and why they chose to use those tools. The 'progressives' in the Territory Administration generally agreed that it would be better to absorb the energies of Indigenous leaders into community development schemes, focussing on rural communities, villages and hamlets, by providing administrative machinery geared to give maximum emphasis to the economic, political and social aspects of Indigenous advancement. This chapter, and the two following, emphasise the importance of community development programs to the overall objective of Australian (Chifley Labor and Menzies Liberal/Country) Government policy for TPNG; explaining their genesis, assumptions and intent. These schemes were designed in Canberra or Port Moresby but played out on the ground in the villages where local people embraced them with some alacrity. Community development schemes, such as cooperatives and local councils, are explored in later chapters, where the autonomy of Indigenous people and diverse factors of climate, geography and population density forced the Australian Government to adjust their carefully laid plans.

---

2   John Black cited in Bill Gammage, *The sky travellers: Journeys in New Guinea 1938–1939* (Carlton: Melbourne University Press, 1998), 229.
3   On 26 June 1945 Australia signed the UN Charter, which included acceptance of the UN Trusteeship Council monitoring of Australian management of TPNG. 'External Territories of the Commonwealth', 30 September 1946, Papers of John Black, MS8346/11/7/1, National Library of Australia (NLA).

The chapter is broken into two sections. The first provides a snapshot of the difficulties faced by the provisional administration in the aftermath of the war. It describes an ineffective administration, riven by internal politics and led by an administrator (Murray) inexperienced in public service procedures, undermanned with untried staff, overwhelmed with the strain of reconstruction and afforded minimal departmental support from Canberra. Despite these handicaps, this section explores the ideas of two mid-level progressive Territory officers, David Fenbury and John Black, who attempted to find practical solutions concerning Indigenous welfare and development. The second section explains the genesis behind, and an insight into, the intent of two key postwar community development tools, cooperative societies and local government councils. The general aim of such programs was to provide the tools to 'develop' the bulk of the population step by step, working in the first place from Indigenous institutions as they existed at the village level, but eventually moving towards a self-supporting local government agency or autonomous economic organisation. The success of such schemes, particularly in the early years, was measured by the extent they overcame inter-village antipathies and affected larger combinations. Cooperatives and councils are community development schemes which reflect much of the pro-Indigenous, proactive state intent of DORCA, were designed during the provisional administration and remained critical to community economic activity during the Hasluck years of 1951–63.

Implementing the 'New Deal': The early years

The Territory Administration was primarily focussed on reconstructive efforts in the first five years following the end of the Pacific War. In terms of basic development objectives, there was little drive for policy implementation from Canberra; senior officials in what was then the Department of Territories (DOT) did not provide any detailed policy instructions to department heads in the provisional administration.[4] On the other hand, it was the efforts of DEA officers, such as Bill Forsyth and John Burton who worked so assiduously at the 1945 UN San Francisco conference to force several important proposals regarding trusteeships, which

---

4   The relevant department was known as the Department of External Territories (DET) from 26 June 1941 until 10 May 1951; the Department of Territories (DOT) was established 11 May 1951. James Griffin, Hank Nelson and Stewart Firth, *Papua New Guinea, a political history* (Richmond: Heinemann Educational Australia, 1979), 19.

would have such a profound effect on the administration of the Territory. The most significant of these was Article 73E, which forced controlling powers to report annually on the progress of the people under their care on social and economic matters.[5] It was this international obligation which often provided the imprimatur for the introduction of progressive 'New Deal' programs. Even in circumstances, for example, the establishment of Indigenous local councils, that senior Territory officials openly regarded as 'fancy dressing designed to placate the United Nations', the UN emphasis on Indigenous political development held sway.[6] Moreover, UN messaging (conclusions and recommendations) was inescapable for Territory officers. Each year the Trusteeship Council published an assessment of the Territory annual reports and every three years an inspection report of their tour of New Guinea, each of which was reported widely in press statements, via department memorandums, and importantly, printed in *Monthly Notes*, a widely read official journal published by the Australian School of Pacific Administration (ASOPA).[7]

Table 2.1: Australian grants (for the year ending 30 June).

Prewar Commonwealth grants		Grants to provisional administration	
1937	$327,491	1946	$505,000
1938	$319,304	1947	$4,037,000
1939	$311,516	1948	$3,734,000
1940	$300,521	1949	$6,393,000
1941	$287,015	1950	$8,369,000
Total	$1,545,847	Total	$23,038,000

Notes: Prewar annual Commonwealth grant to the Territory of Papua was £42,500 (increased from £40,000 in 1935); the Territory of New Guinea did not receive annual grants (line of credit existed for annual shortfalls). Because the annual grant remained at £42,500, inflationary effects reduced the purchasing power by $40,476 for the years 1937–41. Figures are in 1969 Australian dollars (per official compendium statistics for PNG), calculated from the Reserve Bank of Australia (RBA) Pre-Decimal Inflation Calculator.

Sources: DET, *Territory of Papua, Annual report for the year 1940–41* (Canberra: Government Printer, 1941); Statistics Section (DET), *Compendium of statistics for Papua New Guinea* (Canberra: Government Printer, 1969), 45; Reserve Bank of Australia, Pre-decimal inflation calculator, available at: www.rba.gov.au/calculator/annualPreDecimal.html.

---

5   Transcript of oral history, Papers of William Douglass Forsyth, MS5700/8/1/45, p. 104, NLA.
6   David M Fenbury, *Practice without policy: Genesis of local government in Papua New Guinea* (Canberra: The Australian National University, 1978), 46; David M Fenbury, 'Native local government council: Initial problems', 5 February 1952, Papers of David Maxwell Fenbury, MS6747/4/6, NLA.
7   'Administration of the Territory of New Guinea', *South Pacific* 3, no. 2 (1948): 30–35. ASOPA published the first volume of *Monthly Notes* in September 1946; the title changed to *South Pacific* for volume 2 in September 1947. The journal was published monthly until October 1959.

During the war, DORCA had commenced research, and then outlined, in Minister Ward's 'New Deal' speech, the Australian Government's postwar plans for the rapid socioeconomic development of TPNG. The strategy had been sketched, but with the sudden and unexpected end to the war, there were few, if any, detailed plans available to begin implementing new programs. It was not that DORCA plans were completely rejected, but rather, policy development was not prioritised by either Minister Ward or his department. In Australia, there was broad recognition that prewar colonial practice was no longer acceptable.[8] Table 2.1 reveals the level of commitment of the Chifley Labor Government in the early postwar period, and the general acceptance of mainstream Australia for increased funding. This acceptance for a soon-to-be massive injection of funding was an example of the influence of Papua and New Guineans (and their reputation as 'Fuzzy-Wuzzy Angels') as portrayed in films such as Damian Parer's documentaries, and the experience of Australians in military service in PNG. During WWII, more than 500,000 Australians served overseas; many went to PNG. As noted by James Griffin, Hank Nelson and Stewart Firth,

> from a total population of only 7,000,000, they left few families without friends and relatives 'in the islands'. By the end of the war, Australians had learnt about Papua New Guinea—Milne Bay, Kokoda, Coral Sea, Buna, Salamaua, Lae, Wau, Madang, Wewak, Bougainville and Rabaul were more than little-known place names, they had acquired associations only a little less strong than an earlier generation had attached to Gallipoli and Flanders.[9]

The almost twentyfold increase in grants for the five years post-WWII in comparison to the five-year period prior to the war was evidence that, at a minimum, Labor politicians were confident they would not be criticised for financial mismanagement or overreach.[10] Moreover, unlike in the Solomon Islands, where the British did not provide any form of war damage compensation, Commonwealth grants did include provisions for

---

8   Donald F Thomson, 'New deal for Papua', *The Herald* (Melbourne), 22 October 1945, 4. This is just one example of many editorials in the Australian newspapers in this period supportive of the Government's development plans.
9   Griffin, Nelson and Firth, *A political history*, 85.
10 See Table 2.1. Total Commonwealth grants for the period 1937–41: $1,265,847; for the period 1946–50: $22,588,000.

war damage. For the period 1947–50, war damage compensation amounted to $3,304,800, by 1960 this scheme had processed 140,000 claims and paid out $6,670,588.[11]

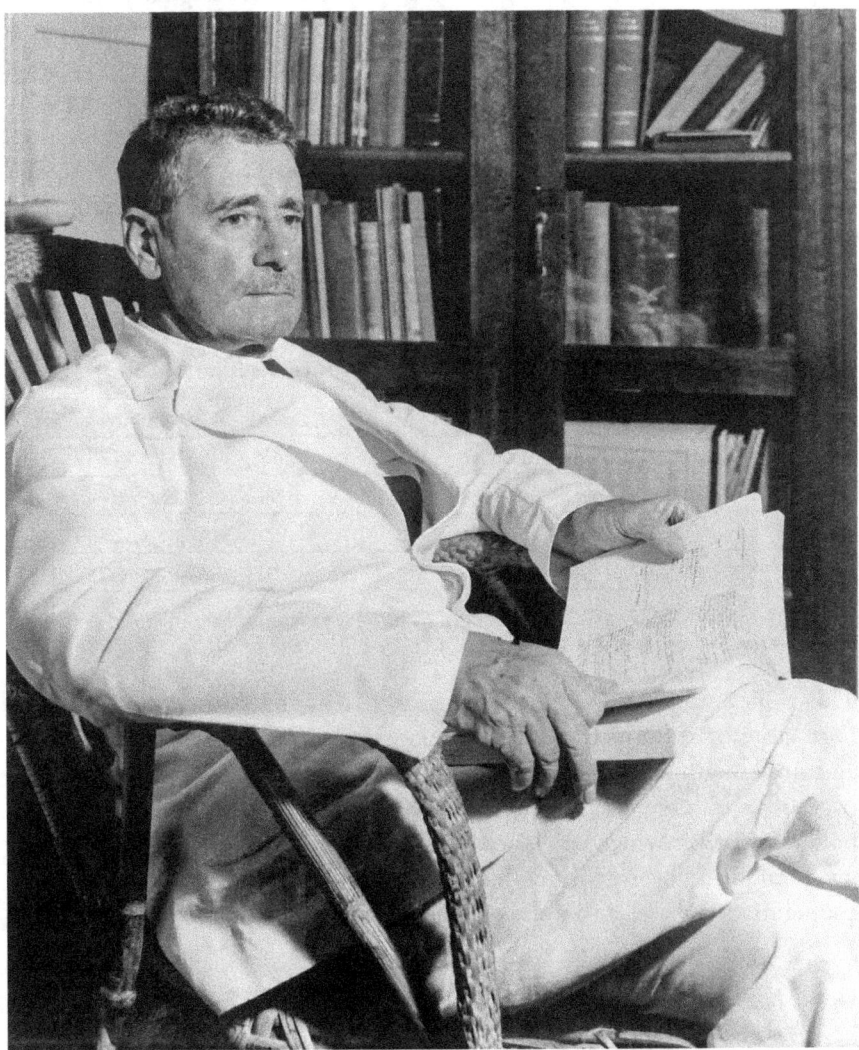

Figure 2.1: Colonel JK Murray.
Source: National Archives of Australia (NAA), A6511, 6, item 8162474.

---

11   The public finance budget line for such expenses was 'native welfare, development, War damage and reconstruction'. For instance, see: Department of External Territories (DET), *Territory of Papua. Annual Report for the Period 1st July, 1947 to 30th June, 1948* (Canberra: Government Printer, 1948), 20; Ian Downs, *The Australian trusteeship: Papua New Guinea 1945–75* (Canberra: Australian Government Publishing Service, 1980), 66.

Two new DORCA initiatives were established early in the postwar period to expand on earlier research: the Pacific Territories Research Council and ASOPA.[12] With the end of the war, by March 1946 DORCA had been disbanded, and with it, the progressive drive in Canberra stagnated under the 'dead hand' of Department of External Territories (DET) Secretary, James Halligan.[13] The research council was brought under the control of Halligan, who demoted it to be a council within ASOPA, effectively quashing policy and research initiatives in Australia.[14] JK Murray, the newly appointed Administrator of TPNG, grew increasingly frustrated with Canberra, and after corresponding with Halligan for several months wrote a letter, in April 1947, directly to the Minister complaining that 'your policy is impossible without an adequate research and training institution of the kind envisaged in DORCA'.[15]

Table 2.2: The effect of the war on public servants, 19 June 1945.

	Papua	New Guinea	Total
Suspended from civil administration	143	443	586
Prisoners of war	Nil	87	87
Retired	21	25	46
Died	4	23	27

Source: 'Notes for Minister', Department of External Territories, Papers of Edward John Ward, National Library of Australia (NLA), MS2396/43A/5.

This policy vacuum was filled, to some extent, by senior officers in the Port Moresby Administration. Although focussed on reconstructive efforts, and undermanned due to war losses (see Table 2.2 and for full details see page 65), retirements and internal division, there were several important policy initiatives which originated from TPNG during this period.[16] These included local government councils, the Highland Labour Scheme (HLS), cooperative societies and a massive expansion of health services under the

---

12   CB Laffan, memorandum 'External Territories Research Council', 22 September 1944, Australian New Guinea Administrative Unit (ANGAU), Papers of Sir Donald Cleland, MS9600/6/4/5, NLA.
13   JV Barry correspondence to Eddie Ward, 13 July 1945, cited in Graeme Sligo, *The backroom boys: Alfred Conlon and Army's Directorate of Research and Civil Affairs, 1942–1946* (Newport: Big Sky Publishing, 2013), 93, 246.
14   Brian Jinks, 'Hasluck's inheritance: Papua New Guinea in May 1951', in *The Hasluck years: Some observations. The administration of Papua New Guinea, 1952–63*, ed. Alan Ward, Tony Voutas and Brian Jinks (Bundoora: Latrobe University, 1977), 18–20.
15   JK Murray cited in Brian Jinks, 'Policy, planning and administration in Papua New Guinea, 1942–1952: With special reference to the role of Colonel J.K. Murray' (PhD thesis, University of Sydney, 1975), 304.
16   Jinks, 'Hasluck's inheritance', 22; Jinks, 'Policy, planning and administration', 351, 403.

auspices of the energetic and domineering department head, John Gunther. Murray used committees extensively as a vehicle for both advice and policy implementation, reasoning it lessened the load and provided a forum for the development of a liberal program.[17] He travelled widely, encouraged younger innovative officers, was actively undermined by many senior officers, had little or no financial or budgetary skill, and oversaw an administration described variously as 'clumsy' by Jinks and 'inefficient' by Ian Downs.[18]

In late 1947, David Fenbury, one officer who benefited from the support of Murray, spent five months in TPNG and noted the lack of staff and supplies which beset Port Moresby, remarking that 'around the departmental headquarters there is an atmosphere of cynicism and despondency'. He wrote that while he was sympathetic to the various supply problems, and the 'ignorance and lethargy at Canberra', he remained 'doubtful if they've got what it takes to do methodical and detailed planning … there's no coordinating body and there's little realism'. By January 1949, in a personal letter to British Colonial Administrator George Cartland, he described the outlook of the administration as 'essentially parochial; the great wealth of British colonial experience remains a closed book to most of them'.[19]

Other factors which limited the effectiveness of the early postwar administration included low wages, which remained close to prewar levels, ineffective recruitment levels, inadequate staff housing and deficient shipping and supply services.[20] Finally, because the Australian Administration was provisional for the years 1945–49 as it awaited final approval for its Trusteeship of New Guinea, in terms of staffing this meant all positions were acting or temporary in nature, which could not help but undermine morale.[21]

---

17 JK Murray, 'In retrospect–Papua–New Guinea 1945–1949 and Territory of Papua and New Guinea 1949–1952', *Australian Journal of Politics and History* 14 (1968): 324, doi.org/10.1111/j.1467-8497.1968.tb00711.x.
18 WEH Stanner, *The South Seas in transition* (Sydney: Australasian Publishing Company, 1953); Huntley Wright, 'State practice and rural smallholder production: Late-colonialism and the agrarian doctrine in Papua New Guinea, 1942–1969' (PhD thesis, Massey University, 1999), 191; Jinks, 'Hasluck's inheritance', 24; Downs, *The Australian trusteeship*, 37.
19 David Fenbury adopted that surname in 1960, in place of the family name of Fienberg, by which he was previously known. To avoid confusion, the more recent name is used throughout. Fenbury, *Practice without policy*, 8–22.
20 Prewar wages paid in the Territory of Papua were below those of the Territory of New Guinea. In the combined Provisional Administration, the wage level was raised to that of the Territory of New Guinea. Sub-Committee, Agendum 38, 'Funds for Administration', 29 June 1945, Reconstruction Policy and Post-War Planning, CP637 [44], National Archives of Australia (NAA).
21 Jinks, 'Policy, planning and administration', 519.

PREPARING A NATION?

Territory officers prioritising the Indigenous population

Criticism of the provisional administration understates the effort of many people at this time to implement the ideals and principles espoused by the 'New Deal' and Trusteeship Council. Two mid-level public servants of this period, John Black and David Fenbury, provide an interesting insight into the attitudes of progressive Territory officers who were charged with implementing the Chifley Labor Government's development plans.

John Black joined the New Guinea service in 1933, became famous as an officer on the Hagen–Sepik patrol from March 1938 to June 1939, and served with distinction in the Australian New Guinea Administrative Unit (ANGAU) administration, but regarded his contribution to postwar policy as his most important work.[22] He first met DORCA director Alf Conlon in June 1943 and worked under him at the School of Civil Affairs from March to September 1945 before Conlon appointed him Military Governor of Labuan and Sarawak (Borneo). In mid-1946, Murray controversially selected the progressive (and DORCA-associated) Black as Director of Policy Planning and Research, a move which drew criticism from acting Department of District Services and Native Affairs (DDSNA) Director JH (Bert) Jones, the Papuan Public Service Association and the expatriate magazine *Pacific Islands Monthly*. Both Minister Ward and Murray stood by this appointment. Black's influence on the DDSNA in the early postwar period was substantial. For instance, in a handwritten note attached to his personal papers held in the National Library of Australia, Black stated that he wrote practically all DDSNA circular instructions for distribution to all patrol officers under the signature of Jones.[23]

He told historian Bill Gammage his proudest achievement was how:

> We stopped them [prewar conservative officers] putting the clock back ... [they could] never go back to the old exploiting labour laws or neglect native health, education and political and economic development as they had pre-war.[24]

---

22   Gammage, *The sky travellers*, 226–29.
23   Papers of John Black, MS8346/11/6, NLA.
24   Gammage, *The sky travellers*, 226–29.

During this period he travelled widely and stressed the importance of providing equality of opportunity for ambitious Papuans and New Guineans to both field staff and local people.[25] For instance, in a circular he wrote to all field officers in November 1946, Black underlined the importance of mutual understanding and respect between the administration and local people, not only as an enabler of Indigenous agency, but as the basis of positive future relations.[26] Two months later, in another circular, Black reiterated the primary role of a patrol officer was as 'a teacher who fosters native development'; this required patient and sympathetic explanation, because it would 'ensure that the community gets that necessary experience in managing its own affairs'.[27] He believed a racial barrier, accentuated by an authoritative administrative machine, aloofness of the European, lack of knowledge of vernacular languages, frequent change of staff and an underappreciation for the capacity of local inhabitants, was the reason for Indigenous lack of enterprise, and the potential capacity for subversive activity.[28]

Critics within the administration at this time accused Black of having the opposite effect: instead of providing confidence and opportunity, Black's support, on occasion, morphed into cases of local leaders agitating and expressing anti-administrative or micro-nationalist sentiment. In Black's personal papers, there is a fascinating series of letters and official correspondence regarding a local leader, Apelis Mazamak, from the village of Munawai, New Ireland. Mazamak toured and gave lectures with Black in 1947 to local people, speaking of community effort and Indigenous opportunity. Later, however, Mazamak was accused of quoting extracts from newspapers regarding Indonesian independence, advocating for early independence and stirring up sectarian anti-Catholic sentiment.[29] Black was criticised for inciting Mazamak's propaganda, although an alternative explanation, and a theme explored in Part 2 of this book, is that the behaviour of Mazamak, rather than being that of a subversive, did not conform to Western expectations of the compliant 'native'.

---

25   JR Black, correspondence to Director DDSNA re: Report Samarai 1 of 1946/7, 16 September 1946, p. 4, Papers of John Black, MS8346/11/1, NLA.
26   JR Black, Circular, 'Maintenance of native confidence', 1 November 1946, Papers of John Black, MS8346/11/2, NLA.
27   Circular instruction no. 42 of 46/47, 'The principles of native administration and their application', 15 January 1947, DDSNA, Papers of John Black, MS8346/11/6, NLA.
28   Black, correspondence re: Report Samarai 1 of 1946/7.
29   IF Downs to Director DDSNA, 8 January 1950, critical of Black's role in inciting sectarian strife, Papers of John Black, MS8346/12/15, NLA. For a succinct summary: Graham Hassall, 'Religion and proto-nationalism: Apelis Mazakmat and "traces of mild sectarian strife" in New Ireland', *Baha'i Library Online*, February 2001, accessed 22 June 2019 at: bahai-library.com/hassell_apelis_majakmat_ireland.

In March 1947 Black wrote what he described as a basic policy directive, 'The Aim of Policy'. This document demonstrates how durable the progressive ideas of DORCA proved to be, as what was outlined in the war period, was echoed, but framed, around policy platforms by Black, and later implemented to varying degrees of success by the postwar administration. Furthermore, to Black and other progressive officers, the principles of the Trusteeship Council at the UN were essential to any future direction of government policy, that the 'era of development primarily directed by European enterprise and implemented by cheap labour has ended with Allied Victory'. Black argued that mutual benefit for both Australia and Papua and New Guineans was possible, explaining that working with 'us as partners and citizens bound by the ties of mutual interest' was a 'sincere interpretation of the ideals of Trusteeship'.[30]

In practical terms, given the low education standards of local people, Black explained that policy implementation had to be directed towards village developmental projects, specifically the introduction, development and marketing of cash crops on an individual and communal basis; improvement of subsistence crops; encouragement of Indigenous business enterprises in transport, sawmills and similar; introduction of producer/consumer cooperatives; provision of machinery for local government; and government policy to encourage sound interracial relations based on interdependence of interest.[31]

Black's words of warning were oft repeated over the years by others within the administration, including David Fenbury who joined the New Guinea service in September 1937 and retired as Secretary of the Department of Social Development and Home Affairs in March 1973. During this period, he also enlisted in the Australian Imperial Force in October 1941, was posted to ANGAU in November 1942 and led guerrilla operations in Japanese-held territory for the duration of the war.[32] Fenbury described how, shortly after the ceasefire, he was ordered to report to Alf Conlon and was told he was to be sent on assignment to Tanganyika and later, seconded to the British Colonial Office, London.[33]

---

30   JR Black, 'The aim of policy', 7 March 1947, pp. 1–2, Papers of John Black, MS8346/12/15, NLA.
31   Circular Instruction 50 of 1946/47, 'Native agitation and social unrest', 26 June 1947, DDSNA, p. 2, Papers of John Black, MS8346/11/6, NLA.
32   He was promoted to captain, awarded the Military Cross and mentioned in despatches. Ian Downs, 'Fenbury, David Maxwell (1916–1976)' in *Australian Dictionary of Biography*, 14th ed. (Melbourne: Melbourne University Press, 1996).
33   Fenbury, *Practice without policy*, 16.

Table 2.3: Selection criteria for attachment to Colonial Office.

Order of Selection	Officer	Territory
1	CJ Millar	New Guinea
2	DM Fenbury	New Guinea
3	FWG Anderson	Papua
4	DGN Chambers	New Guinea
5	AT Timperley	Papua
6	FNW Shand	New Guinea
7	TG Aitcheson	New Guinea
8	FH Moy	New Guinea

Notes: Selection criteria: Officers must be under the age of 33 and have completed seven years of service, including attendance at the prewar course of training at the University of Sydney. JB McKenna (Papua) was originally selected but hospitalised. There were 52 officers considered.
Source: DM Cleland, 'Attachments to Colonial Office', 25 November 1944, Papers of Sir Donald Cleland, MS9600/6/4/6, NLA.

Plans to send Territory officers overseas to learn British colonial practice had been in train since at least July 1944. The original plan was for officers to spend four months in a colony and two months in London. Fenbury spent close to 18 months away, arriving back in Australia in April 1947. Even though only Fenbury and John Millar (later appointed Cooperatives Registrar) participated in the program, the influence of these secondments was significant as both men became central figures in the administration's postwar focus on community development.[34]

Fenbury and Black, both energetic and progressive Territory officers, maintained a lively correspondence during the 1940s, their letters full of Territory gossip and enlightened ideas on colonial development policy.[35] For example, in a number of personal letters to Black written from the Colonial Office in London in late 1946, Fenbury became increasingly frustrated at the 'traditional [British] weakness for regarding political progress (which is cheap) as more important than social and economic progress (which are not cheap)'. He wrote of 'political "progress" without corresponding economic and social progress is worse than useless'.[36] A few weeks later, Fenbury

---

34 DM Cleland, 'Personal diary visit to LHQ 9-7 to 27-7-44', p. 6, Papers of Sir Donald Cleland, MS9600/4/19, NLA.
35 Keith McCarthy and Jim Taylor also corresponded with Black/Fenbury on progressive colonial development ideas.
36 Fenbury to Black, 11 October 1946 and 20 December 1946, Papers of John Black, MS8346/11/2, NLA.

wrote to Black and warned that if the administration hoped to succeed in an economic strategy based on Indigenous cash cropping, then practical socioeconomic progress demanded two essential elements: extensive road building to allow produce to reach markets, and a system of government close to the common people capable of managing local services in a way which would help raise the standard of living.[37]

Fenbury was a prodigious writer and thinker on colonial problems. In September 1952, writing under the pseudonym 'Kiap', he drafted an article for the expatriate journal *Pacific Islands Monthly*. In this paper, he dismantled the logic of a plantation economy, especially those expatriates whom he regarded as 'little better informed on fundamental TPNG problems than the average Australian', who continue to argue that the Territory's 'future start and end with the necessity for a cheap, plentiful and docile supply of native labour'. Fenbury pointed out the lack of labour for such a program (either in the Territory or Australia), and that it did not conform with Australia's trusteeship commitment. Instead, he suggested ways to tackle the Territory problems which, in brief, included encouraging/subsidising capital enterprise; growing food for local consumption; subsidising research into the mechanisation of the copra industry; and making a concerted effort to raise the standard of living by emphasising agricultural development.[38] In essence, much of what Fenbury outlined in this article bears the hallmark of Australian development strategy during the 1950s.

In April 1956, he wrote a paper titled 'Notes on native policy' which summarised many of his ideas and concerns that were also evident in his personal papers from the early postwar period. The crux of Fenbury's paper was a fundamental question: In which direction did Australia desire the Indigenous population of the Territory to evolve? He feared it was unrealistic to expect TPNG to stand completely on its own given the inherent problems of land tenure, difficult terrain, limited natural resources, multiplicity of languages and the lack of truly arable land.[39] He doubted whether it was even possible, given these issues, to develop a self-sustaining capitalist economy, encompassing an adequate social welfare and education system. Furthermore, Fenbury reminded his readership that any policy decision

---

37 Fenbury, 'Notes on local government in British Tropical Africa 1947', July 1947, Papers of David Maxwell Fenbury, MS6747/2/2, NLA.
38 DM Fenbury, pseudonym 'Kiap' (draft), to *Pacific Islands Monthly*, Papers of David Maxwell Fenbury, MS6747/3/1, NLA.
39 Clearly Fenbury was unaware of the large mineral deposits and other natural resources which exist in TPNG.

regarding the development of the territories must align with Australia's own strategic interest. Fenbury then speculated that the unalterable facts of geography, coupled with the limiting factors mentioned above, meant that Australia could not afford to shrug and turn away from TPNG: 'We dare not'. As such, Australia was committed to TPNG indefinitely unless forced out by superior foreign armed forces or by internal pressures sponsored by outside influences. This meant the priority of the Australian Government had to be the satisfaction of the Indigenous population; it must aspire to manage affairs so that its continuing presence was regarded by the 'advancing Indigene' as essential to their continuing wellbeing.[40]

An interesting aspect, or perhaps a cynical reading, of this document is the way it spells out the underlying duality of the postwar colonial development plan. The headline story is the promotion of self-development, of improved welfare and sociopolitical and economic opportunities for local inhabitants. But as this paper indicates and is replicated in the 'New Deal' planning documents of the Pacific War period, strategic security was the most important aspect of Australian and TPNG relations. The aim of this policy was to further bind the territories to Australia: grant money and administration officers were to become indispensable to the raising of living standards. Australia benefited by creating a stable and peaceful island to govern, providing an ideal platform to maintain TPNG as an effective security barrier.[41] Regardless of this interpretation, the ideas of these two Territory officers also reflect the influence of trusteeship and 'New Deal' ambition, the prioritisation of Indigenous welfare and improved living standards, but framed in terms of mutual benefit for both Australia and Papua and New Guineans.

---

40   Fenbury, 'Notes on native policy', Department of Native Affairs, 17 April 1956, pp. 2–10, Papers of David Maxwell Fenbury, MS6747/3/5, NLA.
41   Key 'New Deal' planning documents: HC Coombs, 'The future of the territories', 26 October 1943, Ministry of Post-War Reconstruction, A989 [1943/735/144/3], NAA; WD Forsyth, 'Notes on the rehabilitation and reconstruction of New Guinea, Papua and Nauru', DEA, 10 November 1943, CP637/1 [44], NAA.

The genesis for community development: Cooperatives and local councils

Cooperative societies

The impetus for the introduction and formalisation of cooperative societies in the Territory as an important community development vehicle was not the Australian Government, but rather, the missions. In March 1947, Reverend Clint of the Portland Rectory (NSW) made initial enquiries with Minister Ward regarding support for Mission Cooperatives in TPNG. When Ward did not respond, Clint made direct representations to Prime Minister Chifley. Pressed into action, Minister Ward met Reverend Clint in Sydney on 15 May 1947 and expressed surprise at the sudden level of interest in cooperatives by village communities, particularly those in the Northern District.[42] Clint explained in this meeting that, because there was no legal machinery for cooperatives in the Territory, these enterprises were at risk from 'commercial sabotage'. CT Cockshott, an agricultural officer, was sent by Ward to meet, firstly, the Registrar of NSW Cooperative Societies and then, on 21 October 1947 in Port Moresby, Department of Agriculture, Stock and Fisheries (DASF) Director Cottrell-Dormer.

Cockshott was instructed to 'find out as much as possible in the short time available, concerning the registration, organisation, and operation, of cooperative societies'.[43] This rush to introduce cooperatives as a community development vehicle was aided by the ready availability of NSW legislation. On 20 July 1948, to appease Bert Jones, the Minister approved the creation of Cooperative Section within DDSNA, and three months later announced the *Co-operative Societies Ordinance 1948*.[44] Despite warnings from the Crown Law Officer that the legislation was too advanced for local conditions, Registrar John Millar pushed hard for 'the legislation to go through as it stands'.[45] The decision to base the ordinance on Australian legislation, purely

---

42 By 1947 the Anglican Mission at Gona had a subscription base in excess of £2,000.
43 Correspondence February–June 1947 between Reverend Alf Clint, Prime Minister Ben Chifley, Minister Eddie Ward, EH Burgmann Bishop of Goulburn and CT Cockshott, A518 [E840/1/4 part 1], NAA.
44 DET, 'Co-operative Societies Ordinance 1948', Press Release, 29 October 1948. Briefing document for the Minister, 'Organisation of native co-operative movement', 29 September 1948, A518 [E840/1/4 part 1], NAA.
45 Millar correspondence to BJ Surridge (Colonial Office) in London, 21 June 1947, A518 [E840/1/4 part 1], NAA.

because it was readily available, proved to be a mistake. The framework was overly elaborate for local conditions which had to account for dividends, legal set-up, lending ability and bookkeeping requirements.[46]

Table 2.4: Cooperatives: Primary organisations (year ending 31 March).

Year	No. of societies	Members	Turnover
1951	119	20,688	$223,500
1952	109	22,172	$378,000
1953	153	37,818	$789,000
1954	182	53,891	$1,240,000
1955	198	54,250	$1,945,000
1956	224	61,385	$2,006,000
1957	214	64,035	$2,054,000
1958	222	61,733	$1,504,000
1959	220	72,730	$1,634,000
1960	218	71,651	$2,324,000
1961	219	74,140	$2,364,000
1962	245	78,192	$2,228,000
1963	272	85,451	$2,287,000

Note: Prior to 1951 there was no system of cooperative marketing.
Source: Statistics Section, *Compendium of statistics for Papua New Guinea* (Canberra: Government Printer, 1969), 34.

Why, and how, Murray made his October 1947 announcement, and the resultant rushed and poorly designed 1948 *Co-operative Societies Ordinance*, provides an interesting snapshot in how the Australian Government (both Liberal and Labor) would often misstep regarding the coordination and implementation of community development schemes. Firstly, the sudden motivation for the introduction of cooperatives appears to have been due to the postwar interest of missions in the movement. As is demonstrated in later chapters, this was not an isolated incident. For instance, the administration rushed, and bypassed their own speciality section (Native Authorities: NAS) with the sudden introduction of local councils in Milne Bay, resulting in a lack of coordinated effort and a fracturing of the trust between local people and the government. In the case of cooperatives, the lack of coordination, which Jones tried to mitigate by forcing the Co-operative Section within the

---

46   Jinks, 'Policy, planning and administration', 504; John D Legge, *Australian colonial policy* (Sydney: Australian Institute of International Affairs, 1956), 217.

confines of DDSNA, caused some wavering on the intent of cooperatives as a community development vehicle. Because cooperatives were expected to foster and encourage Indigenous economic expansion, a better fit would have been within the DASF, not DDSNA, who were primarily concerned with law and order, pacification and administrative control.[47] Secondly, cooperatives are an excellent example of social trusteeship, of the state ameliorating the risk and dangers of free-market capitalist or spontaneous economic activity.

Regardless of the failings of the original 1948 legislation, and the misplaced enthusiasm for aligning village 'native' communal thinking with a communal profit project, cooperative societies were an important development tool for introducing Western concepts of business management and providing an avenue for raising capital.[48] Table 2.4 highlights the popularity of cooperative societies as an Indigenous economic enterprise; in the period 1951–63 membership grew fourfold, and turnover increased almost tenfold. In December 1952 Hasluck affirmed his commitment to cooperatives, regarding them as 'an important instrument of native economic development'.[49]

The underlying motive for cooperatives as a development tool was their expected ability to increase both household production and consumption, while ameliorating the risk of migratory labour, which threatened to destroy traditional village society. Cooperatives represent a fascinating shift in Australian thinking from pre- to postwar. Prewar, the Australian Government's economic plan was based on plantation labour which, at least to some extent, could be viewed as extractive colonialism. The postwar shift to Indigenous village production and cooperative societies is a fundamental move away from such concepts towards the 'New Deal'/UN trusteeship emphasis on Indigenous economic opportunity.

Local government councils: A control measure?

> The local government system, first established in 1950, was initially regarded by the headquarters of the then Department of District Services and Native Affairs as political window dressing, primarily

---

47 Wright, 'State practice', 196.
48 Paul Hasluck, *A time for building: Australian administration in Papua and New Guinea, 1951–1963* (Carlton: Melbourne University Press, 1976), 156–57.
49 Hasluck cited in Commerce Branch Press Release, 'Native co-operatives in Papua and New Guinea', 16 December 1952, Department of Territories (DOT), A518 [E840/1/4 part 2], NAA.

designed to placate the U.N. Trusteeship Council, and possibly useful as a sop to relatively advanced communities exhibiting some signs of restlessness.

David Fenbury, *Practice without policy*, 254

During the war, both ANGAU and army directorate officers advocated for local government councils as a community development tool. On 26 January 1945, ANGAU headquarters issued a circular which proposed the introduction of village councils to assist in providing more effective 'native administration', foster communal interest and develop a 'feeling of responsibility amongst natives'. The pre-existing system of luluais and village constables was not to be replaced; instead, councils were expected to assist them in control of village affairs.[50]

During this period, anthropologist and DORCA officer Ian Hogbin had written a long paper on the prewar experience of councils in both nearby Solomon Islands and, with some success, Rabaul and Madang.[51] His paper was later referenced by David Fenbury as a major stimulus for the introduction of local government council policy.[52] Towards the end of the war, and in the early postwar period, the framework for the establishment of local councils was founded. Although later there was much debate over the primary role of councils, either as an adjunct to district administration or as a training vehicle to teach Indigenes political education, it is quite clear the original intent of councils was to expand existing indirect rule by collecting villages into a system of area management, which would better provision local communities with economic, medical and civic services.

During the provisional administration and early Hasluck period, there was persistent discussion regarding potential repercussions from a sudden devolution of colonial political responsibility. Government policy was firmly against establishing an Indigenous elite where political development was seen to be a balancing act between encouraging political independence and discouraging anti-colonial sentiment. A poorly timed exit, one that did not provide for adequate civil and economic structures, could encourage colonial unrest, and in the late colonial stage, was regarded as inevitable

---

50   ANGAU HQ, Circular 17, 'Village councils', 26 January 1945, Papers of John Black, MS8346/11/6, NLA.
51   Herbert Ian Hogbin, 'Local government for New Guinea', *Oceania* 17 (1946): 38–65, doi.org/10.1002/j.1834-4461.1946.tb00142.x.
52   Fenbury, *Practice without policy*, 22.

if political advancement outstripped economic and social development.[53] For instance, in June 1947, Black wrote of the harsh lessons the British had learnt by not recognising the close relationship between their 'subject's political, economic and social advancement, and if one of these elements is out of step then it can lead to undesirable outcomes'.[54] David Fenbury, with his customary caustic turn of phrase, and an eye always to the potential for local councils to absorb both Indigenous discontent and promote autonomous action, wrote of his concern for such misalignment, warning a 'politically disgruntled educated elite would emerge whilst the majority are still diseased and ignorant subsistence gardeners'.[55] Both Black and Fenbury agreed it would be better to absorb the energies of Indigenous leaders into an area of administrative machinery geared to give maximum emphasis to the economic and social aspects of Indigenous advancement. Black, in his 1947 circular, argued that development policy should be realistic, and given the low levels of literacy, practical efforts should be directed through village developmental projects such as local councils supported by administrative machinery to train villagers in their operation.[56]

Fenbury was aware of the rumours following anthropologist Ian Hogbin's 1946 article of the impending establishment of local councils, and by early 1949 DDSNA Director Jones had advised him of his likely role in supervising and implementing such a program. Given the shortage of staff, and with District Commissioners 'already fully occupied', Jones wrote to Fenbury in June 1949, explaining the likelihood that a specialised section would be established to administer local councils.[57] On 17 December 1949, Fenbury was appointed Senior Native Authorities Officer, responsible for the introduction of local government councils to TPNG, a role he regarded primarily to provide area machinery and local funds for extending and coordinating services at the village level. While councils played an important role at a local level, they were not intended to have equal authority with the Legislative Council or the administration, and initially, did not form part of the total system of government, could not pass laws applying to the

---

53 Fenbury, 'Native local government', 24 October 1953, par. 7, Papers of David Maxwell Fenbury, MS6747/3/5, NLA.
54 Circular 50 of 1946/47, 'Native agitation and social unrest', 26 June 1947, DDSNA, Papers of John Black, MS8346/11/6, NLA.
55 Fenbury, 'Native local government', 24 October 1953, par. 11.
56 Circular 50, 'Native agitation'.
57 Jones had temporarily relinquished DDSNA departmental head duties to concentrate on planning. Fenbury, *Practice without policy*, 18–22, 29.

whole of the Territory, or employ constabulary.[58] Despite being consistently met with resistance in the first six years of the program (which resulted in only 10 councils being gazetted), in the following decade, councils were to become a critical factor in the overall government effort to advance a measure of socioeconomic and political autonomy to Indigenous people at a local level.[59] Ironically, for much of this period of exponential growth in councils, Fenbury had, in something of a melding of local and international policy, moved to New York to work at the UN Trusteeship Division as an area specialist. Nevertheless, much of the ideas and strategy he outlined early in his tenure with NAS proved effective in the later rapid expansion of councils.[60]

Fenbury was disappointed in the term 'village' inserted in the title of the 1949 ordinance, arguing it was a misnomer as the administration planned on implementing an 'area council' approach.[61] He explained that 'local government policy of native administration will only become real to the extent that it succeeds in overcoming inter-village antipathies and effecting larger combinations'.[62] Fenbury's analysis of TPNG society appeared wedded to a notion that it remained untouched, enclosed and primitive. He argued that the small and disparate nature of TPNG societies meant local councils would, out of necessity, be artificial in character. Fenbury's analysis is problematic, given that pre-colonial alliances between often widely dispersed villages and communities were significant in many places in TPNG.[63] But further, he pointed to the practical implications of inserting an alien social, economic and political concept on a traditional community. He wrote that we must:

---

58   The Legislative Council power was with the colonialist. Of the 29 members, 17 were administration officers, a further nine nominated by the administrator (three each from the missions, commerce and Indigenous Papua and New Guineans) and three non-officials elected by expatriate voters. Brian Jinks, *New Guinea government: An introduction* (Sydney: Angus and Robertson, 1971), 111; Scott MacWilliam, *Securing village life: Development in late colonial Papua New Guinea* (Canberra: ANU Press, 2013), 84, doi.org/10.22459/SVL.05.2013.
59   John T Gunther, 'Native local government', 22 June 1959, Papers of David Maxwell Fenbury, MS6747/3/6, NLA.
60   Fenbury was at the UN (New York) from June 1956 to July 1958. Fenbury, *Practice without policy*, vii.
61   In 1954 the term 'village' was removed, and the ordinance was renamed as the *Native Local Government Ordinance*. Fenbury, *Practice without policy*, 29.
62   Fenbury to DDSNA Director, 'Comments on the Village Council Ordinance', 28 December 1949, Papers of David Maxwell Fenbury, MS6747/3/5, NLA.
63   John Barker has written about such pre-colonial alliances and how colonial models of village government were imposed before WWII. John Barker, 'Village inventions: Historical variations upon a regional theme in Uiaku, Papua New Guinea', *Oceania* 66 (1996): 211–29, doi.org/10.1002/j.1834-4461.1996.tb02552.x.

fit into our system of government a primitive people whose culture, values and institutions differ markedly from our own, we need to lead them to a condition where they can pay for their own social services and assume responsibility in management of their own affairs, and we cannot do this by imposing an alien system from above.[64]

What is troubling about Fenbury's analysis is that he ignores, or diminishes, previous European–Indigenous relations; his sweeping generalisations regard all local communities as isolated and primitive. He does not account for the more than 50 years of mission and expatriate contact, the five years of war and three separate occupiers (in some instances) and intermittent colonialism (in some places), as well as indentured labour on the islands and along the coast of the mainland.

More perceptively, Fenbury explained the short-term success of the program relied on it being acceptable both to elderly non-hereditary conservatives and a growing middle class of 'younger progressives', who had, 'thrown up by the recent war, experienced a different form of culture contact'.[65] He argued that the breakdown of traditional social elements was inevitable; his analysis and prescription to overcome this problem was most interesting, a scenario played out in Part 2 of this book. Fenbury considered the problem of integration, of effecting a system of 'voluntary combinations of authority with jurisdiction over a larger group than a single village'.[66] The artificiality of the arrangement was, according to Fenbury, unavoidable because there was 'no precedent for it in traditional [Indigenous] social organisation', considering the notion of a multiple series of minor councils based on the 'village' as completely 'unworkable'.[67]

Fenbury has described in his memoir, *Practice without Policy*, how, during the provisional administration, it was common practice to link local councils with 'Native' courts.[68] During the 1950s this association was the cause of both frustration and friction for Fenbury with senior government bureaucrats, including Minister Hasluck. Fenbury believed local courts and councils should be controlled by Indigenous authorities; the opposing view, based on both substantive and procedural matters, was that courts should be kept separate from the executive. Hasluck, whose views on this matter

---

64 Fenbury to DDSNA Director, 'Comments on the Village Council Ordinance', 28 December 1949, Papers of David Maxwell Fenbury, MS6747/3/5, NLA.
65 Fenbury, 'Comments on the Village Council Ordinance'.
66 Fenbury, 'Comments on the Village Council Ordinance'.
67 Fenbury, *Practice without policy*, 34.
68 Fenbury, *Practice without policy*, 34–36.

were inherently assimilationist, to progressively meld Indigenous society into Western civic and political systems, argued for an independent and 'educative' court system, one where he could decree uniform consistency, despite the clear difference between the systems of law of Europeans and villagers. In a sense, this debate was an uncertain marriage between the aims of assimilationists and the protection of culture, although in Fenbury's case, his reasoning was as much pragmatic and overcoming resistance to the introduction of local councils. Nevertheless, the issue was eventually settled in 1961 when, following the Derham Report, a decision was made to integrate 'Native' and lower courts within a framework like the Australian legal and local government system.[69]

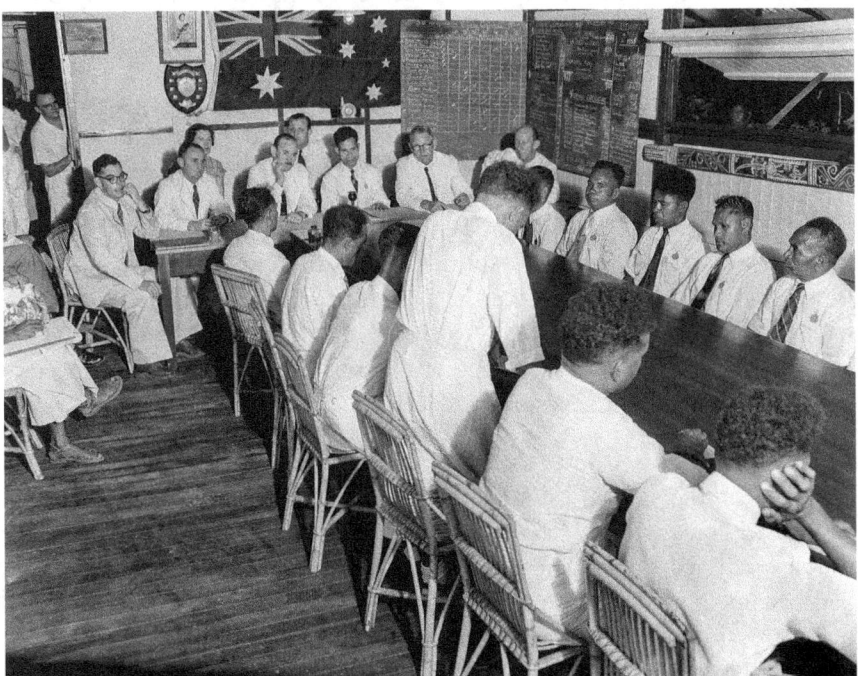

Figure 2.2: Paul Hasluck attending a meeting of the Hanuabada Local Government Council, Port Moresby.
Source: NAA, A1200, L18788, item 11181704.

---

69 Fenbury, 'Notes on political development', 18 August 1965, Papers of David Maxwell Fenbury, MS6747/2/6, NLA.

Fenbury envisaged local councils as incorporating a 'whole-of-government' operation at a ground level, in the villages, and this included a judicial system. While his views on traditional society were primitivist, it is worth highlighting how progressive Fenbury was in his acceptance of local customs while at the same time seeking to graft them onto larger development principles. He acknowledged that, to the trained legal mind, it may appear 'distasteful' to give such responsibility to 'untutored Indigenes'. But from 'an Indigenous point of view a witness has the opportunity to tell their story in his own way to a bench who is fully conversant with native customary usage'.[70] Fenbury regarded as a guiding principle, that it was best to separate the council executive from the local judiciary, which would also have the added benefit of appeasing both the conservative and progressive elements of a local community. Elders, who have an 'intimate knowledge of local customary law', may be dissuaded from protesting against the new political entity if they provided most of the personnel for the local court bench, effectively reaffirming their traditional status, while the younger 'progressives' should be given an outlet on the council executive.

In this extensive memorandum, Fenbury was arguing against a policy of straight-out assimilation, fearing the disintegration of tribal discipline and Indigenous institutions. Instead, he explained, the bulk of the population had to advance step by step, 'working in the first place from native institutions as they exist at village level', and eventually moving towards a self-supporting local government agency.[71]

The creation of a separate 'specialist' section within DDSNA exacerbated tensions and personal animosities within the department and the administration generally.[72] Headed by Fenbury, NAS implementation of the new council policy threatened the autonomy to which many officers had become accustomed in the days of village administration.[73] Directors of technical departments, including progressive individuals such as John Gunther (Public Health) and William Groves (Education) would not agree to their departmental officers assuming subordinate roles in a structure dominated by 'semi-literate bushwhackers'.[74] Jones explained to Fenbury

---

70   Fenbury, 'Notes on political development'.
71   Fenbury, 'Comments on the Village Council Ordinance'.
72   Fenbury, 'Native local government', 24 October 1953, para. 58, Papers of David Maxwell Fenbury, MS6747/3/5, NLA.
73   AL Epstein, *Matupit: Land, politics and change among the Tolai of New Britain* (Canberra: Australian National University Press, 1968), 259–60.
74   Gunther describing the lack of education of district and patrol officers. Fenbury, *Practice without policy*, 78.

that he had 'silenced District Commissioners' objections to the idea by asking them what they knew about the policy?'. Fenbury, who suffered the consequences of this determined internal opposition to the separate section, told Jones that he believed 'many senior officials regarded the new council's policy as dangerously premature fancy dressing designed to placate the United Nations'. Furthermore, he expected the change of policy would elicit sharp opposition from a 'variety of White interests, including religious missions', and assumed he would be a target for enmity.[75]

During the early 1950s, the section struggled due to insufficient staff, and a lack of understanding or appreciation by most field and technical officers of the value of local councils in district area management. Fenbury planned to staff NAS with 14 experienced officers, graduates of the ASOPA long course, which covered the various colonial systems of 'indirect rule in their studies'. However, in what was probably an example of the dire shortage of staff, and of overall inability to support well-intentioned development programs with adequate resources, Fenbury obtained only one recruit.[76] He complained that:

> local government policy is coming to be regarded by field staff generally as a fanciful superstructure that is being superimposed on a tried-and-true system of native administration by a handful of specialists with little else to do.[77]

In 1953, Administrator Donald Cleland recommended the disbandment of the NAS, although with the Minister's support it continued in existence until 1956.[78]

The first four councils—Vunamami and Reimber (New Britain District), Hanuabada (Central District) and Baluan (Manus Island)—were gazetted in September 1950. In the following five years, primarily due to staff shortages and lack of support from senior administrative officials, the expansion of councils ground to a virtual stalemate.[79] From 1956, the government, and Hasluck in particular, impressed upon the administration the critical importance of local councils. The government announced area administration would become a general policy, the change linked to

---

75 Fenbury, *Practice without policy*, 46.
76 The recruit was Harry Plant. On 4 August 1950, due to the unrest from the Paliau Movement on Manus Island, the section obtained the services of Jim Landman. Fenbury, *Practice without policy*, 45.
77 Fenbury memorandum November 1954, cited in *Practice without policy*, 83–87.
78 Fenbury *Practice without policy*, 87.
79 There were several amalgamations of smaller councils to create larger and more financially sustainable organisations.

a departmental reorganisation which removed the impression that local government was a specialist activity.[80] This change coincided with Fenbury's move to the UN in New York; however, in many ways, the resultant expansion was based on his ideas laid out in the first half of the decade.

Table 2.5: Establishment of local government councils, 1950–54.

Council	District	Gazetted
Vunamami	New Britain	14 September 1950
Reimber	New Britain	14 September 1950
Hanuabada	Central	14 September 1950
Baluan	Manus	28 September 1950
Rabaul	New Britain	7 June 1951
Ealeba	Milne Bay	23 November 1951
Vunadadir	New Britain	28 November 1952
Livuan	New Britain	21 January 1953
Tavara	Milne Bay	16 September 1954

Source: Annual Reports (1950–55) for Territory of Papua and Territory of New Guinea, held at the National Library of Australia.

Table 2.6: Expansion of local government councils, 1951–63.

Year	No. of councils	No. of councillors	Population in council areas	Average no. of people per councillor
1951	5	89	17,900	201
1952	6	92	19,000	206
1953	8	145	28,413	195
1954	8	178	30,260	170
1955	9	211	38,124	180
1956	10	277	49,400	178
1957	16	389	76,655	197
1958	24	638	146,436	230
1959	28	780	187,421	240
1960	39	1077	265,352	247
1961	43	1223	309,547	253
1962	59	1723	501,664	291
1963	77	2234	696,845	312

Source: Jinks, *New Guinea government*, 117.

---

80   Allan M Healy, 'Native administration and local government in Papua, 1880–1960' (PhD thesis, The Australian National University, 1962), 361–62.

In 1959, John Gunther, now Assistant Administrator, instructed all officers that local councils were 'never intended to be counterparts to the municipal type of local government in Australia, instead they are area instrumentalities organised along lines calculated to fit into evolving circumstances of Indigenous communities'.[81] The drive to expand local councils meant that in the seven years from 1956, there was a sevenfold increase in the number of councils (10 to 77) and a fourteenfold increase in the population covered by councils. For instance, in 1956 there were 178 people per councillor (often the size of a village); by 1963 the number of people per councillor had increased to 312. This was a significant change to customary or prewar colonial practice, more aligned to area management as envisaged by Fenbury. However, as Hank Nelson has noted, in practical terms, it often led to villagers losing interest as meetings took place out of sight of villages and were often concerned with things not related to daily village management.[82]

Conclusion

While the provisional administration proved in many ways to be ineffectual, this chapter has primarily focussed on the attempt to implement a radical change from prewar rule, one which emphasised comprehensive local community development. One example: the work of the more progressive officers in the administration to wed 'New Deal' and UN trusteeship humanitarian intent with a practical roadmap for policy implementation. These ideas demonstrate how durable the progressive ideas of DORCA, and in international terms the DEA, proved to be regarding social trusteeship: of protecting, educating and providing opportunity to subjugated peoples.

The broad conception was to advance at a local level, through community development agencies, the living standards of local people, and furthermore, accord them an opportunity to play an active role in their economic, social and political future. The programs were remotely conceived, paternalistic, Western-orientated and assumed that such programs could work in all environments. Given such a base, it was inevitable problems would arise. Cooperatives were an immediate success, but later, in many cases, as enthusiasm waned, cooperatives struggled to prove viable, and often left local people frustrated and disenchanted with the Australian Government.

---

81 Gunther, 'Native local government', 22 June 1959.
82 Hank Nelson, 'Filling in some gaps and building for a nation', in Ward, Voutas and Jinks, *The Hasluck years*, 75.

Local councils were handicapped in the early postwar period by internal administrative division and, as such, took many years to expand. However, in the mid-1950s, councils were strongly supported by Minister Hasluck, who regarded them as an important administrative tool for political education. Community development programs such as cooperatives and local government councils maintained local people in the villages. It is an illustration of how the Australian Government promoted a progressive liberal development agenda but framed it within a covert containment strategy. Not only were they able to deliver a colonial development program without promoting an Indigenous elite, but they were also able to monitor the autonomous actions of local people and quash those who did not conform to Western expectations of the compliant 'native'.

3

Administering the 'New Deal' from the Extreme Centre

This, and the following chapter, explain the philosophical underpinning of Minister Paul Hasluck's development beliefs, the Australian objective in the Territory of Papua New Guinea (TPNG) and the strategies Hasluck employed to implement the Menzies Government program. There were many thousands of Australian and Papua New Guinean personnel involved in postwar development; however, it was Hasluck who sat at the pinnacle: he directed, harangued, obtained the financial means and outlined the broad objectives, and simultaneously was transfixed by the minutiae of detail. He was precise, belligerent and the single most influential policymaker to contribute to the development of TPNG.

The change of government in December 1949 from Labor to Liberal/Country did not, to all intents and purposes, provide any significant revision in policy.[1] Instead, and although only partially successful, Hasluck went about a fundamental reorganisation and building up of the strength and efficiency of the administration. While sympathetic to the demands of postwar reconstruction and the previous government's overall objective, he was critical of their bureaucratic and administrative incompetence, and regarded the postwar period as a missed opportunity. Therefore, although there was minimal change to strategy, he was focussed on policy effectiveness and prioritising Indigenous socioeconomic, educational and political advancement.

---

1   Commonwealth (Australia), *Parliamentary debates*, House of Representatives, 1 September 1954 (Paul Hasluck).

Figure 3.1: Commonwealth Bank in Papua New Guinea, Minister for Territories, Paul Hasluck on an official party visit to a village in the Highlands, 1955.
Source: National Archives of Australia (NAA), A1200, L18992, item 7558662.

This chapter explores the underlying motive which informed Hasluck's developmental beliefs, especially social trusteeship, assimilation and public administration. While Hasluck held the classical liberal belief of individualism, it was somewhat tempered by protective and ameliorative concern for the vulnerable or disadvantaged.[2] Hasluck promoted an interventionist development program against the extremes of capitalism, expanding on the positive benefits of assimilation which moved away from prewar 'protection' to instead promote welfare and social advancement. This chapter concludes with an examination of Hasluck's view on public administration, and the structure of Territory Administration, before describing how the lack of staff and structural issues in the bureaucracy hampered the implementation of policy.

---

2   Commonwealth (Australia), *Parliamentary debates*, House of Representatives, 30 September 1959 (Paul Hasluck).

3. ADMINISTERING THE 'NEW DEAL' FROM THE EXTREME CENTRE

This and the following chapter have been written from a Eurocentric perspective, focussed on how Australia designed and implemented development policy. Research for this chapter, drawn primarily from government archives, illustrates how little the Australian Government expected, or recognised, Indigenous autonomy. Faith in Australian expertise and ignorance of Papua New Guinean entrepreneurship would later prove a major failing, forcing the government to radically adjust and introduce new development programs. Therefore, while this chapter fixates on Hasluck and Australian planning and implementation of postwar development policy, the absence of Indigenous input encapsulates the basic disconnect between the coloniser and the colonised.

Change of government

For much of the 20 years following the end of World War II, the intent to prioritise Papua New Guinean welfare became increasingly bipartisan. As described by Griffin, Nelson and Firth:

> [Minister] Spender and his successor in 1951, Mr (later Sir) Paul Hasluck, paid more than lip-service to the objective of Papuan New Guinean welfare. Just as Labor had not opposed private enterprise, the non-Labor government did not oppose generous welfare paternalism.[3]

The defeat of the Chifley Labor Government in December 1949 provided hope to expatriate planters for a change of Australian policy, for a move in favour of 'free enterprise'.[4] Some academics, including Brian Jinks, have argued this was in fact what happened with the installation of Liberal party stalwart, Percy Spender, as External Territories Minister.[5] The new minister visited the Territory from 29 March to 13 April 1950, and made a substantial statement to the House of Representatives on 1 June 1950. Following his tour of TPNG, the expatriate magazine *Pacific Island Monthly* described his visit as 'notable and refreshing' and paid particular attention to

---

3   James Griffin, Hank Nelson and Stewart Firth, *Papua New Guinea, a political history* (Richmond: Heinemann Educational Australia, 1979), 110; John D Legge, *Australian colonial policy* (Sydney: Australian Institute of International Affairs, 1956), 196.
4   A congratulatory message was sent to Spender from the Planters Association. Scott MacWilliam, *Securing village life: Development in late colonial Papua New Guinea* (Canberra: ANU Press, 2013), 79, doi.org/10.22459/SVL.05.2013.
5   Brian Jinks, 'Policy, planning and administration in Papua New Guinea, 1942–1952: With special reference to the role of Colonel J.K. Murray' (PhD thesis, University of Sydney, 1975), 494.

Figure 3.2: Percy Spender, New External Territories Minister, December 1949.
Source: NAA, A1200, L12797, item 11386997.

Spender's positive comments regarding private enterprise.[6] Yet, as John Legge has pointed out, in Spender's broad-ranging June 1950 speech, he did not reject the humanitarian ideals of the New Deal.[7] In this speech, he directed Australian policy to prioritise:

1. The welfare and advancement of the native peoples and their increasing participation in the natural wealth of the Territories.

2. The development of the resources of the Territory to the point ultimately where the area will be economically self-supporting and thus advance the Territory and its inhabitants and supply the needs of Australia ...[8]

Spender's action fits with his reputation as somewhat of an outrider in 1940s liberal/conservative circles who, according to historian David Lowe, had a history of siding 'with the state's overriding powers in the interests of development and security, whilst trying to safeguard individual freedoms'.[9] Therefore, while it was not surprising that Spender was more enthusiastic towards private enterprise than Ward, in reality his stated intention remained how best to mould capital to benefit Papua New Guineans and the Territory at large.[10] True to his beliefs, he did not reject the 'New Deal'; rather he remained committed to providing 'proper safeguards' against the potential disruptive effects to Indigenous people of spontaneous capitalism.[11] Furthermore, as pointed out by Hasluck himself, Spender's emphasis on private enterprise was rejected by Hasluck 18 months later. He describes how, after early visits to the Territory, in terms of economic matters and

---

6 'Papua-N. Guinea under review: Visiting Minister promises many reforms and clear-cut policy', *Pacific Islands Monthly* 20, no. 9 (April 1950): 10.
7 The speech was 11,000 words in length. Legge, *Australian colonial policy*, 196. Brian Jinks was not as effusive, describing the speech as 'pretentious'. Brian Jinks, 'Hasluck's inheritance: Papua New Guinea in May 1951', in *The Hasluck years: Some observations. The administration of Papua New Guinea, 1952–63*, ed. Alan Ward, Tony Voutas and Brian Jinks (Bundoora: Latrobe University, 1977), 25.
8 Percy Spender, 'Australia's policy in relation to external territories', 1 June 1950, CP637/1 [21], National Archives of Australia (NAA).
9 For example, in 1944 when Spender sided against his colleagues and argued in favour of the Labor government 'powers' referendum. David Lowe, *Australian between empires: The life of Percy Spender* (London: Pickering and Chatto, 2010), 3.
10 Spender, 'Australia's policy in relation to external territories'.
11 For more details on the Spender period as External Territories Minister, see: Huntley Wright, 'State practice and rural smallholder production: Late-colonialism and the agrarian doctrine in Papua New Guinea, 1942–1969' (PhD thesis, Massey University, 1999), 205; MacWilliam, *Securing village life*, 79; Legge, *Australian colonial policy*, 198; WEH Stanner, *The South Seas in transition* (Sydney: Australasian Publishing Company, 1953), 128.

a plan to attract Australian enterprise, he turned away from the lead given by Spender, citing plans to attract Australian enterprise as unrealistic.[12] In September 1954, Hasluck told the Commonwealth Parliament that:

> by and large, the situation in Papua and New Guinea did not call for any striking revision in policy … what it did call for was a fundamental re-organisation and building up of strength and efficiency of the Administration, so that it could make the policy effective in action.[13]

Therefore, the change of government in December 1949 from Labor to Liberal/Country did not provide any significant revision in policy. In the speech he wrote for Sir John Northcott to open the Territory's Legislative Council in 1951, Hasluck explained that he had to:

> soften any opposition and especially reduce the dismay and resistance that had been generated by the way in which the so-called 'Ward–Murray' policy had been presented to the planters and traders.[14]

In time these naturally conservative voters would become quite disappointed by what they perceived as Hasluck's lack of advocacy for their 'rights'. He believed in the broad outlines of the 'New Deal', but his approach was more conciliatory, and he regarded it as his role to 'persuade the influential people in the Territory'—planters, traders and missionaries—to think about coming change.[15] Former administrator JK Murray agreed that there was a 'continuance of policy, in relation to Indigenous people, for the prioritisation of their socioeconomic, education and political advancement, and protection against the extremities of capitalism'.[16]

Underlying Hasluck's constructivist intent, the use of state power to negate the destructive characteristics of capitalism, was a belief in the positive benefits of assimilation.[17] Anna Haebich has noted that Hasluck's attraction to humanitarian or social justice issues was primarily due to the influence

---

12   Paul Hasluck, *A time for building: Australian administration in Papua and New Guinea, 1951–1963* (Carlton: Melbourne University Press, 1976), 128.
13   *Parliamentary debates*, 1 September 1954 (Paul Hasluck).
14   Hasluck, *A time for building*, 43.
15   Hasluck, *A time for building*, 44.
16   JK Murray, 'In retrospect—Papua–New Guinea 1945–1949 and Territory of Papua and New Guinea 1949–1952', *Australian Journal of Politics and History* 14 (1968), 322, doi.org/10.1111/j.1467-8497.1968.tb00711.x.
17   Huntley Wright, 'A liberal "respect for small property": Paul Hasluck and the "landless proletariat" in the Territory of Papua and New Guinea, 1951–63', *Australian Historical Studies* 33, no. 119 (2002): 60, doi.org/10.1080/10314610208596201.

of his parents who were devoted Salvation Army officers.[18] Will Sanders has explored Hasluck's longstanding interest in the circumstances of Aboriginal Australians and how, as Minister for Territories, apart from overseeing the 'native affairs branch' of the Northern Territory (NT) administration, he became a driving force within the Commonwealth for advancing Indigenous welfare, and restoration of their legal status to equality with other Australians. Sanders explained that, to Hasluck, assimilation was inevitable as a social process and it was logical for a government to constructively support this progression.[19] MacWilliam has written perceptively of the major differences between conditions for the Indigenous populations of both the NT and TPNG, but also the similarity for state constructivist policy.[20] Hasluck wrote a minute on 22 April 1954 which reinforced the positive characteristics of assimilation in relation to governance and eventual political self-determination of Papuans and New Guineans:

> [There are] two distinct forms of government: the 'general', overall responsibility to Australian standards and a special 'native' government which is working to and within the former, and which has the dual task, firstly, of adapting and applying our rules of government to the present standards of these undeveloped native peoples; and secondly, of gradually raising these standards to the point where they can be largely 'assimilated' into the general community and governed in the same way.[21]

In TPNG, Hasluck's belief in assimilation was factored against the potentially destructive aspects of settler capitalism; it was a form of intentional development which moved away from prewar 'protection' to instead promote welfare and social advancement.[22] In this sense, assimilation was a tool to wed Australian economic and civil concepts with Papuan and New Guinean culture and sentiment.

---

18 Anna Haebich, 'The formative years: Paul Hasluck and Aboriginal issues during the 1930s', in *Paul Hasluck in Australian history: Civic personality and public life*, ed. Tom Stannage, Kay Saunders and Richard Nile (St Lucia: University of Queensland Press, 1998), 95.
19 Will Sanders, 'An abiding interest and a constant approach: Paul Hasluck as historian, reformer and critic of Aboriginal Affairs', in Stannage, Saunders and Nile, *Paul Hasluck in Australian History*, 106–9; Paul Hasluck, *Shades of darkness: Aboriginal Affairs, 1925–65* (Melbourne: Melbourne University Press, 1988), 86.
20 Scott MacWilliam, 'Anti-conservatism: Paul Hasluck and Liberal development in Papua New Guinea', *Australian Journal of Politics and History* 65 (2019): 89, doi.org/10.1111/ajph.12535.
21 Hasluck, 'Native local government', 22 April 1954, para. 2, *Papers of Sir Donald Cleland*, MS9600/15/10/1, NLA.
22 Wright, 'State practice', 212.

Figure 3.3: Paul Hasluck at a village in the Highlands in 1955.
Note: Hasluck was a frequent visitor to TPNG and wrote of his pleasure of visiting the small villages and hamlets of the territories.
Source: NAA, A1200, L18993, item 11163489.

One example of Hasluck's assimilationist intent was the February 1954 direction to the public service commissioner for preparatory work to begin for an Auxiliary Division, to allow young Indigenous officers to be trained on the job.[23] By July 1955 an amendment to the *Public Service Ordinance* came into operation, providing for the establishment of the new division, although in practice it did not begin operations until January 1957, with the approval of 28 new candidates (see Table 3.3). Minimum salary rates were equivalent to the higher categories of administrative servants, and auxiliary officers were able to qualify, by examination, for the main division of the public service.[24] Hasluck described the division with some pride, commenting that:

---

23 Hasluck, *A time for building*, 254.
24 Assistant Secretary, 'Native employment in Papua New Guinea', 26 February 1959, p. 2, Native labour 1955–60, A452 [1959/5852], NAA.

quite a number of significant men in political life in Papua and New Guinea, 15 years later, when the country moved towards independence, were men to whom I had given their first chance to learn about government by my decisions in 1956.[25]

In terms of ideological motivation and the role of the state, Hasluck appears to have been influenced by a confluence of liberal ideas of which Fabianism, it could be argued, was at one end of a spectrum.[26] An alternative explanation for this meeting of minds could be what historian Alexander Zevin has recently described as the liberal 'extreme centre'. Emanating out of Britain and the US during the 1930s, and in response to the Great Depression, he argues liberalism was a conducive factor in bringing together people of different political creeds. Zevin defines liberalism of this period as non-threatening, adaptable, efficient and potentially effective as a vehicle to cure social ills such as poverty and inequality. Furthermore, it appealed to the Americans, in particular Franklin Roosevelt, who promoted his 'New Deal' policies as liberal in an attempt to disassociate from Republican 'progressives' or what he regarded as the more extreme social democracy.[27] In terms of the main drivers of Australian policy in postwar TPNG, liberalism as an 'extreme centre' aligns with Alfred Deakin's 'ethical state', what Walter James defined as 'a liberal polity where freedom was associated not solely with individualism, but with state intervention to assure conditions where a level of liberty could be meaningfully enjoyed by all'.[28] Therefore, liberal moderates such as Percy Spender and especially Paul Hasluck were able to align classical liberal imperatives of individualism and reward for effort with the constructive hegemony of state developmentalism, one advocated by the original architects of Ward's 'New Deal'.

Paul Hasluck was appointed Minister of the newly formed Department of Territories (DOT) on 11 May 1951, he remained in that office until December 1963.[29] Ian Downs, who on occasion clashed with Hasluck, nevertheless praised him as a legendary expatriate figure who was 'the sole

---

25 Hasluck, *A time for building*, 249.
26 Hasluck's direct links to Fabianism are tenuous at best; he wrote of his admiration for British Fabians, particularly British colonial secretary Arthur Creech Jones, whom he met during a series of meetings in the lead-up to the United Nations San Francisco conference of 1945. MacWilliam, *Securing village life*, 31.
27 Alexander Zevin, *Liberalism at large: The world according to the* Economist (London: Verso, 2019), 15, 166.
28 Walter James, *What were they thinking: 150 years of political thinking in Australia* (Sydney: University of New South Wales Press, 2010), 109.
29 The Department of Territories replaced the Department of External Territories (DET), and the new department encompassed the Northern Territory and all Australian external territories.

catalyst for positive change in the Territory'. To Downs, Hasluck seemed to have asked nearly every question himself in his quest for what was best and to have acted on most of them to public satisfaction.[30] James Sinclair, who worked on the ground in TPNG during the Hasluck period, regarded Australia and TPNG as 'fortunate having a man of Hasluck's intellectual calibre and integrity as Minister for such a long period', that on balance his policies were enlightened and beneficial.[31]

In terms of public administration, Hasluck described himself as an 'Inspector-General', and although he believed in clearly delineated chains of authority and allocation of responsibilities, was obsessed with control.[32] In *A Time for Building*, Hasluck explained how the Territory Administration and the Canberra Department often differed in their views about what should be done and how it should be done. Consequently, he reasoned, it was his role to break this deadlock and he would often use this prerogative to make decisions.[33] Rachel Cleland, the wife of long-term administrator, (later Sir) Donald Cleland, described how Hasluck's:

> attention to detail led him to keep a close watch on progress. This tendency increased administrative difficulties, especially as Hasluck did not have a good appreciation of the logistics of a situation or of what it was possible to do in a given time. More seriously, he had poor appreciation of what was wise. This was largely because he lacked a feeling for the time needed by a people being administered to develop a readiness to meet change and absorb it. His own sense of urgency blinded him to these aspects.[34]

---

30   Ian Downs, *The Australian trusteeship: Papua New Guinea 1945–75* (Canberra: Australian Government Publishing Service, 1980), 217.
31   James Sinclair, 'Australian colonial administration of Papua New Guinea—1951–1963: A field staff point of view', in Ward, Voutas and Jinks, *The Hasluck years*, 52.
32   Geoffrey Bolton, *Hasluck: A life* (Crawley: University of Western Australia Press, 2015), 128, 302; Hasluck, *A time for building*, 407; MacWilliam, 'Anti-conservatism', 97.
33   Hasluck, *A time for building*, 407–8.
34   Rachel Cleland, *Papua New Guinea: Pathways to independence* (Perth: Artlook books, 1983), 148.

Figure 3.4: Rachel and Donald Cleland (right and second right) with Governor-General William Slim in 1959.
Source: NAA, A1200, L33830, item 7494981.

In an unpublished reflection following the retirement of Cleland, David Fenbury delivered a fascinating, if caustic, commentary on minister–administrator relations. Fenbury, who was quite likely to be writing from a position of frustration or personal enmity, regarded their distinctive personal characteristics as a defining feature in the dominance of Canberra over Port Moresby. Fenbury described Hasluck as a strong, single-minded minister who disliked bureaucrats, a 'historian with firm theoretical convictions regarding the evolution of primitive societies and inexorable trend of events in the post-war colonial world', who had little love for the pomp and ceremony of British colonialism, a pedantic fondness for precise language, a critical eye and a highly developed ability to read official papers. According to Fenbury, 'Hasluck regarded Cleland as essentially timid, vacillating, and slow to grasp the realities of an emerging colonial situation. He gave Cleland hell', leaving the 'administrator vulnerable to the metropolitan government pressures much more so than in a British colony'.[35]

---

35 Fenbury, (unpublished) 'New Guinea's Cleland in retrospect', submitted to *The Australian* 15 January 1967 under the pseudonym 'Pyrex'. Papers of David Maxwell Fenbury, MS6747/2/7, National Library of Australia (NLA); Hasluck, *A time for building*, 15.

Figure 3.5: The administrator, Donald Cleland, breakfasting outside house 'Kiap' Fatmilak, New Ireland, in 1954.
Source: NAA, A6510, L1287, item 764338.

In January 1964, after Hasluck had moved to the Defence portfolio, he reflected on the role of the minister in relation to policy implementation. He spoke of the importance of providing clear leadership on policy, but in reality 'policy is made and shaped and translated into action by day-to-day decisions', and while the overall objective remains clear and constant, the more limited objectives can be varied or discarded.[36] MacWilliam has described how, to Hasluck, policy was inseparable from administration; 'policy development' took place as a result of a succession of facts performed by a wide range of people.[37] The minister would invariably first obtain advice from internal reports or external academics, although as pointed out by Downs, the 'recommendations in these reports usually reflected Hasluck's own policy and were used in support of a particular course of action'.[38] To Hasluck, the Canberra department was stronger and needed firmer handling than the Territory Administration, reasoning they had

---

36   Hasluck, 'Present policies and objectives', 6–10 January 1964, Papers of Sir Donald Cleland, MS9600/16/11/3, NLA.
37   MacWilliam, *Securing village life*, 87; Hasluck, 'Proposed staff re-organisation', Department of Territories (DOT), M1776 [vol. 1], NAA.
38   For example, the 1953 *Spate report*, a general survey of TPNG by Oskar Spate (Geography), Trevor Swan (Economics), Belshaw (Anthropology), academics from The Australian National University; 1961 *Derham report* on the judiciary by David Derham, Melbourne University Professor of Jurisprudence. Downs, *The Australian trusteeship*, 97.

greater knowledge of public administration, could more closely consult other government departments and were more familiar with other branches of government. According to Hasluck, they could work more effectively and would often do the work of the administration despite his efforts to ensure they had the freedom to carry out policy. His reputation as an 'interfering' minister stemmed from both his willingness to step in if department officers overstepped their position in relation to the constitutional separation of them, and propensity for constant personal monitoring of policy development.[39]

As has been noted by other historians such as Nigel Oram and Allan Healy, Hasluck by his own admission was totally ignorant of colonial administration and TPNG before coming to the job.[40] During his 13 years as Territories Minister, he never visited another colony and gave the impression that TPNG as a colonial territory existed in complete isolation. He made no attempt to learn from the British—even on technical matters, according to Healy; many of his ministerial minutes,

> represent attempts to work out policies from scratch, with no acknowledgement of the fact that similar problems elsewhere had, over the years, produced a wide range of responses, successful and unsuccessful, that could have served as guides and warnings.[41]

Oram, a former senior officer in the British Colonial Office in Kenya and later a member of the *Pangu Pati* in the 1960s, spoke to an official from DOT who said they were not bound to follow British precedent. To Oram this seemed ludicrous as, worst case, the British 'had made every possible mistake in one or other of their many colonies and that something might be learned from them'.[42]

Healy described Hasluck as totally dedicated to one model of development, a misapplied evolutionary theory in which Indigenous people graduate along a straight line: from primitive to civilised.[43] This is an interesting analysis by Healy, especially regarding the administration's actions and attitude toward a nonconforming Indigene. Part Two of this book investigates this most difficult and contradictory aspect of Australian

---

39   Hasluck, *A time for building*, 56–57, 152, 201.
40   Hasluck, *A time for building*, 6.
41   Allan Healy, 'Hasluck on himself', in Ward, Voutas and Jinks, *The Hasluck years*, 33; Nigel Oram, 'Canberra and Konedobu under Hasluck and the Colonial Office—a comparison', in Ward, Voutas and Jinks, *The Hasluck years*, 79.
42   Oram, 'Canberra and Konedobu', 36, 46, 79.
43   Healy, 'Hasluck on himself'.

postwar rule in TPNG: how government policy, broadly informed by liberal and progressive thinking, clearly articulated eventual political autonomy but only when it fitted within particular colonial development paradigms. Where an Indigenous leader or group manipulated government programs to suit their own community in a way not envisaged by the government, then the government's reaction was often officious and aggressive. This attitude can be understood in the evolutionary terms described by Healy in which the 'native' is regarded as helpless and promotes the concept of a benevolent coloniser or neighbour. The result increased tension on the ground, undermined government messaging and divided efforts at improving the lived experience of local people.

During the Hasluck years (1951–63), Commonwealth grants exceeded $255 million (2019 equivalent $3.1 billion[44]) with an average growth of 14 per cent, while internal revenue grew from $4.7 million to $18 million during this period.[45] As indicated in Table 3.1, the size of the Commonwealth grant as a proportion of overall consolidated government expenditure was minuscule (0.63 per cent). And yet, over the 12-year reign of Hasluck, he was able to triple the size of these grants as a proportion of the Commonwealth budget, eventually rising to 1 per cent by 1963.[46] The machinery of government was conducted along the following lines: the Minister of Territories instructed the administrator of the Australian Government's policies and objectives for TPNG. The minister was supported in the implementation of these instructions by an executive council; the Legislative Council, empowered to make ordinances for peace and good order; a judicial system, including a supreme court and 'Native Village Courts and Tribunals'; and a public service divided into 11 technical departments responsible to the Government Secretary.[47]

---

44 Reserve Bank of Australia, 'Inflation Calculator', accessed 11 February 2020 at: www.rba.gov.au/calculator/annualDecimal.html.
45 All figures are in 1969 Australian dollars.
46 As an example, in 1952 the Australian Broadcasting Commission's (ABC) budget was $12,185,485 compared to the TPNG grant of $10,568,618. By 1963, the ABC budget was $33,995,923, whereas the TPNG grant had reached $40,000,414. Commonwealth of Australia, 'Budget' for 1951/52 (p. 10) and 1962/63 (pp. 12 and 40), *Archive of budgets*, accessed 24 September 2020 at: archive.budget.gov.au/.
47 'Reorganisation of the Central Executive of the Administration', 16 July 1953, p. 1, Papers of J.K. McCarthy, MS5581/3/21, NLA.

Table 3.1: Australian grants (for the year ending 30 June).

Year	Commonwealth expenditure	PNG grants	Per cent of Commonwealth expenditure	Growth	Internal revenue	Growth	Total revenue
1952	$3,093,104,954	$10,568,618	0.34%	24.00%	$4,781,734	8.40%	$15,350,352
1953	$2,878,704,611	$9,314,044	0.32%	(11.87%)	$4,868,666	1.82%	$14,182,710
1954	$2,792,629,383	$10,843,966	0.39%	16.43%	$5,938,804	21.98%	$16,782,770
1955	$3,033,188,538	$14,256,578	0.47%	31.47%	$6,308,704	6.23%	$20,565,282
1956	$3,063,818,850	$16,863,798	0.55%	18.29%	$7,726,648	22.48%	$24,590,446
1957	$3,435,520,908	$18,893,180	0.55%	12.03%	$8,307,420	7.52%	$27,200,600
1958	$3,430,417,914	$21,592,982	0.63%	14.29%	$9,450,062	13.75%	$31,043,044
1959	$3,300,469,496	$22,957,820	0.70%	6.32%	$11,209,494	18.62%	$34,167,314
1960	$3,537,431,578	$25,616,564	0.72%	11.58%	$13,187,856	17.65%	$38,804,420
1961	$3,956,992,188	$29,593,296	0.75%	15.52%	$14,904,200	13.01%	$44,497,496[a]
1962	$3,977,582,930	$34,586,796	0.87%	16.87%	$15,411,598	3.4%	$49,998,394[a]
1963	$4,009,766,216	$40,000,414	1.0%	15.65%	$18,048,722	17.11%	$58,094,136[a]
Total	$40,509,627,566	$255,088,056	Average: 0.63%	Average: 14.22%	$120,143,908	Average: 12.66%	$375,231,964

Notes: All figures in 1969 Australian dollars. [a] denotes additional loans (1961: $1,103,330; 1962: $993,552; 1963: $1,976,794). Percentage increase based on 1951 Australian grant of $8,523,303 and internal revenue of $4,410,883. Internal revenue includes: customs duties, direct taxation, licence fees, land taxes and public utilities.

Source: Statistics Section (Department of External Territories), *Compendium of Statistics for Papua New Guinea* (Canberra: Government Printer, 1969), 46–48; Commonwealth of Australia, 'Budget' for year 1951/52 and 1962/63, Archive of Budgets, archive.budget.gov.au/; Commonwealth of Australia, *Report to the General Assembly of the United Nations on the administration of the Territory of New Guinea: From 1st of July, 1950 to 30th June, 1951* (Canberra: Government Printer, 1950), 84.

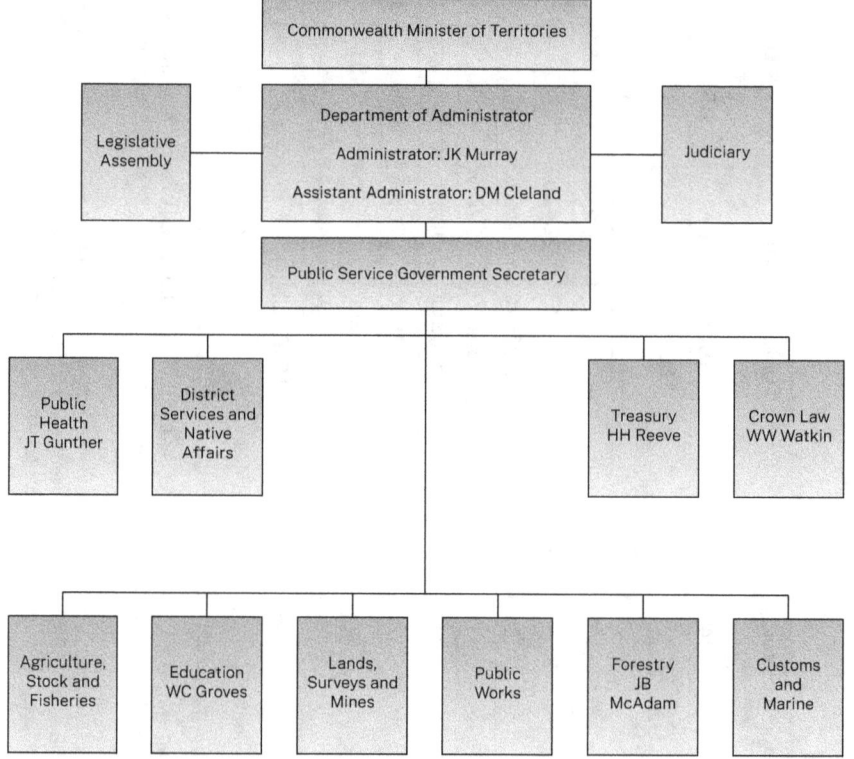

Figure 3.6: Territories Department, 1952.

By 1969 there were 16 departments, including: Trade and Industry; Posts and Telegraphs; Information and Extension Services; Labour; Social Development and Home Affairs; Business Development; and Transport.

Source: Ian Downs, *The Australian trusteeship: Papua New Guinea 1945–75* (Canberra: Australian Government Publishing Service, 1980), 87; Brian Jinks, *New Guinea government: An introduction* (Sydney: Angus and Robertson, 1971), 136; Department of Territories, *Territory of Papua, Annual Report for the period 1st of July, 1951, to 30th June 1952* (Canberra: Government Printer, 1952), 15.

In practical terms, as Hasluck explained, the government decision had to filter through the Canberra department to the administrator, and 'from the Administrator down to an officer in the field, who then told a group of people in words of his own and in a manner of his own what the Government wanted done or had already done itself'. Apart from concerns of decentralisation and 'loss of message', this form of administration, according to Hasluck, 'tended to favour an authoritarian and presidential form of government'.[48]

---

48 Hasluck, *A time for building*, 415.

In terms of designing and implementing government policy, several issues arose regarding the structure of the Territory Administration: the role of the District Commissioner (DC); the lack of coordination at a district level; and insufficient staff numbers. The long-term objective of the administration was to govern for the whole Territory, with the same laws, rights, opportunities and obligations for all people. Therefore, the system of district administration was focussed purely on the control, coordination and development of one group of people. It was transient in nature, governed by social and political circumstances, location and time. Although, as Hasluck acknowledged in a personal letter to Cleland of March 1959, unlike other departments whose administrative tasks could be easily defined, district administration required officers at headquarters and in the field to be of 'a high level of intelligence' and should be provided with the full understanding of government intent.[49]

The DC was the senior executive officer of a district, responsible to the Government Secretary for the coordination of all activities except 'Native' administration, for which they were responsible to the Department of District Services and Native Affairs (DDSNA) Director.[50] During the 1950s, the influence of district administration waned.[51] DDSNA was divided into two departments, District Services (DDS) and Native Affairs (DNA), the role of the DC was restricted to that of a coordinator, while technical officers dealt directly with district representatives of their own departments.[52] In the early postwar period, patrol officers remained the dominant government presence in the villages;[53] however, as other technical departments strengthened, they became increasingly involved in village affairs, diluting, to some extent, the dominance of district administration. Furthermore, problems arose over the practical authority of a DC regarding the activity of personnel from technical departments. At the 1957 DC Conference, the Assistant Administrator, John Gunther, criticised department heads for not informing DCs of their plans and activities within a district. New Britain DC John Foldi explained how, from a district perspective, technical departments tended to 'form themselves into water-tight cells and resent interference from people who were non-technical'.[54]

---

49   Hasluck to Cleland, 3 March 1959, Papers of Sir Donald Cleland, MS9600/15/10/3, NLA.
50   'Reorganisation of the Central Executive of the Administration', p. 2.
51   Hasluck to Cleland, 7 October 1958, Papers of Sir Donald Cleland, MS9600/15/10/3, NLA.
52   Downs, *The Australian trusteeship*, 137–47.
53   Health and Agricultural officials also provided an important government presence.
54   Territory of Papua and New Guinea, 'Summarised report of proceedings at the District Commissioners' Conference', 11–14 March 1957, pp. 1–3, Papers of J.K. McCarthy, MS5581/4/24, NLA.

PREPARING A NATION?

In July 1956, Keith McCarthy, a Territory official of long experience (1927–69), and at the time an executive officer in District Services, wrote of the dysfunctional relationship which existed between those designing government policies and those charged with implementing them. In particular, he complained that at a district level, DCs were 'left functionally in the air', often not advised of important plans and left unsure of their functional role. He argued it was not possible to write a singular plan for the whole Territory, given 'the variation of terrain and in the numbers and development of their people', and recommended that the senior officer be firstly informed of government strategy, but even more importantly, be the person to approve plans on the ground; this would ensure a continuity of aims in a district for many of the objectives spaced over a number of years.[55]

Table 3.2: Public service, Auxiliary Division and administrative patrols.

Year	Europeans in public service	Indigenous in Auxiliary Division	No. patrols	No. patrol days
1946	643	N/A	N/A	N/A
1947	975	N/A	N/A	N/A
1948	1,022	N/A	167	3,461*
1949	1,174	N/A	323	6,420
1950	1,314	N/A	283	6,205
1951	1,280	N/A	301	6,999
1952	1,293	N/A	384	8,517
1953	1,447	N/A	402	9,657
1954	1,675	N/A	400	12,471
1955	1918	N/A	451	11,853
1956	2,196	N/A	421	10,638
1957	2,700	N/A	449	11,214
1958	2,989	188	409	9,768
1959	3,236	248	542	11,853
1960	3,804	350	668	14,501
1961	4,274	582	736	16,471
1962	4,293	592	894	20,015
1963	4,453	928	1,085	21,642

Notes: * Papua only. The Auxiliary Division numbers only represent those Indigenous workers employed as a Division Four Public Servant; this does not include, for instance, Indigenous teachers or medical assistants.

Source: Jinks, *New Guinea government*, 103, 131, 141.

---

55   JK McCarthy, 'Department of the Administrator', 23 July 1956, pp. 1–4, Papers of J.K. McCarthy, MS5581/4/24, NLA.

During the 1950s, the administration spent approximately 22 per cent of Territory revenue on salaries and allowances for the Territory public service.[56] And yet, a major hindrance to the effectiveness of the administration remained: firstly, the lack of staff and secondly, the excessive amount of clerical work required of a patrol officer.[57] James Sinclair remarked how, over the whole postwar period, the government was never able to establish a full field strength, in fact, it generally hovered around 60–65 per cent.[58] This, even though public servants in TPNG were paid a higher salary and were entitled to better allowances than those of a similar rank in Australia, a recognition of the more difficult tropical conditions and also to tempt Australians to work in the Territory in a period of very low unemployment in Australia.[59] Therefore, while Table 3.2 indicates a sevenfold increase in European public servants and a dramatic rise in Indigenous officers from 1958, there was always a significant number of positions which remained unfilled. The problem caused by a combination of budgetary constraints, insufficient infrastructure (housing, office accommodation and transport), generous recreation entitlements and study leave demands.[60] The increase in patrolling, particularly post-1953, reflected the completion of station rebuilding, newly penetrated areas (Highlands), and the slow increase in staff numbers which had been contained due to Commonwealth budgetary constraints in 1951/52.[61] One problem resulting from both the lack of staff and the continued push from Hasluck to accelerate uncontrolled areas of work was that, at times, junior officers were placed in positions they were not ready to command.[62] Hasluck later reflected that he struggled over the

---

56 Public Service Commissioner, *Annual report for the Year ended 30th June, 1958 to the Minister of State for Territories*, p. 18, Papers of Sir Donald Cleland, MS9600/16/11/2, NLA.
57 RJ Daugherty, 'Economy in administration', 2 February 1956, p. 1, Papers of J.K. McCarthy, MS5581/4/24, NLA.
58 In Milne Bay the average was 45 per cent; Sepik 54 per cent. Sinclair, 'Australian colonial administration', 54.
59 For most of the 1940s, the 1950s and the 1960s, Australia's unemployment rate never climbed above 2 per cent. Peter Martin, 'The unemployment floor', ABC Local Radio, *AM* program broadcast, 23 July 1999. James Sinclair, *Kiap: Australia's patrol officers in Papua New Guinea* (Sydney: Pacific Publications, 1981), 45.
60 ASOPA exams which were regarded as compulsory for promotion. Sinclair, *Kiap*, 150.
61 Establishment of public service positions was 1,625 but was limited to 1,400. Hasluck, 'Public service of Papua and New Guinea', 10 December 1951, Papers of Sir Donald Cleland, MS9600/15/10/1], NLA; figures from Brian Jinks, *New Guinea government: An introduction* (Sydney: Angus and Robertson, 1971), 103.
62 Sinclair, 'Australian colonial administration', 54; Jinks, *New Guinea government*, 131.

decision to extend administrative control due to an inexperienced field staff and his lack of faith in the ability of DDSNA leadership to formulate a practicable plan.[63]

Conclusion

In terms of political and social advancement, the rhetoric of Ward's 'New Deal', while short on detail, did provide a consistent platform for the socioeconomic development of the territories for both the Chifley Labor and Menzies Liberal/Country governments. When Hasluck was installed as Territories Minister 18 months after the change of government from Labor to Liberal/Country, he did not foresee any significant revision in policy. This chapter has argued that the genesis for these ideas stratified a broad political consensus, from Fabian policymakers of the Labor left to the progressive wing of the Liberal party. In this way, the postwar Australian objectives in TPNG can be understood as emanating out of an 'extreme centre' of liberalism, one which balanced individualism with state intervention, although on balance favoured universal development over individual liberty.

This chapter has explored the character, drive, thoughts of and ambition of Minister for Territories Paul Hasluck. His domineering personality, intellectual and bureaucratic rigour, and power of office (unique in the Commonwealth at the time) ensured his status as the most significant expatriate figure of the postwar period. Despite Hasluck's undoubted capacity as an administrator, he consciously chose to work in complete isolation from the experiences and knowledge of other colonial administrations. This attitude would waste resources on the ground in the Territory as Australia repeated errors to similar problems elsewhere. Australian development policy under Hasluck reflected the positive benefits of assimilation, and while empathetic to Indigenous concerns and welfare, was not informed by Papua New Guinean input.

---

63   Hasluck, *A time for building*, 78.

4

The Australian Objective: Understanding the Hasluck Development Pyramid

This chapter maps the overall Australian objective in the Territory of Papua New Guinea (TPNG), and how Hasluck's gradualist ethos and belief in uniform development shaped and influenced the way this objective was delivered. Paul Hasluck believed in building a broad base, both in terms of nation-building projects, such as universal English language and access to health or other government services, and in institution-building projects, such as a sustainable public service, independent judiciary and political competency. Time and again Hasluck reaffirmed Australia's trusteeship commitment for eventual Indigenous self-rule and emphasised the importance of managing this scenario to its best advantage.[1] In practical terms, this meant continued preservation of Indigenous land tenure, encouragement of local people in assuming responsibility in government, and promotion of Indigenous economic and social advancement based on the utilisation of household labour or smallholder agricultural production.[2]

---

1   Examples of where the Minister outlined his vision and ambition for the development of TPNG: August 1956 'Progress in New Guinea'; May 1958 'The legend of remote control'; Paul Hasluck, 'Progress in New Guinea', New Guinea speeches, articles and notes, M1775 [2], National Archives of Australia (NAA); Paul Hasluck, *A time for building: Australian administration in Papua and New Guinea, 1951–1963* (Carlton: Melbourne University Press, 1976), 209–11.
2   Paul Hasluck, 'Native local government', 22 April 1954, para 12, Papers of Sir Donald Cleland, MS9600/15/10/1, National Library of Australia (NLA).

Figure 4.1: Paul Hasluck on an official 1955 visit to the Territory Administration, Port Moresby.
Source: National Archives of Australia (NAA), A1200, L19000, item 11163490.

To Hasluck, the development of TPNG and the Australian ambition of a stable, non-threatening and easily controlled people to the north had to be managed within a gradualist program of progressive change. To meet this ambition, this chapter introduces a theoretical model, the Hasluck Development Pyramid, to explain Australian development strategy. The pyramid comprises five levels, each level representing a stage towards the ultimate attainment of self-government. Based on an evolutionary appeal to steady advancement, the model argues Hasluck instituted a 'demand-driven' development policy for TPNG, one which would provoke Indigenous interest in civic, economic and political self-governance.

Hasluck and the Australian objective in TPNG

In April 1954 Hasluck wrote what he described as a 'general statement of Australian policy in TPNG'; this declaration mirrored much of the 'Ward–Murray' objectives, but interestingly, was not only a pragmatic statement, but one which framed the long-term health of Australia–TPNG relations as its most critical factor. Although, as Hank Nelson has written, while Hasluck acknowledged he could envisage a time when Papuans and New Guineans would seek self-government and a measure of independence, until at least 1958, he was unclear on what form, and what date, this would take.[3]

In simple terms, Hasluck believed the Australian Government's objective had to be the mutual security and prosperity of both Australia and TPNG, a joint ambition, in which policies would encourage an attachment by the peoples of both nations, specifically by 'speech, culture, form of government, economic interest, and sentiment'. This bond would help satisfy a second consideration, mutual security. Hasluck argued security was not a one-way street; the large northern island could not be regarded merely as a security bulwark for Australian benefit. Instead, the benefit to local people of a continued Australian presence had to be fostered in terms of 'security benefit' to them, such as the risk of land expropriation, loss of eventual self-government and domination by any other power.[4] In other words, just as David Fenbury and John Black had argued, it was vital Papua New Guineans could see the benefit of a long-term association with Australia.

In practical terms, this meant continued preservation of Indigenous land tenure, encouragement of local people in assuming responsibility in government, and promotion of Indigenous economic and social advancement. While this is not the usual action of an Australian liberal government, it is an example of postwar economic reality for the late colonial period: smallholder production, United Nations (UN) trusteeship protection of Indigenous rights, and repercussions in places such as Kenya of riots and a landless proletariat. While preservation of land tenure made sense on a practical level, Hasluck's attitude fluctuated between maintaining an economic

---

3   In a 1958 speech to the Australian Institute of Political Science, Hasluck gave the impression he was thinking of anything but a fully independent state. Hank Nelson, 'Filling in some gaps and building for a nation', in *The Hasluck years: Some observations. The administration of Papua New Guinea, 1952–63*, ed. Alan Ward et al. (Bundoora: Latrobe University, 1977), 76.
4   Hasluck, 'Native local government', 22 April 1954.

policy which wedded Indigenous households to their land (and hence their community), and later attempts to replace customary land tenure with one comparable to the Australian freehold system.[5] Hasluck has argued that prior to his appointment there had been minimal research into customary land tenure. Hank Nelson, on the other hand, notes the many anthropologists who had written at length about landholding by Melanesian peoples by 1950, and suggests this is another example of Hasluck either ignoring or being unaware of resources outside the official files.[6]

Hasluck's 1954 statement of Australian policy, and its reiteration of the trusteeship commitment was followed up in a number of speeches during the 1950s, culminating in an address to the House of Representatives on 23 August 1960.[7] In this speech, Hasluck acknowledged the increased international interest in the Australian Administration of TPNG, given recent upheavals in the colonial world, and outlined the achievements of the administration, the success of which he attributed to a 'record of two governments'. He defended the policy of Australia by quoting Article 73 of the UN Charter and the 'sacred trust of the obligation to promote to the utmost ... the wellbeing of the inhabitants of these territories', and 'recognised the principle that the interests of the inhabitants of these territories are paramount'. One line in his speech explains much of Hasluck's gradualist methodology, making the argument that 'political independence on its own is of limited value unless the people have the capacity to use their independence to their own advantage'. He also warned of the tragic consequences if subjugated people are not fully cognisant of the workings of public institutions:

> if there is not fair dealing, probity and regard for the public measure on the part of those who attain power and a measure of trust among those who are governed. This means a system of law and order, institutions for the administration of justice, hospitals, schools, houses, roads, services of various kinds and the means to provide food and livelihood for the population. History shows with tragic clarity that the past failures of colonialism have not simply been the withholding of self-rule but failures to give the people the means or the capacity for living on their own.[8]

---

5   Huntley Wright, 'State practice and rural smallholder production: Late-colonialism and the agrarian doctrine in Papua New Guinea, 1942–1969' (PhD thesis, Massey University, 1999), 62.
6   Nelson, 'Filling some gaps', 66–68.
7   Hasluck, *A time for building*, 210; Hasluck, 'Progress in New Guinea', New Guinea speeches, articles and notes, M1775 [2], NAA.
8   Hasluck, *Australian policy in Papua and New Guinea: Statement in the House of Representatives* (Canberra: Government Printer, 1960), 7–9.

4. THE AUSTRALIAN OBJECTIVE

It is interesting to note, and probably a reflection of the cautious approach advocated by Hasluck, that the delivery of these public services and institutions remained almost solely in the hands of the coloniser; secondary schools were almost non-existent, law and order were moving increasingly towards a homogenous 'town' central model (and away from villages), and while an Auxiliary Division of the public service had been established, numbers remained low.

Finally, Hasluck linked his gradualist intent and pragmatic nature with the Australian objective, arguing that:

> from the point of view of Australia, in this part of the world, it is of the highest importance that we should have good relations with an independent and self-governing New Guinea. We have that in mind for we are entitled to consider our own security and our own proper self-interest. If we fail to make sound preparations for their independence—politically, administratively and economically—they may fall in the first years of their independence into such disorder and trouble that instead of being a blessing their independence will be a tragedy for them. We will be held accountable for their ills, and goodwill between us will suffer.[9]

Nigel Oram has argued Hasluck's trenchant belief in the importance of Australian institutions laid the foundations of Papua New Guinea's (PNG) administrative and economic structure. It also resulted in the replacement of a colonial system of direct and personal rule (district administration/patrol officers) with one remote and incompatible with Indigenous cultural institutions.[10] Explicitly, he did not want a Papuan or New Guinean to be placed in a position of subservience to the more fortunate of their fellow countrymen, those who had economic or educational opportunity merely due to location and longstanding European contact. Gradual development meant a slowdown of economic development in the more developed coastal areas until Indigenous people from, for example, the Highlands could share in it on a more equitable footing.[11] The Australian objective in TPNG reiterated UN trusteeship ambition, and while Hasluck defended his cautious and pragmatic approach as the most suitable model for establishing legitimate workable public institutions, it also exacerbated colonial control and limited Indigenous autonomy.

---

9   Hasluck, *Australian policy*, 9.
10 Nigel Oram, 'Administration, development and public order', in *Alternative strategies for Papua New Guinea*, ed. Anthony Clunies Ross and John Langmore (Melbourne: Oxford University Press, 1973), 5–6.
11 Hasluck, *A time for building*, 217–18.

This gradualist ethos was incorporated into a broader philosophy of uniform development, of encouraging a greater homogeneity among the Indigenous population and building a genuine sense of nationalism. Universal development, it was argued, was expected to pre-empt the emergence of a particular group whose economic demands might threaten Indigenous households. It was a policy to accelerate development in areas so they could catch up, while not restricting the continued progress of the more 'advanced' groups.[12] At a more esoteric level, during Hasluck's 1960 parliamentary speech in which he referred to the divided nature of pre-colonial TPNG and its detrimental impact on national unity, the people were:

> originally divided into hundreds of small groups speaking different languages and living in a state of fear and enmity towards the other … There is nothing yet even faintly resembling a sense of nationalism or sense of community over the whole Territory.[13]

The diversity of the Indigenous population was regarded as an impediment to future independence and an argument for universal development. As pointed out by MacWilliam, 'the pursuit of homogeneity was also apparent in education, health and agricultural extension policies and programs'.[14] While not a focus of this book, Hasluck regarded education policy as essential to nation-building. The policy of universal primary education (at the expense of an expanded secondary education) was designed to ensure people from as wide a range of areas as possible had equality of opportunity in eventual self-government. It was also a way of ensuring Africa's problems of a small, educated elite were not replicated in TPNG. In 1958, Department Secretary Cecil Lambert outlined this objective by explaining how education policy should advance Indigenous people:

> socially, economically and politically towards a state where they will be capable of managing their own affairs and providing for themselves the best standards of living which the physical resources of their country and their own capabilities can provide.[15]

---

12   Hasluck, *A time for building*, 164–65; Wright, 'State practice', 219; Scott MacWilliam, *Securing village life: Development in late colonial Papua New Guinea* (Canberra: ANU Press, 2013), 77, doi.org/10.22459/SVL.05.2013; Brian Jinks, 'Policy, planning and administration in Papua New Guinea, 1942–1952: With special reference to the role of Colonel J.K. Murray' (PhD thesis, University of Sydney, 1975), 642; Ian Downs, *The Australian trusteeship: Papua New Guinea 1945–75* (Canberra: Australian Government Publishing Service, 1980), 126–28.
13   Hasluck, *Australian policy*, 9.
14   MacWilliam, *Securing village life*, 94.
15   CR Lambert, 'The needs, methods and specific difficulties to be considered in developing the educational program for the Territory of Papua and New Guinea', Papers of Sir Donald Cleland, MS9600/15/10/3, NLA.

In a practical sense, this suggested maximum emphasis on agricultural and technical training at the expense of higher education and opportunity to advance within the administration.

In terms of nation-building, the objective of education, according to Hasluck, was 'mass literacy in English'.[16] This reflected Hasluck's oft-repeated opinion that only two cultural influences could assist the Indigenous Papua New Guineans to achieve a sense of unity, without doing damage to themselves or to Australia: the English language and the Christian religion.[17] Hasluck feared faux-nationalism, one fostered in an artificial way by Europeans or 'stimulated among the native peoples themselves by colour consciousness or antipathy to Whites'. In a private letter to Cleland of April 1956, Hasluck reasoned these movements (presumably he was referring to the newly colonised nations of Africa):

> do not survive independence; they do not create a strong enough unifying element, and they tend to become mere political slogans by which inexperienced and often unscrupulous coloured leader mismanages the affairs of the coloured majority.[18]

The philosophy behind universal development was to guard against such developments, both as a precautionary measure and as a foundation for an eventual viable and equitable self-government.[19] Ken Inglis, in what amounted to a somewhat uncomfortable paternal summation, argued the policies of the Australian Government, of universal development, created TPNG 'nationalism'; from an Indigenous perspective, they were born in a village, learnt from elders their family and language groups; and from the Europeans, that they lived in a territory, country, nation.[20]

---

16   Department of Territories (DOT), minutes of 'Conference of Mission Representatives', pp. 2, 5 October 1956, *Papers of Sir Donald Cleland,* MS9600/15/10/2, NLA.
17   For example: Hasluck's last official speech as minister to the Summer School of the Council of Adult Education on 6 January 1964 was titled 'Present policies and objectives'.
18   Hasluck to Cleland, 4 April 1956, p. 2, Papers of Sir Donald Cleland, MS9600/15/10/2, NLA.
19   Hasluck, 'Native welfare is a big N. Guinea task', *The Sydney Morning Herald*, 5 August 1952, 2; Hasluck, *A time for building*, 78.
20   Ken S Inglis, *Papua New Guinea: Naming a nation*, The Academy of the Social Sciences in Australia: Annual lecture (Canberra: The Australian National University, 1974), 6.

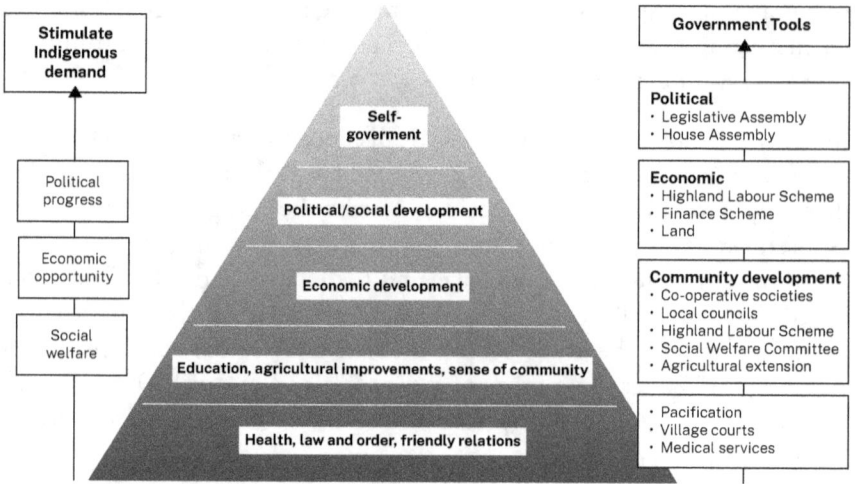

Figure 4.2: Hasluck Development Pyramid.
Source: Author's depiction.

In May 1958, in an address to The Australian National University (ANU) 'New Guinea Society', Hasluck explained his rationale for a 'demand-driven' development policy for TPNG, one which would provoke Indigenous interest in civic, economic and political self-governance. In this speech, which was later quoted extensively in his memoir, *A Time for Building*, Hasluck argued his administration had always prioritised—in fact, had consistently shaped government policy towards—the ultimate goal of Indigenous self-government, and even more emphatically, a 'self-government of a country in which the Indigenous people are the vast majority'.[21] To understand Hasluck's development ideas it is useful to use the concept of a hierarchical pyramid, one comprising five levels, each level representing a stage towards the ultimate attainment of self-government. Contained within most of Hasluck's speeches and ministerial minutes was not only an evolutionary appeal to steady advancement, but a specific push to move Indigenes from one stage of development to the next. This model reflects the theoretical ambition, not necessarily the reality, of what happened on the ground in TPNG.

In fact, the overall impetus for gradual and universal development was a recognition of the disparate and diverse lived experience of local people: language, culture contact, population density, geographic and climatic

---

21 Hasluck, 'The legend of remote control', 12 May 1958, cited in Hasluck, *A time for building*, 210.

conditions. The Indigenous experience of colonial rule and development intent varied depending on locale and gender; people were at different 'stages' of development, and therefore, the applicable government developmental tool had to be directed at a local community level. Hasluck recognised this and was especially insistent on economic development planned and encouraged at a local basis, reasoning it the most effective way to gain villager confidence and allay fears. In a June 1956 ministerial minute, Hasluck directed socioeconomic development 'in local areas [be] determined in each case according to the communal affinities which exist therein and the physical characteristics of the land'.[22] Therefore, the homogeneity of this model, while reflecting a macro strategy, should also be broken down to reflect the expected experience of people in a local region, community or village. As part of this model, Hasluck also regarded the drift towards towns as inevitable; improved technical and clerical education supported producers' demand for a stable work force.[23]

According to Hasluck, at each level, targeted development programs would stimulate needs and wants, beginning at a basic or physiological level, in which the government provided basic health and civic services. The next step was to strengthen and broaden community bonds by focussing on socioeconomic development in the villages. Specifically, community development schemes such as rural progress societies, cooperatives and local government councils, in combination with universal primary education (English language priority) and new agricultural concepts, would enable local inhabitants, in theory, to participate in a modern economy. Once this need had been met, and people became increasingly aware of the opportunities available, they would demand education in social and political affairs. The assumption was that as new skills were learnt, from first contact and pacification through to working in the public service or in their own business, local people would be empowered to demand self-government.[24]

The model assumes the minister always had Indigenous-controlled self-government as the ultimate goal. From a teleological standpoint, there is a danger of relying on Hasluck's personal reflections in *A Time for Building*. And indeed, Tony Voutas, among others, has argued one needs to be careful in assessing Hasluck's contribution based on this memoir because, although

---

22 Paul Hasluck, 'Native economic development in Papua New Guinea', Policy on native economic development, June 1956, M331 [73], NLA.
23 Hasluck, 'Wages policy', 26 April 1961, Native labour 1960–61, A452 [1961/25], NAA.
24 Hasluck, *A time for building*, 195.

a valuable resource, he generally gave the impression he was 'just a little too modern and too constant', or more succinctly, 'more enlightened than everyone else'.[25] However, in reviewing his ministerial papers and speeches, Hasluck, while not specifying a date for independence, was consistent in his ambition for eventual Indigenous self-rule.[26] In one of his first speeches as minister in November 1951, he explained that:

> with the aid of Commonwealth instrumentalities, it is hoped that New Guinea will develop first towards greater participation in the local management of purely local affairs, and eventually beyond that to some form of self-government.[27]

In terms of meeting this eventual goal, and placating mainland concerns regarding 'two races living together', Hasluck outlined a roadmap, an assimilation which would progressively move away from segregation and race-based laws. He argued that if Australia succeeds:

> we will see ... a more politically conscious and politically active native population who, very gradually, over a number of generations, will take an increasing interest both in running their own enterprises and in taking a share in their own government.[28]

Hasluck's preference for gradualism is evident from early into his ministry, later, in September 1956, he expanded on the nature of this administrative task. Principally, he reiterated the overall objective was to advance 'its inhabitants to self-government', but significantly, emphasised the more important task of building a society based on Western principles: justice, freedom and representation. To Hasluck, it was the Australian responsibility to patiently guide local people in this endeavour, without failing to acknowledge they 'have their own culture'. He envisaged a blending of cultures based on a 'common standard of material welfare and Australian social economic and political practice but preserving and enriching all that is best in their cultural heritage'.[29]

---

25 Tony Voutas, 'Preface', in Ward et al., *The Hasluck years*, 4.
26 Downs, *The Australian trusteeship*, 94.
27 Speech reprinted in Paul Hasluck, 'A policy for New Guinea', *South Pacific* 5, no. 11 (January 1952): 225–27.
28 Hasluck, 'A policy for New Guinea', 225–27.
29 Hasluck, 'Australia's task in Papua and New Guinea', Roy Milne Memorial Lecture, 10 September 1956, Papers of J.K. McCarthy, MS5581/4/29, NLA.

Table 4.1: Public service, 1961–64.

Year	Expatriate	Asian/ mixed	Indigenous permanent	Indigenous temporary	Auxiliary Division	Total	Per cent Indigenous
1961	4,273	264	1	26	582	5,146	11.8
1962	4,388	227	39	18	692	5,364	14.0
1963	4,719	238	113	12	928	6,010	17.5
1964	5,068	193	172	18	1,204	6,655	21.0

Notes: The *Public Service (Papua New Guinea) Ordinance 1963* came into operation on 10 September 1964. It made full provision for the appointment of Indigenes to permanent staff; the Auxiliary Division was abolished and the staff from this division was absorbed into the new structure, together with a large number of administration servants. By 1968 Indigenous staff totalled 12,066 out of a total of 18,540 (65.1 per cent).

Source: Statistics Section (Department of External Territories), *Compendium of statistics for Papua New Guinea* (Canberra: Government Printer, 1969), 37.

His message remained remarkably consistent. For example, in January 1964 he described how the objective of self-government would be achieved by a path of peaceful progressive change, in circumstances which provided a reasonable prospect of local people having both the will and the capacity to make autonomous choices, which would be effective for the benefit of Papuans and New Guineans. In response to criticism from both the UN and Australian journalists for the slow progress towards independence (and lack of target dates), Hasluck argued the practical application of 'building a public service and helping a country become financially self-sufficient are more difficult than creating representative institutions or drafting constitutions'.[30] Hasluck's rhetoric did not quite match the deeds of the government, as demonstrated in Table 4.1, Indigenes made up only 11.8 per cent of the public service in 1961 and while growing steadily towards the end of Hasluck's reign, still only accounted for one in five by 1964. Again, Hasluck restated the importance of Western traditions and conventions to a sustainable Indigenous self-government, and this meant stimulating demands and needs of local people for a better standard of living, gainful employment, economic activity and political representation.[31]

---

30 Hasluck, 'Present policies and objectives', pp. 5, 6–10 January 1964, Papers of Sir Donald Cleland, MS9600/16/11/3, NLA.
31 Hasluck, 'Present policies and objectives', p. 6.

PREPARING A NATION?

Stage one: Health, law and order, and friendly relations

Figure 4.3: On 7 April 1961, Paul Hasluck opened the Madang General Hospital. The guard of honour was made up of hospital orderlies and infant child and maternal health nurses.
Source: NAA, A1200, L38803, item 11919955.

The spread of administrative control in the postwar period resulted in the end of tribal fighting in the Highlands (and the freeing up of manpower), the introduction of Western concepts of law and order, and the provision of modern health services. In many parts of the Territory the first stage of development had been completed by May 1951 when Hasluck came to the ministry. One example, the 1947 nutrition survey, undertaken by Commonwealth Health Department officers, recommended the incorporation of greater amounts of protein-rich foods and a wider variety of plant crops in Indigenous diets.[32] This is an example of how science informed colonial policy and greater cooperation between agricultural,

---

32 Commonwealth Department of Health, *The New Guinea nutrition survey expedition* (Sydney: 1947), 3–4, 12.

educational and health services.[33] Functionally, the survey provided a foundation for policymakers to design essential or 'basic' development work, effectively linking health and development aims.[34] Hasluck has written in quite emotional terms of the effect the suffering endured by villagers with various tropical ailments had on his mindset; he attributed their physical welfare needs as the starting point for his personal interest and advocacy for public health policy. Pragmatically, he also explained that in terms of developing friendly relations there was no greater way of gaining the trust and acceptance of local people than when someone who is expected to die is saved by Western medicine.[35]

Table 4.2: Extension of government influence.

	Restricted area (sq. km)	Percentage of total land mass
1950	87,192	18.3%
1951	69,036	14.5%
1952	47,715	10.0%
1953	42,734	9.0%
1954	35,224	7.4%
1955	29,785	6.3%
1956	25,620	5.4%
1957	21,308	4.5%
1958	18,415	3.9%
1959	17,560	3.7%
1960	14,465	3.0%
1961	26,785*	5.6%
1962	21,953	4.6%
1963	11,753	2.5%

Note: * Method of classification changed. Restricted area: Europeans (missionaries, traders and recruiters) banned until the area was under control. Total area of PNG 475,366 km².

Source: Brian Jinks, *New Guinea government: An introduction* (Sydney: Angus and Robertson, 1971), 103.

---

33   Joseph Morgan Hodge, *Triumph of the expert: Agrarian doctrines of development and the legacies of British colonialism* (Athens, OH: Ohio University Press, 2007), 7–17.
34   MacWilliam, *Securing village life*, 52.
35   Hasluck, *A time for building*, 100–1. In terms of the emotional impact of public health policy, see Chapter 11 of *A time for building*.

PREPARING A NATION?

Figure 4.4: An example of the harsh environment patrol officers dealt with in the early postwar period of 'pacification'.
Source: Photographer J Fitzpatrick (1948). NAA, A1200, L9709, item 6849434.

The first major decision Hasluck made in November 1951 was to endorse Spender's instruction to bring the whole of the Territory under control by December 1955; most of this work would be done in the Central Highlands and the high remote headwaters of the Sepik River.[36] Hasluck explained 'the pacification of an area and the establishment of government influence were an essential starting point for all other measures to promote the welfare of the people'. Further, it provided a means to introduce people to Western ideas of law and order to newly unrestricted areas, eliminate tribal fighting and demonstrate the strength of government authority.[37]

---

36   James Sinclair, 'Australian colonial administration of Papua New Guinea—1951–1963: A field staff point of view', in Ward et al., *The Hasluck years*, 53; Percy Spender, 'Australia's policy in relation to external territories', p. 18, 1 June 1950, CP637/1 [21], NAA.
37   Hasluck, *A time for building*, 76, 78.

Pacification and Western concepts of law and order in TPNG are in themselves contested terms; for instance, villagers under plantation labour laws, those press-ganged into assisting with the war effort, or those who had their land taken by the Germans and then the Australians in East New Britain. Nevertheless, penetration work was very popular with patrol officers who often had to be held back from pushing too deeply into the new country. James Sinclair explained that it was Hasluck who made the policy decisions to make expansion possible, and those in the field knew their efforts were watched and appreciated.[38] On the other hand, this policy put a strain on available administrative capacity due to a lack of experienced officers. Ian Downs also criticised the 'urgency of this objective', speculating it contradicted Hasluck's policy of balanced development and political gradualism.[39] On this point, Downs may have misread Hasluck's intention. To Hasluck, exploratory patrols and pacification were the essential first steps, establishing the base for development and providing an opportunity to advance with the rest of the Territory.

Stage two: Education, agricultural improvements and sense of community

Stages two and three of Hasluck's pyramid are closely aligned, primarily directed at community development as part of the broader philosophy of uniform development: of maintaining people in their villages, achieving mass literacy, awakening interest in a higher material standard of living, and moving inexorably towards managing their own political affairs.[40] The aim was for the gradual improvement of the standard of living for Indigenous peoples through their own voluntary efforts, the idea to grow outwards from the village as 'demand' or interest for more autonomy arose. In speaking of agricultural extension work, Hasluck expressed the view that its most import objective was, 'in co-ordination with facets of policy and administration, to consolidate the village unit as the core of development'.[41] This aligned closely with longstanding government policy; for instance,

---

38 Sinclair, 'Australian colonial administration', 53; Hasluck, *A time for building*, 82.
39 Downs, *The Australian trusteeship*, 99, 126; Hasluck, *A time for building*, 79.
40 Hasluck, *A time for building*, 95.
41 Department of External Territories (DET), 'Extract of discussions held in office of the Minister for Territories', 1–2 February 1956, p. 2, Advancement of native agriculture 1954–6, A518 [C2/1/1], NAA.

a planning document from 1944 argued that, insofar as the aim of policy was to protect and improve Indigenous welfare, 'the village economy must be regarded as the basis on which to build'.[42] Hasluck's ideas were not unique; instead it was the power he yielded, combined with his intellectual and bureaucratic rigour, which made his contribution so important.

Ten years before Hasluck made his comment regarding the village as the central component of development policy, in March 1946, Department of Agriculture, Stock and Fisheries (DASF) Director William Cottrell-Dormer had proposed a practical roadmap for the utilisation of household labour as the primary economic development model for the Territory. Dormer is an example of a technician utilising science and expertise to manage the perceived problems and disorder generated by colonial rule.[43] Dormer advocated for a mixed-farming agricultural model where the principal basic unit of the community would be the rural family who, securely settled on its smallholding, could produce food and other crops for its own use and for export. These individual landholdings would produce adequate subsistence for a family and sufficient income from cash crops to satisfy other wants and needs and for the payment of taxes levied for the maintenance of social services.[44] Hasluck not only agreed with this policy but pushed for improved agricultural methods to produce surpluses which could 'and should be turned into cash'. During these discussions, and in comments which provide an excellent example of Hasluck's support for interventionist and intentional development, the Minister said:

> that while we cannot stop change, our aim should be to guide it, perhaps to accelerate it at this point or slow it down at that point; to defer as far as possible, changes, until the basic understanding of the natives is greater; to maintain local custom.[45]

Much like education policy, in terms of impact on the ground in the villages, the agricultural extension program suffered from a lack of resources and produced a wide variation in the status of Indigenous farming in

---

42   Directorate of Research and Civil Affairs (DORCA), 'Inter-relationship of the New Guinea and Australian economies', July 1944, p. 2, Papers of Sir Donald Cleland, MS9600/7/4/17, NLA.
43   For more on this topic see: Hodge, *Triumph of the expert*.
44   William Cottrell-Dormer, 'Proposed plan for Department of Agriculture, Stock and Fisheries', 9 March 1946, Papers of John Black, MS8346/11/7/1, NLA.
45   DET, 'Extract of discussions held in office of the Minister for Territories', p. 1.

the Territory.⁴⁶ The numerical weakness of DASF made it impossible to secure the continuity of both research and extension work in the villages. As pointed out in the March 1953 *Spate Report*:

> men must go on leave, and transfers are necessary to fill the gaps; and six months absence of a man who has got to know the local people, their outlook and their problems, may wreck a promising development.⁴⁷

It should be noted that this was not particular to Australia: shortages of skilled personnel were a feature of postwar conditions in many countries. Furthermore, colonial powers such as Britain enjoyed a great advantage over Australia because the colonial public service had been developed over a long period.⁴⁸

Table 4.3: Agricultural extension officers.

Extension officers	1956	1957	1961
Agricultural officers	45ᵃ	44ᵃ	175ᵇ
Indigenous agricultural assistant	62	79	82
Indigenous agricultural trainee	268	266	743

Notes: ᵃ Expatriate officer; ᵇ Expatriate and Indigenous officer.
Source: DASF, 'The present state of native agricultural advancement in Papua and New Guinea', 30 June 1957, Advancement in native agriculture 1950–59, NAA, A452, 1960/8266; DASF, 'Objectives of five-year programme—Agricultural Extension', June 1962, p. 1, NAA, A2063, A6.

Two 1954 departmental briefs to the Minister praised the work of the extension officers and the impact their advice had on living standards in terms of both health and economic benefits, while acknowledging that the lack of qualified agriculturalist officers was hampering Territory-wide plans.⁴⁹ In fact, the later report of June 1954 made the somewhat astonishing admission that, even after a proposed five-year recruitment drive, 'it would not be possible to provide adequate services to natives in some areas (e.g. the

---

46 Department of Agriculture, Stock and Fisheries (DASF), 'The present state of native agricultural advancement in Papua and New Guinea', 30 June 1957, Advancement in native agriculture 1950–9, A452 [1960/8266], NAA.
47 Oskar Spate, Cyril S Belshaw and Trevor Swan, *Some problems of development in New Guinea* (Canberra: The Australian National University, 1953), 28.
48 Nigel Oram, 'Canberra and Konedobu under Hasluck and the Colonial Office—a comparison', in Ward et al. *The Hasluck years*, p. 80.
49 DOT, 'Encouragement of agricultural development', January 1954, Folders of Ministerial briefing notes, M335 [3], NAA.

PREPARING A NATION?

Highlands Districts)'.⁵⁰ By November 1954 Hasluck's frustration at DASF over its failure to recruit or train extension officers had reached its limit, and in a tersely worded minute, threatened to ask the Department of District Services and Native Affairs (DDSNA) to recruit their own agricultural officers in opposition to DASF. Hasluck would not brook failure in this area; he regarded agricultural work and community development among the most 'basic requirement of our work in the Territory', and essential in both the protection and advancement of the local population.⁵¹

Figure 4.5: Teacher trainees assembled on the playing field of Popondetta, Educational Centre, 1955.

Note: The caption given by the administration to this photograph is an excellent example of administration propaganda. It reads as follows: 'Students enjoy every phase of school life to the full and for many the journey to Popondetta is the first time they travel beyond the immediate environment of their villages'.

Source: NAA, A1200, L188760, item 7558743.

---

50   In 1954 there were 27 European agricultural officers; the proposal was to expand to 85 by 1960. DOT, 'Lack of extension officers', A518/1 [C2/1/1], NAA.
51   Hasluck, 'Native agricultural extension work in Papua and New Guinea', 20 May 1955, Advancement of native agriculture 1954–6, A518 [C2/1/1], NAA.

On the important subject of education policy, there is insufficient room in this chapter to adequately explain the factors which led to the failure of the government to adequately prepare students for secondary and tertiary study, to prepare an 'educated elite' to govern in independence. Some of the factors which led to this policy failure include a lack of prewar investment in education; an ineffective director of education; postwar shortage of teachers in Australia; widespread concern, shared by Hasluck and officials in both the army directorate and provisional administration, of an Indigenous elite hijacking future development to meet their individual needs, and not for the benefit of the mass Indigenous population; and the ameliorative effects of creating a landless proletariat. Of these factors, Hasluck wrote of his regret in not removing William Groves as Director of Education and the difficulty of recruiting teachers. On the point of an Indigenous elite hampering colonial development, an alternative reading was that the government prioritised control over Indigenous autonomy: if a local person or group did not fit within an expected narrative, then they were regarded as a renegade element. In terms of positive intent, he forcefully advocated for universal primary education as a means of strengthening communication bonds, protecting the local community and preparing a base for future secondary education.[52]

Hasluck, in a minute of 24 February 1955, with growing frustration at the lack of action by the Education Department, set the immediate tasks of education policy as including teaching all children in controlled areas to read and write in English, and for vocational training to be aligned with both primary school curriculum and in response to the developing needs of the people. Hasluck wrote that:

> next to teaching reading and writing to establish a means of communication, I think the most urgent need in the primary schools in the 'new areas' is to reinforce what other departments do to improve hygiene, to ensure the understanding and co-operation of the native peoples in what we are trying to do to establish law and order and to combat disease, and to teach them to grow better food and use it more wisely.[53]

---

52 Hasluck, *A time for building,* 220–25.
53 Hasluck, 'Education in the Territory', 24 February 1955, Education and Advancement of Native Women Policy, A452 [1960/8272], NAA.

His opinion mirrored much of what army directorate officer, Camilla Wedgewood, wrote in August 1945, in what became an influential paper on education policy for the Territory, and in particular the importance of universal primary education and the threat of education to the village unit. Her primary concern, and one echoed by Hasluck among others, was the potential creation of a class of 'educated unemployables', or a landless proletariat. The danger, as experienced in other colonial territories, was education as a transformant means for the more intelligent and ambitious young men to leave the village but face a scenario of few suitable employment prospects. Wedgewood pondered whether, given primary production was the most likely economic activity for most of the population, education policy should recognise the benefit of universal primary instruction as social rather than individual. As a first step, Wedgewood argued for the maintenance of village life, of progressively educating adults in ideas and techniques alongside education of children.[54] In terms of universal primary education, both Wedgewood and Hasluck aspired to protective measures against the threat of modernity, while prioritising education policy as most effective as part of a whole of administration effort, but one primarily focussed on village or community level.

Stage three: Economic development

Hasluck, who never wavered in his evolutionary and paternalistic theory of colonial development, regarded it as Australia's duty, as a colonial power, to instigate socioeconomic advancement for the benefit of Papuans and New Guineans. As late as October 1961, in a speech to the Economic Society of Australia and New Zealand, he argued:

> some territories are dependent, not because some power has denied them their rights, but because, in fact, they do not have the capacity to administer their affairs; they cannot defend themselves; they cannot feed and clothe themselves or provide services for their community and they do rely on someone else to help them do all these things.[55]

---

54 Camilla Wedgewood, 'The aims of native education and the incentives which lead the natives to desire it', Papers of Ian Downs, MS8254/11/8/2, NLA.
55 Paul Hasluck, 'The economic development of Papua and New Guinea', *Australian Outlook: The Australian Journal of International Affairs* 16 (1962): 5, doi.org/10.1080/10357716208444101.

Hasluck's argument assumed the inevitability of economic development, critiqued Indigenous Papuans and New Guineans as helpless (despite a long history of trade, rich cultural diversity and successful subsistence farming), and promoted the benevolent intentions of the coloniser. Hasluck's view accords with what Roger Keesing has criticised as a general lack of recognition by development 'experts' for the richness of a subsistence-based life. Keesing argues there was a 'consistent denigration of subsistence agricultural production, and a concomitant stress on the commitment of labour and land to cash-crop production and the dismantling of customary land tenure'.[56]

In this same speech, Hasluck recognised the danger of social change wrought by modernity and capitalist intent, one where the villager went 'from the security and protection of the group to a competitive, unpredictable world of rising and falling prices and fluctuating employment'.[57] James McAuley described this as the paradox of development where, on the one hand, benefits accrue—better hygiene, housing, nutrition and medical care, improved literacy and intellectual culture—but there is a cost when the needs of economic production accentuate economic considerations at the expense of other sociocultural values.[58] For instance, cash cropping and land ownership could enforce economic differentiation between families and individuals, especially in the case of a tree crop, which has an economic life of 20 or more years. This phenomenon was not usually applicable to subsistence agriculture, when reciprocity and land sharing between families allied by marriage could overcome the disadvantage of poor land.[59]

Toward the end of his speech to the Economic Society, Hasluck expressed his commitment to 'self-help' community development, arguing the social consequences of initiative coming from outside could result in:

> freedom from old social restraints before he accepts new social restraints or even knows anything about them. He obtains material benefits of economic development without having learnt any of the realities of sustained effort, capacity or industry to pay, limits on markets and so on.[60]

---

56   Roger M Keesing, 'A tin with the meat taken out', in *Pacific Islands trajectories: Five personal views*, ed. Ton Otto (Canberra: The Australian National University, 1993), 38, 47.
57   Hasluck, 'The economic development of Papua and New Guinea', 19.
58   James McAuley, 'Paradoxes of development in the South Pacific', *Pacific Affairs* 27 (1954): 146–47, doi.org/10.2307/2753623.
59   Maurice Godelier, 'Is the West the model for humankind? The Baruya of New Guinea between change and decay', in Otto, *Pacific Islands trajectories*, 60–63.
60   Hasluck, 'The economic development of Papua and New Guinea', 19–20.

Hasluck's reasoning assumed subsistence farmers lacked an economic incentive to produce a surplus, to generate a financial profit, because of their reliance on self-sufficiency in local foods.[61] And yet, David Fenbury noted in June 1957, any significant improvement in Indigenous living standards was heavily dependent upon the effective extension of social services sustained through maximum development of a cash economy.[62] Therefore, as it was clearly vital to administration plans for local people to be enlisted in productive activities in the Western economy, the administration had to stimulate Western wants and ambitions.[63] In 1959 Hasluck emphasised the central role of community development projects (local councils, agricultural extension work, cooperative societies) in introducing such ideas, explaining an individual project's worth could not be measured solely on its socioeconomic impact on the community, but also the effect they have in the development of new attitudes and habits.[64]

Furthermore, Hasluck argued there had to be, for the sake of the long-term structure of the ownership of economic activities, Indigenous participation in all aspects of economic enterprise. This fitted with the overall ambition, the pinnacle of the pyramid, of economic and political self-sufficiency, and therefore the 'measurement of success in economic development would be social consequences as well as in the statistics of export production'. On this basis he rejected a planned economy, explaining he 'believed them [Indigenes] to be an individualistic and somewhat materialistic people', and therefore would respond to a program which promoted self-development and self-participation, where they 'would find an incentive in doing things for themselves and for their own direct benefit'.[65] Hasluck's model of development presumed that once people have been exposed to new efficient farming techniques, benefited from Western goods and been educated in the opportunities available to them if they produce surpluses, they would, step by step, willingly participate in a money economy.

---

61   Ernest Fisk, 'The economic structure', in *New Guinea on the threshold: Aspects of social, political and economic development*, ed. Ernest Fisk (Canberra: Australian National University Press, 1966), 25–27.
62   Fenbury to Hasluck, June 1957, 'Rural economic development in New Guinea', Papers of David Maxwell Fenbury, MS6747/2/3, NLA.
63   James McAuley, 'Defence and development in Australian New Guinea', *Pacific Affairs* 23 (1950): 380, doi.org/10.2307/2752744.
64   Memorandum from March 1959 cited in Hasluck, *A time for building*, 268.
65   Hasluck, *A time for building*, 129–31.

Stage four: Political and social development

Figure 4.6: Paul Hasluck at the official opening of the Legislative Council in November 1951.
Source: NAA, A6513, 4, item 9627099.

In terms of political and social development, the administrative policy was twofold, both informed by gradualist and universalist intent. At a nation-building level, the government introduced the Legislative Council in November 1951, expanded its role and reach in 1960, and eventually in 1964, with increasing external pressure, established the House Assembly for nationwide elections. Progress was slow; Hasluck admitted he could be accused of gradualism, 'of taking one step after another', but this also fitted with his ethos of ensuring 'political change was the outcome of growth and not the cause of it'. Political autonomy, however, as is explored in Part Two of this book, was only encouraged if it fitted within expected colonial development paradigms. From Hasluck's perspective, political advancement had to be established from a strong base; he used the analogy of a tree to explain his strategy as one of 'growth' in which the policy focussed on the 'roots, trunk, branches, leaves and not just the fruit'.[66] Therefore, it was

---

66   Hasluck, *A time for building*, 240.

at a local level where most political development activity focussed. This was predominantly in the guise of local councils, but also through other community development schemes such as cooperative societies, women's advancement committees and agricultural committees, who were expected to introduce and operate as democratic organisations. It was anticipated that these government initiatives would provide both practical education in delivering a service or producing a commodity for market, and the basic framework in public and civic responsibility.

Whether local councils were primarily a vehicle for area management, providing socioeconomic services to a local community, or instead training Indigenes in self-government has been the cause of much discussion. Below is a summary of the differing views; however, in terms of this chapter, what is most interesting is how the debate highlights the close link between economic and political development. The purpose, according to a 1952 DDSNA circular, was for local councils to provide a medium for teaching Indigenes a measure of responsibility in local affairs, establish area machinery and local funds for extending social services, and educate local people in efficient management practice and the cost of providing such services, all of which were ultimately preparing Indigenous people to understand and participate in the Territory's political system. The circular acknowledged there was an important educational aspect to the policy, and officers were encouraged to allow a measure of autonomy and expect a level of mistakes.[67] Therefore, the official policy was to both educate in political and civic affairs, and deliver government services at a local level.

Although, as RS Parker has noted, despite being advertised for their practical political education, councils were kept within the administrative framework, equipped with humble functions, and had few rights to experiment or make their own local rules: all this in the interests of 'national' consistency and uniformity.[68] On the other hand, it is clear Hasluck favoured local government as a political development tool because it did not require formal education to be successful.[69] Huntley Wright argued that instead of training people for self-government, a council's main purpose was to support

---

67 Circular 141 of 1951/52, 'Native local government', 4 February 1952, DDSNA, Papers of David Maxwell Fenbury, MS6747/4/1, NLA.
68 RS Parker, 'Economics before politics—A colonial phantasy', *Australian Journal of Politics and History* 17 (1971): 208, doi.org/10.1111/j.1467-8497.1971.tb00837.x.
69 Downs, *The Australian trusteeship*, 136.

4. THE AUSTRALIAN OBJECTIVE

the government's overarching economic commitment to the productive capacity of households.[70] Wright's opinion contrasts with that of Hasluck, who, in *A Time for Building*, wrote that councils were:

> promoted as a first step towards self-government and as a measure in political education. Through it we introduced the people to the practice of choosing their own representatives to handle their own affairs, to the means of conducting an election, holding a meeting in an orderly fashion, keeping a record of what was done, deciding on a tax for themselves and deciding how the revenue should be used, by employing their own staff to work for the whole community and paying their wages out of money provided by the community. We taught them to expect their representatives to account for what they did on behalf of the community. All these ideas were new to them.[71]

Wright's argument is based on the original intent of local councils, and most especially the advocacy of David Fenbury, who clearly viewed them as a way of connecting local people and issues with far-sighted policies of economic development, and as a means of delivering area management of administrative services. Fenbury expressed these concerns in numerous long and eloquently written documents. One example, from a personal letter he wrote to Hasluck in late 1956, criticised the administration's failure to align traditional land tenure with cash crop production. Fenbury argued local councils were an ideal mechanism to deliver government services and could assist in the work of economic transition as part of the general policy of promoting individual cash cropping on a non-customary tenure.[72] His fear, as expressed in another reflective piece from this period, was avoiding the 'normal or classical' colonial agrarian problem which, he believed, would lead inevitably to political instability as demonstrated in British East Africa. He pointed out how DDSNA, in 'promoting a native local government policy with a solid economic bias, has pioneered a new approach to this land-tenure problem'.[73]

---

70 Wright, 'State practice', 35.
71 Hasluck, *A time for building*, 234.
72 Fenbury to Hasluck, December 1956, Papers of David Maxwell Fenbury, MS6747/3/6, NLA.
73 Fenbury, 'UN: reflections on the Territory elections', 1957, pp. 24–27, Papers of David Maxwell Fenbury, MS6747/2/3, NLA; Sumar Singh, *A cost analysis of resettlement in the Gazelle Peninsula* (Canberra: New Guinea Research Group, 1967).

Hasluck did not agree with this premise, writing in a minute of 4 April 1957, that:

> for the immediate present, the government believes that the most fruitful efforts for the political advancement of the Indigenous people can be made in the field of local government and it is an instruction on policy that increasing efforts shall be devoted to this work.[74]

At the same time, Hasluck agreed with Fenbury regarding the ability of councils to mediate classical colonial problems (including dictatorship). Whereas Fenbury argued local councils could assist in economic transition, Hasluck expected councils to be a vehicle to accustom Indigenes to 'the idea of representation, responsibility of government to the people and a public service that carried on the tasks of administration for the benefit of the whole country'.[75]

Conclusion

Hasluck's Developmental Pyramid explains how the minister expected administrative activity, and especially community development schemes, to stimulate Indigenes to work towards eventual self-rule. The aim was to ensure, step by step, that local people had the opportunity to participate in self-government, and furthermore, that provisions were made to establish and staff the necessary civic and economic institutions for a sustainable Westminster democracy. To Hasluck, the final goal was political self-rule, and a strong, long-term and ongoing relationship between Australia and TPNG. The method he employed was informed by gradualist intent, incorporated into universal and nation-building programs built on a broad base which, at its core, primarily focussed on development activity at a local level.

Part One of this book has necessarily been written from a Eurocentric and gender-specific perspective.[76] It has explained the Australian objective for the development of TPNG, of how Australia designed the policies, implemented the programs, spent the money, 'advanced' the prehistoric

---

74   Hasluck, minute, 4 April 1957, cited in Hasluck, *A time for building*, 251.
75   Hasluck, *A time for building*, 240.
76   The only prominent female voice informing development policy in the early postwar period was Camilla Wedgewood.

people of TPNG, and brought independence to TPNG. However, Part Two explores, and challenges, this Eurocentric narrative of Australian dominance of postwar development in the lead-up to independence in 1975. The actions of local people and the impact of local conditions are explored in four case studies, uncovering how autonomous actions and conditions forced the Australian Government to radically adjust and introduce new development programs.

Part Two: Indigenous Influence: Local Conditions and Autonomous Actions

CASE STUDY: CHIMBU

5

Chimbu: Australia's New Deal Problem?

The Chimbu (or Simbu) case study explores how the postwar development of this subdistrict was profoundly shaped by regional characteristics, broadly: scarcity of land suitable for commercial agriculture, high population density and a local population who demanded equality of opportunity to raise their living standards. The Chimbu postwar experience is an example of the varied and diverse Indigenous response to an Australian policy that was designed in Canberra/Port Moresby and was manipulated on the ground to suit local circumstances. Patrol officers were expected to implement the progressive 'New Deal' plans of the Australian Labor Party, but it quickly became evident that the unique features of Chimbu and a lack of government resources would play a significant role in the postwar experience of the subdistrict.

Chimbu is the name of a place and a people, it is unique as a region within the Territory of Papua New Guinea (TPNG), as many people speak variants of a single language. The basic culture, views and values of Chimbu were much the same throughout the subdistrict.[1] The topography of Chimbu is rugged and irregular, with elevation ranging from 1,600 to 4,000 metres (Mount Wilhelm), the landscape is unstable due to high erosion.[2] In most

---

1   There are 13 vernacular languages in Chimbu: Kuman is the most widely spoken. Paula Brown, 'Chimbu leadership before provincial government', *Journal of Pacific History* 14 (1979): 100, doi.org/10.1080/00223347908572368; John Nilles, 'The Kuman of the Chimbu Region, Central Highlands, New Guinea', *Oceania* 21 (1950): 25, doi.org/10.1002/j.1834-4461.1950.tb00171.x.
2   Diana Howlett, R Hide and Elspeth Young, *Chimbu: Issues in development* (Canberra: Development Studies Centre, Monograph no. 4, The Australian National University, 1976), 71–75.

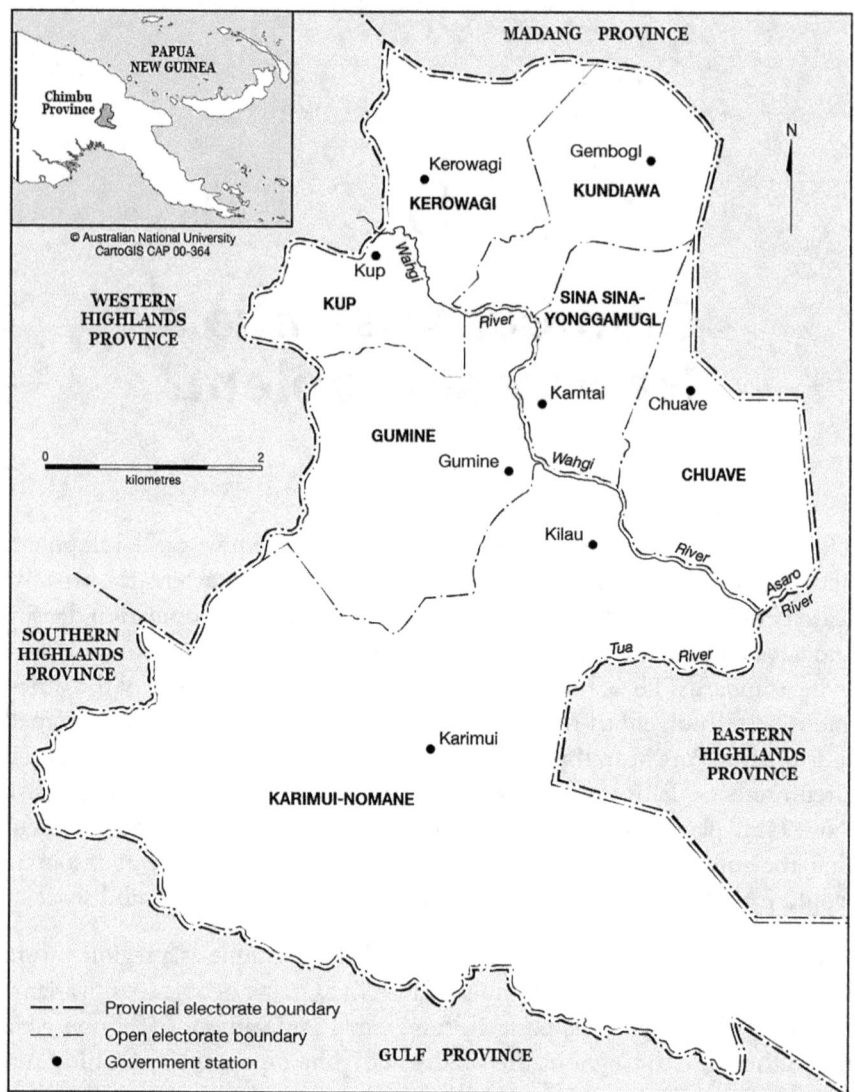

Map 5.1: Chimbu Province.
Source: CartoGIS Services, College of Asia and the Pacific, The Australian National University (ANU).

of Chimbu, there were no villages as such; houses were usually lined in small hamlets along the tops of knife-like ridges. In 1964, Cadet Officer Murray Tomlinson described how:

> the little flat land that is available is kept mainly for gardening purposes and thus is not used for building sites. In the days of tribal fighting houses built on these steep ridges were much easier to defend.[3]

This chapter follows how these patrol officers were immediately confronted with how little Australian influence there was in the region, and where it was noticeable, it was poorly administered. In this way, instead of introducing progressive socioeconomic and political programs, officers were forced to contend with the particularity of high population density and insufficient arable land for the agriculture development planned for in the 'New Deal'. These factors profoundly affected the contested colonial space between the local population and government officials. On the ground, as explained by the Hasluck Development Pyramid, the administration extended its reach with the time-consuming task of first contact and pacification.

However, the next step, introducing agroeconomic programs which anchored local people to their village, was hampered by local conditions. As seen through the patrol reports, and explained in this chapter, officers were consumed with attempting to marry government strategy for smallholder production with options available to the administration. In January 1950, the Australian Government established the Highland Labour Scheme (HLS), premised on obtaining local labour for coastal plantations and, somewhat dubiously, as an opportunity for Highlanders to earn some income. It was a program aimed at addressing short-term economic concerns and was in complete opposition to the government's economic strategy for village-based cash cropping. It is also an example of the tension within the government regarding forced labour, as in some respects this program reinstates a form of indenture system. While introduced in this chapter, the HLS is the major focus of Chapter 6 and explains how this colonial development program would have a profound impact on Chimbu society.

The experience of the Chimbu subdistrict in the postwar period undermines the argument that socioeconomic and political change was a one-way process initiated by the colonial state. Instead, postwar Chimbu development

---

3   Murray Tomlinson, Report 1 of Patrol Reports, Chimbu District, Gumine, 1964–1965. p. 1, National Archives of Papua New Guinea (PNGA).

must be viewed as an interdependent relationship between the aims of the Australian Administration, the regional characteristics on the ground and the demands of the Chimbu people.

Conditions on the ground at the end of the Pacific War

At the end of the war, the population of Chimbu was a staggering 140,000. The people shared the same basic cultural values, language (variants of Kuman), views and expectations.[4] The postwar period saw an immediate change in power relations, as the government attempted to establish a colonial administration; local people had to adjust to new rules and new sources of power. The administration had to contend with, in the words of the 1956 United Nations (UN) Visiting Mission, a people who:

> seem to have sublimated their energies into a demand for progress which is probably not excelled in any other part of the Territory, and the Administration will have to keep ahead of it.[5]

On 1 December 1944 Koningambe, bossboy of Suinga hamlet, reported to Lieutenant Ken Jones of an attack on his people by the Gembogl clan, resulting in the death of two of his men and a general outbreak of tribal warfare.[6] Jones had only arrived in the subdistrict of Chimbu in the previous fortnight and had, to this point, not been issued with instructions regarding limits of patrol activity. Chimbu was under the direct control of the District Officer (DO) for Hagen, George Greathead, who had reasonably expected Jones would be content to familiarise himself with the immediate surrounds of the Kundiawa patrol post.[7]

Jones left Kundiawa on 9 December 1944, travelling north-east through the Chimbu valley by jeep accompanied by seven police constables. At Kerowagi, an Australian New Guinea Administrative Unit (ANGAU) substation and Lutheran Mission Station, Jones collected supplies and

---

4   Ian Downs, correspondence to Director Department of District Services and Native Affairs (DDSNA), 28 February 1953, Eastern Highlands District (EHD) Quarterly Report, Box 869 [DS 29-16-30], PNGA.
5   United Nations Visiting Mission to Trust Territories in the Pacific, *Report on New Guinea* (New York: UN Trusteeship Council, 1956), 65.
6   KW Jones, Report 5 of 1944/45, Patrol Reports, Chimbu District, Kundiawa, 1940–1950, PNGA.
7   George Greathead, HQ Northern Region, ANGAU, 7 March 1945, Chimbu District, Kundiawa, 1940–1950, PNGA.

30 carriers before proceeding in a north-westerly direction by foot, arriving in the Gembogl division on 14 December 1945. Jones was immediately confronted with villagers armed and apparently looking for a fight; moving forward it became apparent the main contingent of the group had moved higher up the mountain. Jones decided to halt for the night, and several headmen agreed to sleep in the patrol camp, promising that their men would come down the following morning. During the night, these leaders disappeared, and Jones had little choice but to head into the mountains. With six police, Jones followed a bridle path, hoping to make contact; one hour into this climb they were ambushed by a shower of spears. Police fired shots to scatter the attack and over the next week, Jones arrested and 'pacified' the warring tribes.[8]

Greathead, an experienced officer who had arrived in TPNG in June 1933 and had worked since 1938 in the Southern Highlands surrounding Mount Hagen, was unhappy with the circumstances which had placed a young officer in danger.[9] And he blamed administration policy for this situation. He pointed to 'the happy position prevailing in the Hagen subdistrict during the past five years, with only one case of tribal fighting' because the scope of patrol activity had been confined to an approximate radius of 10 kilometres. In fact, Greathead had refused a suggestion from the district office in Madang to double this radius. He reasoned the attack on Jones a consequence of an administration spread too thin. If the government was incapable of providing adequate services, then it was better to not make contact, to disrupt local communities with haphazard patrolling. Greathead argued:

> a similar policy in the Chimbu sub-district in 1935 would have made possible a more permanent consolidation of government influence. The position, however, has been that for the best part of nine years one officer has been permitted to undertake obligations towards something like 250,000 uncontrolled natives; but the unfortunate aspect is that incoming O.I.C's [Officers in Charge] of the Sub-District are called upon to bear the brunt of previous maladministration.[10]

---

8 Jones, Report 5 of 1944/45.
9 Judy Tudor, ed., *Pacific Islands year book and who's who*, 9th ed. (Sydney: Pacific Publications, 1967), 580.
10 Greathead, 7 March 1945.

Figure 5.1: Women bringing food to the Chimbu Police Post in the early days of its establishment in 1937. The post can be seen in the background.
Source: National Archives of Australia (NAA), A1200, L25793, item 7594952.

This lack of resources would become a recurring theme during the postwar development of not just the Chimbu subdistrict, but throughout the Territory. The military had withdrawn in February 1946 and until the end of April there was no administrative presence in Chimbu. In September 1946, the Central Highlands District (CHD) was proclaimed, with Jim Taylor appointed DO stationed at Goroka. The new district encompassed 10 subdistricts, although the administration was only operating in five: Kainantu, Bena, Chimbu, Hagen and Wabag. The Chimbu subdistrict consisted of five officers: Assistant District Officer (ADO) HL Williams, two patrol and two medical officers.[11]

At a district level, within a month of arrival, Taylor was questioning the administration commitment to the Highlands. Taylor was quite concerned regarding the 'native situation in Chimbu', that it was deteriorating because of a lack of experienced staff, and he was keenly awaiting the arrival of an experienced officer, ADO Jack Costelloe, in January 1947. On the one hand, Taylor complained,

---

11   Jim Taylor, November 1946, Monthly reports Central and Eastern Highlands, Box 869 [DS 29-16-3], PNGA.

critics may aver that too much has been undertaken [and yet] the highlands contain a virile population that is inspired with a desire to progress. The people are setting the pace and it is imperative that the Administration should keep up with them.[12]

On the other hand, in response to Taylor, Department of District Services and Native Affairs (DDSNA) director Bert Jones acknowledged the problem but instructed that until 'the necessary funds will be made available, you must continue to restrict your activities to the normal routine administration you are at present engaged in and so ably organising'.[13] Taylor's comments and Jones's response reflect a persistent problem throughout the postwar period, whereby when the desire or actions of local people, especially where their agency is autonomous, challenges government control, the government inevitably pushes back and attempts to contain. Too often—sometimes due to a lack of resources, at other times, because of unimaginative administration—the potential to harness the capacity of local people was not grasped.

Williams was the first administrative officer to arrive in Kundiawa in April 1946 following the withdrawal of the military, and immediately commenced a patrol to familiarise himself with the subdistrict. What became obvious was the 'density of population' and lack 'of consolidation which had been effected during the past years of administration'. One example of this maladministration was in the opinion of Williams, 'the disgraceful amount of labour' wasted on worthless road construction. He was so incensed that he banned any further roadworks for at least six months, except in cases of extreme emergency.[14]

Williams was also confronted with an inadequate and undermined system of indirect rule among the local population. While on the surface there existed a system of 'boss boys' approximate to those in operation in other districts, with some investigation Williams discovered District Services had never officially instituted a village leadership system.[15] While Williams was unable to uncover how the system was established, it was in fact the prewar District Officer for Chimbu, Ian Downs, who appointed several local 'boss boys'. These leaders were recognised by a white porcelain ring on their

---

12   Taylor and Jones correspondence, January/February 1947, December 46 Monthly Report, Box 869 [DS 29-16-4], PNGA.
13   Taylor and Jones correspondence, January/February 1947.
14   HL Williams, Report C1/46, Madang, p. 3, Chimbu District, Kundiawa, 1940–1950, PNGA.
15   Williams, Report C1/46, p. 3.

foreheads.[16] Downs, an active officer, had limited impact primarily due to the onset of war, although he did choose two notable people as administrative representatives. Ambagarawagi (authority over Kewandegu) and Bage (Goglme) were highly regarded as local leaders, and would in the postwar, work closely with government officers to introduce 'New Deal' initiatives.[17] In spite of these noteworthy appointments, by the time Williams arrived in 1946, the porcelain ring had become a highly sought-after item of personal decoration. In fact, these rings became a tradeable commodity. Williams described how many of the rings worn came to the bearer in return for 'a bag of sweet potato and not as recognition of outstanding service to the administration or of high status within the group'.[18]

The Australian Government's economic development of TPNG was based on gradual development of 'Native' agriculture (conversion from subsistence to cash crop farming) and encouraging smallholder gardens. In March 1946, Department of Agriculture, Stock and Fisheries (DASF) Director William Cottrell-Dormer had outlined an agroeconomic plan based on:

> mixed-farming on individual small-holdings capable of producing adequate subsistence for a man and his family and, in addition, sufficient cash crops to obtain the money necessary to him for the satisfying his other wants.[19]

Given that Australian plans for the socioeconomic viability of the Territory relied on sufficient arable land for both subsistence and cash crops, patrol officers were immediately aware that in parts of the Chimbu, these plans were not feasible. The subdistrict was remote, had a harsh (steep) environment, and featured scattered settlements and what appeared a traditional land tenure system incompatible with cash cropping. This problem was further magnified by what government officers regarded as inefficient farming methods, a lack of arable land and too high a population density to support cash cropping. Furthermore, because most of the population lived in the north, Australian efforts were concentrated in this portion of the

---

16   Bill Standish, 'Simbu paths to power: Political change and cultural continuity' (PhD thesis, The Australian National University, 1992), 64.
17   Paula Brown, *Beyond a mountain valley: The Simbu of Papua New Guinea* (Honolulu: University of Hawai'i Press, 1995), 126–34, doi.org/10.1515/9780824840761.
18   Williams, Report C1/46, p. 3.
19   William Cottrell-Dormer, 'Proposed plan for Department of Agriculture, Stock and Fisheries', 9 March 1946, p. 5, Papers of John Black, MS8346/11/7/1, National Library of Australia (NLA).

subdistrict.[20] Opportunities for southern people were limited due to this administrative decision. For instance, while patrols to the south were still dealing with first contact and 'pacification', the people of the north were introduced to cash cropping and the HLS.

Table 5.1: Northern Chimbu: Population land density.

Census division	Population (1971/72)	Area below 2,400 m	Population density/km	Acre per person below 2,400 m
Kundiawa	30,169	228 km²	132	1.87
Sinasina	25,372	204 km²	124	1.99
Gumine	40,641	922 km²	38	6.50
Kerowagi	31,973	376 km²	52	4.75
Gembogl	22,370	89 km²	60	4.11
Chuave	29,311	539 km²	50	4.94
Total	179,836	2,358 km²	76.27	3.23

Note: 1 km² is equivalent to 247.1 acres.
Source: Diana Howlett, R Hide and Elspeth Young, *Chimbu: Issues in development* (Canberra: Development Studies Centre, Monograph no. 4, The Australian National University, 1976), 93.

Defining overpopulation involves some subjective consideration, but at a minimum is the presence of too many people for the land to support above starvation level. It should be noted that agricultural knowledge has changed dramatically from the 1940s to the present. There is in fact viable cash cropping in South Simbu today; however colonial development strategy was premised on the agricultural knowledge of the time.[21] In terms of subsistence farming, geographer Harold Brookfield argues shifting or long-fallow cultivation demands across TPNG averaged no more than half an acre per head.[22] Whereas in terms of improving living standards, a survey by ADO Len Bailey and agricultural officer Jim Barrie in 1956 concluded that overpopulation existed in Chimbu because there was insufficient land for cash cropping.[23] The geographer Diana Howlett estimated 10 acres

---

20 Ninety-four per cent of the population live in the north: a population density 15 times higher than in the south. In square kilometre terms: 61 persons per square kilometre in the north to 4 in the south. Howlett, Hide and Young, *Chimbu: Issues in development*, 90–91.
21 Australian Government, 'Cocoa in PNG climbing to new heights', *Australian Centre for International Agricultural Research*, 23 December 2020, accessed 2 March 2019 at: www.aciar.gov.au/media-search/blogs/cocoa-png-climbing-new-heights.
22 Harold C Brookfield, 'Population distribution and labour migration in New Guinea', *Australian Geographer* 7 (1960): 237, doi.org/10.1080/00049186008702352.
23 Harold C Brookfield, 'Two population problem areas in Papua–New Guinea', *South Pacific* 9 (1959): 135.

of arable land was required for cash cropping, and while cultivation does occur at higher altitudes above 2,400 metres above sea level, in Chimbu this was not general practice.[24] Therefore, to calculate overall population density it should be calculated on land under 2,400 metres. In northern Chimbu, while individual census divisions range significantly, the average land per person was 3.23 acres.[25] In 1951, the Sinasina Census Division, just south of the subdistrict headquarters, Kundiawa, had an average of only 1.5 acres of arable ground available per head.[26]

In a patrol of the Kerowagi Census Division in April, ADO John Wakeford pointed out that even in an area which, on the surface, appeared to have sufficient land capacity, he predicted future problems. Wakeford described the Wahgi valley as encompassing 23,040 acres with a population of 7,343 people: three acres per person. However, there were other considerations:

> ground made useless through erosion, roads, areas taken up by buildings, and areas in which there is heavy timber; consideration must also be given to an application on behalf of the Roman Catholic Mission at Mingende for an agricultural lease of some 800 acres. With all these factors taken into consideration, the area of land per person has now been reduced to just over two acres per person. This is considered insufficient for their needs.[27]

In addition, Wakeford considered the implications of an impending surge in population given the end of tribal warfare and provided there were no further outbreaks of disease, such as dysentery, which had killed hundreds of people in 1944. Wakeford suggested:

> it will have the effect of decreasing the amount of land for each person, and also decrease the resting period of the land which is at present available, which in turn means a decrease in production in both quality and quantity.[28]

In response to this report, DDSNA acting director Charles Rich acknowledged the problem of land alienation but reminded Wakeford the 'territory belongs to the native peoples and we must see to it that they have sufficient for all their needs'.[29]

---

24   Diana Howlett, *Papua New Guinea: Geography and change* (Melbourne: Thomas Nelson, 1973), 111.
25   Howlett, Hide and Young, *Chimbu: Issues in development*, 94.
26   DE Kelaart, Report 2 of 1951/52, p. 10, Chimbu District, Kundiawa, 1950–1952, PNGA.
27   JE Wakeford, Report 2 of 1948/49, Chimbu District, Kundiawa, 1940–1950, PNGA.
28   Wakeford, Report 2 of 1948/49.
29   MCW Rich to Central Highlands District Office, 14 November 1949, Chimbu District, Kundiawa, 1940–1950, PNGA.

While officers praised the gardening proficiency of the local people, they could also see an opportunity to introduce more efficient methods of agricultural production. Chimbu practised shifting cultivation. Officer William Sippo explained how:

> [once] a new garden is planted, quick-growing casuarina trees are planted also, and a new garden is not again planted on that area until the trees are large enough to cut down for firewood. The exact number of years is unknown.[30]

While agricultural officers regarded this as inefficient and planned to improve yields with intensification programs, they were also mindful that new techniques had to be introduced as 'present methods would soon drain the soil of all plant nourishment'.[31]

When the provisional administration took control of Chimbu in April 1946 it was immediately apparent to the patrol officers how little Australian influence they had in the region. Things did not radically change in the short term, as the administration continued to suffer from a lack of staff, hampering any development ambitions. Furthermore, as already discussed, the 'New Deal' was prefaced on agriculture development in the villages; this however proved very difficult in Chimbu due to high population density and insufficient arable land. From late 1948, the government began to introduce new programs to address this problem.

In September 1947, patrol officers Harry West and Frederick Reitano were selected to attend the Australian School of Pacific Administration (ASOPA) long course; this left the subdistrict dangerously understaffed: only ADO Jack Costelloe and officer Craig Symons remained.[32] In what became a series of repeated calls, Jim Taylor pleaded with headquarters for more staff, describing the 'Chimbu sub-district is most difficult to control'. In fact, between Taylor and his later replacements as District Officer, George Greathead and Ian Downs, almost every report deplored the lack of government resources.[33] While the Australian administration were, by

---

30 WG Sippo, Report 1 of 1949/50, p. 4, Chimbu District, Kundiawa, 1950–1952, PNGA.
31 HL Williams to DDSNA Director, 6 March 1952, Chimbu District, Kundiawa, 1950–1952, PNGA.
32 Monthly Report, September 1947, Monthly reports Central and Eastern Highlands, Box 869 [DS 29-16-13], PNGA.
33 Monthly Report, November 1947, Monthly reports Central and Eastern Highlands, Box 869 [DS 29-16-14], PNGA.

1948, developing plans for the introduction of cooperative societies and local government councils, at a local level in the Central Highlands, the lack of resources meant officers such as Dick Kelaart were reporting:

> only thirty days were available for the census and administration of over 14,000 natives ... it is estimated 80 per cent of the working time was spent on the census, and practically all that was left of the writer's time was spent in the Courts of Native Affairs. Very little time indeed was available for general discussions with the natives and for any close inspections.[34]

During the 1930s, in order to 'protect the primitive inhabitants of the undeveloped Central Highlands' and enable the foundations of 'ordered government', commercial and other influences were banned under the *Uncontrolled Area Ordinance*.[35] However, on 27 April 1948, 18 months after the proclamation of the CHD, Jim Taylor wrote that 'it has become patent in that time that we, as a government, are retarding the people's development by the continuance of restrictions' and that the region must be opened up to economic opportunities. By contrast, in Goroka in the early 1950s land sales to expatriates were regarded as an economic measure.[36] In this case, Taylor was arguing for a relaxation of restrictions to enhance control measures of local people. He pointed out that:

> it is difficult for persons not resident in this district to realise the numbers of the inhabitants with whom we are in contact, say 240,000, three times the population of New Britain. Even if the district were fully staffed, it would only be possible for the Administration to scratch the surface, as it were. Hence the need for an increased European population.[37]

---

34 Kelaart, Report 2 of 1951/52, p. 2.
35 The Central Highlands remained closed in New Guinea until 1948, and in Papua until 1939. Department of External Territories (DET), 'Employment of Highland natives in coastal areas', 26 January 1950, p. 1, Native labour from Highlands, A452 [1957/2748], National Archives of Australia (NAA).
36 Land could only be acquired from Indigenous owners through the Administration (Lands Department) and only if the Indigenous owners were willing to sell it. In the Highlands, due to the inability of the Lands Department to process such sales, the District Commissioner (Ian Downs) was, according to Paul Hasluck, bypassing this department and finalising land sales. The minister stopped the sale of land in the Highlands at a local level in September 1953. Only the Lands Department could make such decisions regarding land alienation, and their overriding consideration was expected to be Indigenous welfare and 'preservation of the capacity for local people to make their own decisions on the use of their resources'. Paul Hasluck, *A time for building: Australian administration in Papua and New Guinea, 1951–1963* (Carlton: Melbourne University Press, 1976), 121–24.
37 Taylor to Director Jones, 27 April 1948, March 1948, Monthly Reports Central and Eastern Highlands, Box 869 [DS 29-16-19], PNGA.

Figure 5.2: Villagers in Goroka deriving a cash income from their natural timber stands.
Note: This wood is pit-sawn and has been carried to the road for transport to Goroka after it has been measured and paid for by the District Services officer on his weekly visit to all groups along the route of the road.
Source: NAA, A1200, L18798, item 7558749.

The non-official European community were expected to provide an example of socioeconomic development and 'educate' the people, using the word in its broadest sense.[38] Paul Hasluck, Minister for Territories, stated to the 1953 UN Visiting Mission that European settlement was essential because it is a 'question of farming by example and instruction and showing the natives how the resources of the Territory can be used'.[39] This was not possible in Chimbu. Until this point, the only land alienation in Chimbu had been government and mission stations, and even this was regarded as too much, with ADO Williams arguing that it was 'absolutely essential that no further alienation of ground be permitted'.[40] George Greathead, who replaced Jim

---

38 Taylor to Director Jones, 27 April 1948.
39 United Nations Visiting Mission to Trust Territories in the Pacific, *Report on New Guinea* (New York: UN Trusteeship Council, 1953), 15.
40 HL Williams to DDSNA Director, 6 March 1952.

Taylor as Eastern Highlands District (EHD) District Commissioner agreed, and further, recommended against the admission of non-administration personnel.[41] Simply, Chimbu did not have sufficient arable land to support its local population, let alone an expatriate community.

Table 5.2: Administration control or influence in the Central Highlands, 1949–54.

	1949	1953	1954
Fully controlled	16.3%	60.6%	62.3%
Uncontrolled	26.8%	15.15%	8.7%

Sources: Department of External Territories (DET), *Report to the General Assembly of the United Nations on the administration of the Territory of New Guinea: From 1st of July, 1953 to 30th of June, 1954* (Canberra: Government Printer, 1954), 127; DET, 1949 Annual Reports, Central Highlands District, p. 15, Box 869, National Archives of Papua New Guinea (PNGA).

Government strategy was to prioritise pacification and establishment of government influence; as outlined in the Hasluck Development Pyramid, this was the essential starting point for all other measures to promote the welfare of local people.[42] However, expansion of government reach in the Highlands was incapacitated by a lack of resources. The CHD Annual Report for 1949 estimated only 16 per cent of the region comprising the future EHD as 'fully controlled': where the rule of law was deemed to exist. More than a quarter of the region was considered 'uncontrolled': first contact was regarded as potentially hazardous. In 1950 there were only two patrols of Chimbu completed.[43] By 1951 the administration had acknowledged the CHD as too large, unwieldly and poorly resourced to be effectively administered, and divided it into three districts: Western, Southern and Eastern Highlands districts. The Eastern Highland District (or EHD) comprised three subdistricts, from east to west: Kainantu, Goroka and Chimbu.[44] By July 1954, the change of administrative structure had produced dramatic success for the rule of law, with more than 62 per cent

---

41   Greathead to IF Champion, 7 December 1950, Report 2 of 1950/51, Chimbu District, Kundiawa, 1950–1952, PNGA.
42   Hasluck, *A time for building*, 76, 78.
43   DET, *Report to UN General Assembly on New Guinea on the administration of the Territory of New Guinea: From 1st of July, 1949 to 30th June, 1950* (Canberra: Government Printer, 1950), 93.
44   Charles Hawksley, 'Constructing hegemony: Colonial rule and colonial legitimacy in the Eastern Highlands of Papua New Guinea', *ReThinking Marxism* 19 (2007): 198, doi.org/10.1080/08935690701219025.

of the population regarded under control and 14 patrols of the subdistrict.[45] On his installation as EHD District Commissioner, Ian Downs was concerned with the situation facing the administration:

> It is quite clear that the degree of control and the solidarity of administrative settlement in this district is already dangerously thin. To press on with expansion when all around us there are obvious signs of actual decay and contraction in our organisation seems to be against the evidence in relation to our priorities. We have no trafficable main road; we are already committed to checking the names of more than 650 persons per day seven days a week for 52 weeks in order to merely maintain our census records. Our four hospitals have each exceeded on occasions a daily average of 500 patients per day, and even radio communication system is totally unrelated to our local requirements because we cannot communicate direct to our out-stations. Missionaries have actual stations in areas where we cannot even maintain regular patrols. We have done virtually nothing for the economic development and education of 242,000 people under census.[46]

By 1953, 20 years after the first patrols through the region of Chimbu, the Australian administration had established a rudimentary system of centralised control in the densely populated north of the subdistrict. These included a semblance of law and order, an emphasis on hygiene controls, an expansion in medical aid posts and the appointment of more village leaders (luluai). In terms of economic and political development, regional characteristics forced the administration to radically change tack and introduce alternative systems of development. It is little wonder that by this stage local people were dubious of Australian rule. While the Australian Government held firm views in relation to the protection of Indigenous labour rights and favoured a village-based economy, the short-term reality of a stagnant economy and the pressing need to reconstruct and develop the economy led it to establish the HLS.

---

45 Department of Territories (DOT), *Report to the General Assembly of the United Nations: From 1st of July, 1953 to 30th June, 1954* (Canberra: Government Printer, 1954), 125.
46 Ian Downs, July–September 1952, EHD Quarterly Report, Box 869 [DS 29-16-30], PNGA.

PREPARING A NATION?

The Highland Labour Scheme

The decision to establish this new program was at odds with a government strategy which favoured the village (and household) as the socioeconomic and political unit of choice. It was a measure of how seriously the Australian Government took the inherent problems in Chimbu that it would continue with this program well into the 1960s, one which actively denied Chimbu the opportunity to enter the cash-cropping economy. It is clear the postwar administration had immediately recognised the potential labour resource in the Highlands. On the one hand, high population density meant less arable land for individuals to farm according to government strategy. On the other, this high population was also a potential labour resource.

As early as 1946, Jim Taylor had recommended the recruitment of Highland labour to work in Port Moresby. This was rejected over health concerns, particularly the risk of a malaria outbreak which was believed to be almost non-existent in the Highlands.[47] Ongoing concerns over the shortage of Indigenous labour forced the administration to make representations to the Acting External Territories Minister, Cyril Chambers, during his visit to the Territory in early 1949 for a relaxation of the prohibition over Highland labour.[48] To coastal employers desperately short of labour, the Highlands was the last great untapped source for recruitment. A meeting of department heads for Public Health (John Gunther), DDSNA (Bert Jones) and 'Native' Labour (John McKenna) decided to introduce recruiting of Highland Indigenous labour, specifically indentured labour, for use in coastal areas. The administration undertook to manage the recruitment process at no fee, and justified the scheme on the basis that highland people should have an 'opportunity to work on the coast and enter an economy pattern available to others'.[49]

On 22 December 1949, McKenna approved the HLS, rescinding the 1946 *Native Labour Ordinance* ban in relation to labour recruitment in the Central Highlands. Labour would become available for recruitment from 1 January 1950. The government applied strict conditions including a program of vaccination against various infectious diseases including tuberculosis, typhoid, whooping cough and tetanus; examination as to labourers' fitness

---

47 Jim Taylor, February 1947, Monthly Reports Central and Eastern Highlands, Box 869 [DS 29-16-6], PNGA.
48 DET, 'Employment of Highland Natives in Coastal areas', 26 January 1950, p. 2, Native labour from Highlands, A452 [1957/2748], NAA.
49 JT Gunther, 'Native labour from Central Highlands', 15 December 1949, A452 [1957/2748], NAA.

for employment by a medical practitioner; labourers to receive antimalarial tablets; penicillin to be kept on hand at each centre of Highland labour; and any abnormal disease to be immediately reported to the Director of Public Health.[50]

The original approval to re-examine the question of Highland labour restrictions was approved by the Chifley Labor Government which, however, in opposition questioned such measures. On 9 March 1950, less than three months after the election of the Liberal-Country party, Labor's Kim Beazley (Senior) quizzed newly established External Territories Minister Percy Spender in Parliament over the change in policy. Beazley asked rather pointedly whether it was true 'as reported, that there is jubilation among the planters at the prospect of getting 20,000 natives from the highlands?' Spender, in response, essentially requoted the previous government's policy and the protective measures to justify the course being taken.[51]

The scheme allowed officers to accept as 'volunteers' men aged 16 to 45 for 12 to 18-month contracts. In 1952, the period of employment was raised to two-year terms, but such was the concern of the disruptive nature to family life, Highland officers were successful in forcing terms back to 18 months.[52] In practical terms, this meant patrol officers were expected to examine individual villages for their labour potential, and limit recruitment to a maximum of 25 per cent of men from any age group (and minimise potential harm to the village economy).[53] In the villages, families had to cope with the men's absence, while at the same time, the government continued to pressure villages to transition from subsistence farming to cash cropping. For example, officer Robert Mellor noted in August 1952 the 'particular stress placed on the families of absentee natives. In nearly every case, the brother or parents of the indentured labourer take care of his wife and family'.[54] Every patrol included in the census a report on the numbers and percentage of 'absent migrant labourers', and where numbers were above the maximum threshold, often patrol officers had to justify to their superiors the reason for such discrepancy.

---

50 Department of Native Labour, 'Employment of Highland native workers', A452 [1957/2748], NAA.
51 Commonwealth (Australia), House of Representatives, *Parliamentary debates*, 7 March 1950 (Percy Spender).
52 In 1958 labour agreements were reset at two years. R Gerard Ward, 'Contract labor recruitment from the Highlands of Papua New Guinea, 1950–1974', *International Migration Review* 24 (1990): 290–96, doi.org/10.1177/019791839002400204.
53 DET, 'Native Labour Control', 17 May 1945, pp. 1–2, Native labour policy including review 45–56, A452 [1959/5851], NAA.
54 RHC Mellor, Report 4 of 1952/53, p. 3, Chimbu District, Kundiawa, 1952–1953, PNGA.

Table 5.3: Age group and marital status.

Age	1957
Below 20 years old	19.81%
20–30 years old	64.53%
Over 30 years old	14.12%
Marital status	
Single	74.02%
Married	25.98%

Source: Harold C Brookfield, 'Native employment within the New Guinea Highlands', *The Journal of Polynesian Society* 70 (1961): 309.

Harold Brookfield studied the census records for the Highlands in the period 1956–58. His findings indicate the HLS provided labour to the Bismarck Archipelago and Madang plantations, the Morobe goldfields and Papuan rubber plantations, and casual labour in smaller numbers to Port Moresby, Milne Bay and the Gulf region.[55] The majority of labourers were unmarried young men in their late teens and early twenties. They were employed in an unskilled capacity at minimum wages on short-term contracts.[56]

While the length of contract was restricted to protect the labour force from exploitation, it also reinforced a system of unskilled labour. The government had, until this point, failed to provide any substantive educational and technical training: length of tenure was the only reliable pathway to upskill and move to higher-paying employment positions. By December 1957, the government had recognised this problem and established a register for skilled and semi-skilled workers who could be re-employed on an individual basis.[57] Another government decision, the restriction of land alienation in densely populated areas (such as in Chimbu), also had poor socioeconomic implications for local people. When the government overturned the ban on European land alienation in the Highlands the European population was approximately 200; by 1959 this was 1,400.[58] In Chimbu, the European population was restricted to administration staff and missionaries. European

---

55   Brookfield, ' Population distribution and labour migration', 239.
56   Harold C Brookfield, 'Native employment within the New Guinea Highlands', *Journal of Polynesian Society* 70 (1961): 309.
57   TPNG, 'Skilled and semi-skilled Highland workers', 28 December 1957, Native labour from Highlands, A452 [1957/2748], NAA.
58   Brookfield, 'Native employment', 303.

settlers in places such as Goroka established coffee plantations which created casual employment. This meant many Highlanders could choose to work for wages close to home, whereas Chimbu had to venture far from home to find work. According to anthropologist Paula Brown, employment on the European-owned coffee plantations was far less restrictive, where the impact on village life was minimised by constant interaction with friends and family.[59] Therefore, in terms of social disruption and economic opportunity, the experience of Chimbu was skewed by government decisions which, on the face of it, were to protect them from regional particularity: a lack of arable land and high population density.

Table 5.4: Number of workers employed in the Highlands, 1951–52.

	1951	1952
Employed in district	2,981	2,280
Employed outside district	4,216	6,148
Total	7,147	8,428
Employed in New Guinea	5,363	5,882
Employed in Papua	1,784	2,546

Sources: United Nations Visiting Mission to Trust Territories in the Pacific, *Report on New Guinea* (New York: UN Trusteeship Council, 1953), 22; DET, *Report to UN General Assembly on New Guinea on the administration of the Territory of New Guinea: From 1st of July, 1949 to 30th June, 1950* (Canberra: Government Printer, 1950), 52.

The 1953 UN Visiting Mission reported that of the 35,838 Indigenous people employed in New Guinea, 5,882 (16.4 per cent) were Highlanders. This reveals a remarkable uptake of labour in a short period of time. Furthermore, those people employed outside their home districts came almost entirely from the Highlands or Sepik. In the case of the Highlands, a further 2,546 people were employed in the Territory of Papua, which means that 6,148 or 72.9 per cent of Highlanders were employed outside the district.

Table 5.5 provides some interesting insights into the movement of casual labour from the densely populated central Chimbu, particularly the high proportion of labourers (31.7 per cent) who continued to work on the coast seven years after the scheme's commencement. The competition for places in the labour scheme remained highly valued among the Chimbu, primarily due to the lack of other economic opportunities. For example, in

---

59 Paula Brown, *The Chimbu: A study of change in the New Guinea Highlands* (London: Routledge, 1972), 87.

November 1957 Otto Alder departed the government station of Kundiawa for the nearby Central Census Division on a 13-day patrol. The central division is close to the administrative headquarters and dissected by the main Highland highway; consequently, local people had close contact with Europeans and economic opportunities. They were regarded as the most progressive in the subdistrict. And yet it was also one of the most heavily populated pockets in the Territory with an average of 0.24 acres available per person for one year's subsistence gardening. Alder reported that 'if the present natural rate of [population] increase continues over the next ten years, the land available to each person will be a square of only 30.6 yards'. The central Chimbu were ideal candidates for the government's agricultural smallholder economic strategy but were opting for the labour scheme. Government officers explained this was due to high population density, a lack of arable land and HLS rules capping labour at one-third of a village's male population.[60] It also clearly demonstrates the government considered the scheme the most viable economic option for many Chimbu.

Table 5.5: 1957 absentee labour statistics, Central Census Division.

Location	Absent labourers	Percentage
Goroka (EHD)	17	3.3%
Kainantu (EHD)	52	10.1%
Coast	163	31.7%
Kerowagi (Chimbu)	17	3.3%
Kundiawa (Chimbu)	33	6.4%
Elsewhere Chimbu	60	11.7%
WHD	140	27.2%
SHD	7	1.3%
Police	25	4.8%
Total	514	100%
Central Census Division labour potential	2,450	20.9%

Notes: WHD = Western Highland District, SHD = Southern Highland District.
Source: OF Alder, Report 8 of 1957/58, Central, Chimbu, EHD, Appendix B, PNGA.

---

60   Population in this census division was 9,809, growth was 340 or 3.59 per cent per annum. Otto Alder, Report 8 of 1957/58, p. 7, Chimbu District, Chimbu, 1957–1958, PNGA.

Conclusion

The Territory Administration had limited control of the Chimbu district at the end of the war, was poorly resourced and struggled to align Commonwealth development plans with the inherent characteristics of the subdistrict. The early priority for the subdistrict was establishing a base for development; this meant most of a patrol officer's time was spent on exploratory patrols and pacification. However, in terms of introducing 'New Deal' development plans, it became quickly apparent to the administration that a singular strategy of community development and maintaining people in their villages was not suitable to Chimbu.

The government's Territory-wide strategy was to consolidate the village unit as the core of development, and to develop outwards from the village as 'demand' or interest for more autonomy arose. However, regional characteristics in Chimbu forced the government to radically change tack and introduce an alternative system of development. This new program, the Highland Labour Scheme, was established to address two problems: overpopulation in the Highlands, which limited economic opportunity as the government perceived it, and labour resources to plantations on the coast. The impact of the new program in the villages is explored in much greater detail in Chapter 6, although it is worth pointing out that additional government regulations in Chimbu meant a far higher proportion of Chimbu worked on the coast compared to other Highlanders. This decision exacerbated the socioeconomic and political impact of the labour scheme in the villages; Chimbu could not work on plantations and easily return home. Local communities adjusted to fewer young men, and when these young men returned, it was with new ideas which would challenge existing political and economic structures. The reaction to this new contested colonial space by the returnees, customary leaders and government officers is explored in the following chapter.

6

Highland Labour Scheme: Indigenous Opportunity or Government Solution?

The Highland Labour Scheme (HLS) was introduced by the Australian Government on 1 January 1950 and, as detailed in the previous chapter, was a program aimed at addressing short-term economic concerns and was in complete opposition to the government's economic strategy for village-based cash cropping. This chapter provides a case study of this government initiative and the profound impact it had on Chimbu society and, to alleviate specificity of Chimbu, how it transformed over time into a migratory labour scheme.

HLS returnees posed a dilemma for the administration. On the one hand, returnees brought back new agricultural techniques, an enthusiasm for cash cropping and a demand for a money economy. However, experiences on the coast and in the plantations expanded awareness of alternative sociopolitical systems. This new knowledge enabled some returnees to challenge pre-existing traditional social systems, and in effect, represented a political threat to the administration's indirect rule. Primarily young, single males, they acted in a manner which directly suited themselves and their communities and which did not accord with Australian expectations, effectively undermining administration influence.

PREPARING A NATION?

Effect of the HLS on the ground in Chimbu

The first cohort of labourers were recruited in early 1950. Officer Geoffrey Burfoot set out on 21 March 1950 for a five-month patrol of the southern portion of the subdistrict. Burfoot's patrol was specifically instructed to recruit coastal labour, and he reported an 'overwhelming response', signing up 1,828 locals and registering a further 1,652 names. Burfoot advised that 'all natives were informed that the period of contract was for one year and I strongly advise against any extension of this period of initial contract'.[1] Dick Kelaart's patrol of central Chimbu in late 1950 reported a further 764 people in employment outside the district, which represented 22.4 per cent of the male population.[2] By July 1951, Assistant District Officer (ADO) Ken Jones had calculated 'to date about eight thousand natives have left the sub-district to work, and it is estimated that nearly half of this number have returned'.[3]

Attracted by the opportunity, these labourers were the first generation of Chimbu to travel to the coast and get to know white men, experience plantation working conditions, and be exposed to Pidgin and Indigenous Papuans and New Guineans from other places. Paula Brown spoke with many of these men in later years; she found they usually reflected on receiving small items such as a laplap, towel or blankets, they would reminisce about their first experience of travelling in trucks and planes, and perhaps eating unusual food. Brown interviewed Waine of Bamugl (near to Kundiawa) who had left his village in 1951 and was employed as a 'boss boy' on a coconut plantation off the Madang coast (Karkar Island). Waine reflected on the financial reward, of how 'at the end [we] were taken to Goroka and got five kina and had to walk with our money to Kundiawa then. We bought shirts, tomahawk, paint'.[4] A 13 September 1954 press release from the Department of District Services and Native Affairs (DDSNA) outlined a number of problems faced by Chimbu when they arrived on the coast. There was minimal guidance from employers, Chimbu complained other Indigenous people were unfriendly, that they were often misled and,

---

1   This was 23.5 per cent of the male population. GR Burfoot, Report 1 of 1950/51, Chimbu District, Kundiawa, 1950–1952. p. 1, National Archives of Papua New Guinea (PNGA).
2   DE Kelaart, Report 3 of 1950/51, p. 8, Chimbu District, Kundiawa, 1950–1952, PNGA.
3   KW Jones, correspondence to District Commissioner (DC), Eastern Highlands District (EHD) 11 July 1951, Chimbu District, Kundiawa, 1950–1952, PNGA.
4   Paula Brown, *Beyond a mountain valley: The Simbu of Papua New Guinea* (Honolulu: University of Hawai'i Press, 1995), 194, doi.org/10.1515/9780824840761.

6. HIGHLAND LABOUR SCHEME

because of language barriers, unable to explain problems or difficulties that arose. They also complained the lack of recreation opportunities and were left to their own devices during leisure hours in a country completely strange to them.[5]

Patrol officer observations of the labour program differ quite considerably, some were quite effusive and focussed on the potential of HLS to alleviate growing concerns around population pressure and promote development programs through these newly 'educated' young leaders. Other officers became increasingly concerned about the breakdown of traditional social systems such as inflation of bride-price, increases in divorce, ignoring traditional community customs and the usurping of traditional leadership. In July 1952, Bert Jones instructed all officers that 'special attention should be paid to the effects of coastal employment upon returning natives, and their resultant influence upon the local population'.[6]

An early response to the Jones instruction was from officer Tony Keogh, who was conducting a patrol of the Dom census division. Keogh, a young but highly regarded patrol officer, had travelled south-west over the Wahgi River on 17 July 1952 for a two-week patrol.[7] He first observed that the region had:

> been visited by few patrols since the end of the war. In fact, according to the natives, only one patrol has visited all villages of the Dom group, at the one time, during that period.[8]

Keogh pointed out that although numbers were insufficient to have a noticeable effect, there were warning signs of potential future problems:

> At present, the older natives seem to view the comparative sophistication of the repatriates with some suspicion and the prestige which the labourers hold in the eyes of the younger natives has the appearance of being rather 'a sore point' with them. In years to come … the introduction of new customs and ideas which the labourers will inevitably bring back with them might well develop into a problem of some proportions.[9]

---

5   'Employment of Highland Labour, particularly Chimbu', 13 September 1954, p. 1, Native labour policy including review 45–56, A452 [1959/5851], National Archives of Australia (NAA).
6   JH Jones to Eastern Highlands DC, 30 July 1952, Report 1 of 1952/53, Chimbu District, Kundiawa, 1952–1953, PNGA.
7   Ian Downs to DDSNA Director, 17 December 1952, Report 8 of 1952/53, Chimbu District, Kundiawa, 1952–1953, PNGA.
8   AM Keogh, Report 1 of 1952/53, p. 5, Chimbu District, Kundiawa, 1952–1953, PNGA.
9   Keogh, Report 1 of 1952/53, p. 5.

Later in the year, while patrolling Koronigl in the far north-west of the subdistrict, Keogh confirmed his previous warning when local medical assistants reported to him that the community was rife with internal dissension. Keogh's interest was piqued not just by the village tension, but the fact that local officials were reluctant to bring such matters to his attention. He pondered whether 'pride' meant he could not trust the leaders to fully inform him of developments. He was less concerned about the disputes, regarding them as 'a manifestation of their comparative sophistication, rather than a normal continuation of traditional grudges'. He blamed this on the repatriated labourers, as now there were sufficiently high numbers:

> to have an appreciable bearing on the native situation and enable the more unscrupulous of them to trade on the simplicity of their officials so as to bring up again old tribal grievances.[10]

Unsurprisingly, the scheme was received enthusiastically by the younger men who regarded it as a chance to get away from 'the humdrum group life' and earn some income, although to government officers it was evident a breakdown in traditional social structures was possible. The general scenario described in the reports: young men would leave the valley to work, and after earning an income and buying some possessions at the trade stores, would begin to realise they were no longer dependent for a living on the help of their clan or sub-clan.[11] Many of these returnees would struggle to settle down to their old way of living; often they had no sooner returned than they would be away seeking more work. Those who remained were accused by village elders of disobeying orders, and not pulling their weight in community work.[12] For example, during a June 1960 patrol of the Upper Chimbu, officer Peter Hardie reported that while preparations were underway for a major pig-killing festival (an event where clans from across the valley were expected to participate) there was almost no interest from the coastal returnees. Hardie described how they had abandoned traditional customs and dress and would neglect any work they were not forced to do.[13]

Village elders would complain to patrol officers such as George Ball of how these young men returned from the coast with 'money and a complete air of indifference to group officials and to the older people of the group'.[14]

---

10   Keogh, Report 1 of 1952/53, p. 5.
11   PA Hardie, Report 6 of 1960/61, p. 1, Chimbu District, Gembogl, 1960–1961, PNGA.
12   RHC Mellor, Report 4 of 1952/53, p. 5, Chimbu District, Kundiawa, 1952–1953, PNGA.
13   Hardie, Report 6 of 1960/61, p. 2.
14   GF Ball, Report 17 of 1956/57, p. 2, Chimbu District, Chimbu, 1956–1957, PNGA.

On the other hand, while the situation was clearly deteriorating, there remained strong sentimental ties which bound people to their land and relatives. The village leaders also remained important regarding marriage; many of the younger men struggled to find a wife except in the traditional manner, which required help, especially in the matter of pigs (owned mainly by the older men) from the clan.[15]

In fact, the HLS was having a profound effect on marriage; patrol reports from this period make constant reference to rising divorce rates. While patrol officers had received some anthropological training at the Australian School of Pacific Administration (ASOPA), these reports reflect a purely Eurocentric understanding of marriage. Clearly Chimbu, at this time, held a different understanding of marriage, not a matter of simple monogamy, whereas these patrol officers regarded divorce as a threat to social order, citing two reasons for this. One, although not part of this study, was the missionary insistence on the end of the local widespread practice of polygamy, or 'divorce consequent upon baptism', and two, problems arising from men spending extended periods away from home.[16] For instance, during a patrol of Upper Chimbu in September 1954, John Gauci reported some concern about the rapidly increasing divorce rate. Gauci described how the patrol came across:

> several instances where a husband was divorced soon after his departure for the coast. His ex-wife remarries. A few instances were encountered where the first husband, having returned from the coast, the wife remarries him, divorcing her second husband. These happenings, if they increase, could well be damaging to their social structure.[17]

In July 1955 Robert Mellor elaborated further, speculating the reason women pressed for divorce was that they regarded themselves as abandoned.[18] By 1957 patrol officers were consciously choosing single men. The patrol reports portray the 'native' without morals, framing Australia as the benevolent coloniser who would provide appropriate guidance. They were full of comments such as how 'they were not keen on married men going as in at least half the cases of wives being left, the wife promptly finds

---

15 Hardie, Report 6 of 1960/61, p. 2.
16 AA Roberts to DC Eastern Highlands, 11 March 1953, Report 12 of 1953/54, Chimbu District, Kundiawa, 1953–1954, PNGA.
17 J Gauci, Report 1 of 54/55, p. 1, Chimbu District, Chimbu, 1954–1955, PNGA.
18 RHC Mellor, Report 18 of 1954/55, p. 3, Chimbu District, Chimbu, 1954–1955, PNGA.

herself a new husband'. In December 1957, Michael Neal, after patrolling Elimbari (south-east Chimbu) forecast future problems as a 'result of marriages of wives to husbands away at work on the coast'. Neal explained that a considerable amount of time and patience were expended by himself and those involved in straightening exchange payments and settling the many domestic disputes that occurred prior to and since the husband's arrival home.[19]

The response of the district administration was, to some extent, quite pragmatic. ADO James West encapsulated this attitude:

> illegitimate babies, immorality in the form of mistresses, coupled with the neglect of the younger men to participate in communal activities indicate an increasing breakdown in traditional practices. Such a breakdown is acceptable as there occurs change from traditional to a money economy however the immorality aspect is most disturbing.[20]

And yet, by December 1952, the deterioration of village leadership influence was an active concern of both patrol officers and district leadership.[21] An unforeseen impact of the HLS was a change in social and political dynamics on the ground in the village where young, newly returned villagers were challenging pre-existing social structures. Officers were describing coastal returnees as 'laplapped, peroxide-haired, sophisticates' who were viewed with considerable respect by the younger people, whereas these young people regarded village elders as old-fashioned and unsophisticated. The government reacted by making every effort to increase the prestige of the leaders. However, as Keogh pointed out, if the area did not have the 'presence of one really dominant personality amongst them', then the administration was fighting an uphill battle.[22]

Furthermore, some imaginative leaders utilised the HLS to shore up their political base and promote the interests of family members. On a three-week patrol of central Chimbu in August 1952, Noel Fowler encountered many returnees wearing laplaps and using European cooking utensils. Fowler was the first officer to describe in the Chimbu patrol reports that

---

19 MV Neal, Report 10 of 1957/58, p. 4, Chimbu District, Chimbu, 1957–1958, PNGA.
20 J West to EHD District Office, 8 November 1960, Report 6 of 1960/61, Chimbu District, Gembogl, 1960–1961, PNGA.
21 BB Hayes to EHD District Office, 8 December 1952, Report 8 of 1952/53, Chimbu District, Kundiawa, 1952–1953, PNGA.
22 AM Keogh, Report 8 of 1952/53, pp. 9–10, Chimbu District, Kundiawa, 1952–1953, PNGA.

many of the returned labourers were agitating to become officials. He also noted a growing awareness of the problem among the leaders themselves. Fowler described how Luluai Siume and Kwatininem 'were in firm control ... shoring up their leadership by sending their sons and younger brothers to the coast'.[23] Throughout Chimbu many leaders encouraged family members to do terms as coastal labourers, policemen and medical orderlies, or they sent their sons to school in an active attempt to influence future succession plans.

Within a very short period, leaders had recognised a change in power dynamics, in political realities. As with much of Melanesia, the path to power had primarily relied on a big-man leadership system which rewarded ability and success with prestige and power. As Paula Brown noted, because resources in land and forest were limited, two primary areas of tribal success were war and ceremony: war meant land could be won, and ceremony was an opportunity to display success and to feast.[24] The political realities of postwar development, and particularly the challenge posed by the HLS, led the 'more intelligent and powerful' village officials to utilise opportunities provided by the administration in an attempt to maintain political power.[25] The autonomous actions of these leaders, and the active manipulation of administrative policy to suit themselves and their community, was a consistent theme throughout the postwar period. Moreover, the reaction of the administration was to actively contain and control circumstances on the ground, to quash any destabilising elements and to support Papuans and New Guineans who acted as the coloniser expected.

By late 1952 patrol officers were reporting that economic interactions with Chimbu were changing; a rising demand for cash was replacing the barter system. ADO Basil Hayes regarded this transformation as a signal of Chimbu's growing sophistication and praised the 'returned labourers as having much to do with the new trend'.[26] This praise was an example of how Australian attitudes to local people's agency or initiative was less about the attitude and more about the action. On the one hand, they were quite critical, or at least concerned, at actions by coastal returnees when it challenged pre-existing traditional hierarchical social systems; one could surmise as a threat to indirect rule and the administration losing control of the local population.

---

23   HF Fowler, Report 3 of 1952/53, p. 3, Chimbu District, Kundiawa, 1952–1953, PNGA.
24   Paula Brown, 'Chimbu leadership before provincial government', *Journal of Pacific History* 14 (1979): 103, doi.org/10.1080/00223347908572368.
25   Keogh, Report 8 of 1952/53, p. 10.
26   BB Hayes to EHD District Office, 8 December 1952, Report 8 of 1952/53.

While new economic concepts, the introduction of cash money and new agricultural processes were a direct challenge to pre-existing systems, the administration response was generally quite positive. In other words, local people were 'behaving' in a manner encouraged by the administration, that is, supporting cash cropping as an economic system based around the Indigenous smallholder. Positive patrol comments regarding the potential of coastal labourers to subvert or undermine traditional leadership was a later phenomenon, post-1956, as officers became increasingly frustrated at the slow pace of change. The patrol reports provide a perfect example of how the administration expected the local population to behave. Therefore, when searching and analysing the actions or autonomy of local people, the complaints from officers often refer to such agency, merely because they are demonstrating actions contra to administration instruction and creating an unstable element in the community.

One instance was when the newly appointed ADO for Chimbu, Basil Hayes, departed Kundiawa for a six-week tour of northern Chimbu on 5 January 1953, his comprehensive report praised by both Eastern Highlands District (EHD) District Commissioner (DC) Ian Downs and DDSNA Director Allan Roberts. Hayes was quick to note the disruptive behaviour of returned labourers, complaining they lacked sufficient work ethic. He recommended, as a short-term measure, that a limit be placed on contracts to just one term, reasoning that it was not worth the 'undesirable effects of the abrupt impact of new ideas on traditional native belief and custom'. However, when it came to economic acculturation and the transition away from traditional forms of wealth towards an acceptance of a money economy by the local people, he was most effusive in his praise for returnee labourers. Hayes noted Chimbu were increasingly requesting to be paid in cash for food and manual labour, and how:

> much of this can be attributed to the large number of natives from this area who have served periods on the coast, many of whom can, for instance, be heard valuing kinas in terms of so many shillings rather than pigs or other items of native wealth.[27]

In response to reports such as the one by Hayes, the administration instigated a program of 're-orientation' classes for returned labour. The plan was aimed at providing a positive outlet in the form of agricultural economic development, to 'stave off the frustration of confinement

---

27   BB Hayes, Report 12 of 1952/53, pp. 8–9, Chimbu District, Kundiawa, 1952–1953, PNGA.

inherent to many of the mission-controlled societies'.[28] For instance, while patrolling Yongamugl (north-east of Kundiawa) in September 1953, Robert Mellor was, like most administrative officers during this period, focussed on introducing coffee as a cash crop. Mellor hoped many ex-Kainantu labourers would be able to start the ball rolling, as 'they have had a good deal of experience in coffee planting, and have no doubt seen or heard about the prices obtained by some of the Kainantu natives'.[29]

The coastal labourers were, almost immediately on return, exhibiting a desire to initiate change within their community. The administration frowned on and attempted to contain Indigenous actions where it actively undermined traditional social structures, whereas when these young men displayed urgency in the direction of economic development, the administration encouraged this behaviour. In cases where the entrepreneurial energy of coastal returnees challenged administration control, it was quickly suppressed. One interesting example involves Bomai Census Division, a large 'restricted' region in the southern part of Chimbu, which unbeknown to the administration, was infiltrated by returning coastal labourers who, utilising their new-found skills from the coast, took advantage of people whom the administration regarded as a 'vulnerable' group. ADO Bill Kelly's November 1953 patrol was the first to penetrate the southern regions of Chimbu beyond Mount Suauru and the Tua river. Kelly wrote of his concern that ex-coastal labourers were abusing trade relations:

> [they] have been buying from coastal trade stores large white china rings (the symbol of the appointed 'Boss Boy' in the Chimbu Sub-District). On their return home these ex-Labourers have used these rings as an important trading item in the Lower Bomai and appointing pseudo–Boss Boys, complete with ring as a badge, in exchange for lavish gifts of bird of paradise plumes.[30]

Kelly reported that the ring bearers, although issued without authority and with intent to defraud, ironically had contributed towards administration control.[31]

---

28 Downs to DDSNA Director, 24 August 1953, Report 1 1953/54, Chimbu District, Kundiawa, 1953–1954, PNGA.
29 RHC Mellor, Report 4 of 1953/54, p. 5, Chimbu District, Kundiawa, 1953–1954, PNGA.
30 WJ Kelly, Report 7 of 1953/54, pp. 1, 6–7, Chimbu District, Chuave, 1953–1954, PNGA.
31 Kelly, Report 7 of 1953/54, pp. 1, 6–7.

While Highlanders were initially attracted to work on the coast, by the mid-1950s it became more difficult for officers to recruit labour; by September 1954 over 90 per cent of Highland labour was recruited from Chimbu.[32] What became increasingly clear is that, when an individual could remain at home and grow cash crops, they were not interested in going to the coast. This was not the case in the more heavily populated parts of Chimbu.

However, an interesting dynamic began to confront the officers: as the consequences of a lack of young men available to help establish cash cropping became evident, village leaders began to insist on a stop to recruitment. On the one hand, these young men, encouraged by the administration, left to pursue economic opportunity, and yet at the same time, the administration was increasingly focussed on establishing cash crops in the villages. For instance, while patrolling Upper Chimbu in September 1954, John Gauci found village leaders reluctant to allow their young men to leave for the coast. On 16 September 1954, Gauci was in the village of Kalingu when the local headman:

> complained that too many of his line were away at work. Upon investigation the writer discovered that a number having been accepted for work on the coast, the line was still above the overrecruited mark. Later however quite a few more decided to set off and find work here in the highlands as casuals. This left the line somewhat depleted.[33]

What is most interesting about this example is that these young men were acting on their own behalf, choosing to leave and work on plantations without the support of either village leadership or the administration.

Village leaders were becoming increasingly interested in economic development for their people. One example from an April 1957 patrol by George Ball highlights the dilemma for leaders. The leader of the Endugwa group (east of Kundiawa) was Luluai Wadimonco, a highly regarded prime mover in both Chimbu and EHD headquarters. The Endugwa group was considered pro-administration (instead of pro-mission) and supported most initiatives suggested by government officers. Furthermore, Wadimonco's prestige reached beyond his group of villages; as an example, he persuaded the people of both Kumai and Endugwa to supply the labour necessary to build a suspension bridge across the Wahgi River. And yet even Wadimonco

---

32 'Employment of Highland Labour, particularly Chimbu', 13 September 1954, p. 1.
33 J Gauci, Report 1 of 1954/55, p. 4.

complained that coastal recruitment 'cuts their labour force too much and increases discontent among those left behind'. Ball considered this evidence enough for the government to act; that as village leaders of the ilk of Wadimonco expressed concern with the economic stability of their communities, they would increase pressure on the men to remain in the village.[34] And interestingly, officers increasingly respected the wishes of village leaders in terms of labour recruitment. In one case, Peter Wilson reported of his July 1964 patrol of Chuave that at 'every Rest House Village Officials expressed the view that they would prefer if no volunteers would be accepted'. These leaders complained that the returnees never settled down again to do the work expected of them, Wilson wrote of 'respecting their view and as a result no volunteers have been accepted'.[35]

Despite the increasing resistance of village leaders to coastal labour, and the support of officers such as Peter Wilson to accept such wishes, local people continued to volunteer or relocate themselves. The willingness to volunteer was directly related to economic opportunity. For instance, Bill Kelly pointed out to EHD headquarters in February 1956 that 'as local development increases the eligible males will be more loath to leave coffee plots to seek coastal work'. He noted that in areas where considerable aid and guidance had been offered, the drop off in coastal volunteers was noticeable.[36] Whereas Bob Greaney found that while patrolling Gumine in July 1957 he was inundated with requests to go to the coast to earn an income. He felt that, given the land was too steep for most cash cropping 'it is obvious that the only means of fostering development for these people will be through this medium'.[37]

One noteworthy development was villagers paying their own plane fares out to the coast, bypassing both local leadership and administrative instructions. In June 1964, Bill Biscoe reported that he had stopped recruiting from Gembogl because they were over the maximum allowable employment level. However, Biscoe noted 'it is undoubtedly a fact that many are leaving by paying their own plane fares out, which is hard to prevent. Also, it appears that many do not return home after their term of service is over but stay on searching for work'.[38]

---

34   GF Ball, Report 14 of 1956/57, p. 6, Chimbu District, Chimbu, 1956–1957, PNGA.
35   PW Wilson, Report 2 of 1964/65, p. 5, Chimbu District, Gumine, 1964–1965, PNGA.
36   WJ Kelly to EHD District Office, 13 February 1956, Chimbu District, Chimbu, 1956–1957, PNGA.
37   RK Greaney, Report 2 of 1957/58, p. 6, Chimbu District, Chimbu, 1957–1958, PNGA.
38   Biscoe, Report 3 of 1963/64, p. 7, Chimbu District, Gembogl, 1963–1964, PNGA.

PREPARING A NATION?

The developmental intent of the administration in the Highlands during the mid-1950s was expanding. In this way, the Chimbu experience mirrored the expected outcomes of the Hasluck Development Pyramid; the government moved from the pacification phase to the next stage of advancement by offering expanded services in health and education and the introduction of local councils. However, from a patrol officer perspective, the major priority shifted to economic advancement at a local level. This reflects the intention of Paul Hasluck, who argued that it was 'essential [that] the administration was brought right down to the grass roots' by using instruments for economic development at a local basis which would, in turn, allay fears, gain the confidence of the local people and encourage them to work together.[39] Therefore, when officers reported on the prospects of an area during this period, it was, in reality, with a mindset for the potential of village-based cash cropping.

The HLS was, as a policy, in complete opposition to these plans. Firstly, to advance, Highlanders were expected to move away from the village to the remote coast, and secondly, they generally worked on plantations instead of in their own gardens as smallholder farmers. Therefore, for these officers to describe coastal work as the only avenue to economic opportunity, and effectively disregard government plans, it is reasonable to assume they had very serious and genuine concerns for the inherent problems of land and population density in Chimbu.

In the areas of exceedingly high population, patrol reports would openly dismiss the potential of economic opportunity, regarding HLS as at least a short-term fix, in effect a temporary migratory labour scheme. For example, William Lambden, patrolling the heavily populated Yongamugl (north-east from Kundiawa) in October 1957 described the area of having 'little scope for much agricultural economic development'; economic advance would need to rely on coastal work. Lambden noted that Yongamugl not only had a population density of 167.5 people per square mile (3.82 acres per person), but with much of it mountainous and population growth increasing at '15.1 per 1,000 persons the time is not far distant when the Yongamugl will require all their land for the supply of food'. Lambden went further and argued that mass migration was:

---

39   Paul Hasluck, 'Native Economic Development in Papua New Guinea', pp. 1–3, Policy on native economic development, M331 [73], NAA.

the only lasting solution to the problem, but when and if it is brought into operation, these people, living at present under strong clan system, will not like leaving the land of their ancestors.[40]

In September 1956, Bill Kelly described Dom (south-east of Kundiawa) as comprising infertile and difficult land with only 77 acres of coffee planted. Again, population pressure was regarded as severe, accentuated by the 'Dom people being surrounded on all sides by other land-hungry groups'. Not only did Kelly argue that it was unlikely any larger-scale plantings would take place, but that in the future 'the needs for subsistence gardens will be more acute than the need for a cash income'. He suggested there was a pressing need for planned resettlement, and that:

> our present expedient of siphoning off a percentage of the population to the coast as labourers is, at its best, only a temporary solution to problems which are today present and which will become more emphasised in the immediate future.[41]

By advocating for the temporary resettlement of Chimbu, officers such as Kelly wrestled with their conscience over the long-term damage such a program would have on Chimbu. In his September 1956 report to district headquarters, Kelly described Upper Chimbu in a state of helplessness given population density and the rugged terrain; the only obvious solution was to regard it:

> as a source of labour, both for the coast and for highland plantations. This however condemns the male population to a lifetime of unskilled work for low wages and will do little to improve the economic lot of these people.[42]

Harry Pegg, who patrolled Upper Chimbu in August 1956, noted that, given coffee planting had proven unsuccessful, 'what other profitable economic ventures are left to the people?' Options were limited; other cash crops such as passionfruit and peanuts suffered from uncertain markets and the only paid employment, as a pitsaw, was restricted to just a few people. Pegg reasoned the only other means of advancing was to continue working as labourers on Goroka and coastal plantations. Pegg surmised that 'for the present these people will of necessity be forced to be a labouring class'.[43]

---

40 WJG Lambden, Report 4 of 1957/58, p. 4, Chimbu District, Chimbu, 1957–1958, PNGA.
41 WJ Kelly, Report 3 of 1956/57, pp. 3–4, Chimbu District, Chimbu, 1956–1957, PNGA.
42 Kelly to EHD DO, 30 September 1956, Chimbu District, Chimbu, 1956–1957, PNGA.
43 HS Pegg, Report 1 of 1956/57, Appendix B, Chimbu District, Chimbu, 1956–1957, PNGA.

Six months later, Pegg was patrolling Sinasina and wrote plainly of the potential danger the administration may find itself in if it could not find a genuine alternative to labouring. Pegg not only empathised with the Chimbu but described growing discontent and the potential that Chimbu would take matters into their own hands. He regarded it reasonable that Chimbu would demand a higher living standard as they are 'no more money-hungry than Europeans'. Pegg described, in quite sarcastic terms and directed clearly to his superiors, how:

> strange as it may appear, they are no less vocal when they think their rights, actual or imaginary, are infringed. I can see only too well the faces of those who will be asking why they receive no more help in the planting of new coffee plots. After four years of Administration urging, they will desire, perversely perhaps, to plant now no one is desirous of them doing so.[44]

Pegg was concerned the administration did not realise HLS could only be a temporary stopgap. Finally, Pegg outlined the consequences of the government's lack of initiative, of offering 'coolie work' instead of genuine advancement. He warned the 'administration will find itself saddled with a cargo-cult which WILL succeed in amalgamating these people, if only temporarily, as they seek a common goal'.[45] Pegg was supported by his superior, ADO Orm Mathieson, who wrote:

> I fail to see how our administration can operate successfully on a number of individual Sub-District policies instituted from within the respective Sub-District. It is to this type of planning and guidance that Mr. Pegg was referring.[46]

In fact, Mathieson believed Pegg had given a 'timely warning that should not be overlooked', and further, given Pegg's four years' experience in Chimbu, it was applicable to not just Sinasina, but the whole subdistrict.[47] EHD DO Bill Tomasetti's response suggests he was relatively unconcerned, even pointing out that, in the future, surplus rural population may need to voluntarily transfer elsewhere if cash cropping was to be become economically viable. Tomasetti noted his lack of 'faith in comprehensive

---

44 HS Pegg, Report 12 of 1956/57, pp. 5–6, Chimbu District, Chimbu, 1956–1957, PNGA.
45 By the late 1950s, agricultural officers were expected to discourage further coffee plantings. Pegg, Report 12 of 1956/57, pp. 5–6.
46 OJ Mathieson to EHD Head Office, 29 July 1957, Chimbu District, Chimbu, 1957–1958, PNGA.
47 Mathieson to EHD Head Office Goroka, 13 May 1957, Chimbu District, Chimbu, 1957–1958, PNGA.

or total social planning proposed by Mr. Pegg' and argued that 'successful administration consists of keeping just a little in front of local demands'. To be fair to Tomasetti, he also wrote of his concern that 'there must be sufficient balance in the population to ensure normal activities and the accepted division of labour'.[48]

However, the problem remained: labourers from Chimbu were the main source of income, and during the 1950s and 60s there remained little faith that other financial options would become available. For instance, Laurie Bragge, while patrolling Marigl (south of Kundiawa) in November 1962 reported:

> for the young men who wish to work and earn money, the Gumine area has nothing to offer except for the Highland Labour Scheme. As a result, there are large numbers of young men wandering out of the census division all the time seeking work.[49]

Tomasetti's response to Pegg's report mirrors one given to the 1959 United Nations (UN) Visiting Mission. The administrator, Donald Cleland, acknowledged the population pressures in Chimbu and how the problem was being examined. While no decision had been made, Cleland suggested people may be forced to move south into the less populated Wahgi Valley. Of course, what is made clear in a myriad of patrol reports and by the Visiting Mission themselves, despite short-term contracts remaining popular, was how difficult it would be to force people to move when their old customs and beliefs tied them to their land. Nonetheless, the UN Visiting Mission recommended the administration pursue a more rigorous program to resolve the issues around land shortage and population density.[50] These responses suggest an administration under stress and lacking realistic options to solve Chimbu's inherent land and population problems. By the mid-1950s, the HLS appeared increasingly to be the response of an administration focussed on short-term goals.

---

48   WJ Tomasetti to Kundiawa, 23 May 1957, p. 2 and 28 October 1957, p. 1, Chimbu District, Chimbu, 1957–1958, PNGA.
49   LW Bragge, Report 5 of 1962/63, p. 2, Chimbu District, Gumine, 1962–1963, PNGA.
50   United Nations Visiting Mission to Trust Territories in the Pacific, *Report on New Guinea* (New York: UN Trusteeship Council, 1956), 21.

Conclusion

On 30 April 1962, the UN Visiting Mission held a combined meeting with councillors from three local government councils (Waiye/Central, Koronigl, Chuave). One speaker addressed the mission and pointed out that he was dissatisfied with the slow rate of progress in the living standards for Chimbu and suggested that the US be invited to help administer the Territory. His comments were endorsed by four other councillors who spoke of their inability to earn a decent income.[51] After 28 years of colonial control, the Australian Government was struggling to maintain control of the Chimbu subdistrict, their plans impaired by a lack of government resources and an inability to resolve problems with inherent characteristics of Chimbu: population density, lack of arable land, and an energetic population determined to improve their living standards and take control of their destiny. The HLS was initially a government response to a lack of labour for plantations along the coast but morphed into a temporary labour migration scheme to alleviate these regional problems.

The introduction of colonial development programs was expected to gradually stimulate a desire for an improvement of the standard of living for Indigenous peoples while they remained in their villages. However, in Chimbu, while the government persisted with a demand-driven gradualist approach, introducing cash cropping and other socioeconomic programs, it was undermined by the establishment of the labour scheme. For many young people, the reality was to advance they were expected to move away from the village and work on the coast. In this way, the labour scheme did not fit with the gradualist, ground-up, general approach of the Hasluck Development Pyramid. In effect, it created an elite of men who experienced the cash economy and no longer fitted in; they posed a dilemma for the administration. On the one hand, returning coastal workers introduced (and demanded) cash; this was regarded as a positive sign, of growing sophistication, and could be attributed to a government initiative. On the other, coastal returnees often challenged pre-existing traditional hierarchical social systems and, in effect, represented a political and destabilising threat to the administration's indirect rule.

---

51 United Nations Visiting Mission to Trust Territories in the Pacific, *Report on New Guinea* (New York: UN Trusteeship Council, 1962).

The labour scheme added a new dimension to an already contested colonial space. Chimbu people were already dealing with new power dynamics as the Australian Government enforced their rule and new socioeconomic ideas. However, these coastal returnees, and some entrepreneurial leaders, recognised a change in power dynamics, in political realities. They actively manipulated the HLS scheme to suit themselves and their communities, acting in a manner which did not accord with Australian expectations, and effectively undermined administration influence. The government's reaction was to back the existing leadership, consistent with the overarching Australian objective of limiting civil unrest. This case study has highlighted how the Australian Government in Canberra proposed but the Australian on-the-ground administration disposed, in the light of both the wish of the people and sheer pragmatics, development on the colonialists' terms. It has pointed out how some Papuans and New Guineans appropriated these new ideas to suit their own needs. This tension, between colonial intent and Indigenous autonomy highlights the lack of Papua New Guinean input in development planning and diminished the effectiveness of government programs.

CASE STUDY: MILNE BAY

7

Milne Bay: The Emergence of Indigenous Autonomy

Map 7.1: Milne Bay.
Source: Compiled by the 3rd Australian Army Field Survey Company, 1943. Trove, National Library of Australia (NLA), item MAP G8160 s63 (Copy 1).

In the early postwar period, Milne Bay government officials, understaffed and overwhelmed, failed to utilise the opportunity provided by war compensation to address local needs for participation in socioeconomic development. Instead, it was Papuans, inspired by the Kwato Extension Association (KEA), and led by an Indigenous elite created by this institution, who utilised the proceeds from war compensation to establish socioeconomic enterprises of dynamism and vision, a local movement which directly challenged and enforced a change of administrative policy by the Australian Government. The experience of local people to colonisation had engendered an autonomous, independent and driven people, a community not satisfied with a passive role in the development of their villages.

The Milne Bay case study fundamentally explores how colonised people were able to demonstrate a significant measure of Indigenous socioeconomic autonomy, and yet were forced to operate within the strictures of their colonial guardian. While the activity of those involved in operations such as the Milne Bay Development Company (MBDC) was focussed on business operations and expansion, the administration was more concerned with its inability to control events, and local repercussions if these ventures should fail. The drive of Milne Bay people to 'advance', inspired by an educated and determined Indigenous elite, forced the Administration to adjust their policy strategy to suit local conditions. This case study tests the auspices of the 'New Deal' agenda, and whether a Papuan autonomous enterprise could fit within the constrictive hegemony of state developmentalism. It asks whether the government was more concerned with preparing Papuans and New Guineans for self-rule and supporting Indigenous enterprise, or a containment strategy which bound the territories to Australia and the raising of living standards.

This chapter is broken into two parts. The first section describes the immediate postwar situation and the inability of the government to harness war compensation to Indigenous demands. In a case study of the MBDC, the second section explores the genesis behind, the activities of, and the remarkable agency of local people in establishing a local development movement of such ambition, energy and action that it demanded direct intervention of the Territory Administration.

Situation on the ground and the rise of Indigenous enterprise

On 1 March 1946, Assistant District Officer (ADO) Barter Faithorn met with the patrol officer on the ground in Milne Bay, Phil Hardy, to discuss district matters and inspect several disposal depots situated on the northern shore of Milne Bay.[1] Faithorn reported that with the war at an end and most of the military forces leaving, coastal people were returning to their villages and hamlets. One exception was the village of Wagawaga which, located on the southern shore of Milne Bay and adjacent to the American naval base (Gamadodo), continued to be disrupted by military activity.[2]

Phil Hardy had been part of the first intake of 1942 Australian New Guinea Administrative Unit (ANGAU) recruits, and like many of his contemporaries, transferred to District Services as a patrol officer before arriving in Milne Bay in early February 1946. He found an area decimated during the army occupation, with 'millions of feet of the best timbers for building native houses cut down and the area denuded of sago and Nipa palm'. Hardy was issued with four primary objectives: secure the stores of equipment and materials passed on by the military; rehabilitate and support local people evacuated from the area during the years 1942–45; maintain contact with remaining Royal Australian Air Force, Australian Navy and American forces stationed at Milne Bay; and most importantly, investigate and administer war damage compensation claims.[3]

Hardy was working in a region with a relatively long history of European–Indigenous relations: traders, whalers and missionaries had been in regular contact since the early to mid-nineteenth century.[4] In 1888 the discovery of payable gold on Sudest, Misima and Woodlark Islands led to great activity in prospecting in the district. By the commencement of the Pacific War, much of the district had been under administrative control for 30 years.[5]

---

1   Disposal depots stored munitions, fuel and military equipment.
2   BW Faithorn, Report 1 of 1945/46, pp. 1–3, Milne Bay District, Gehua, 1945–1950, National Archives of Papua New Guinea (PNGA). The base could cater for 10,000 men. United States Navy Department, *Building the Navy's bases in World War II* (Washington DC: US Government Printing Office, 1947), 289.
3   WJ Lambden to Director Department of District Services and Native Affairs (DDSNA), 30 March 1946, Patrol Reports, Milne Bay District, Gehua, 1945–1950, PNGA.
4   French missionaries of the Society of Mary established a mission on Woodlark Island in 1847.
5   DDSNA, *Milne Bay District Annual Report 1956/57* (Port Moresby: Government Printer, 1957), pp. 1–3.

In 1946, Milne Bay (Gehua patrol post) was a subdistrict of Eastern District (Territory of Papua).[6] District headquarters was located on the small island of Samarai at the extreme eastern end of the mainland. While Samarai was not the ideal centre for administrative purposes due to its distance from any centre of population, it was an important commercial centre for the district and indeed, the Territory.[7] In 1950 Milne Bay was reclassified as a district, consisting of the eastern extremity of the mainland and the archipelagos of D'Entrecasteaux, Woodlark, Trobriand, Lusancay and Louisiade. There were five subdistricts: Samarai Island, Esa'ala (Goodenough Island), Losuia (Kiriwina, Trobriand Islands), Misima Island and Gehua (Milne Bay). Often referred to as an 'island district', the area comprised approximately 130,000 square kilometres, of which only 18,000 square kilometres was represented by land mass. The enumerated and estimated Indigenous population of the district in 1950 was 86,487 (450 European), of which 16,092 persons lived in the Gehua subdistrict.[8] The topography of Milne Bay is dominated by the diminishing Owen Stanley Ranges; the mountains of mainly rainforest rise quickly from the shore on both sides of the bay.[9]

In the early postwar period, patrol officers of Milne Bay were overburdened with clerical duties: routine court and census work, and complicated war compensation claims, which left no time to establish strong trusting relations.[10] Furthermore, as pointed out in 1956 by District Commissioner (DC) Allan Timperley, 'the Milne Bay District has, since 1946, been sadly neglected' with a chronic lack of officers.[11] For instance, in February 1949, Acting Department of District Services and Native Affairs (DDSNA) Director Ivan Champion reflected on the lack of staffing resources and how, despite efforts over the past 12 months, he could not acquire staff for the Cooperative Section.[12]

---

6   Department of External Territories (DET), *Territory of Papua Annual Report for the period 30th October 1945 to 30th June, 1946* (Canberra: Government Printer, 1946), 15.
7   HC Gaywood, Report 2 of 1954/55, p. 2, Milne Bay District, Gehua, 1953–1955, PNGA.
8   DET, *Annual Report to 30th June, 1946*, 39.
9   DDSNA, *Annual Report for the year ending June 1954* (Port Moresby: Government Printer, 1954), p. 3.
10 Cyril S Belshaw, 'Native administration in south-eastern Papua', *Australian Journal of International Affairs* 5 (1951): 106–8, doi.org/10.1080/10357715108443774.
11 TPNG, *Milne Bay District Annual Report 1956/57*, 34.
12 I Champion, Report 8 of 1947/48, 19 August 1948, Milne Bay District, Gehua, 1945–1950, PNGA.

Figure 7.1: The District Office at Samarai in 1958, the administrative headquarters for the Milne Bay district, Papua and New Guinea.
Note: In the foreground, an agricultural officer talks with a member of the Royal Papua and New Guinea Constabulary.
Source: National Archives of Australia (NAA), A1200, L27299, item 7572888.

In a typical report of the period, Alexander Murison, who had completed a patrol of the eastern cape of Milne Bay in January 1949, argued that villagers in war-damaged areas tended to neglect their gardens and subsist on store food purchased from compensation payments. And yet, in the same report, Murison described a conversation in a village where:

> two men were killed, and one seriously disabled by enemy action during the war and the people asked me, 'We have heard that people killed by the Japanese will not be forgotten by this Government and something will be paid to the relatives'. I acquainted them with the provisions of the War Damage Compensation scheme and assured them that their cases were the most deserving to come to my notice and the matter would have prompt attention.[13]

---

13   AJ Murison, Report 1 of 1948/49, pp. 2–3, Milne Bay District, Gehua, 1945–1950, PNGA.

Clearly, patrol officers had mixed feelings regarding the potential effect of compensation. On the one hand, it could undermine traditional subsistence farming, but on the other, it had the potential to provide a stimulus for economic activity. Furthermore, financial settlements were often quite substantial. In the case of Milne Bay, it appears the compensation scheme was implemented with insufficient knowledge of what was happening on the ground, at least as far as the number of sago palms was concerned. For instance, Milne Bay District Officer (DO) John Foldi reported:

> as I write this, a patrol leaves the station to pay over £5000 in the East Cape Divanai section. The people are being told that this is their great opportunity to band together and supply themselves with useful tools … committed to £50,000 on the North side of the bay and approximately £20,000 on the southern side. Size of the claims is due to coconut and sago palms at ten shilling each. The Barry Report [War Compensation Report] could never have contemplated sago as it existed in Milne Bay.[14]

Finally, officer Dallen, on his patrol of the northern shore of Milne Bay in October 1949, described the complicated dynamics at play for patrol officers. He explained:

> on reflection, it seems to the writer that it would be more accurate to describe these people as suffering from a loss of faith in the administration rather than an anti-government feeling. It is felt that this war damage patrol did much to eradicate this feeling.

However, further on Dallen argues:

> there are a few intelligent and educated natives in the area and they themselves say that the large majority will sit in their villages and fritter away their money in the stores.[15]

In the late 1940s, government officials, understaffed and overwhelmed, failed to utilise the opportunity provided by war compensation to address local needs for participation in socioeconomic development. Instead, local people took matters into their own hands and by 1950 there were local organisations springing up around the bay.

---

14   JR Foldi to DDSNA Director, 22 November 1949, Milne Bay District, Gehua, 1945–1950, PNGA.
15   W Dallen, Report 1 of 1949/50, p. 13, Milne Bay District, Gehua, 1945–1950, PNGA.

Case study: Milne Bay Development Company

Indigenous agency around the bay: 1949–55

In the postwar period the local people who lived along the shore in the Milne Bay subdistrict, influenced by the Kwato Mission, utilised the proceeds from war compensation to establish both primary and secondary Indigenous enterprises. These included a local newspaper, a factory on the southern shore at Wagawaga manufacturing prefabricated houses and furniture, and on the northern shore, a sawmill at Divinai and a communal farm at Ahioma. The ease with which local people from around the large bay worked together was aided by the homogeny of language. The Tawala (Tavara) linguistic area extended from the far east cape, along the northern shore and across to the southern shore to include Wagawaga.[16] While the energy and action were reliant on the self-belief and physical effort of local villagers, the genesis for the drive and organisational skill of local leadership came from the Kwato Mission.

The driving force behind the postwar Milne Bay projects was Cecil Abel of the Kwato Extension Society. An influential believer in Moral Rearmament and 'industrial Christianity', he was a son of Charles Abel, the founder the Kwato Mission.[17] Children were given a general education and trained in manual or domestic skills; the plan was for Papuans to become economically self-sufficient but inoculated by their Christian morality from potential temptations and threats introduced by Western society. The Kwato Extension Association (KEA) fostered technical education, the study of English and loyalty to the mission which, as later actions of the administration demonstrate, was regarded by the government as a threat to their primacy. Christine Weir described Kwato as a unique organisation

---

16   P Donaldson, Report 4 of 1950/51, p. 2, Milne Bay District, Gehua, 1950–1953, PNGA; Bryan Ezard, *A grammar of Tawala: An Austronesian language of the Milne Bay Area, Papua New Guinea* (Canberra: Pacific Linguistics, Research School of Pacific and Asian Studies, The Australian National University, 1997).
17   Moral Rearmament was a revivalist movement. David Wetherell and Charlotte Carr-Gregg, 'Moral Re-armament in Papua, 1931–42', *Oceania* 54 (1984): 177, 185, doi.org/10.1002/j.1834-4461.1984.tb02044.x; Graham Hassall, 'Religion and nation-state formation in Melanesia: 1945 to independence' (PhD thesis, The Australian National University, 1989), 135.

attempting to create an alternate society, an Anglicised elite removed from their villages in the hope of creating the nucleus of a new Papuan society.[18] David Wetherell explained Charles Abel's ambition as attempting:

> to keep converts on the mission head station and thus create an entire Christian society there. To implement this plan Abel embarked on his most controversial venture: the establishment of 'industrial branches' whose objective was: 'to raise the New Guineans to a higher level, and by civilising him to give him the opportunity of the attainment of stronger Christian character'.[19]

Abel argued 'industrial Christianity' would result in a strong independent Papuan Christian, one capable of restructuring their social order. Kwato's methods were, according to Wetherell and Belshaw, a destructive force on traditional Indigenous society, not only removing children from their traditional environment, but actively destroying important village institutions, such as men's houses, and replacing them with Christianity, industry, European manners and sport.[20] Regardless of the evolutionary intent of the Kwato program, Charles, and later Cecil, Abel were clearly aiming at developing an Indigenous 'elite', a policy in direct competition with the Australian Government's more gradualist, universalist program.[21] Yet, as Weir points out, many Kwato graduates, English-educated and sophisticated in their relationships with Europeans, became leaders as political opportunities emerged in the 1950s.[22] Belshaw described how the more sophisticated Kwato Mission population, like those at Wagawaga, had abandoned much of traditional life, the old ceremonial festivals and crafts associated with it, and instead had a relatively clear notion of what they wanted in terms of personal consumption and capital goods.[23] Furthermore, unlike in much of the Territory of Papua New Guinea (TPNG) in the early 1950s, the technical skill of labour developed at Kwato provided a means for local people to consider it feasible for them to establish a relatively sophisticated secondary industry.

---

18   Christine Weir, 'Education for citizenship or tool of evangelism? All Saints Anglican School, Labasa, 1952–1970' (PhD thesis, The Australian National University, 2005), 232.
19   Wetherell and Carr-Gregg, 'Moral Re-armament in Papua', 182.
20   David Wetherell, *Charles Abel and the Kwato Mission of Papua New Guinea, 1891–1975* (Carlton: Melbourne University Press, 1996), 49, 142–48; Cyril Belshaw, 'In search of wealth: A study of the emergence of commercial operations in the Melanesian society of Southeastern Papua', *American Anthropologist* 57 (1955): 8.
21   Paul Hasluck, *A time for building: Australian administration in Papua and New Guinea, 1951–1963* (Carlton: Melbourne University Press, 1976), 195.
22   For example, Merari Dickson (1951 Legislative Council) and Alice Wedega (1961 Legislative Council). Weir, 'Education for citizenship or tool of evangelism?', 235.
23   Belshaw, 'In search of wealth', 12.

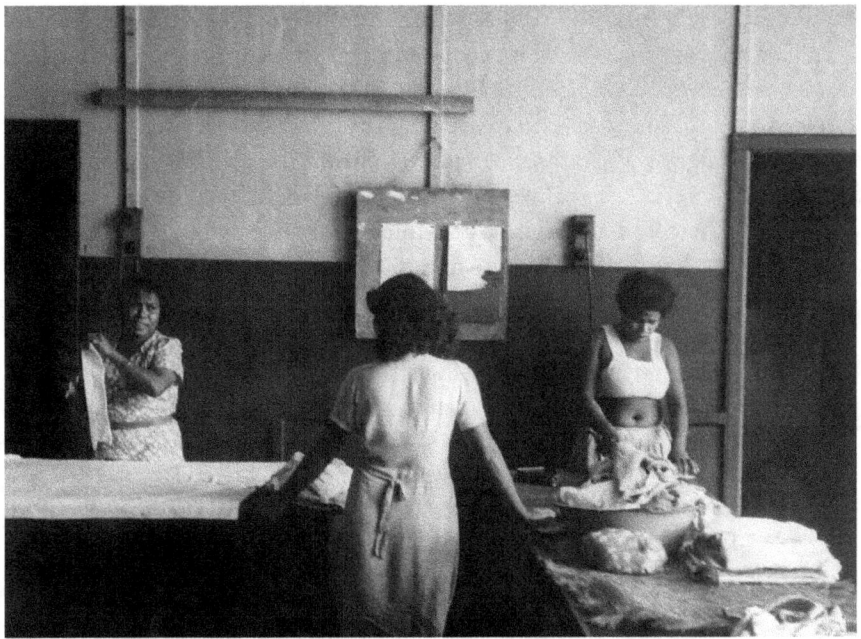

Figure 7.2: According to the caption (1950), 'at Kwato Mission, the girls are taught dress-making and laundering'.
Source: NAA, A6510, 1644, item 6942725.

The Indigenous activity in Milne Bay was at odds with the government's preferred economic vehicle of agricultural household cash cropping. While activity remained in the villages, it was the emergence of an independently minded and capable Papuan, supported by a mission, which directly challenged the Australian colonial dominance on the ground. The mere creation of an Indigenous 'elite' was counter to Australia's universal gradualist program, one which was premised on all Papuans and New Guineans having equality of opportunity to participate in eventual self-rule.

An interesting venture, and one closely aligned to Kwato Mission, was the establishment of an Indigenous newspaper. The editor, Penueli Anakapu, a graduate of Kwato, established the *Papuan Times* in 1948, using surplus paper and a mimeograph machine salvaged from an allied dump, and by 1953, had a weekly circulation of 200 copies and a readership of approximately 1,000.[24] Anakapu, reflecting in July 1951 on the previous

---

24 Prewar, the Kwato Mission had a publication, the *New Guinea Tidings*, though mainly to inform its overseas supporters (see the National Library of Australia's Trove for more details). Ryan Schram, 'The tribe next door: The New Guinea Highlands in a postwar Papuan mission newspaper', *Australian Journal of Anthropology* 30 (2019): 18–24, doi.org/10.1111/taja.12301.

three years of publication, described the ambition of the paper as trying 'to give a true account of what is happening in the world, far and near, and in our own country'. He believed the weekly publication had 'enabled us to know what our countrymen are doing and to feel that we are a part of the country's progress'.[25] As anthropologist Ryan Schram has noted, while the source material was primarily Australian newspapers, writers were able to 'revoice' the colonial narrative and imagine Papuans and New Guineans as agents of change: a powerful demonstration of Kwato's emphasis on acculturation and development of a village elite.[26] Clearly, Kwato-educated local people aspired to be part of, in fact probably lead, a self-governing Territory or nation, an ambition which was not set against their colonisers, but as part of a rapid advancement towards independence.

A sawmill at Divinai (northern shore) was established in the early 1950s by local people without the assistance of any Europeans. Described in the local paper as a people who:

> Listened to their leaders and put together the individual money for their future development, and a few months ago they were able to buy a sawmill.[27]

Within 12 months, officer Pierre Donaldson was praising the mill's operations, pointing to:

> quite a sizeable stack of timber (approximately 4,500 square feet) cut and ready to be shipped to Samarai. Machinery and equipment were in good running condition, and it appears that no trouble has been experienced by the native mechanics operating the plant.[28]

As part of the same patrol, Donaldson stopped at the village of Ahioma (west of Divinai) to report on the communal farm operating as an Indigenous collective society. The enterprise included five acres of land tilled and under cultivation, and approximately 400 acres of land being used as a pasture for cattle supplied by Kwato Mission.[29] Donaldson commended the supervision of local leader, Esekiela Wedega, a graduate of both Kwato

---

25 Penueli Anakapu, 'The *Papuan Times* review', *Papuan Times*, 27 July 1951, 2.
26 Schram, 'The tribe next door', 18.
27 The Kwato Mission, prewar, used local timber and taught carpentry. During the war the allies had more than 10 sawmills operating once the Japanese were ousted. 'A future? Or no future', *Papuan Times*, 25 April 1951, 6.
28 P Donaldson, Report 4 of 1950/51, p. 13, Milne Bay District, Gehua, 1950–1953, PNGA.
29 HD Gaywood to District Office, 5 August 1954, Milne Bay District, Gehua, 1953–1955, PNGA.

and an agricultural course at Abau and felt 'these people are highly deserving of every success in this venture as their ideals and aims are worthy of all possible guidance'.[30]

Wagawaga and the Milne Bay Development Company

Figure 7.3: Interior of the joinery works and factory of the Milne Bay Development Company, 1952.
Source: NAA A1200, L14386, item 1186783.

The idea for the Milne Bay Development Company (MBDC) came from a meeting between Wagawaga village councillors and Cecil Abel in August 1949.[31] The original concept was for a furniture factory, but it quickly expanded to include prefabricated housing, and an ambition to introduce modern fishing and fish/fruit canning, and mother-of-pearl fishing.[32] While many of these ambitions were not realised, and later the business folded, the

---

30 The course at Abau was operated by the Commonwealth Reconstruction Training Scheme. Donaldson, Report 4 of 1950/51, p. 6.
31 Village councillors were government-appointed village leaders in the Territory of Papua; their equivalents in the Territory of New Guinea were luluais and tultul.
32 CS Belshaw, 'Wagawaga: Preliminary conclusions', 25 April 1950, p. 1, Establishment co-operatives 1950–1, A518 [V840/1/4 Part 1], National Archives of Australia (NAA).

sheer scope of the project and dedication to the enterprise from a village of fewer than 300 people forced the Australian Government to accelerate its own development plans for the district.³³

The furniture factory was started and financed by funds collected from the Wagawaga villagers and a small subsidy from the Kwato Mission. The erected factory had open sides and consisted of an office, lathe, plane table, petrol engine and electrical dynamo.³⁴ In December 1949, at a newly created 'Festival of Christmas' held at Wagawaga to promote this community enterprise, the first pieces of furniture manufactured at the factory were sold. As a result of these sales and the subscriptions of approximately £600 raised from other Milne Bay villages (on both shores), there were enough funds to expand production and sponsor a trip to Australia for Abel and two local leaders to plead for support from the Australian Government.³⁵ The dedication of Abel to Indigenous enterprise meant that he not only travelled to Australia in 1950, but had, in 1947, travelled to Britain in the hope of recruiting agricultural instructors for a program to educate Papuans in modern farming techniques.³⁶ The trip to Australia in March 1950 to meet External Territories Minister Percy Spender, and a series of correspondence from Abel to government officials in both Australia and the Territory, portray a group of people dedicated to an Indigenous enterprise of imagination, self-confidence and capacity for self-determination.

The two young Indigenous leaders who accompanied Abel to Australia were Henry Leki and Penueli Anakapu. Leki was the manager of MBDC, a trained engineer and graduate of Kwato, and his leadership, like other Indigenous leaders of the period, had arisen because of the hope he offered for socioeconomic advancement. Leki told Belshaw that:

> many of us have had technical training. Before we didn't know what to do with it for ourselves. During the war we saw that the machines can be organised and controlled to increase wealth. That is what we should be doing. Are we always going to live in this state when we know that something else is possible?³⁷

---

33 Community Development Review Paper, 'Observations and reflections on community development in Milne Bay, Papua', 28 August 1951, p. 5, Native Education 1950–55, A1361 [45/2/1 PART 3], NAA.
34 The building was 24 metres by 12 metres and almost 17 metres high. Belshaw, 'In search of wealth', 44.
35 The Administrator, Murray, attended the opening of the factory. JK Murray to Department of Territories (DOT) Secretary, 10 May 1951, Establishment co-operatives 1950–1, A518 [V840/1/4 Part 1], NAA.
36 A Boss to JK Murray, 9 December 1949, Milne Bay District, Gehua, 1945–1950, PNGA.
37 Belshaw, 'In search of wealth', 43.

A report by the Social Welfare Officer of the Department of Education described MBDC as an endeavour aiming to achieve material wealth which 'certain groups throughout the territory [had] adopted as a "cult" in one form or other'. The officer attributed the ability of Milne Bay people to avoid such pitfalls to its good leadership.[38] Leki had lived most of his life away from Wagawaga at Kwato, was not related to earlier leaders and had little knowledge of local custom and history. On his return, Leki was regarded as the wealthiest man in the village and, acting in the typical fashion of a Melanesian big man, won elders across to his vision by spending a good deal of his personal wealth assisting with the food supply.[39] Therefore, his leadership depended almost entirely for its success upon his personality and his ability to lead his people towards the goals they desired. Abel described Leki, in a letter to Spender as:

> doing a far bigger job as a human engineer at Wagawaga, Milne Bay, where he, with others, is helping to forge a new industrial framework that may give back to his people a purpose in life and perhaps even the very will to live.[40]

While this rhetoric from Abel perfectly encapsulates his evolutionary belief in industrial Christianity, what follows is quite remarkable. The letter points to Abel's broader vision for the modern Papuan and 'his' value to Australia. He warns Spender that these young leaders 'are alive to the danger of Communist infiltration and propaganda', and further, 'in the face of the rising tide of Communism from the North it could be that Australia's most valuable bulwark is a united and grateful people in Papua'. Abel argued:

> these enlightened and responsible Papuans are not only free from inferiority but know how to stop the rot in others. Like Henry they are developing a genius for getting people to pull together, whether white or brown, and to pull in the same direction.[41]

To reiterate the commitment of the community to this project, a translated letter was attached, signed by Wagawaga councillors and elders, and brimming with a subaltern, self-effacing declaration for the wise counsel of their Australian 'masters', and expressing a desire to access new opportunities for village industries.

---

38 Community Development Review Paper, 'Observations and reflections', 1.
39 Belshaw, 'Wagawaga: Preliminary conclusions', pp. 5–7.
40 C Abel to P Spender, 25 February 1950, Establishment co-operatives 1950–1, A518 [V840/1/4 Part 1], NAA.
41 Abel to Spender, 25 February 1950.

During their visit, Penueli Anakapu penned an article for *The Sun* (Sydney) which expressed his admiration for Sydney and detailed the nature and importance of the Wagawaga projects.[42] The visit was clearly quite unique, as indicated by the patronising framing of the article for a mainstream Australian audience. The headline of 'palm tree philosopher' and title which implies the Papuan as incapable of working in the efficient manner of the Sydneysider undermines, rather than promotes, the achievements of the Papuans.

According to the Officer-in-Charge at Gehua, Minister Spender told the Papuans: 'External Territories would back any enterprise that was undertaken that would enable the Native people of Papua and New Guinea to create industries of their own'.[43] Whether the conversation included conditions attached to the offer of support remains unclear. However, as later actions demonstrate, the administration might have been willing to support such a local project, but the enterprise had to be commercially viable, responsibly managed and remain an easily contained small village venture. MBDC did not meet these criteria, lacking adequate business management skills, and the leadership had a vision to expand well beyond a small village-based enterprise. Furthermore, it was an Indigenous enterprise outside the control of the administration, an explicit challenge to colonial hegemony.

Evidently the village leadership and Abel were confident of government support as, on their return, they established formalised business structures and quickly looked to expand operations: the organisation was registered as a company, books of account were created, and a Board of Directors established consisting of Cecil Abel as chairman, with Henry Leki and Joshua Peter. A later visit to the Territory by the Undersecretary for External Territories, John Howse, convinced the villagers to expand from furniture-making to prefabricated houses. By early 1951 MBDC had purchased new sawmilling plant equipment from Australia, and timber from both Kwato Mission and the Indigenous sawmill at Divinai. Cashflow was tight, and while five houses had been sold by May 1951, the revenue was used to pay expenses. Minimal wages were paid while capital was not fully subscribed as potential shareholders continued to wait for war damage compensation.

---

42 Penueli Anakapu, 'Papuan (in no hurry) finds a city that lives by the clock', *The Sun* (Sydney), 26 February 1950, 18.
43 Officer-in Charge (Gehua) to Secretary DET (forwarded by JK Murray-Administrator), 10 May 1951, Establishment co-operatives 1950–1, A518 [V840/1/4 Part 1], NAA.

In a follow-up letter to Spender, Abel asked the government to guarantee a loan from the Commonwealth Bank of £3,500 'to establish a fishing and canning business in the immediate future'. He argued the business would be economically sound once they had received this capital injection along with the £3,500 local people expected to receive for war compensation (which was a prolonged process).[44] A few days later, after speaking with the Inspector of the Commonwealth Bank, John Howse wrote to the Treasurer, Arthur Fadden, and asked 'in view of the great boost which would be given to Island development and to progress in other centres, I should be grateful if you could see your way clear to approve Mr. Abel's request'. This request was rejected by the Treasury Department on 24 May 1950. In later correspondence, the Territory Administrator, JK Murray, argued the project was 'abnormally large for such a small community', and professed to growing apprehension over the financial management of the scheme.[45] His opinion was based on a report from anthropologist Cyril Belshaw who raised concern over the lack of business competency, and an Education Department report which highlighted a lack of labour to maintain such a large project and ensure a high enough return on capital.[46] Howse also arranged with the Department of Commerce and Agriculture for a representative from the Fisheries Department to commence enquiries into the viability of the fishing and canning enterprise.[47]

The establishment of the MBDC in Wagawaga provided an opportunity for a colonised people to demonstrate Indigenous socioeconomic autonomy, and yet they also had to operate within the strictures of their colonial guardian. The activities of those involved in MBDC were focussed on business operations and expansion, while the administration was concerned for the local repercussions if these ventures should fail. This is an interesting attitude from the administration as, within a few years, government-sponsored cooperative societies and rural progress societies would regularly

---

44 The archives do not explain why the compensation was delayed despite repeated questioning by Abel.
45 Series of correspondence: JK Murray to DOT Secretary, 10 May 1951; Cecil Abel to Percy Spender, 24 March 1950; John Howse to Arthur Fadden, 30 March 1950; PW Nette to DET Secretary, 24 May 1950; JK Murray to DET Secretary, 1 September 1950, pp. 1–2, Establishment co-operatives 1950–1, A518 [V840/1/4 Part 1], NAA.
46 After three years of operation no individual had been given training in bookkeeping and there was no system of simplified accounting. Belshaw, 'In search of wealth', 49; Community Development Review Paper, 'Observations and reflections', 5.
47 John Howse to Percy Spender, 28 March 1950, Establishment co-operatives 1950–1, A518 [V840/1/4 Part 1], NAA.

fail. It suggests risk of business failure was only acceptable if it conformed to government strategy. In this case, it was not government-controlled stimulus but rather, the autonomous motivation of local people guided by a mission.

While Belshaw's report raised concern over the financial management, he was effusive in his praise for the men working in the factory who had been encouraged by Kwato to expect:

> a high standard of living, and who have the training and ability to command that standard in private employment. Some of these people have used their savings and have no money left … yet such is their faith in the future that they go on working day after day, and even neglect their gardens to do so. They know that they are at a critical point in their development, fighting for self-respect.[48]

In terms of leadership, Belshaw described Henry Leki as ambitious with a characteristic love for power, but one being used to great advantage for his community. In fact, Belshaw believed 'the community of Wagawaga are as much behind him as any community could be expected to be'.[49] Leki, along with Abel, continued to move around the district and strove to strengthen collaborative ties. For example, in June 1951, they were in Divinai for an inspection of the sawmill project, and Leki spoke of his vision for the MBDC as a vehicle for the development of the whole district, and how they had 'start[ed] a fund for education', not 'for Wagawaga but for the educational work of the district'.[50] Operations continued at a brisk rate with Donaldson visiting the Wagawaga factory in June 1951 where he reported construction of '3 whaleboats, 2 dinghies and one 45-foot cutter' valued at £300.[51]

But, the lack of capital investment, primarily due to the rejected loan application and failure to receive the promised war damage compensation, forced Abel to write again to Howse asking for him to intercede on behalf of the Wagawaga villagers. Abel argued:

> the Wagawaga people are doing most to ensure the success of this project and have decided to invest all their War Damage into this community venture. When the whole issue centres around the wise

---

48   Belshaw, 'Wagawaga: Preliminary conclusions', 6–8.
49   Belshaw, 'Wagawaga: Preliminary conclusions', 6–8.
50   'A visit to Divinai to co-operate more and more with Wagawaga said a Divanai leader', *Papuan Times*, 22 June 1951, 2.
51   P Donaldson, Report 4 of 1950/51, p. 13, Milne Bay District, Gehua, 1950–1953, PNGA.

use of their money they find it difficult to understand why they should be denied the use of their money at a time when it would do them most good.[52]

Despite cashflow problems, the business continued to expand and motivation and belief in the project remained high. The 1952 Annual General Meeting 'passed, with one mind and with cheers', and a determination 'to lift the standard of living of Papuans in this area, and to raise the standard of leadership by giving every Papuan boy or girl who is ready the chance to get the highest possible education'. The Managing Director's report described the extraordinary growth, from one business in 1950 to 12, including prefabricated houses, furniture, boatbuilding, sawmilling, engineers who look after the plant, electric light and water supply, bakery, canework, handicrafts, agriculture and rice growing, large-net fishing and a retail store.[53]

Conclusion

This chapter has described how Papuans from the Milne Bay region, inspired by the KEA and led by an Indigenous elite created by this institution, were the active agents who brought socioeconomic and political change to the district in the early postwar period. While the Australian Government provided substantial war damage compensation, a lack of patrol officers, administration resources and a coordinated approach meant they failed to comprehend, or were physically unable to satisfy, the growing socioeconomic demands of Milne Bay people. Instead, despite being forced to operate within the constraints of their colonial guardian, they were able to demonstrate a considerable measure of Indigenous socioeconomic autonomy. Cecil Abel and an Indigenous elite, graduates from the Kwato Mission, created a new sense of purpose and were able to draw extensive support from villages around the bay, which resulted in a remarkable array of Indigenous enterprises.

On the surface, the Commonwealth Government appeared supportive of these local initiatives, the External Territories Minister provided verbal assurance, and the Assistant Minister acted on the villager's behalf. They

---

52   Cecil Abel to Howse, 11 June 1951, Establishment co-operatives 1950–1, A518 [V840/1/4 Part 1], NAA.
53   'Annual general meeting of the Milne Bay Development Company', *Papuan Times*, 11 April 1952, 4.

were motivated by a desire for Western concepts of better living conditions and were prepared to remain in their villages. And yet, the Commonwealth Treasury and Territory Administration did not provide the necessary support. In fact, as is explained in Chapter 8, the Territory Administration actively undermined the MBDC, which suggests two factors were at play. Firstly, the administration would not take the risk of business failure on an unsponsored Indigenous enterprise. And secondly, the actions of the administration point to a preference for containment and control on the ground. The Australian Government's efforts were focussed on Indigenous advancement—but only on their terms.

8

Indigenous Advancement: Only on the Colonialist's Terms

In the first decade after the end of the Pacific War, Papuans from the Milne Bay subdistrict utilised the proceeds from war compensation to establish both primary and secondary Indigenous enterprises. Their vision, inspired by the Kwato Mission, was to forge a new industrial framework, one which local people would control. This chapter explains the Australian response to this autonomous action, one which did not fit within their expectations of the 'submissive native'. It will detail how, at times, the administration acted in a duplicitous manner which undermined any pretence for Indigenous self-development.

This chapter is divided into two sections. Part 1 explains the growing concern of the administration about the business activity at Milne Bay. It outlines the response of the Australian Government, one clearly motivated by fear it was being usurped as the primary source for improving the living conditions for local people. It details how the administration was unable to implement a coordinated development program for the region due to a lack of planning. However, Part 2 explains how agricultural officer William Cottrell-Dormer and local leader Alice Wedega were able to meld together administrative ambition, Indigenous agency and Kwato doctrine to develop an effective community development vehicle. This interesting example is at odds with the earlier actions of the administration. It is well planned and supported by an experienced skilled government officer who actively worked with local people, utilising their desire for improved living conditions but within the

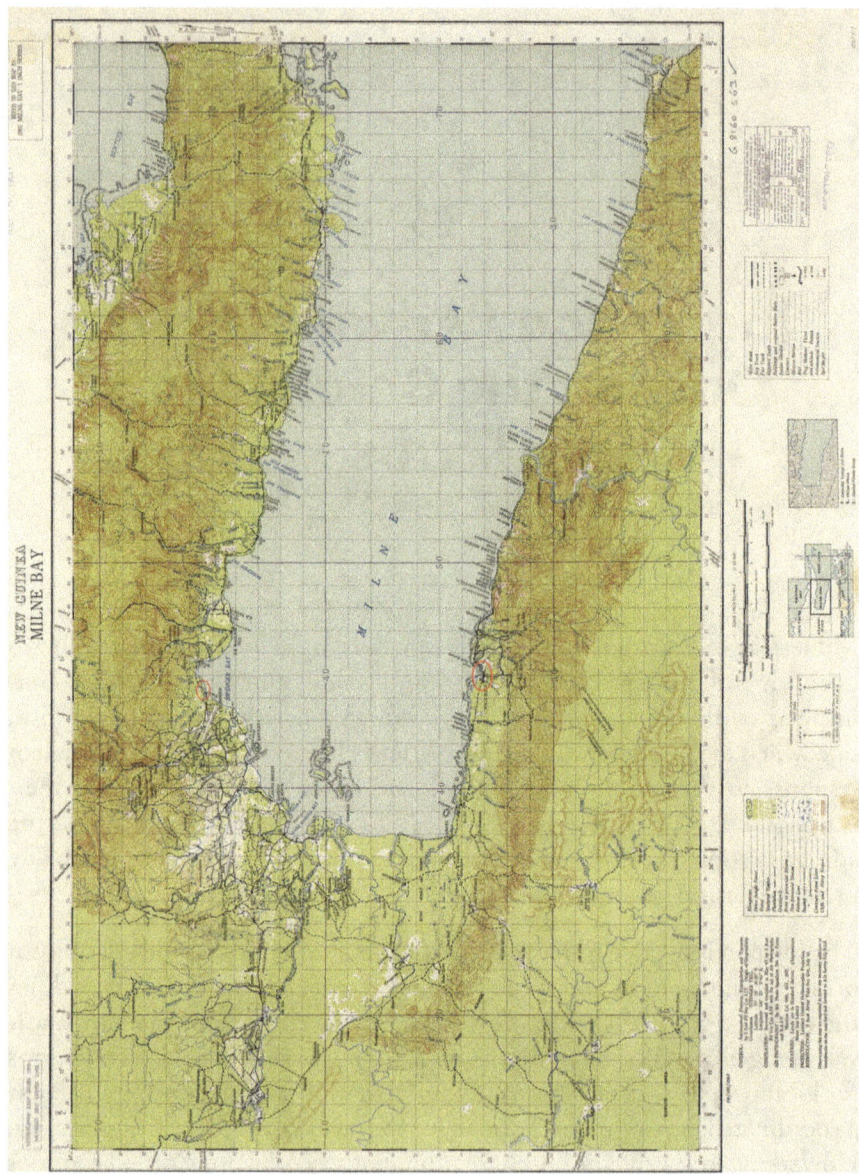

Map 8.1: Milne Bay.
Source: Compiled by the 3rd Australian Army Field Survey Company, 1943. Trove, National Library of Australia (NLA), item MAP G8160 s63 (Copy 1).

8. INDIGENOUS ADVANCEMENT

confinement of colonial control. In some ways it is a perfect example of how Hasluck envisioned development; the government officer applies his technical skill and ensures it is the coloniser who is providing the resources to stimulate Indigenous desire for 'progression'. This chapter considers whether the flurry to set up councils and cooperatives was due to a limited and often inexperienced administrative staff trying to show it was doing something along Hasluck-orientated lines, or if it was a deliberate attempt to dominate and shape a strong mission enterprise.

Administrative concern and action

By mid-1951, the administration regarded the operations and sheer scale of the Milne Bay Development Company (MBDC) with concern, partly because of the poor business organisation behind them, but primarily because it regarded the group, and its attempts to provide welfare services, as a triumph for the Kwato Mission over the administration.[1] In February 1951, the patrol officer stationed at Wagawaga, Harry Plant, had warned that 'the lead has passed from the administration to Kwato mission' regarding the social, political and economic future of the subdistrict.[2] Belshaw, in his April 1950 report noted:

> present policy is to leave areas of strong Mission influence to themselves as much as possible. As an administrative device delegating responsibility, saving manpower, and securing co-operation with vested European authorities, this is no doubt admirable. But when brought into relation with the development of an area as large as Milne Bay, there are obvious defects.[3]

In an October 1950 memo, the district office, in what appears to be confirmation of their growing alarm over their lack of influence in the Milne Bay subdistrict, requested the immediate establishment of statutory councils in the Bay.[4] The administration, in their desire to understand and evaluate the likelihood of success of the MBDC, commissioned four

---
1   Allan M Healy, 'Native administration and local government in Papua, 1880–1960' (PhD thesis, The Australian National University, 1962), 339.
2   HT Plant to Director DDSNA, 1 February 1951, Milne Bay District, Gehua, 1950–1953, National Archives of PNG (PNGA).
3   Cyril S Belshaw, 'Wagawaga: Preliminary conclusions', 25 April 1950, p. 3, Establishment co-operatives 1950–1, A518 [V840/1/4 Part 1], National Archives of Australia (NAA).
4   District Office to IF Champion, Director Department of District Services and Native Affairs (DDSNA), 31 October 1950, Milne Bay District, Samarai, 1949–1953, PNGA.

surveys: the April 1950 Belshaw Report (financial viability); two surveys of the proposed fishing and fish/fruit canning enterprise, one by the Commonwealth Fisheries Department and another by the Department of Agriculture, Stock and Fisheries (DASF) in April 1951; and an investigation by the Social Welfare Officer for the Department of Education.

The Social Welfare Officer reported the people of Wagawaga were obsessed with the community project, where there was 'no mention of the ordinary day-to-day village matters such as hygiene or sanitation. The high grass around the village houses and the broken culvert in the centre of the village' an indication of their obsession. The report, while praising the dedication and leadership of the operation, warned, based on previous experience, that the lack of financial return could ultimately lead to a 'rebellion'. The prime concern was the long gestation period between the significant financial investment and the promised return. The report argued the Ahioma farming project, closer to the soil and the government's agroeconomic plans, was a more worthwhile project and one which would yield quicker results.[5]

In July 1951, Murray again denied an application from Abel, this time for the support of the proposed commercial fishing and fish/fruit canning business. Murray clearly viewed it as a Kwato business enterprise, arguing:

> such projects should be developed by and from the initiative of the Native people themselves, preferably on a small scale in the first instance, growing into a larger enterprise. Considerable harm can be done if a project on the scale proposed by Mr. Abel should fail.[6]

The sheer scale and lack of business acumen were important factors; other reasons included the large purchase of ill-suited fish netting and the world shortage of tin for the proposed canning factory. Belshaw reported that Abel had been too busy to teach local people about business management, leaving control of operations solely in the hands of Leki and village leaders.[7] In the same memo, Murray took the first of two decisive decisions to

---

5   Community Development Review Paper, 'Observations and reflections on community development in Milne Bay, Papua', 28 August 1951, pp. 5, 8–9, Native Education 1950–55, A1361 [45/2/1 PART 3], NAA.
6   Murray referred to the advice of Belshaw as well as Mr A O'Grady (Commonwealth Fisheries Office: Sydney) and Mr RL Childs (an officer in the Department of Agriculture, Stock and Fisheries and a member of the Fisheries Survey Party) in his decision not to support any of the MBDC projects. In the archival file there are extensive reports by all three. Murray to Department of Territories (DOT) Secretary, 30 July 1951, Establishment co-operatives 1950–1, A518 [V840/1/4 Part 1], NAA.
7   Cyril Belshaw, 'In search of wealth: A study of the emergence of commercial operations in the Melanesian society of Southeastern Papua', *American Anthropologist* 57 (1955): 52.

reel in control of the Bay with the appointment of Ernest Graham as the cooperative officer for the area. In conjunction with local government councils (LGCs, Murray's second key decision), the people of Milne Bay took up cooperatives with alacrity. Cooperatives, like LGCs, were an example of the administration's community development plans for the 1950s. The introduction of cooperatives during this period was widespread throughout the Territory of Papua New Guinea (TPNG), and the experience of Milne Bay mirrored much of the rest of the Territory: initial enthusiastic take-up of the concept followed by later financial collapse. Despite the government's fear of Indigenous economic organisations failing, cooperatives would prove a valuable resource as an enabler for economic literacy and political education for a nascent Indigenous elite.[8] It is also an example of the administration willing to risk business failure if it fitted within the strictures of a colonial development program. This was understandable from the perspective of the coloniser as the sole arbiter of development, especially one who actively worked against an Indigenous elite, but hardly the basis for supporting Indigenous autonomy and progression towards self-rule.

However, the early introduction of LGCs and later, Village Agricultural Committees, represent a significant departure from development plans for the administration, one forced upon them by the influence of Kwato and the agency of local people. While the actions of local people of this region were inspired by a specific form of colonisation administered by the Kwato Mission, their attitudes were not unique to Papuans and New Guineans in this period. The case studies of Sepik and New Hanover also explore and explain the actions of autonomous, independent and driven people. They were not necessarily aggressive in opposition to their coloniser, but neither were they satisfied to be passive bystanders in the development of their region, and in fact, the territories. However, the Australian response to these people suggests the maintenance of control was a priority over the rapid advancement of its colonised people.

In Milne Bay, the administration lacked any planned or coordinated approach to socioeconomic development, certainly equal to those of Abel and the MBDC. The government, while not actively undermining the MBDC, regarded the danger of an uncontrolled Indigenous elite, clearly linked to the Kwato Mission, as an undesirable and potentially unstable presence. The response of the administration was one of fear, of attempting 'to rectify

---

8   Brad Underhill, 'Co-operatives and political development in PNG: Colonial failure or unrecognized success?', *Journal of Pacific History* 55, no. 3 (2019): 360–82, doi.org/10.1080/00223344.2019.1665461.

PREPARING A NATION?

an unsatisfactory native situation'.[9] The administrator, JK Murray, accepted the advice of the Milne Bay District Commissioner (DC) in October 1950 who argued a local council established in the area had the potential to arrest the influence of both Kwato and the MBDC.[10]

Figure 8.1: Caption reads as follows (1952): 'Village election, one of the Wagawaga headman strikes a triangle to indicate that the poll is open'.
Source: National Archives of Australia (NAA), A1200, L14365, item 7462810.

---

9   David M Fenbury, *Practice without policy: Genesis of local government in Papua New Guinea* (Canberra: The Australian National University, 1978), 279.
10 District Office to IF Champion, 31 October 1950, Milne Bay District, Samarai, 1949–1953, PNGA.

The decision to introduce local councils was made swiftly and deliberately bypassed the speciality section charged with establishing and managing them (the Native Affairs Section, or NAS).[11] Because local councils were 'voluntary' and had to be economically self-sufficient, NAS relied on extensive consultation in the local community to ensure suitability. Each council had to contain a population sufficient to support revenues large enough to permit it to carry out executive functions including sharing in the cost of local social services. According to acting Department of District Services and Native Affairs (DDSNA) director, Charles Rich, 'experience gained to date indicates that a unit containing fewer than 4000 persons is to be avoided if possible'.[12] In addition, villagers had to be convinced that paying a new council tax would be beneficial to the village in terms of political autonomy and improved services (roads, schools etc.).[13] This did not happen in Milne Bay. The patrol officer on the ground, later appointed as the district Native Authorities Officer (NAO), was Harry Plant, who found himself with the role of suddenly developing a plan to introduce a local council. Moreover, this new council was financially hamstrung from the beginning.[14] Plant, in considering language factors, social cohesion and transport difficulties, recommended a council comprising the village of Wagawaga, Daio, Gwawili, Gamadaudau and Gibara, with a population of only 1,100 people.[15] David Fenbury, the person responsible for introducing councils to TPNG and in charge of NAS, was scathing in his criticism of the rushed and inadequate planning for this new council, noting it was both too small and underprepared.[16] Another consequence of the rushed rollout of government development tools to Milne Bay was the inability of NAS and the Cooperative Section to work together on a comprehensive development program for the area. Instead, cooperatives focussed almost exclusively on trade stores to absorb as much as possible war damage compensation, while the new council was chronically short of funds and administrative support.[17]

---

11 Healy, 'Native administration', 341–44.
12 MCW Rich to SA Lonergan (Government Secretary), 20 January 1950, pp. 1–3, Papers of David Maxwell Fenbury, MS6747/3/5, National Library of Australia (NLA).
13 D Fenbury, 'Comments on Village Council Ordinance', 28 December 1949, p. 3, Papers of David Maxwell Fenbury, MS6747/3/5, NLA.
14 WRA MacSkimming, Report 2 of 1952/53, p. 2, Milne Bay District, Gehua, 1950–1953, PNGA.
15 Only 600 people were eligible to pay tax. Healy, 'Native administration', 337–40.
16 Healy, 'Native administration', 337.
17 Healy, 'Native administration', 341–44.

The Ealeba Native Village Council was established on 23 November 1951 with 13 councillors elected on a proportionate basis.[18] For the first time since the establishment of LGCs, a woman from Gwawili village school (Elenise) stood as a candidate and had the distinction of being elected. Apart from Wagawaga (which used a secret ballot), voting was conducted by open ballot with voters standing behind the candidate of their choice. All males over the age of 17 resident in the council area were liable for a tax while women had the option to place their names on the electoral roll. Local leaders were supportive of this new venture: they did not regard the council as competition but an additional opportunity for government-sponsored development. The Kwato-controlled *Papuan Times*, consistent with their vision for eventual Indigenous self-rule, proclaimed the council as the 'beginning of a new day for Milne Bay'.[19]

The influence of the Kwato Mission on the council elections was significant, probably no more than in the election of the first, and up to that point only, female councillor. The *Papuan Times* reported that Elenise was a graduate of the Kwato Mission, where:

> she learnt to cook, to run the big mission house which was her training school, and when she had finished this part of her training, she chose to become a nurse. She was amongst the first nurses to be trained in the Kwato hospital.[20]

In the lead-up to the council elections, two important Kwato women, Alice Wedega and Halliday Beavis, had spent two weeks visiting village schools and wherever they went they talked with teachers, parents and village leaders.[21] Wedega, who grew up on Sariba Island, a couple of miles across the straits from Samarai Island, had first arrived at Kwato in 1912, and in the postwar period, became a powerful advocate for female participation in the wider community.[22] The *Papuan Times* reported that the Wedega/Beavis tour highlighted:

---

18   'First Milne Bay Council', *Papuan Times*, 23 November 1951, 5.
19   DOT, *Territory of Papua Annual Report for the period 1st of July, 1951, to 30th June 1952* (Canberra: Government Printer, 1952), 25.
20   'Only woman councillor', *Papuan Times*, 23 November 1951, 6.
21   Halliday Beavis arrived in Milne Bay in 1929 and worked as a teacher at the Kwato Mission. She was still at the mission when it closed in 1971. 'Kwato is dead', *Papua New Guinea Post-Courier*, 22 November 1971, 5.
22   Alice Wedega, *Listen my country* (Sydney: Pacific Publications, 1981), 11, 17.

women have a big part to play in the new village life they want to build. This thought for the future of the girls is a very good thing. It is a sign that Papua is really growing. It is a sign of new thinking and real faith in the future.[23]

The Kwato Mission had developed, during the interwar years, a liberal education system with a special emphasis on educating women, and therefore, it was unsurprising there were female councillors from the beginning of LGCs in Milne Bay.[24] Female participation in local government as early as 1951 was unusual and a significant milestone for the administration. It would be almost another four years (March 1955) before Paul Hasluck would direct the administration to start a three-year drive to overcome the lag in the advancement of women.[25] But on the ground in Milne Bay, it was the non-traditional approach of LGCs to local governance that provided the administration with an opportunity to encourage female participation and promote participative self-government.[26]

Kwato and the MBDC did not oppose the establishment of the council; again this was consistent with their conciliatory, but driven, ambition for autonomous opportunity. In fact, the first president of the council was MBDC manager, Henry Leki, and according to Allan Healy, 'the company even lent the money to establish the council'.[27] In August 1952, Daniel Sioni, a senior Kwato leader, toured the council area and praised 'the achievements of each councillor in his area', particularly the fencing of gardens to control damage caused by pigs.[28] Abel was quite effusive regarding the introduction of councils, probably aware that the Kwato-educated elite would play a significant role in council matters, and suggested that the council area should be extended. Prompted by Abel, the area was visited by NAO Plant in late 1952 'with a view to interesting the natives in the Native Village Council scheme'.[29] Officer Ron MacSkimming described the council as 'the most significant development in native affairs', where:

---

23 'What future for our girls?', *Papuan Times*, 26 October 1951, 3.
24 Community Development Review Paper, 'Observations and reflections', 2.
25 Paul Hasluck, *A time for building: Australian administration in Papua and New Guinea, 1951–1963* (Carlton: Melbourne University Press, 1976), 327–30.
26 Healy, 'Native administration', 511.
27 Healy, 'Native administration', 338.
28 'A visitor praises the work of South Milne Bay Council', *Papuan Times*, 8 August 1952, 1.
29 The Buhutu people joined the Ealeba Council in early 1953 but did not improve the finances, as they were poor people and paid little tax. WRA MacSkimming, Report 2 of 1952/53, p. 2.

all villages former village councillors (usually the oldest and most feeble men in the village) have been replaced by representatives elected by taxpayers, who meet once a month at the Council headquarters at Wagawaga. Most of the councillors appear to be progressively-minded, with ideas of their own about development, and if the council is supported in every possible way should be an effective means of lifting the people.[30]

Council elections were held on an annual basis, and when MacSkimming patrolled the area in March 1953, tax collecting was about to commence. MacSkimming also reported that with the addition of an extra patrol officer (from one to two), the administration was able to spend more time patrolling the subdistrict.[31]

Table 8.1: 1952 Ealeba Council budget.

Revenue		Expenditure	
Council tax	£1,260	Administration	£985
Fees and rebates	£15	Medical and sanitation	£25
		Education	£50
		Roads and bridges	£125
		Reserves	£90
Total	£1,275	Total	£1,275

Source: Department of Territories (DOT), *Territory of Papua Annual Report for the period 1st of July, 1951, to 30th June 1952* (Canberra: Government Printer, 1952), 25.

In November 1952, on the one-year anniversary of the Ealeba Council, an official government party, including Minister Paul Hasluck, his wife Alexandra and Acting Administrator Donald Cleland, visited Wagawaga and the surrounding subdistrict. Hasluck, in a speech to the gathered audience, congratulated the villagers on their council who were running their affairs and 'no-one could do it better'.[32] This was a clear endorsement of the government-sponsored local council but interestingly, did include a visit to the MBDC factory. The motivation for the visit to the Indigenous enterprise is difficult to gauge. On the one hand, the government was actively attempting to reclaim dominance and perhaps wanted to align its development model with the success of the Indigenous enterprise. On the

---

30   MacSkimming, Report 4 of 1952/53, pp. 3, 7, Milne Bay District, Gehua, 1953–1955, PNGA.
31   MacSkimming, Report 1 of 1953/54, p. 4, Milne Bay District, Gehua, 1953–1955, PNGA.
32   'Minister & party visit Wagawaga-Rabe', *Papuan Times*, 28 November 1952, 2.

other hand, it may have been for pragmatic reasons, given the dominance of council positions by the Kwato elite. Attitudes on the ground from Indigenous leaders reflect a desire to work together in developing the community. For example, at the official opening of a store and community recreation centre in Wagawaga in October 1953, Councillor Diporo, spoke of how:

> if there was only an M.B.D. or only Cooperatives or only traders it would be a bad thing. If there was only the Government or only the Missions, it would be a bad thing. We need all sides to do their part and should tolerate and welcome the work that the others are doing.[33]

Later, Assistant District Officer (ADO) Harry Gaywood, while patrolling the Ealeba Village Council area in August 1954, commented on the continued popularity of the council despite its failure to produce tangible results. Although sponsoring an atmosphere of enterprise, Gaywood warned that the council was 'in some danger of dying of inaction' primarily a result of neglect from NAO Harry Plant.[34] Gaywood's summation had merit, even though he failed to name the underlying reasons for the poor performance: insufficient funds, too small a council population, and internal dissension.[35] In terms of Gaywood's criticism of Plant, it is unfair, but probably true. Plant had moved to the north shore in June 1953 to begin consultations on a new council and, at least to Gaywood, not paid sufficient attention to the performance of Ealeba. On the other hand, how could Plant be blamed when the administration continued to suffer from a chronic shortage of staff, and as a result, by 1956, had resorted to closing the Gehua patrol post for 12 months? In fact, there was only one 38-day patrol of the Gehua subdistrict for the whole year, and even this was completed by the NAS officer.[36] This problem was not resolved until June 1957 when officer Maxwell was transferred to the new station at Sineada (East Cape).[37]

---

33   'Papuan Private Company opens, called "D.G" at Wagawaga', *Papuan Times*, 1 October 1953, 1–2.
34   H Gaywood, Report 2 of 1954/55, pp. 6–7, Milne Bay District, Gehua, 1953–1955, PNGA.
35   Healy, 'Native administration', 346.
36   TPNG, 'Milne Bay District Annual Report 1956/57', pp. 7–8.
37   DF Sheekey to Samarai District Office, 28 September 1957, Milne Bay District, Milne Bay, 1956–1957, PNGA.

Table 8.2: 1956 Ealeba Council budget.

Revenue		Expenditure	
Council tax	£1,963	Administration	£444
Fees and rebates	£215	Medical and sanitation	£117
c/f balance	£1,010	Education	£42
		Roads, bridges, wharves	£361
		Community development	£365
		Other*	£986
		Reserve's c/f 1957	£873
Total	£3,188	Total	£3,188

Note: * Councillor personal emoluments and transport.
Source: DOT, *Territory of Papua Annual Report for the period 1st of July, 1955, to 30th June 1956* (Canberra: Government Printer, 1956), 26–28.

The reason Plant moved to the north shore was to expand the council population base in the whole Milne Bay region. His original strategy was to establish four councils around the Bay with one central treasury based at Wagawaga: Erskenia Taupiri, the Ealeba treasurer, was both trained and experienced in keeping the council books.[38] Plant established the Tavara Village Council on 11 September 1954 on the northern shore of Milne Bay, the area so large that the population of 3,337 required 31 councillors. The joint treasury concept was not used because of concerns over financial supervision (insufficient staff) and the relative lack of savings expected from overheads.[39] The administration acknowledged the activities of both councils were hampered by a lack of numbers, and a decision was made to merge both councils to form one greater council for the whole Milne Bay area.[40]

Decline of Kwato and the MBDC

There were underlying problems which, by late 1953, had begun to destabilise and undermine community development on the southern shore of Milne Bay. Firstly, Cecil Abel had resigned from Kwato Extension Associate

---

38 'The formation of New Councils in Milne Bay', *Papuan Times*, 19 June 1953, 1.
39 D Fenbury, 'Financial mergers of local government units', 12 November 1952, p. 2, Papers of David Maxwell Fenbury, MS6747/3/5, NLA.
40 Territory of Papua New Guinea (TPNG), *Milne Bay District Annual Report 1956/57*, pp. 13–14, DDSNA, PNGA.

(KEA) in April 1951. This was because, according to David Wetherell, of the announcement of his engagement to marry Semi Bwagagaia, the granddaughter of a clan elder who owned Kwato Island. And although he continued to be involved with the MBDC until its collapse, and lived nearby at Gamadaudau, his direct political influence in the region, and that of the Kwato Mission, began to diminish from this point.[41] Secondly, the leadership of Henry Leki was undermined after being accused of adultery.[42] Another setback was the closure of the Indigenous paper, *Papuan Times*; the last edition was printed on 2 September 1954.

Moreover, the existence and decline of the MBDC had serious effects on the council, for it dominated the attention of most councillors. In a Native Authorities memo of December 1952, Fenbury had blamed Kwato and the MBDC for what he regarded as a hostile attitude towards the administration and warned that unless Plant was given 'strong support', he should be withdrawn and the Ealeba Council abolished.[43] In January 1954, growing concern over the leadership of the council led Milne Bay DC Mick Healy to caution councillors over their lack of direction.[44] This appeared to have little effect, as a July 1954 tour by Kwato leader Halliday Beavis (to celebrate 25 years living in Milne Bay) left her quite disappointed. She described Indigenous 'enterprises which had been running when we left [3 years earlier with Wedega] have been given up through lack of co-operation from the village people themselves'. Those that had closed included a village agricultural experiment, a cooperative store, a sawmill and a mission school 'because the building had fallen into disrepair and the village people were too lazy to build a new one'.[45] The closure of the Wagawaga factory and the *Papuan Times*, and the failure of the local council, meant momentum for local Indigenous enterprise and government-sponsored development had reached a low ebb by 1955. Fortunately, into this breach stepped an agricultural officer with a vision to develop the region with the support of all government agencies and importantly, the inclusion of local people.

---

41 After the collapse of MBDC, Abel worked on a plantation and for the Copra Marketing Board. In 1963 he moved to Port Moresby, and joined academic staff of the newly founded Administrative College, where he taught political science. David Wetherell, *Charles Abel and the Kwato Mission of Papua New Guinea, 1891–1975* (Carlton: Melbourne University Press, 1996), 233–35.
42 Healy, 'Native administration', 346.
43 D Fenbury, 'Affairs of the M.B.D.C.', 22 December 1952, cited in Healy, 'Native administration', 345.
44 'D.C. urges leadership in village councils', *Papuan Times*, 28 January 1954, 1.
45 Halliday Beavis, 'Growth and growing pains of Milne Bay', *Papuan Times*, 8 July 1954, 5.

Village women and agricultural committees: A coordinated approach

On 15 June 1950 ADO Gregory Nielson requested 'someone to go and live in the area and get the rice-growing project under way. This is technical work and up to the Department of Agriculture'.[46] In response, the department's head of Agricultural Extension Services apologised, explaining 'the field staff of this department is still well below future requirements and the need for making available an experienced officer for agricultural work in this area is impossible'.[47] The district had to wait until 17 August 1953 for the appointment of former DASF Director, William Cottrell-Dormer, as Regional Agricultural Officer.[48] Despite his late arrival to Milne Bay, Cottrell-Dormer was able to develop a coordinated multi-departmental approach to agricultural community development. His most significant contribution, Village Women and Agricultural Committees, used existing village and clan structures, and were encouraged to support and develop interdependent relations with government development agents including agricultural extension officers, cooperative societies and local councils. In a 1959 address to the Wewak Agricultural Extension Conference, Cottrell-Dormer outlined his strategy and experiences in the introduction of these programs. He suggested a coordinated approach to communal development, one which considered the chronic shortage of administrative officers. New community organisations should, according to Cottrell-Dormer, be integrated with those groups already functioning for the welfare of the people: missionary or Indigenous enterprises, local councils, cooperative societies.[49] Cottrell-Dormer's aim was for a coordinated approach to agricultural extension, and so he introduced a clear chain of command: headquarters were responsible for policy decisions and to obtain technical information, which were to be passed on to field staff, who were to then transmit information to local people through the Village Agricultural Committees. Importantly, villager feedback was encouraged and was to be passed from the extension officers back to headquarters.[50]

---

46   GF Nielson to Director DDSNA, 15 June 1950, Milne Bay District, Gehua, 1945–1950 PNGA.
47   CC Marr to Director DDSNA, 8 July 1950, Milne Bay District, Gehua, 1945–1950, PNGA.
48   'New Milne Bay Agricultural Officer', *Papuan Times*, 27 August 1953, 1.
49   W Cottrell-Dormer, 'The Village Committee organisation', September 1959, pp. 3–4, Papers of William Cottrell-Dormer, MS3762, NLA.
50   Cottrell-Dormer, 'The Village Committee organisation', pp. 5–6.

8. INDIGENOUS ADVANCEMENT

Cottrell-Dormer believed in the benefits of agricultural education for Indigenous farmers, arguing it was the best way to capitalise on their land resources and empower them to successfully enter the cash-cropping economy.[51] This fitted with the government's overall economic strategy for the Territory based around household agricultural production. Cottrell-Dormer had previously been at the forefront, although with decidedly mixed results, of agricultural development programs such as Rural Progress Societies and the Mekeo rice-growing project. These were based less on financial and economic management and more on a whole-of-community effort.[52] The genesis for Village Agricultural Committees was founded on these same communal principles; moreover, he believed individuals had a moral duty to help improve and advance their community.[53] Healy noted how these principles aligned closely with those espoused at Kwato and had been advocated during the establishment of the MBDC, and therefore he found immediate support from the Kwato-trained Indigenous elite.[54]

In September 1954, Harry Gaywood discussed the matter of agricultural development and the ideas of Cottrell-Dormer with the people of Wagawaga and surrounds. Despite the difficulties surrounding MBDC, he found a people who remained determined to better their living standards. They advised Gaywood of their willingness to move towards commercial farming and to work in closer synergy with the administration. Gaywood reaffirmed Dormer's new approach and how it was 'an integral part of the general effort of the administration on their behalf'.[55]

The most revolutionary aspect, one which attracted both universal interest and support, was the establishment of Village Women's Committees, undoubtedly facilitated by the influence of Kwato. The Kwato doctrine of acculturation and its liberal education emboldened many village women to become leaders in their community and feel comfortable working closely with the Australian Administration. Women like Alice Wedega understood Western economic demands and had the tools and confidence to mediate between the administration and local villagers. Furthermore, the influence of the Kwato Mission and Indigenous elite normalised the practice of village women participating in an external communal venture such as the

---

51 Kim Godbold, 'Didiman: Australian Agricultural Extension Officers in the Territory of Papua and New Guinea, 1945–75' (PhD thesis, Queensland University of Technology, 2010), 82.
52 Healy, 'Native administration', 656.
53 Cottrell-Dormer, 'The Village Committee organisation', 3.
54 Healy, 'Native administration', 658.
55 H Gaywood, Report 2 of 1954/55, p. 3.

MBDC or Village Women's Committees. This was not the case in many parts of the Territory. Kwato-educated Anne Dickson-Waiko has written about the gendered ideology of the colonial state, and how most village women had little or no contact with the government: they 'remained independent throughout the colonial era because they subsisted beyond the pale of developing colonial enclaves', whereas, in areas where Kwato had a strong presence, the impact of colonialism was significant because it actively engaged with women.[56]

Cottrell-Dormer reasoned that since so much of agricultural work was done by Indigenous women it would seem folly not to include them. He believed:

> it filled a serious gap in the mass education of local people and provided a valuable medium for the work of social welfare and further, an entrée for DASF into the activities of women in village communities.

Figure 8.2: Alice Wedega talking with girl guides in 1958.
Source: NAA, A1200, L27346, item 7572885.

---

56 Anne Dickson-Waiko, 'Women, nation and decolonisation in Papua New Guinea', *Journal of Pacific History* 48 (2013): 179–80, doi.org/10.1080/00223344.2013.802844.

Cottrell-Dormer employed Alice Wedega as a part-time field worker and in his 1959 speech described Wedega as:

> a member of staff of Kwato Mission, and a Papuan who is widely travelled, has an excellent knowledge of English and is dedicated to the advancement of native women … Her task will be to make patrols and help the Women's Committees to understand their functions and duties and also to assist in their training.[57]

In her book, *Listen My Country*, Alice Wedega reflected on her experience working with Cottrell-Dormer. She explained that after travelling around the district it became evident to Cottrell-Dormer 'that the women were better gardeners than the men, so he came to Kwato to ask if some of the women there could go and help him'. Over a period of two and a half years they visited 100 villages, spending up to one week in each village. Cottrell-Dormer would call the men together and introduce new farming techniques and crops:

> He would then form a committee at each village which would meet every three months to discuss results and find out what else they needed to know from the Agricultural Department. Mr. Cottrell-Dormer continuously travelled from village-to-village, meeting members of the committee and observing how they were progressing. While this was going on with the men, Penipeni [another woman employed] and I would call the village women together, get to know them and find out what their problems were.[58]

According to Cottrell-Dormer, the fundamental objective of the Women's Committee was to provide better opportunities for the 'coming generation', which he interpreted as 'improving the environment in which they [were] reared'. While Cottrell-Dormer had the sense to work with women who the people knew and trusted, it was a pity he did not allow them to know more of the introduced methods of agriculture and crops. Some of the activities the committees were encouraged to undertake included curtains and shelving in their homes, village latrines, organising infant welfare mornings, operating village bakeries and running handcraft schools for children.[59] It appears that despite a recognition by Cottrell-Dormer that women were better farmers, they were not directly instructed in new agricultural practices.

---

57 Cottrell-Dormer, 'The Village Committee organisation', 3–4, 7, 9, 15.
58 Wedega, *Listen my country*, 81–82.
59 Cottrell-Dormer, 'The Village Committee organisation', 20–21.

In April 1957 Agricultural Committees began forming local associations, entirely of their own volition, to collect money, which was used, for instance, to establish communal copra driers. This Indigenous resourcefulness was in effect overtaking the role of cooperatives and LGCs, and according to Healy, 'tended to alarm the Native Affairs department and to worry Cottrell-Dormer'. Moreover, the committees/associations spread at a much faster rate than councils, and this meant they became a substitute for local government in many areas.[60] For example, by late 1959 the administration was reporting that there were over 300 Village Women's Committees in the Milne Bay District, although it should be noted the committees also worked with the Milne Bay council to produce a booklet printed in English and local vernaculars on the aims and work of the Women's Committees.[61]

While tensions and a lack of coordination between administration departments persisted into the 1960s, this was not the case in Milne Bay, where there was widespread recognition in the government of the success of Cottrell-Dormer's program. The administrator, Donald Cleland, on a tour of the district in 1960, directed that every departmental representative in the district was to integrate their plans with the overall rural extension program. He instituted monthly meetings of senior officers to be held in the district and told the DC that local council expansion must accelerate to keep up and be coordinated with the Village Agricultural Committees. Both Belshaw and Healy are critical of administrative implementation of government development programs, especially the lack of coordinated strategy. In contrast, they are full of praise for the village committees, the first attempt by the administration to formalise a local mechanism of the interdepartmental committee type.[62] Cottrell-Dormer's passion and capacity to implement a coordinated approach to agricultural extension work, coupled with the unique local conditions created by the KEA, and the drive of Milne Bay people to better their living standards, forced the administration to adjust their policy and implementation strategy. This would be a noteworthy achievement on its own, but this was the second time within a decade that the people and circumstances existing in Milne Bay had forced a change of government development strategy.

---

60 Healy, 'Native administration', 660.
61 Department of External Territories (DET), 'Report on advancement of women', 19 November 1959, p. 3, Education and Advancement of Native Women policy, A452 [1960/8272], NAA.
62 Healy, 'Native Administration', p. 663.

Conclusion

This case study of Milne Bay in the postwar period has demonstrated how a colonised people, despite being forced to operate within the strictures of their colonial guardian, were able to demonstrate a significant measure of Indigenous socioeconomic autonomy. Cecil Abel and an Indigenous elite, graduates from the Kwato Mission, created a new sense of purpose and were able to draw extensive support from villages around the Bay, which resulted in an extraordinary array of Indigenous enterprises. However, instead of harnessing this energy, the administration acted in a manner which indicated they feared being usurped. The most striking action was Murray's decision not to contact the NAS, which had been provisioned to introduce local councils to the Territory.

The administration's strategy in Milne Bay was hampered by critically low staff levels and a lack of planning. When comparing the Milne Bay experience with the theoretical expectations of the Hasluck Development Pyramid, the assumptions of Australian colonial development practice become quite clear. Firstly, it is a perfect example of the government's universal gradualist strategy, one which actively discouraged the promotion of an Indigenous elite. Secondly, it was assumed the administration would be the dominant source of development impetus and were infused with sufficient resources to establish and maintain programs. This scenario, in which local people took the initiative and the administration struggled with inadequate resources to maintain development momentum, would also play out in two other case studies in this book: Sepik and New Hanover. The experience on the ground suggests that despite the positive 'New Deal' agenda informing policy, and the genuine efforts of many administration officers, the assumptions inherent in Australia's colonial development strategy favoured a containment strategy which bound the territories to Australia and limited the raising of living standards.

CASE STUDY: MAPRIK

9

Sepik: 'If You See a European, Don't Call Him Masta'

> I held a meeting only. I did not start anything then. I took the frond of a coconut. I stood up and I broke the twigs one at a time. I said, look, if you don't come together this will happen ... You, yourselves must come together. If you see a European, don't call him masta. It doesn't matter about the colour of his skin, black or white. All must come together.
>
> Pita Simogun, 1947 meeting at Makupini with village leaders[1]

The introduction of cash cropping and business enterprises to the Sepik District in the postwar period was not at the behest of the Australian Government. Instead, it was through the actions of local people who commenced planting and establishing commercial operations along the coast from late 1947. Indigenous diplomatic links and ex-police networks passed the knowledge of these new ideas to the inland people of the Maprik subdistrict, who travelled to the coast to either work and stay, or to bring back business knowledge to their home village.

This chapter explores the early postwar period, 1945–52, and particularly the dissonance between the entrepreneurial activity of Sepik Indigenous leadership and an Australian Administration understaffed and overwhelmed with postwar reconstruction, pacification and war damage compensation. Primarily through the energy, action, vision and networks of Pita Simogun,

---

1   Pita Simogun, 5 December 1972, cited in Bryant Allen, 'Information flow and innovation diffusion in the East Sepik District, Papua New Guinea' (PhD thesis, The Australian National University, 1976), 425.

PREPARING A NATION?

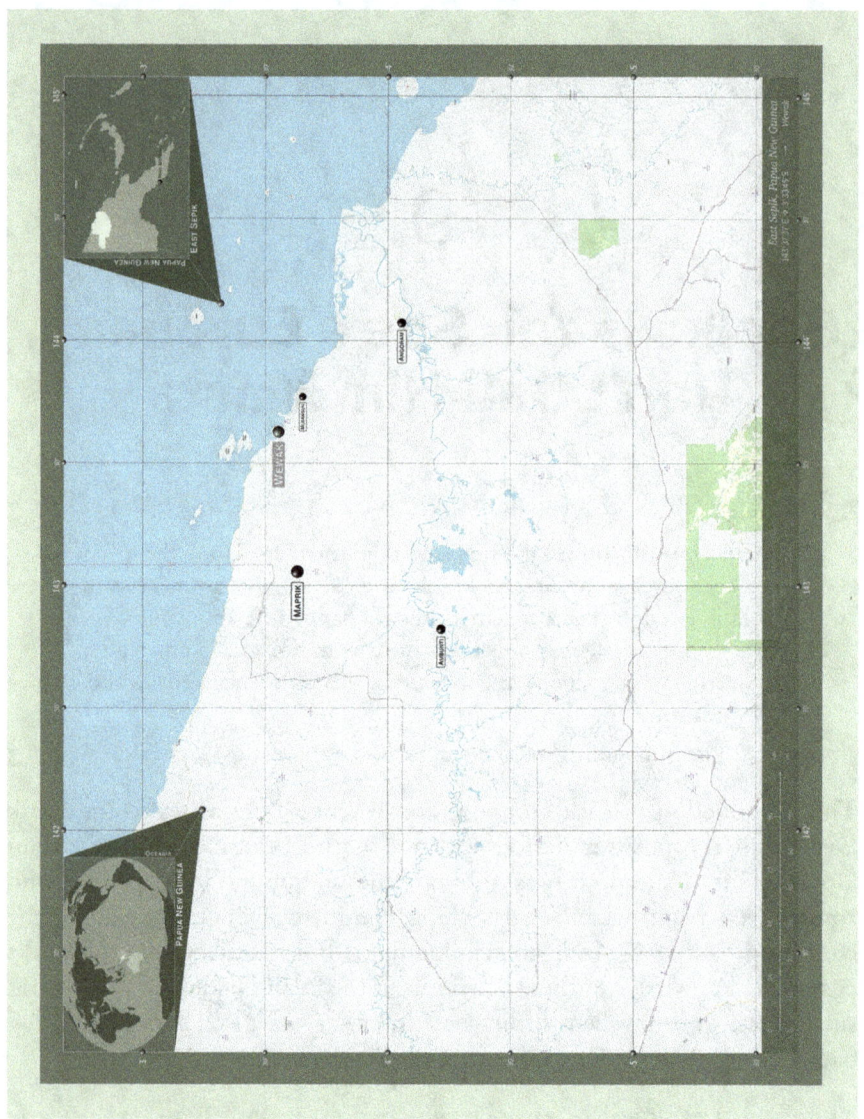

Map 9.1: East Sepik Province.
Source: Shutterstock.

local people were able to move ahead of the administration in the introduction of cash cropping and business opportunities. Interestingly, the attitude of the administration to Simogun's efforts as a leader of an autonomous Indigenous enterprise differed significantly from that experienced in Chimbu, Milne Bay and New Hanover. Much of this can be attributed to his non-confrontational messaging: work together, become independent and self-improve. Simogun was one of only a few Indigenous leaders explicitly supported and promoted as an 'elite' by the Australian Government, and in this way, was able to garner assistance from the administration for his rice cropping and transport business. While this business proved quite successful, particularly in the early years, it was more important as an inspiration for both local coastal people and those from the inland foothills of the Maprik subdistrict.

The Sepik case study describes a contested colonial space of leadership, vision, energy and mismanagement. Consistent with Milne Bay, it was local leadership and a non-confrontational approach which stimulated development practice in the region. On the coast where Simogun resided, government support for Indigenous community ventures was quite substantial and fitted within an early development phase of government strategy. However, inland, despite being inspired and approved by Simogun, government officers were sceptical of the autonomous activities of local people. It suggests an attitude in parallel with those displayed in the other case studies, where there was limited support for any activities on the ground unless established by the coloniser. While the 'New Deal' and, later, Territories Minister Paul Hasluck espoused a pro-Indigenous agenda, it was framed around a compliant local population and fitted with a strategy of containment and gradualist progression.

1945–51: Autonomous Indigenous activity and an overwhelmed administration

During the colonial period, the Sepik District was one of the largest and most densely inhabited in the Territory, covering an area of 78,200 square kilometres, and in 1954 had an enumerated population in excess of 250,000.[2] At this time the district consisted of four subdistricts: Wewak

---

2 In July 1966, the Sepik District was split into East and West Sepik Districts. Maprik subdistrict now lies in the former. D Cleland, 'Administrator's tour of the Sepik District October 7th to 16th, 1954', Papers of Sir Donald Cleland, MS9600/12/1, National Library of Australia (NLA).

(coast); Aitape (west); Maprik (inland foothills) and Angoram (Sepik River).[3] This case study largely focusses on the most heavily populated subdistrict, Maprik, which, until World War II (WWII), had very little contact with the Australian Administration.[4] The region was effectively cut off by the Prince Alexander Ranges and Torricelli mountains which rise sharply from the coast, the mountains covered in a thick forest, with sudden sharp rises and narrow ridges that made the country difficult to travel. Inland, in the Maprik subdistrict, the land falls away to rolling hills and kunai grasslands leading southwards to the Sepik River.[5]

From an Australian perspective, due to a poorly handled transfer from military to civil management, the provisional administration was immediately on the back foot regarding operations along the north coast of New Guinea. An Army Liaison group, chaired by Kenneth McMullen of District Services, commenced duties with the First Australian Army Headquarters at Lae on 14 January 1946. They were charged with the responsibility of arranging the handover of Madang, Morobe and Sepik from the army to the provisional administration on 18 February 1946 on a walk-in-walk-out basis. Given the immensity of the task, it is little wonder that six weeks proved insufficient. McMullen criticised the army's 'complete lack of interest', which left Indigenous labourers stranded on the cancellation of their contracts and stretched administration personnel to a point where positions were not filled. There were limited commercial firms operating in the area and minimal food resources due to the destruction of village gardens. The administration was stretched, and in some places, left officers stranded as general storekeepers for the entire population.[6]

The effect of the war on local people, in terms of the physical and emotional toll, was profound. The Japanese landed at Wewak in December 1942, establishing themselves along the coast in 1943, but did not enter the Maprik hinterland until mid-1944.[7] While early relations between the Japanese and Sepiks appeared friendly on the coast, by the time the Japanese had been pushed inland by the Australians their actions betrayed

---

3   Department of District Services and Native Affairs (DDSNA), *Annual Report for the year ending June 1954* (Port Moresby: Government Printer, 1954), 20.
4   In June 1966 over one third of the Sepik District population lived in the Maprik subdistrict. Richard T Shand and W Straatmans, *Transition from subsistence: Cash crop development in Papua New Guinea* (Port Moresby: The Australian National University, 1974), 92.
5   KC Jones, Report 2 of 1949/50, p. 1, East Sepik District, Wewak, 1949–1953, National Archives of Papua New Guinea (PNGA).
6   Liaison Group Report, August 1946, Papers of Ian Downs, MS8254/20/45, NLA.
7   Allen, 'Information flow', 85.

the increasingly desperate circumstances they faced.[8] Both Richard Curtain and Bryant Allen have described how the Maprik people were trapped by the savage military action of both the Australian and Japanese troops.[9] The consequence for these people was total physical devastation of their surroundings. For instance, in late October 1945, approximately a month after the Japanese had been cleared from the area, Lieutenant Grainger Morris described how, during the occupation, villagers had moved out of the area, but 'now they have returned to find their gardens eaten out by the Japs … all livestock has gone, a few wild pigs in the bush are their only meat supply'.[10] Other patrols noted how Australian bombing raids had not only endangered Sepik lives, but destroyed villages and gardens throughout the subdistrict.[11]

The Japanese forced people, in ruthless style, to move away from villages into scattered hamlets and away from their food source. James Rogers wrote of Japanese troops roaming the countryside in bands of approximately 40 men, living off the local gardens and livestock. In the case of a Sepik refusing to supply pigs,

> they simply shot the owner of the pig and went their way. Any village who was successful in hiding its pigs from these troops had their houses and gardens destroyed by the frustrated Japanese.[12]

Furthermore, not only had villagers witnessed the Australians overrun by the Japanese but were also victims of the Australian Army's harsh recruitment measures to 'gain as many labourers as possible from each village'. While officer Geoff Herkes reassured the local population that 'the days of compulsory recruiting are over', he continued to struggle in his endeavours to reassert administrative control over the subdistrict.[13] The end result was a disparate and frightened local population, Rogers noted, 'the natives have now developed the practice of fleeing into the jungle whenever anyone who is not a native is sighted'.[14]

---

8   Michael Somare, *Sana: An autobiography of Michael Somare* (Port Moresby: Niugini Press, 1975), 1–3; Richard Curtain, 'Dual dependence and Sepik labour migration' (PhD thesis, The Australian National University, 1980), 198–200.
9   Allen, 'Information flow', 85–89; Curtain, 'Dual dependence', 197–201.
10 G Morris, Report 3 of 1945/46, p. 1, East Sepik District, Maprik, 1945–1953, PNGA.
11 MJ Denehy, Report 2 of 1949/50, p. 2, East Sepik District, Yangoru, 1949–1953, PNGA.
12 JM Rogers, Report 2 of 1947/48, p. 5, East Sepik District, Maprik, 1945–1953, PNGA.
13 G Herkes, Report 2 of 1945/46, p. 5, East Sepik District, Maprik, 1945–1953, PNGA.
14 JM Rogers, Report 1 of 1947/48, p. 6, East Sepik District, Maprik, 1945–1953, PNGA.

On the other hand, those Sepiks who had helped or supported the Australian forces were often quick to demand compensation. John Wakeford, in an April 1946 patrol, complained of returned soldiers 'making trouble against the administration; their attitude being that, but for them, we should have lost the fight'.[15] By March 1948, Rogers was warning of an impending avalanche of war damage claims. And despite the enormous strain it put on officers in terms of workload, they realised how important such a program was in restoring villagers' faith in the administration. Herkes reiterated this, reporting on the great numbers of claims submitted and how the 'people were therefore greatly impressed to learn that the government intended to replace or recompensate their losses'.[16] Although as Wakeford explained, in those parts of the subdistrict with no former labourers, the concept of money was foreign, and as such, the gesture was wasted. In these situations, it was payment in kind that the local people wanted, which only non-existent trade stores could alleviate.[17]

Sepik District Officer (DO) Horace Niall wrote repeatedly to administration headquarters throughout this period to express his dismay at the proportion of an officer's time taken up by investigating war damage claims. For instance, in May 1948 he complained that Rogers's March patrol included an investigation of 1,537 war damage claims, remarking this was in addition to:

> normal routine patrol work amongst the people who are timid and barely under control [which] requires great tact and patience as well as hours of work in the hot, humid Sepik Plain.[18]

To Niall, the administration would not be able to devote sufficient time to postwar development and civic rule until all war damage investigations were complete.[19] Fortunately, Niall's fears were not realised, as war compensation claims were not settled until August 1954, and by this stage, the Australian Government was supporting road-building and agricultural development programs throughout the subdistrict.[20]

---

15   JE Wakeford, Report 1 of 1945/46, p. 8, East Sepik District, Maprik, 1945–1953, PNGA.
16   Herkes, Report 2 of 1945/46, p. 8.
17   Wakeford, Report 1 of 1946/47, p. 12.
18   HR Niall to DDSNA Director, 19 July 1948 and 22 May 1948, East Sepik District, Maprik, 1945–1953, PNGA.
19   Niall to DDSNA Director, 19 July 1948 and 22 May 1948.
20   Finalisation of the war damage compensation scheme occurred in August 1954. FV Reitano to Wewak District Commissioner (DC), 4 August 1954, East Sepik District, Maprik, 1953–1956, PNGA.

Figure 9.1: Mahuru Rarua-Rarua in 1959 addressing the Papua and New Guinea Legislative Council.
Note: Seated to his left is the New Guinean Member, Pita Simogun.
Source: National Archives of Australia (NAA), A1200, L31454, item 7803998.

Although this case study is primarily focussed on the experience of Maprik people in the postwar period, the genesis for much of what happened originated in the coastal village of Dagua, the home of Indigenous leader, Pita Simogun.[21] In 1947 Simogun returned home for a short break from police duties, setting in motion an economic movement of such dynamism that it quickly spread along the Sepik coast and into the adjoining Maprik subdistrict. Simogun worked on a German plantation as a young man before joining the 'Native' Constabulary. During the war, he volunteered for special duty with an intelligence unit on enemy-occupied West New Britain and was eventually awarded the British Empire Medal (BEM) for outstanding service. He visited Australia twice during the war, once for military training, and the other to observe smallholder farming techniques.[22]

---

21   August Ibrum Kituai, *My gun, my brother: The world of the Papua New Guinea Colonial Police, 1920–1960* (Honolulu: University of Hawai'i Press, 1998), 195–99.
22   'This New Guinea native leader helped Australia against Japs—awarded BEM', *The Courier-Mail*, 15 February 1954, 2.

This latter visit proved instrumental in the formation of Simogun's village-based agricultural economic plans. For instance, Simogun told Bryant Allen how he would analyse production techniques:

> In my head, I worked out what was happening. I thought, I think he does it like this and this and so on. You see? I would see a man planting wheat, or rice, or sugar cane, or growing cattle. My eyes would see it and then I would hear just a little of his talk and together I could see how they were doing it.[23]

By 1946 he was a sergeant-major of police at Aitape (Sepik), the highest rank to which a Papuan or New Guinean could rise at that time.[24] Simogun was a tall, charismatic, powerfully built man, eloquent and courteous in a quiet confident manner, equally at home in a Sepik village or at a European official function.

Simogun is more widely known as one of the three Indigenous leaders first appointed to the Territory of Papua New Guinea (TPNG) Legislative Council in November 1951. The other two Indigenous members were Merari Dickson and Aisoli Salin. Simogun was an active participant of the Legislative Council despite the fact he could neither read nor write English, and who, apart from his village dialect, spoke only Pidgin.[25] However, for the purposes of this chapter it was Simogun, through persuasion and personal eloquence, who became the driving force for the establishment of cash cropping, road development and civic responsibility along the coast and into the Maprik subdistrict.[26] Utilising his police ties, Simogun met with former and serving policemen, including future village leaders such as Kokomo, Anton, Augen and Pita Tamindei, to outline his vision to take advantage of war damage compensation and establish Indigenous business enterprises.[27] Ira Bashkow described the attitude and operation of Simogun's close followers as resembling a quasi-military organisation.[28] Bill Crellin

---

23   Allen, 'Information flow', 431.
24   'This New Guinea native leader helped Australia'.
25   J Hammond, 'Three "Fuzzy-Wuzzies" join Legislative Council: Natives help to make New Guinea's laws', *The Daily Telegraph*, 2 January 1952, 8.
26   'This New Guinea native leader helped Australia'.
27   Kokomo was the first president of the Dreikikir Local Government Council (LGC). In 1968 he was elected to the House Assembly. Augen was the long-term president of the Supari Rural Progress Society (RPS). Pita Tamindei was president of Maprik LGC (1958) and 1964 House Assembly Member. Allen, 'Information flow', 340, 425, 429; TPNG, *The members of the House Assembly, 1964* (Port Moresby: Department of Information and Extension Services, 1964), 13.
28   Ira Bashkow, 'The cultural and historical openness of Bernard Narokobi's "Melanesian Way"', *Journal of Pacific History* 55, no. 2 (2020): 194, doi.org/10.1080/00223344.2020.1759410.

noted the immediate effect of Simogun's arrival where, for the first time, the 'many hamlets banded together to facilitate the growing of rice, a new crop, and to these people, a new idea of producing something primarily for a cash return'.[29] Simogun told Bryant Allen that he simply 'brought them together and spoke about getting some people to come here and help us. I told them. You can plant coconuts, or whatever you like, work the soil'. During this visit Simogun spoke with people from his local community about utilising war damage compensation, asking for £5 each. In this way he raised £1,500 which he put:

> in a metal cabinet which had belonged to the Japanese, locked it up and gave the key to my wife. I went off to Manus and later Rabaul. I came back in 1949.[30]

Simogun's development strategy was based on two core ingredients. One, village-based commercial activities aimed at improving living standards, and two, for local people to work together, not in opposition or subservience to the Europeans, but as a cohesive group working alongside the Europeans. Speaking in the Legislative Council in late 1952, Simogun reiterated his approach, pointing out that many of his fellow Sepiks were anxious to play a part in the agricultural development of their country, and if voluntary efforts did not have the desired effect 'a little gentle persuasion should be used'. In fact, he stated it plainly: 'enforcement would be of real and lasting benefit to my people', and the administration should proactively assist in this agricultural development; effectively deciding what should be planted and where and seeing that projects were carried out.[31]

Simogun and the Dagua farmers established a community development enterprise, the *Dagua Kompani*, with minimal support from the government. Rice cultivation started in 1948 in the Wokinara hills, six kilometres south of Dagua.[32] Approximately 3,000 villagers were involved in the project by June 1950; funds raised purchased agricultural equipment, tools and processing machinery.[33] Agricultural Officer Bob Pulsford explained how initial funds were primarily raised through war damage compensation

---

29 W Crellin, Report 5 of 1953/54, p. 2, East Sepik District, Wewak, 1953–56, PNGA.
30 Allen, 'Information flow', 425.
31 'Native development—and native recruiters', *Pacific Islands Monthly* 23, no. 4 (November 1952): 108.
32 Oskar Spate, 'The rice problem in New Guinea', *South Pacific* 7 (1953): 735.
33 Department of External Territories (DET), *Report to the General Assembly of the United Nations on the administration of the Territory of New Guinea: From 1st of July, 1949 to 30th June, 1950* (Canberra: Government Printer, 1950), 29–30.

but as momentum grew, a substantial contribution came from police and labourers, some of whom continued to work in Rabaul and Port Moresby.[34] Initially, the villagers planted rice, and then peanuts, cocoa and coconuts. Simogun appealed to District Commissioner (DC) Niall for a cooperative society but was rejected due to a lack of funds; the Co-operative Registrar, John Millar, instead suggested a Rural Progress Society (RPS).[35]

Table 9.1: 1957 Sepik rural progress societies.

Society	Members	Capital	Rice — paddy (lbs)	Peanuts (lbs)
Wosera (Maprik SD)	919	$2,620	21,798	–
Mitpim (Maprik SD)	1,418	$4,780	90,686	1,957
Waigahum	1,600	$5,126	32,377	278
Supari (Maprik SD)	2,649	$7,225	64,221	2,240
Bauimo (Maprik SD)	3,909	$11,519	20,000	–
Kanum	1,008	$14,387	20,656	47,830
Kreer	483	$8,131	–	58,304
Dagua	637	$10,468	24,972	30,070
Total	**12,623**	**$64,256**	**122.6 ton**	**62.8 ton**

Note: Figures in 1969 Australian dollars.
Source: Department of Agriculture, Stock and Fisheries (DASF), *Agricultural extension work and advancement of native agriculture: Report for the year ending 30 June 1957*, p. 18, Advancement in Native Agriculture 1950–9, A452 [1960/8266], NAA.

Kim Godbold, in her comprehensive history of agricultural extension services, wrote of the Department of Agriculture, Stock and Fisheries (DASF) Director William Cottrell-Dormer's ambition for an RPS as a simplified first step towards an eventual fully fledged cooperative society. The RPS was registered under the Native Economic Development Ordinance and was expected to submit trading accounts and balance sheets to the Co-operative Registrar on a six-monthly basis. In practice, these returns were prepared by the agricultural officer.[36] Dormer proposed a strategy which would encourage Papuans and New Guineans 'towards self-reliance in a changing world'. He argued such a scheme would provide the methods and techniques to exploit 'their natural resources to better advantage and

---

34 RL Pulsford, 'Rice in the Sepik OIC Rural Progress Societies Sepik', 3 June 1952, p. 10, Development of Territories: Agricultural village-rice production 1952–7, A518 [AM927/4], National Archives of Australia (NAA).
35 Allen, 'Information flow', 426.
36 Kim Godbold, 'Didiman: Australian Agricultural Extension Officers in the Territory of Papua and New Guinea, 1945–75' (PhD thesis, Queensland University of Technology, 2010), 178–80.

by these means to improve their living standard'.[37] And, like cooperative societies, the concept was a means for local people to contribute capital and purchase relatively expensive equipment such as village rice-milling units.[38] Both cooperatives and progress societies were agroeconomic community development tools expected to introduce and stimulate economic activity beyond a local community. These ventures fit perfectly within the Australian Government's gradualist development strategy as outlined by the Hasluck Development Pyramid.

The RPS movement proved particularly successful in both Sepik and Madang and became the central community development scheme for the administration in these two districts. For instance, in 1950 there were three societies with a total capital of less than £1,000. By 1954 this had grown to 31 societies with a total capital of £23,000, and in 1953 alone, more than 339 villages came under a society's influence in Sepik and Madang. By 1952, the Dagua RPS (formerly *Dagua Kompani*) was at its height in terms of commercial activity, operating a motor transport business, a commercial sawmill and growing cash crops such as rice and peanuts.[39] Simogun had begun working closely with Pulsford, who provided technical and business management in support of the RPS.[40] Pulsford explained how they would work together to overcome 'stubborn resistance manifest in active non-cooperation', encouraging the participation of village leaders in the village-based development message. Simogun's attitude of working with the administration was matched by Pulsford who regarded Simogun's ability to 'take a wide view' an invaluable aid in the expansion of cash cropping through the Sepik District.[41]

Profits were ploughed back into community ventures, including major roadworks such as the Dagua–Wewak Road, a Catholic church and a residential school staffed by a European teacher from the Education

---

37 W Cottrell-Dormer, 'Native Rural Progress Societies—an experiment in social and economic development', 17 September 1949, Address by Director DASF to Conference of District Offices, CP637/1 [30], NAA.
38 'Native agricultural extension, training and education', May 1955, p. 6, Advancement of Native Agriculture 1954–6, A518 [C2/1/1], NAA.
39 The Dagua RPS would eventually collapse. According to Simogun it was because villagers sold their cash crops to European traders for higher prices than offered by the RPS. CG Littler, Report 3 of 1955/56, p. 3, East Sepik District, Wewak, 1953–56, PNGA.
40 Allen, 'Information flow', 426.
41 RL Pulsford, 'Rice in the Sepik', 3 June 1952, p. 4, Development of Territories: Agricultural village-rice production 1952–7, A518 [AM927/4], NAA.

Department.⁴² The society's success was promoted throughout the Territory. The *Papuan Times* reported the innovative method used to raise funds for the new school: instead of selling their rice crops 'they fed all the people who came from different villages to help with the building'. The society also purchased 'a launch built at the Kwato mission [Wagawaga] workshops to transport rice for processing'.⁴³ William Stokes described Simogun as an embryo businessman, one who had:

> stirred his people out of their post-war lethargy (induced by free food and War Damage payments) by making them build better villages and endeavouring to eradicate the many petty squabbles between the various hamlets.⁴⁴

Bill Crellin, in a 1953 report, explained the particularities of the Dagua system, one which would spread throughout the adjoining Maprik subdistrict. Villages would band together, contributing their 'labour on a week and week about basis, that is, a week in the rice fields at Dagua, and then a week in their own private gardens'. Everyone, bar a few elderly people, participated in the rice venture. Each village had an individual plot within the main Society Garden, the produce from this plot credited to the group which worked it.⁴⁵ During this period, villagers approached Assistant District Officer (ADO) Fred Reitano for the reinstatement of the unofficial village councils under the leadership of Simogun. Despite the support of the ADO, it was explained 'that this was not administration policy and that in any case Simogun did not want the position'.⁴⁶ In local matters, Simogun was not interested in political leadership; his focus was a mix of community action and business opportunities. On a personal level, his business interests extended to a store at Wewak, a small fleet of trucks and the sanitary disposal service for the town.⁴⁷ In terms of community leadership, Simogun was most concerned with the autonomous participation of Sepiks in their social, political and economic future.

---

42 'This New Guinea native leader helped Australia'.
43 'Dagua Village built new school', *Papuan Times*, 24 April 1953, p. 1.
44 W Stokes, Report 1 of 1950/51, p. 5, East Sepik District, Wewak, 1949–1953, PNGA.
45 Crellin, Report 5 of 1953/54, p. 2.
46 FV Reitano, Report 1 of 1951/52, pp. 1–2, East Sepik District, Wewak, 1949–1953, PNGA.
47 Spate, 'The rice problem in New Guinea', 735.

9. SEPIK

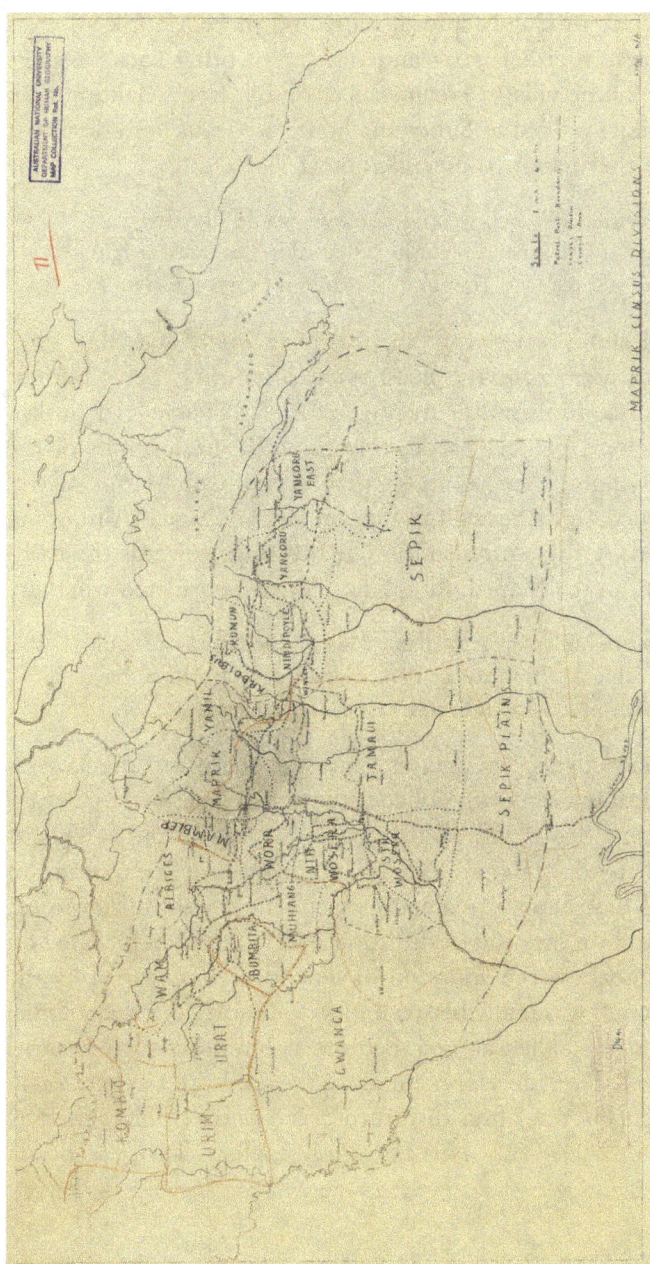

Map 9.2: Detailed map of East Sepik province.
Notes: The Sepik District capital (Wewak) is located on the coast. Villagers from the Maprik subdistrict would cross the Prince Alexander Range to work or cash crop in the environs of Wewak and to the north at Dagua or transfer to New Britain.
Source: Shutterstock (Royalty Free Stock illustration 2280761767).

As news of the success in Dagua spread, more and more Maprik villagers travelled to the coast to either work and stay, or to bring back business knowledge to their home village. For instance, Kesbik from Makupmanip village (near Dreikikir) walked to Simogun's home in Dagua, and despite it being the first time they had met, described how:

> we talked, they talked. Then we said, 'Yes, we would like this stuff. So, we will take it and go and plant it'. They said, 'Oh that's alright. You take some and plant it. You do it like this and this and so on'.[48]

Stokes, patrolling Kaboibus (west of Yangoru) in February and May 1951 explained how returnees from the coast were promoting new business concepts and a pro-administration message around hygiene and health. He described how local people, particularly those in the foothills of the Prince Alexander Ranges, were planting small experimental crops of rice and peanuts obtained from Simogun's rice project at Dagua. Almost no support was offered by the administration at this stage towards the cash-cropping movement in the Maprik subdistrict. Stokes considered whether:

> if some cheap rice hullers were available for sale, [perhaps] rice could become a valuable addition to the diet. Already several natives have approached me to buy rice hullers for them.[49]

The transfer of knowledge, of new ideas, from the coast into the Maprik hinterland was a combination of ex-police networks, as described by Bryant Allen, Ron May and Scott MacWilliam, among others, and language, cultural and familial ties.[50] Bryant Allen's comprehensive 1976 study of Dreikikir region of East Sepik explained how the movement of new ideas had a profound effect on innovation diffusion. Allen's research focussed on information flow and how the adoption of new ideas was shaped by the manner of how contact was made between New Guineans and the colonial power. This relationship, Allen argued, became a communication channel for the dissemination of new development ideas; the result, an acceleration in the desire for change, but one often 'disturbed or inadequate' due to the way subjugated people perceived it.[51] This case study explores this contention,

---

48   Allen, 'Information flow', 383.
49   Stokes, Report 6 of 1950/51, pp. 1-3; Report 3 of 1950/51, pp. 2-4, East Sepik District, Yangoru, 1949-1953, PNGA.
50   Scott MacWilliam, *Securing village life: Development in late colonial Papua New Guinea* (Canberra: ANU Press, 2013), 69–70, doi.org/10.22459/SVL.05.2013; Allen, 'Information flow', 188–89; Ron May, *State and society in Papua New Guinea* (Canberra: ANU ePress, 2004), 177.
51   Allen, 'Information flow', 6.

specifically how the 'messaging' from both the colonial administration and Indigenous leadership shaped the actions and attitude of the Maprik population to economic development.

John Terrell described the partitioning of language in the Sepik District as:

> perhaps more extreme than anywhere else in the world. People in neighbouring communities may speak not only mutually unintelligible languages but also languages that are so markedly different from one another that they are assigned by linguists to entirely separate language families.[52]

For instance, in the Maprik subdistrict, there are 13 language groups, the largest the Abelam, centred on the Maprik township and environs with a population in 1974 of approximately 30,000 people.[53] Adjoining this group to the north-west are the Mountain and Southern Arapesh language groups who speak the But (or Yamil) language, widely regarded by the administration 'as one of the most complicated of native speeches'. This language group extended over a very wide area, from the coast at Dagua into the Sepik plains at Yamil (south of Maprik).[54] Bernard Narokobi, the lawyer, scholar, politician and Arapesh man wrote of diplomatic links or 'link people' who would trade along the coast and with inland people. Narokobi explained how 'new skills and knowledge often passed from one community to another along these channels'.[55] Greg Bablis suggests Narokobi's explanation could apply in explaining how Simogun's business message expanded across the mountain ranges and into the Maprik subdistrict. Bablis argues:

> when Simogun started gathering local support in the 50s and 60s for the people themselves to build the 'road', the Westcoast Highway that now bears his name, his reasons and explanations would have resonated with people.[56]

---

52 John R Terrell, 'Language, ethnicity, and historic material culture on the Sepik coast', *Fieldiana Anthropology* 42 (2011): 16, doi.org/10.3158/0071-4739-42.1.5.
53 William R Stent, 'An interpretation of a cargo cult', *Oceania* 47, no. 3 (1977): 204, doi.org/10.1002/j.1834-4461.1977.tb01287.x.
54 Language spoken by both Simogun and Augen. Zweck, Report 3 of 1949/50, pp. 5–6, East Sepik District, Maprik, 1945–1953, PNGA.
55 Bernard Narokobi, *Lo bilong yumi yet = law and custom in Melanesia*, ed. Ron Crocombe, John May and Paul Roche (Goroka: University of the South Pacific, 1989), 28–29.
56 Personal email communication with Greg Bablis 30 May 2020.

Ira Bashkow expands on this point, arguing the road was a recognition of the distinctive way Arapesh people regarded particular 'passageways as not only practical travel conduits but also as axes of war alliances, identity symbols, political channels, and constellations of highly valued exchange and social relationships'.[57]

The rapid spread of new agricultural practice from the coast into the Maprik subdistrict was not a government-sanctioned program. Geographer and adviser to Minister Hasluck, Oskar Spate, warned of an impending resource problem in the Maprik subdistrict due to the 'result of propaganda from Simogun's circle'. He pondered how the agricultural department would cope with the necessary extension work given the area's agricultural station, Bainyik, was perpetually understaffed. Spate described a chain reaction which could be difficult to control:

> from contacts in Port Moresby, Dagua learns of the Mekeo; Yangoru learns from Dagua; and how long will it be before areas remote from Yangoru clamour in their turn for help which cannot be given without overstraining the resources, in men and material, of the Administration? Yet the ideas that rice is a good thing to grow, that it will bring money, that it can be grown by machines with little effort, that it is the function of government to supply machines, are spreading rapidly. Somehow the Administration must come to terms with this new movement, if it is not to fall back into frustration.[58]

Conclusion

The circumstances faced by the colonial administration in the Maprik subdistrict in the early 1950s illustrate both the willingness of New Guineans to engage in new agricultural development concepts and how underprepared the government was on the ground to either control or promote such drive. On the one hand, it is clear Sepik people were not opposed to, and would willingly engage with, the 'New Deal' and Hasluck village-based agroeconomic strategy. Pita Simogun's pro-administration conciliatory development message was readily accepted by villagers along the coast and inland and, like the people of Milne Bay, their activity was directed towards an improvement in their living standards. In this case study, the impetus for such ideas was an Indigenous group, led by Simogun who

---

57 Bashkow, 'Bernard Narokobi's "Melanesian Way"', 190.
58 Spate, 'The rice problem in New Guinea', 736.

had, as had policemen and ex-soldiers, witnessed new Western concepts of wealth, power and efficiency. Unlike in Milne Bay, the vision outlined by Simogun was acceptable on several fronts to the coloniser. Firstly, it was an agricultural village-based strategy, as outlined by the Hasluck Development Pyramid and the 'New Deal'. Secondly, Simogun was an acceptable Indigenous voice, respected by both local people and the coloniser: there was no threat to power dynamics in the villages.

However, as Spate warned, the administration was unprepared for the spread of these new agricultural development concepts. They were not in control of the messaging, and therefore could not easily put in place a strategy to establish and monitor a cash-cropping scheme. The Maprik subdistrict was woefully understaffed with poor roads and isolated communities; the government could not compete with the efficiency of the Arapesh communication networks. Chapter 10 continues the Sepik case study; it explores the government's reaction, and whether Spate's prediction of impending chaos and disappointment would be the predominant postwar experience for Maprik people.

10
Village Rice Development: Co-opting Indigenous Enterprise

In July 1951, the recently installed Minister of Territories, Paul Hasluck, on a visit to Sepik was inspired by expanding Indigenous cash cropping and directed the establishment of a government-sponsored village rice scheme. This program fitted with the Hasluck Development Pyramid; it was a form of interventionist and intentional community development which promoted the village economy. The stimulus for cash cropping and Indigenous business activity was, as described in Chapter 9, Pita Simogun and a group of former policemen who rapidly spread new agroeconomic ideas along the Sepik coast and inland to the Maprik subdistrict. The Territory Administration was not in control of the establishment and spread of economic development; instead, it was forced to react to the New Guinean initiative. The Sepik case study is an interesting example of the colonial government co-opting an initiative from New Guineans. The acceptance of an Indigenous autonomous venture by the coloniser was not the experience of Papuans or New Guineans from other districts. In this case, it was acceptable because the ideas stemmed from a non-confrontational, pro-administration Indigenous leader and was a scheme which aligned closely with the government's village-based gradualist program. Subsequently, the way economic development was introduced to Maprik would have a significant impact on the success, or not, of cash cropping in the subdistrict.

This chapter explains the genesis and ambition of the village rice scheme and how it aimed to strengthen and broaden community bonds by enabling Sepiks to participate in the modern economy. It was the government's attempt to formalise Indigenous-inspired cash cropping within the auspices of a colonial development program. While rice production was to be grown as a cash crop, it was not sold as an export crop; instead, it was for internal use as part of the administration's efforts to improve nutritional standards and create a viable economy. The introduction and implementation of the government scheme are explored in a case study of the Supari Rural Progress Society (RPS). Members of this society maintained strong links with the coast, and with Simogun in particular, and in this way, the chapter explores the 'messaging' from both the colonial administration and Indigenous leadership and how these shaped the actions and attitudes of the Maprik population towards economic development. By the end of the decade, local people, frustrated but determined, abandoned rice for coffee, in the hope of improving living standards and becoming economically self-sufficient.

The government reacts to Maprik cash cropping

The village rice scheme was expected to strengthen and broaden community bonds by focussing on socioeconomic development in the villages, and to enable Sepiks to participate in the modern economy. The scheme was reliant on agricultural extension officers; rice would improve subsistence and dietary levels while providing a basis for cash crop farming. Crucially, the initiative for rice growing and cash cropping was not from the government; instead, they were attempting to build upon an already expanding network of rice gardens spreading from the coast into the Maprik surroundings. At no stage during the almost decade this scheme operated would the government overcome this handicap; they could never fully control the narrative, problems of insufficient planning, poor rice selection, lack of resources and the cognisant frustration of local people, due primarily to the origin of the rice-growing concept.

10. VILLAGE RICE DEVELOPMENT

Figure 10.1: Clearing land for dry rice in 1952 in the Sepik District.
Source: Photograph taken by RN Cochrane (agricultural department). National Archives of Australia (NAA), A1200, L20159, item 7527661.

Within three months of his appointment as Minister of Territories, Paul Hasluck had visited the Territory of Papua New Guinea (TPNG) twice, touring the Sepik as part of his second tour from 26 July to 8 August 1951. Hasluck was 'greatly impressed by the way in which many native villages had commenced rice production' and directed the administration to immediately focus its attention on this commodity. On 5 May 1952, he issued a ministerial directive outlining a village-based rice production scheme for Madang and Sepik, explaining that:

> in view of the general importance of food production, the difficulty of obtaining rice supplies from Australia and the value of rice as a village food, I think we should make a special project of expanding village rice production to some thousands of tons in the Madang and Sepik districts within the next three or four years. I am certain this can be achieved. There is no land difficulty and no labour difficulty and the interest of the natives seems already to have been aroused and a good deal of experience in rice cultivation in village gardens has been achieved.[1]

---

1   P Hasluck, 'Agricultural production in New Guinea', 5 May 1952, Development of Territories: Agricultural village-rice production 1952–7, A518 [AM927/4], National Archives of Australia (NAA).

Rice production was to be grown as a cash crop, but not sold as an export crop; instead it was for internal use as part of the administration's efforts to improve nutritional standards and create a viable economy. Walter Poggendorff, a rice specialist from the New South Wales Department of Agriculture, visited Maprik in March 1952 to evaluate the economic potential of rice.[2] While his report recommended mechanised flood plain production as the most effective method of attaining self-sufficiency in rice, he nevertheless supported a simplified village-based community scheme (such as an RPS) as a means of coopting Indigenous interest and for the capitalisation of equipment.[3] Hasluck reflected in *A Time for Building* that 'uppermost in my mind' was to ensure sufficient food for a rapidly growing population, which translated to 'no major diversion of land for the production of export crops'. The rice strategy aimed to reduce imports on basic food commodities, promote healthier village diets, encourage village-based economic development, improve agricultural efficiency and eliminate the risk of global price market fluctuations.[4] As argued by Scott MacWilliam, the Hasluck directive is a perfect example of the Australian Government's emphasis on smallholder production in conjunction with state supervision.[5] You could not have one without the other; therefore, for the rice program to work it was reliant on adequate administrative support in the form of technical advice, seeds and nurseries, mechanised equipment, marketing outlets, transport, roads and communication.

On 3 June 1952, in response to Hasluck's directive, Department of Agriculture, Stock and Fisheries (DASF) Director Larry Dwyer accepted the program as envisaged by the minister, but warned of a lack of basic data on resources such as soil and climate conditions. On the one hand, Hasluck was pushing for some immediate action, inspired by the autonomous activity of the Sepiks, but on the other, the administration was unprepared, and this would prove critical in the eventual failure of this program. One example of the administration attempting to provide some semblance of planning and research was a directive from DASF Assistant Director, CC Marr, who had toured Maprik with Poggendorff. He instructed the Bainyik Agricultural Officer (AO) to establish 'small plots every few miles adjoining the main

---

2   'Much rice can be grown in N. Guinea', *Pacific Islands Monthly* 22, no. 9 (April 1952): 80.
3   Walter Poggendorff, *Visit to Papua and New Guinea: Rice production* (Canberra: Department of Territories, 1953), 45.
4   Paul Hasluck, *A time for building: Australian administration in Papua and New Guinea, 1951–1963* (Carlton: Melbourne University Press, 1976), 130.
5   Scott MacWilliam, *Securing village life: Development in late colonial Papua New Guinea* (Canberra: ANU Press, 2013), 153, doi.org/10.22459/SVL.05.2013.

road between Maprik and Marui' as a first step in determining 'potentiality of the country for producing [dry-paddy] rice'.[6] By this stage, of course, rice and peanut crops were already spreading throughout the subdistrict.[7]

An RPS was regarded as the most suitable organisational structure. It provided for a mechanism to collect sufficient funds, ensure adequate financial management controls, and provide a central location to monitor the proper use of equipment (and minimise damage).[8] It was a community development tool, part of the government's gradualist approach to development in the villages. In this case, the administration was not introducing agricultural development; rather it was attempting to contain and control Indigenous autonomous activity.

While an RPS would provide the organisational structure, it was the extension officer who would provide the impetus for increased production with technical advice in sound land use patterns and crop production. Extension officers during patrols were expected to distribute planting material of improved varieties to existing crops and encourage the planting of new crops, both improving economic and nutritional standards.[9] However, Dwyer faced a problem of supplying 'staff for extension duties [which] is well before our minds at this Headquarters'.[10] He recognised he faced a conundrum in carrying out the scheme. While extension officers were vital to the expansion of the program, appointments were difficult because they were limited to finding a person 'with the required amount of experience [and academic qualifications] to perform duties in the field without spoiling the natives or their confidence in this Department'.[11] He could not just employ anyone and, in the short- and medium-term it proved impossible to recruit suitable candidates; patrol reports repeatedly refer to the dire shortage of extension officers. In an October 1952 DASF memorandum, Dwyer provided an estimate on both administrative resources and expected production results for the village rice scheme. One glaring target was not

---

6   CC Marr, 'Village rice production: Sepik Plains', Department of Agriculture, Stock and Fisheries (DASF), 5 August 1952, p. 3, Advancement of Native Agriculture 1954–6, A518 [C2/1/1], NAA.
7   AT Timperley to Department of District Services and Native Affairs (DDSNA) Director, 21 January 1953, East Sepik District, Yangoru, 1949–1953, National Archives of Papua New Guinea (PNGA).
8   RL Pulsford, 'Rice in the Sepik OIC Rural Progress Societies Sepik', 3 June 1952, p. 6, Development of Territories: Agricultural village-rice production 1952–7, A518 [AM927/4], NAA.
9   'Native agricultural extension, training and education', May 1955, p. 2, Advancement of Native Agriculture 1954–6, A518 [C2/1/1], NAA.
10 At this time there was only one agricultural officer (RF Crickard) for the whole district.
11 REP Dwyer, 'Preliminary report on rice production in Sepik and Madang', 3 June 1952, pp. 3–8, Development of Territories: Agricultural village-rice production 1952–7, A518 [AM927/4], NAA.

reached: the estimated 20 extension officers required for the rice scheme. By June 1954 only two full-time and four part-time staff were employed; by August 1955 two officers had resigned (replaced by one machine inspector); by June 1956 there were eight DASF officers working part-time on rice.[12]

Table 10.1: 1952 milling unit.

Equipment	Cost
Anco mill (capacity 500 lbs per hour)	$441
Diesel generator	$1,388
Thresher	$370
30 ft x 4" belt	$55
Bolts etc.	$3
Total	$2,257

Note: Figures are in 1969 Australian dollars (per official compendium statistics for PNG), calculated from the Reserve Bank of Australia pre-decimal inflation calculator, available at: www.rba.gov.au/calculator/annualPreDecimal.html.
Source: RL Pulsford, 'Rice in the Sepik OIC Rural Progress Societies Sepik', 3 June 1952, Development of Territories: Agricultural village-rice production 1952-7, A518 [AM927/4], NAA.

An important aspect of the program was the establishment of decentralised (society) milling, firstly to encourage village-based industry and secondly, to overcome transport limitations and poor roads; the timely introduction of mill equipment was therefore critical. Unfortunately, there was a significant time lag between ordering machinery and delivery. Equipment had to be ordered from England with long delays due to inefficient bureaucracy, then once a machine arrived in Port Moresby it could take up to a year to reach the Sepik District. Bob Pulsford described how he once 'found three Peg Drum Threshers in the Madang Government Store and was told they had been there for nine months. They were addressed to Agriculture, Wewak, Bainyik and Aitape respectively'. He recommended the district build up a reserve of hand equipment and machines to alleviate this problem, and prepare to establish larger central mills with a European manager as the scheme expands.[13] On 30 July 1953, Department of District Services and Native Affairs (DDSNA) Director Roberts wrote of his concern about the

---

12   REP Dwyer, DASF Memorandum, 'Native agriculture—Village rice production. Madang and Sepik districts', 21 October 1952; Department of External Territories (DET), For the minister, 'Native village rice production project in Madang and Sepik districts', 3 August 1955; DASF, 'Report on native village rice production—Madang and Sepik districts', 30 June 1956, Development of Territories: Agricultural village-rice production 1952–7, A518 [AM927/4], NAA.
13   Pulsford, 'Rice in the Sepik', 3 June 1952, pp. 6–8.

10. VILLAGE RICE DEVELOPMENT

delay in the arrival of hulling machinery, warning 'this could have serious repercussions on native administration generally throughout the sub-district'.[14] By early 1954, 27 power-operated village rice-milling units had been purchased by the administration for Sepik and Madang.[15]

From 1957, once roads and transport facilities had improved, mills were removed from remote villages and replaced with a large central mill at Bainyik and Yangoru which, invariably, became a source of considerable disappointment to villagers and was one cause for a loss of interest in the crop. There is no recognition in the files of how the possession of a mill appeared to be a mark of prestige and a sign of participation in modernity. Instead, reports were concerned that the decentralised mills strategy was failing, the smaller RPS (many unofficial) were forced to amalgamate with larger societies registered under the *Co-operative Societies Ordinance*. These societies purchased vehicles to transport growers' paddy to the new and larger centralised rice mills.[16] Only later did officers note how the removal of a rice mill from a village and subsequent loss of prestige had a dramatic impact on the 'people's enthusiasm for rice growing'.[17]

On the other hand, decentralised small-scale milling was expensive, inefficient and unreliable. In addition, the unregulated spread of rice paddies translated into different types of rice often grown in the same garden plots. These different varieties of rice grown presented difficulties in processing and contributed to the breakdown of machines. The autonomous nature of the Dagua-inspired rice-growing movement hampered the ability of the administration to control cash cropping in the Maprik subdistrict. The government was playing catch-up, and this had enormous ramifications on the outcome of agricultural development in the villages. Societies lacked the skilled manpower to maintain and repair the equipment, breakdowns were frequent, and led to continued reliance on an undermanned agricultural department.[18] Because of a lack of staff, planning and technical support, combined with overinflated villager expectations, cash cropping often became a source of disappointment and frustration for both Maprik people and administration officers.

---

14   AA Roberts to Wewak DC, 30 July 1953, East Sepik District, Yangoru, 1949–1953, PNGA.
15   Donald Cleland, '1954 opening legislative council address', 13 May 1954, p. 17, Papers of Sir Donald Cleland, MS9600/17/12/1, NLA.
16   William R Stent, 'An interpretation of a cargo cult', *Oceania* 47, no. 3 (1977): 207, doi.org/10.1002/j.1834-4461.1977.tb01287.x.
17   RK Treutlein, Report 6 of 1960/61, p. 6, East Sepik District, Maprik, 1960–1961, PNGA.
18   Richard T Shand and W Straatmans, *Transition from subsistence: Cash crop development in Papua New Guinea* (Port Moresby: The Australian National University, 1974), 107, 110–16.

It was the actions of the Sepik leaders who most influenced the direction of postwar development in the early years. The attitudes of officers on the ground reflected a cynicism, or concern, for potential problems if an Indigenous enterprise faltered, and they, already stretched with minimal resources and excessive demands, simply did not have the capacity to deal with such outcomes. For instance, in June 1954, Sepik District Officer (DO) Sydney Elliott-Smith wrote to headquarters to advise of the appointment of a cadet patrol officer to the Maprik subdistrict, although it still left him with both Yangoru and Dreikikir patrol posts unmanned. The staff situation was dire, as Elliott-Smith noted: while he,

> hoped to place officers at both these centres, it was not easy. I still have leave commitments and Green River, Vanimo and Burui, together with additional staff at Ambunti and Wewak, to find.

Roberts accepted the reality of the situation, writing that,

> until the staff position improves it can only be expected that as much as humanly possible be done in the way of regular and effective patrolling with the field staff available and this appears to be the case in this sub-district at the present time.[19]

Frustrated patrol officers regularly complained at the lack of patrols by agricultural staff. Elliott-Smith was particularly critical of such comments; he would not only remind his officers of the importance of a unified approach but ask for some tolerance as 'their staff situation is worse than District Services and under the circumstances the officers concerned are doing the best they can'. For instance, in 1950 the Bainyik station was occupied by an extension officer for a period of less than six weeks over a 10-month period.[20] As Table 10.2 illustrates, for the majority of the 1950s, in a period when agricultural community development was a priority of government, there were three or fewer agricultural officers in the Maprik subdistrict. While this circumstance was not unique to Australia, it is open to criticism for deliberately choosing a village-based agroeconomic development strategy when it surely knew technical expertise would be limited.

---

19 The area was not patrolled for more than two years (1952–54). Reitano to Elliott-Smith, 4 August 1954; Elliott-Smith and Director DDSNA: correspondence 3 and 9 June 1954, East Sepik District, Maprik, 1953–1956, PNGA.
20 Elliott-Smith to Director DDSNA, 18 August 1954, East Sepik District, Maprik, 1953–1956, PNGA. For more details see: Kim Godbold, 'Didiman: Australian Agricultural Extension Officers in the Territory of Papua and New Guinea, 1945–75' (PhD thesis, Queensland University of Technology, 2010), 142.

Table 10.2: Agricultural extension officers, Maprik subdistrict, 1950–63.

Year	Extension officers	Agricultural field workers	Total extension staff
1950	1*	–	1
1951	1*	–	1
1952	2	–	2
1953	2	–	2
1954	2	–	2
1955	3	–	3
1956	3	18	21
1957	3	19	22
1958	3	20	23
1959	4	20	24
1960	2	20	22
1961	4	20	24
1962	6	20	26
1963	3	20	23

Note: * Based in Wewak with periodical visits to Maprik.
Source: Richard T Shand and W Straatmans, *Transition from subsistence: Cash crop development in Papua New Guinea* (Port Moresby: The Australian National University, 1974), 132.

While many gardeners had worked outside the subdistrict, in the main, technical knowledge and advice came from extension officers. Inadequate levels of administrative staff (agricultural and district services) had major consequences for the implementation of government programs, hampering the ability to adequately resource village gardeners, monitor events and institute suitable controls. Problems were manifest; just one example was at the Supari RPS where record-keeping was poor: there were no records of who worked and for how long, which, of course, led to confusion over payments and even who were members of the society.

Case study of Supari Rural Progress Society

In early 1952, Kokomo, a village leader from Dreikikir (far west of Maprik), and Augen, from Albiges (near Maprik township), visited Simogun on the coast, inspired by the success of the Dagua enterprise. Both men had been in the police with Simogun and regarded him as their natural leader. Augen, who spoke the same language as Simogun (But Arapesh), asked 'how do we start a society, how do we get committee, how do we get a society at Maprik, as you have here at Dagua'. In response, Simogun explained the Dagua business concept, provided some rice seed to Augen and directed them to 'start business in your villages. So, we started it'.[21]

The effect was immediate. Stokes, patrolling through the area west of Maprik in March 1950, commented on the progressive nature of the Albiges area in direct contrast to its southern neighbours. He thought it was due to Albiges being part of the Arapesh linguistic area and reported that many villagers had 'visited Simogun's Agricultural Project at Dagua and were very impressed'.[22] Augen returned from his meeting with Simogun and established several business enterprises with the support of the paramount luluai, Terapen. Described by Alex Zweck as 'enterprising', Augen purchased from landowners the right to 'cook salt' from a local spring and sell it to the locals while also managing a trade store near the airstrip.[23] Rice was planted in secrecy, but once it was harvested, Augen called a meeting of Southern Arapesh villages and initiated what would become the Supari RPS. The land was cleared and a rice garden was cultivated. Allen described how this rice garden became a showcase garden for local people to witness the potential benefit of planting and cultivating rice. The scheme was framed by Augen as an instrument of change which would produce the same living conditions as in Europe; because of its central location to Arapesh communication networks, news of the venture spread quickly over a wide area.[24]

In October 1952, Alan Jefferies reported on the activity underway at the recently established Supari RPS, the influence of the Dagua system quite evident with communal gardens (adjacent to the former airstrip) 'worked' by several families on a rotating basis. Jefferies was effusive in his praise for the operation but concerned with what had become a problem at Dagua, the high ratio of manpower to production. Because large groups would congregate to plant gardens of rice and peanuts, the financial returns were inevitably small. Jefferies reasoned this lack of tangible reward would threaten the long-term viability of the project. He also commented on the differences in attitude between Albiges (including Supari) and Mamblep people (close to Maprik), and how these 'villages showed little interest in

---

21 Bryant Allen, 'Information flow and innovation diffusion in the East Sepik District, Papua New Guinea' (PhD thesis, The Australian National University, 1976), 189, 348, 427.
22 W Stokes, Report 14 of 1949/50, p. 5, East Sepik District, Maprik, 1945–1953, PNGA.
23 AJ Zweck, Report 3 of 1949/50, p. 4, East Sepik District, Maprik, 1945–1953, PNGA.
24 Allen, 'Information flow', 191, 198.

cash cropping'. Mamblep is part of the Maprik language group and did not have a direct connection with Simogun's circle; there was no 'link person' with the coast to disseminate this knowledge.[25]

The Dreikikir villages joined the Supari RPS in mid-1954. These members, beside growing their own small plots of rice close to home, would visit Supari quite regularly, which often meant a two-day walk, to cultivate communal gardens owned by the Supari village.[26] Despite poor record-keeping, by January 1954 there was £500 (subscriptions cost 20 shillings) in the bank which was used to purchase two rice mills, one placed at Supari, and the other near Dreikikir (Brukham).[27] Dreikikir was remote and as such relied on the influence of local leaders and ex-police networks to establish cash cropping; it also maintained ceremonial links with Supari, a Southern Arapesh village.[28] Furthermore, leaders such as Anton complained of a lack of support from patrol officers in the early 1950s. Anton recalled one conversation with an officer in an interview with Bryant Allen:

> I said, 'Kiap. This is my money and I want you to help me with it'. He said, 'I don't know about this'. I asked, 'Why not?' I have been to Rabaul and Madang. I have seen the way it works … He became annoyed. He said, 'If you do this your money will disappear for nothing. There is no money in this area. Who is going to buy the things from you?'. I said, 'I just want to try'. Kiap, 'No. I will not help'. I was angry, but I went home.[29]

Anton would eventually be supported by more senior officers, Assistant District Officer (ADO) Rupe Haviland in Maprik and DO Horry Niall in Wewak, but suspicions remained with those officers on the ground.[30] For instance, in April 1954, officer Frank Martin wrote openly of his reservations, questioning the intentions of the more business-oriented leaders such as Kokomo and Anton, suggesting 'the money [might] find its way into their pockets'.[31]

---

25   AC Jefferies, Report 1 of 1952/53, pp. 3–4, East Sepik District, Maprik, 1945–1953, PNGA. Concern over labour–production ratio and financial results is discussed in multiple patrol reports. See: CG Littler, Report 3 of 1955/56, p. 3, East Sepik District, Wewak, 1953–1956, PNGA.
26   In 1958 Dreikikir established an independent Rural Progress Society (RPS). FJ Martin, Report 11 of 1953/54, East Sepik District, Maprik, 1953–1956, PNGA.
27   Allen, 'Information flow', 202–3.
28   AT Timperley to Director DDSNA, 21 January 1953; FJ Martin, Report 9 of 1953/54, p. 4; J Preston-White to Director DDSNA, 18 June 1955, East Sepik District, Maprik, 1953–1956, PNGA; Allen, 'Information flow', 189.
29   Anton, cited in Allen, 'Information flow', 357–58.
30   Anton, cited in Allen, 'Information flow', 357–58.
31   Martin, Report 11 of 1953/54, 3–4.

Table 10.3: 1958 Maprik subdistrict rural progress societies.

Society	Census division
Supari	Albiges, north-west of Maprik
Dreikikir	West Maprik subdistrict
Mitpim	Maprik region
Yekere-Ninepolyle	East and south-east of Maprik (Yangoru) region

Note: These societies, capitalised by contributions from growers, purchased the peanuts and provided the transit and storage to Bainyik agricultural station. DASF would then purchase the nuts-in-shell, hull, sort and grade them and transport them to Wewak.

Source: Shand and Straatmans, *Transition from subsistence*, 98.

In May 1955, Arthur Carey warned of two major problems confronting Supari and the development of larger-scale production. First was the continued small per capita production caused by communal planting and a lack of financial incentive to grow more than what was required to meet current needs. Second, inefficient hulling, due to the quality of the machines and the variety of rice grown, resulted in rice having to be reprocessed (milled three or four times to produce a suitable end-product).[32] The ignorance of the kinds of rice and the requirements of the crop and its milling are an example of expectations and interest outrunning government support and infrastructure. Ron Neville reported 15 varieties of rice within a seven-mile radius, there was clearly a need to introduce a standardised type. By the mid-1950s, the administration was issuing instructions to patrol officers such as Frank Martin to focus on eliminating the practice of communal farming. Martin was expected to hold meetings throughout the area and emphasise the administration's expectation of the family unit as the producer unit of choice.[33] The result of this propaganda is difficult to determine as patrols in the late 1950s give different accounts of whether the Albiges people continued to farm communally. In February 1959, cadet officer Graham Black described Augen's efforts to encourage cash cropping and road building as most forceful. He reported on a significant increase in individual garden plots which had reduced 'disputes regarding payments for crops'.[34]

---

32 AT Carey, Report 6 of 1954/55, p. 7, East Sepik District, Maprik, 1953–1956, PNGA.
33 Elliott-Smith to Director DDSNA, 27 July 1954, East Sepik District, Maprik, 1953–1956.
34 G Black, Report 9 of 1958/59, pp. 3, 9, East Sepik District, Maprik, 1958–1959, PNGA.

On the other hand, a year later, Harry Redmond reported 'cash crops are grown on a village communal basis, [but they] have been encouraged to work crop gardens on the basis of one acre to one family unit'.[35] Why there were such widely differing views is open to speculation; however, it should be noted that when Redmond visited Supari, Augen had contracted tuberculosis and was in hospital (where he would remain for two years).[36] In all likelihood, Augen had portrayed a 'positive' development to the young officer (Black), most probably to emphasise his success in changing people's minds towards administrative policy and individual gardens. Karen Brison's 1991 study of the Dreikikir region highlighted the extraordinary faith these people had, and continue to have, in community development and prosperity. Local people told Brison that individual gardens only 'give people a little private spending money', whereas communal gardening could 'lift up' the whole village.[37] This attitude is consistent with most Sepik people, who continued to plant communal gardens of their own accord, despite the active discouragement of agricultural and patrol officers.

Sorcery was often a cause of problems between those promoting business activities and those opposed. The Dreikikir region was well-known as a source of sorcery: Elliott-Smith wrote,

> sorcery or sanguma is an evil throughout the Dreikikir area and it is essential that it be discouraged, Dreikikir men are found as far afield as Boiken on the Coast, acting as tutors of the art as a lucrative fee.[38]

Throughout the subdistrict, officers were incredulous at the 'effectiveness of sorcery [which] has to be seen to be believed'. Redmond described how 'practically every death recorded during the patrol was attributed by the people to the work of sorcerers'. This belief had a direct effect on the ability of village officials to impose their authority upon their fellow villagers because 'they feared to incur enemies who might employ the services of professional sorcerers to bring about the death of the officials'.[39] Bill Stent, an agricultural officer during the early 1950s in the region and later academic, wrote of Cargo Cults which were established in the early 1970s

---

35 HJ Redmond, Report 6 of 1959/60, p. 3, East Sepik District, Maprik, 1959–1960, PNGA.
36 Augen would pass away in 1967.
37 Karen Brison, 'Community and prosperity: Social movements among the Kwanga of Papua New Guinea', *Contemporary Pacific* 3 (1991): 326, 338.
38 Elliott-Smith to Director DDSNA, 27 July 1954, East Sepik District, Maprik, 1953–1956.
39 HJ Redmond, Report 1 of 1960/61, p. 10, East Sepik District, Maprik, 1959–1960, PNGA.

in the subdistrict.[40] He explained in this article how villagers considered magic and ritual as crucial to the success of their gardening project. Stent wrote that:

> If, despite all precautions, there is a crop failure then it will be attributed to sorcery. All deaths are due to sorcery and so too are such things as unfavourable rains. Thus it is necessary for an individual to keep on good terms with his neighbours so that he will not become the subject of sorcery for any breach in moral responsibilities will inevitably be repaid through it.[41]

In January 1955, such tensions were evident at Supari when officer Max Duncan visited the site. He wrote of the people's genuine fear of 'sanguma and poison', and how all the men of the surrounding area had been warned 'that whoever helped Augen with the rice growing etc. would die as those who were against the rice project would work "Poison" against them'. Duncan reported that even Augen himself had been threatened, and the threat proved effective; almost nobody was working the rice gardens. Duncan arrested those responsible and argued for strong punishment as a way of example and eradication throughout the subdistrict.[42]

The handling of sorcery created a conundrum for the administration. Officers would hold meetings to explain the fraudulent practice of sorcery, and how the administration regarded them as imposters. Native Affairs Director Allan Roberts instructed officers to 'make every effort to convey to the assembled people his reasons for so doing [jailing an offender] without, if possible, confirming to a greater degree their belief in the practice'.[43] The administration hoped that by jailing a sorcerer it would, at a minimum, 'remove their presence from the villages, show the disapproval of the administration, and attempt to shield the younger people from their influence'. The most effective measure against sorcery, according to many officers, was a strong mission presence because they could maintain a constant presence and provide an alternative belief system.[44] Despite these efforts, sorcery remained (and remains) a weapon of choice for traditional

---

40   Stent, 'An interpretation of a cargo cult', 208.
41   Stent, 'An interpretation of a cargo cult', 211.
42   MR Duncan, Report 4 of 1954-55, pp. 3–4, East Sepik District, Maprik, 1953–1956, PNGA.
43   AA Roberts to Wewak District Officer (DO), 4 January 1960, East Sepik District, Maprik, 1959–1960, PNGA.
44   JA Wiltshire, Report 10 of 1961–62, Appendix 6, East Sepik District, Maprik, 1961–1962, PNGA.

leaders throughout the colonial period; it was an effective method for them to retain prestige and a semblance of control as new development schemes were introduced.[45]

Other crops

From the mid-1950s, peanuts and coffee were introduced as crops which could be exported to Australia and were promoted in the villages by agricultural extension workers as an alternative to rice.[46] Officers spruiked the benefits of peanuts as both a cash and subsistence crop. For example, on an August 1956 patrol, Ron Neville introduced peanuts as an 'off-season crop', encouraging villagers to re-sow harvested rice plots with peanuts, reasoning it would not only provide increased income, but improve both the soil and their diet.[47] This type of attitude was criticised by Department Secretary Cecil Lambert for undermining the village-based rice scheme.[48] Clearly, Lambert was either unaware or was willing to ignore the problems associated with the rice project—poor soil, transport issues, milling problems, low prices—and the effect it was having on the morale of local people reliant on the expertise of the Australians.

Table 10.4: Supari RPS peanut production.

Year	Quantity (tons)
1957/58	9.8
1958/59	42.3
1959/60	28.5
1960/61	8.0

Note: Assumes average yield of 700 lb per acre.
Source: Shand and Straatmans, *Transition from subsistence*, 97.

Peanuts had a short commercial life in the subdistrict: peak interest encompassed no more than 1,200 farmers and 400 acres planted in the subdistrict. Across the Territory, peanut sales boomed in the years

---

45 B Bunting to Wewak DO, 16 November 1961, East Sepik District, Yangoru, 1961–1962, PNGA.
46 Richard Curtain, 'Dual dependence and Sepik labour migration' (PhD thesis, The Australian National University, 1980), 205–6.
47 RT Neville, Report 1 of 1956–57, p. 14, East Sepik District, Maprik, 1956–1957, PNGA.
48 Lambert to Cleland, 'Rice development', 30 December 1957, p. 3, Development of Territories: Agricultural village-rice production 1952–7, A518 [AM927/4], NAA.

1958–60, before collapsing dramatically when global markets fell.⁴⁹ The Supari experience mirrored that of the rest of the Territory. In 1957/58, the Supari RPS produced 9.8 tons of peanuts, in the following year this more than quadrupled (42.3 tons), by 1961, production had fallen back to 8 tons, and was negligible by 1962.⁵⁰ Redmond reported:

> the failure of rice and peanuts to provide an economic outlet reached a culmination during the past six months and no further plantings can be expected in these annuals, especially with the present poor returns being paid by the Society.⁵¹

Instead, he explained that for the remainder of the year, he would attempt to establish a 10–12 acre block of coffee in each village.

Table 10.5: Albiges coffee tree planting.

Year	Coffee trees
1962	616
1964	36,473
1968	133,245 (267 acres)

Note: 1961 Supari RPS produced 904 lbs of coffee parchment.
Source: Shand and Straatmans, *Transition from subsistence*, 114–15.

In contrast to rice, coffee was introduced through a DASF extension program. Coffee was planted as early as 1948 in Dagua but was found to be unsuitable and failed to attract interest. In 1952 coffee experimentation began at Bainyik: Robusta (used for instant coffee) was selected because of its capacity to grow below 1,500 ft altitude.⁵² The 1956 United Nations (UN) mission reported the administration plans for coffee to be the principal cash crop in the 'alluvial belts of the Sepik Plains and in the foothills of the Prince Alexander and Torricelli ranges'.⁵³ However, as with other development plans, administrative incompetence stifled the expansion of plantings in the Maprik subdistrict. There were no seedlings to support extension activities. The reality was that while rice would take five months from planting to

---

49   Territory peanut production: 1959/60 $44,048; 1960/61 $8,325. Figures in 1969 Australian dollars. Department of Native Affairs (DNA), *Annual report of the Co-operative Section, 1st April 1960 to March 1961* (Port Moresby: Government Printer, 1961), 38.
50   Shand and Straatmans, *Transition from subsistence*, 97.
51   Redmond, Report 1 of 1960/61, p. 2.
52   Allen, 'Information flow', 208.
53   United Nations Visiting Mission to Trust Territories in the Pacific, *Report on New Guinea* (New York: UN Trusteeship Council, 1956), 51.

procure new seeds, coffee took three to four years.⁵⁴ The administration did not have a seed bank; officers became increasingly frustrated at the lack of seeds. Villages would plant shade trees in preparation for coffee seeds, but they were not available. Local people were again the victim of a lack of planning. Somehow Augen managed to secure some seeds for Supari, and by March 1958 Carey was able to report the trees were thriving. It took until 1960 for seed to become widely available across the subdistrict; by the end of the year there were 250 gardens planted. At Supari, tree planting was slow, a total of only 616 trees by 1962, but the numbers exploded to 36,473 in 1964, and by 1968 there was 267 acres of coffee gardens in Albiges.⁵⁵

Bobby Bunting, ADO at Maprik, noted the positive reception to 'propaganda being sent on coffee and its suitability to the native way of life'. In general, patrols were reporting the support for the coffee program from village elders. Bunting reasoned, unlike annuals, 'the growing of coffee and its harvesting is something which is not opposed to the traditional native life in any important manner'. Bunting doubted the motivation to grow coffee was based purely on financial return—he accepted most villagers were quite cynical about administration claims after the failures of rice and peanuts—rather, it was a pragmatic decision because it was 'a more suitable crop and one which will give better returns'.⁵⁶ Despite earlier setbacks, coffee cultivation provided new hope to local people as an avenue for economic advancement.

Unlike rice, coffee (and peanuts) was susceptible to global market prices. Farmers planting coffee risked the vagaries of the market with harvest five to six years after planting—a significant risk, further magnified by challenges to land tenure. Coffee is a permanent tree crop, which meant its introduction removed the land upon which it is planted from other crops for at least one generation. For this reason, rice remained attractive to many villagers unwilling to plant a long-term crop such as coffee.⁵⁷ The fact that these people were willing to undertake such a risk as growing coffee, especially after the failures of previous crops, underlines their faith in and dedication to economic self-sufficiency.

---

54 Coffee was first planted in 1957 by Kinbangua and Jame villagers in the Maprik census division.
55 AT Carey to Wewak DO, 4 March 1959; G Black, Report 9 of 1958/59, p. 9; AT Carey, Report 5 of 1958/59, Appendix C, East Sepik District, Maprik, 1958–1959, PNGA; Shand and Straatmans, *Transition from subsistence*, 114–17.
56 B Bunting to Wewak DO, 23 May 1961, East Sepik District, Maprik, 1960–1961, PNGA.
57 Shand and Straatmans, *Transition from subsistence*, 133–40.

Failure of the village rice plan

By December 1957, it was clear the high hopes held by the government for the rice plan had not materialised. A report from the Primary Industry Branch blamed staff shortages, a falling off of interest because of more attractive prices for other crops such as peanuts, and soil nutrient deficiencies on the Sepik plains.[58] In 1953 some experiments were carried out in the Sepik country which proved the plains sterile, and in the intervening years the agricultural department had commenced experiments to ascertain the possibility of fertilisers as an enabler of economic production.[59] This failure to pre-test the soil before the introduction of rice as a cash crop is a clear indication of the administration's inadequate planning, and the rush to catch up with the planting activity of Maprik villagers.

Table 10.6: Yield per acre.

Crop	Tons per acre
Rice	1
Sweet potatoes	5
Taro	5
Yams	5
Tapioca	8

Source: Agricultural Section of DET, 'Agronomic aspects of the place of rice in the dietary scale of Papua and New Guinea people', 20 January 1958, p. 1, Development of Territories: Agricultural village-rice production 1952–7, A518 [AM927/4], NAA.

The administration encouraged the production of brown rice because it was nutritionally superior. However, it was discovered that the storage ability of the rice was greatly reduced due to the oil content of the brown rice outer layers which would quickly turn rancid. Furthermore, based on yields per acre, it was more productive in terms of labour input and food unit output per acre to grow root crops and leguminous food crops. Traditional subsistence crops, yams and taro, yielded five times the crop output of rice.[60]

---

58 DET, 'Papua and New Guinea—rice action plan', 19 December 1957, pp. 1–2, Development of Territories: Agricultural village-rice production 1952–7, A518 [AM927/4], NAA.
59 WL Conroy cited in 'Discouraged by cheap "foreign" production: Rice industry in Papua-N. Guinea', *Pacific Islands Monthly* 28, no. 2 (September 1957): 138.
60 Agricultural Section of DET, 'Agronomic aspects of the place of rice in the dietary scale of Papua and New Guinea people', 20 January 1958, p. 1, Development of Territories: Agricultural village-rice production 1952–7, A518 [AM927/4], NAA.

10. VILLAGE RICE DEVELOPMENT

Rice was introduced into the Maprik subdistrict as a cash crop, and although it was not sold as an export crop, it was expected to provide a reasonable financial return for local people. However, the rice price was held artificially low by government policy. The freight costs of sending rice from Port Moresby to the outposts were averaged and a uniform price for rice declared which was applicable to all districts of the Territory. In July 1955, Sepik DO John Preston White described how villagers would inevitably compare prices with 'the first quality Australian brown rice shipped to Wewak and airfreighted to Maprik and there sold at a profit in the trade stores of the area'. He recommended the retail price per pound at Maprik of the Australian brown rice be arbitrarily fixed at a more reasonable figure to help offset this problem.[61] Department Secretary, Cecil Lambert conceded that 'if they [had] received a price based on the true cost of delivering Australian rice to Wewak, there would be more incentive to grow rice'.[62] Furthermore, the prices paid to villages accounted for transport and market costs, and because these tended to fluctuate, aggravated farmers considered the price paid by the DASF as unfair.[63]

Poor roads, communication and transport problems resulted in large stockpiles sitting in storage. In 1952, Alan Jefferies explained how important roads were in both practical and economic terms for the rice project. The few roads available could only take a lightly laden jeep and to all intents and purposes were useful only for passengers. Heavy cargo relied on human porterage, and as a result was expensive and unnecessarily arduous. The cost of transporting stores from Maprik to Dreikikir, a mere 30 miles, was enormous and yet necessary, there being no airstrip at Dreikikir.[64] Road development relied on voluntary labour contributed by the village people involved in the scheme. A 1956 report warned that everything possible should be done to supply adequate transport. It argued that local people had made a:

> very considerable contribution to this road development and it is up to the administration to make use of the roads in providing advice and assistance for the improvement of their agriculture.[65]

---

61 JP White to Director DNA, 22 July 1955, East Sepik District, Maprik, 1953–1956, PNGA.
62 Lambert to Cleland, 'Rice development', 30 December 1957.
63 MJ O'Connor, Report 2 of 1959/60, p. 9, East Sepik District, Maprik, 1959–1960, PNGA.
64 Jefferies, Report 1 of 1952/53, p. 2.
65 DASF, 'Report on native village rice production—Madang and Sepik districts', 30 June 1956.

The 1959/60 *Co-operative Annual Report* described the roads in the area as among the worst in the Territory. The report blamed the recent closure of the Bauimo RPS (4,010 members) on 'expensive transportation of produce, mainly peanut by air to Wewak, and the expense of collecting rice padi and peanuts from members by vehicle'.[66]

On 24 January 1958, CS Christian, Chief of the Division of Land Research and Regional Survey, CSIRO (the Commonwealth Scientific and Industrial Research Organisation), was approved by the minister to carry out an investigation of the rice-growing industry. Christian concluded the implementation of the village rice scheme was too broad in scale and the available staff could not, or did not, have sufficient time to service the areas involved. Christian's recommendations were to promote rice as a subsistence crop, a valuable insurance against crop failure or seasonal periods when food was scarce.[67] While rice production reduced during the peanut boom of 1957–60; during the 1960s there was a steady increase in production and by 1970 it had reached nearly 2,000 tons per annum.[68] Village-based rice production failed to live up to the expectations of both Maprik villagers and the administration, but did provide a modicum of benefit as both a cash and subsistence crop.

Conclusion

As this case study has described, the introduction of cash cropping in the postwar period to the Sepik District and the Maprik subdistrict was one of dynamic Indigenous leadership, vision and energy, but also one hampered by a lack of personnel, physical resources and transport, as well as mismanagement. The origins of the cash cropping and business activity came from the coastal village of Dagua under the leadership and guidance of Pita Simogun. His message was to work together and to become independent, and as in Milne Bay, it was not one of confrontation, but one which expressed self-recognition and a desire to self-improve. It was a message acceptable to the colonial government. Simogun's message spread

---

66   DNA, *Annual Report of the Co-operative Section, 1st April 1959 to March 1960* (Port Moresby: Government Printer, 1961), 9.
67   Cleland to Lambert, 'Rice report—C.S, Christian', 4 February 1960, p. 2; DET, 'Figures and notes on rice requested by the Minister', 9 January 1958, p. 2, Development of Territories: Agricultural village-rice production 1952–7, A518 [AM927/4], NAA.
68   Stent, 'An interpretation of a cargo cult', 207.

through inland diplomatic networks inspired by the early success of the Dagua RPS; Indigenous autonomy was at the forefront of socioeconomic development of the Maprik subdistrict.

Hasluck's response to the expansion of rice growing along the coast and into the hinterland reflected his evolutionary belief in community development. Already these people were displaying signs of awakening from a subsistence lifestyle; there was a desire to 'advance' towards economic independence, a crucial step before eventual political self-government. The government's inability to harness the autonomous activity of village people was due to a lack of planning, co-ordination and resources. The subsequent problems of transport, communication, poor soils, and lack of staff and seeds can, to some extent, be explained by the government's initial mishandling of the introduction of economic development and the desire of Indigenous people to have what the Europeans had: autonomy and better living standards.

Inevitably, the introduction of new ideas and ways of living were influenced by local characteristics and form of messaging. In this case, Indigenous diplomatic networks preceded the Australian Government and proved to substantially influence the manner, and effectiveness, of agricultural development to the Sepik region. Therefore, local people's hopes and desires were shaped by early ideas from Simogun's circle but reinforced and reimagined by patrol and agricultural officers. This mishmash of ideas and knowledge, coupled with both internal and external factors such as market prices, poor soil, elderly enmity to change, and poor management, meant many Maprik people were left frustrated and disappointed by their involvement. The experience on the ground did not meet their expectations. However, the desire for change, for improved living standards, was reflected in the acceptance of a new crop, coffee, which provided a new hope for economic self-sufficiency.

CASE STUDY: NEW HANOVER

11
New Hanover: Colonial Control and Indigenous Sociopolitical Agency

The administration regarded the people of New Hanover as dangerous and unsettled people, and this attitude informed much of the development programs for the island. Local leadership was headed by Singerau, luluai of Baikeb, a dynamic, forceful and entrepreneurial person who proactively manipulated government programs to benefit himself and the community. The administration maintained a fractious relationship with him but, nevertheless, relied in a pragmatic manner on his ability to inspire local people to adopt new socioeconomic ideas. This New Hanover case study explains this tension, one of colonial control, development and repeat disappointment. The actions of Singerau and the people of New Hanover reflected frustration at the failure of colonial development but also demonstrated their remarkable gift for creativity, innovation and belief in their own sociopolitical agency.

The New Ireland District (NID), situated in the Bismarck Archipelago and located off the New Guinea mainland east of New Britain, comprised the islands of New Ireland, New Hanover, Feni, Lihir, Djaul, Fead, and the Saint Matthias and Tabar groups. District headquarters was located at Kavieng on the northern tip of New Ireland, the district broken into two subdistricts, Namatanai and Kavieng. The Kavieng subdistrict included two patrol posts: Dalum and Taskul (east coast of New Hanover).[1] This case

---

1 Department of District Services and Native Affairs (DDSNA), *Annual Report for the year ending June 1954* (Port Moresby, Government Printer, 1954), 29.

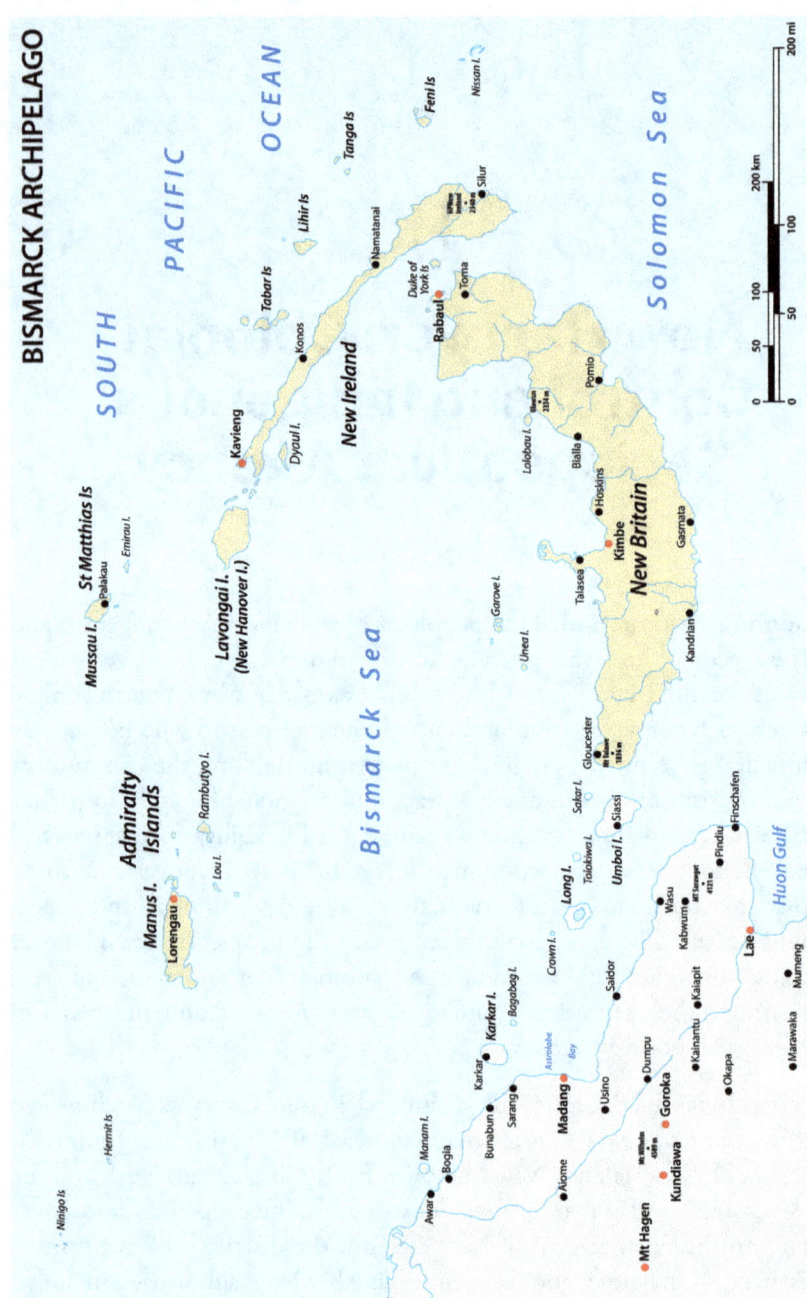

Map 11.1: The Bismarck Archipelago.

Notes: The Bismarck Archipelago encompasses an area of 49,700 km². New Hanover Island is located 37 km north-west of the New Ireland District capital, Kavieng.

Source: VectorStock.

study largely focusses on New Hanover, a large island (1,087 km²) which, in 1946, had a population of 6,382.[2] Linguistically, the whole island and surrounding islands and islets (12,000 people) spoke the Tungag language, and according to patrol reports of the time, 'shared the same beliefs and followed the same cultural practices'.[3] New Hanover was also called Lavongai, a term used to denote the people, the entire island, the administration census division, and a southern coastal village.[4]

There was minimal development on New Hanover prior to the end of World War II (WWII); in fact, until 1920 the colonial administration had placed the island in quarantine due to a leprosy epidemic.[5] One early action sanctioned by both the German and Australian administrations was the forced resettlement of inland peoples along the coast. The colonialists' aim was to centralise and control local populations, but on the ground, it resulted in a fracturing of social cohesiveness and loss of traditional usufruct rights over land, the latter leaving inland people vulnerable to the disposition and the charity of the land-owning coastal clans.[6] Although only 36 kilometres from New Ireland, transport and weather conditions could mean a three-day trip, which left the people of New Hanover relatively isolated and encouraged an independent, internally focussed community.

This chapter explores conditions on the ground after the war, and how the administration dealt with what they considered a restless and unsettled people. They employed large and officious patrols to maintain control, eliminate potential flashpoints and ward off concerns over an inexperienced and undermanned workforce. This chapter also introduces Singerau, who would become the most influential Indigenous leader in New Hanover during the period 1947–60, a primary agent for socioeconomic development on the island. One early postwar community development scheme introduced in New Hanover was 'unofficial' local *Kivungs* (councils). The aim was to recruit and control newly engaged, and potentially dangerous, young men in a government-sponsored program aimed at 'reviving' local Indigenous

---

2   CW Kimmorley, Report 4 of 1947/48, p. 5, New Ireland District, Kavieng, 1946–1948, National Archives of Papua New Guinea (PNGA).
3   William Longgar, 'Towards a theology of land for the New Guinea Islands' (PhD thesis, Asbury Theological Seminary, 2006), 63; Graeme Were, 'Pattern, thought and the construction of knowledge: The question of the kapkap from New Ireland, Papua New Guinea' (PhD thesis, University College London, 2003), 50. FP Kaad, Report 12 of 1949/50, Appendix A, New Ireland District, Kavieng, 1949–1951, PNGA.
4   J Cochrane, Report No. 4 of 1956/57, p. 9, New Ireland District, Kavieng, 1956–1957, PNGA; Bloomfield, Report 7 of 1959/60, p. 3, New Ireland District, Kavieng, 1959–1960, PNGA.
5   Longgar, 'Towards a theology of land', 16.
6   Cochrane, Report 4 of 1956/57, p. 9; Bloomfield, Report 7 of 1959/60, p. 6.

authority. The scheme was 'unofficial' because it was primarily a subdistrict strategy with almost no administration planning, support or monitoring. It was under-resourced and a poor imitation of the official program in nearby New Britain. This chapter concludes with a focus on the economic development program for New Hanover. Copra was widely grown in New Hanover and therefore an easy choice for the administration to use for introducing cash cropping to local villagers. However, it was also a notoriously unstable commodity and presented a potential danger, considering local people were unaccustomed to the vagaries of global commodity markets.

The New Hanover case study explores an underlying tension, a contested colonial space of contrasting and confused ambition between the Lavongai and the colonial administration. The government introduced political, social and economic development to New Hanover, some of which could be considered a mere front for maintaining control of disruptive people. The Milne Bay postwar experience exposes the dichotomy of Australian postwar colonial development practice: socioeconomic advancement or containment of disruptive dangerous elements in the local community.

An impatient 'dangerous' people

The Bismarck Archipelago was the site of brutal fighting during WWII, the major islands of New Britain, New Ireland, New Hanover, the Solomons and Emirau regarded as important strategic assets for naval and airborne forces.[7] New Hanover felt less the impact and fury of war as the Japanese never occupied the island. One reason, recounted by Dorothy Billings, was because Sister Clematia from the Anelaua Mission had marched leprosy patients down to the beach to ward off such approaches.[8] Therefore, to all intents and purposes, the Lavongai retained their wealth, and with few exceptions their villages were left intact.[9] Reverend CF Gribble wrote movingly of his first visit to New Hanover after the war, and how, despite being riddled with machine-gun fire, and on the whole worthless, there stood 'one remaining building in the whole New Guinea District at the close of the war'.[10]

---

7   Patrick Nason, 'Sounding sovereignty: The politics of presence in the Bismarck Archipelago' (PhD thesis, Columbia University, 2018), 21–22.
8   In 1932 a leper colony was established on Anelaua Island (nearby to New Hanover). EM Holland, 'Leprosy in New Guinea', *International Journal of Leprosy* 4, no. 2 (1936): 171–76; Dorothy Billings, *Cargo cult as theater: political performance in the Pacific* (Lanham: Lexington, 2002), 19–20.
9   Rev. AR Gardner, 'Stormy present! Piled high with difficulty', *The Methodist*, 8 February 1947, 1.
10 Rev. CF Gribble, 'New Guinea journey', *The Methodist*, 27 August 1949, 1–2.

Figure 11.1: Sister Clematia and Mr McGuigan watching the unloading of a barge in 1947 on New Hanover.
Source: National Archives of Australia (NAA), A6510, 1588, item 6942669.

While the Japanese did not occupy New Hanover, plantations were abandoned and many Lavongai fought in the Allied Intelligence Bureau (AIB), helping to gather information about the Japanese and harassing the enemy.[11] Those returning from AIB duties were experienced in armed conflict and had witnessed the extraordinary wealth, power and efficiency of the Japanese, American and Australian armed forces. As in the Sepik, leaders emerged on the island, having either fought in the war or served in the New Guinea Police Force, as enablers on their own terms of the Australian Government's socioeconomic development plans.

---

11   Neville K Robinson, *Villagers at war: Some Papuan New Guinean in World War II* (Canberra: The Australian National University, 1981), 10.

Figure 11.2: Anelaua Leprosarium staff, including priest, European sisters, New Guinean sisters and lay brother, 1947.
Source: NAA, A6510, 1761, item 6942829.

The first patrol after the resumption of civil administration was a whole of island patrol by Ken Jones in October/November 1946. The recently installed District Officer (DO), Jack Read, instructed Jones to undertake an unhurried patrol, warning him that disturbing reports had reached him of local people agitated and generally unsettled. He wrote to Bert Jones (Director of Native Affairs) and described a 'resourceful and sophisticated people who are still unsettled from the devastation of war and the successive changes of government since 1942'. The grievances centred around wage-pegging and price-fixing in respect of labour, material and produce, and had generated anti-colonial sentiment. Read reported a fervour 'such that some of the [white] residents here were even apprehensive of an outright uprising'. In view of the threat of hostility, a show of 20 police accompanied the patrol. Plans were also made to establish a patrol and police post at Taskul on the far east coast, the current site of a medical post.[12]

---

12   WJ Read to JH Jones (Director DDSNA), 5 December 1946, 26 February 1947, New Ireland District, Kavieng, 1946–1948, PNGA.

Figure 11.3: Taskul station seen from the Officer's house in 1947.
Source: NAA, A6510, 1302, item 7582431.

Problems continued to plague the administration on New Hanover despite the establishment of the Taskul Patrol Post. In one example, Jack Read sent an officer to investigate what was described as a potential 'cargo cult' which was espousing 'the supposed return of the Americans', noting 'these people who are very prone to exaggerated fervour if not corrected quickly by an officer on the spot'.[13] The Islanders' early postwar interest in the return of the Americans is most noteworthy on two fronts. Firstly, the people of New Hanover were later to become infamous for their protest vote for US President Johnson in the 1964 Papua New Guinea (PNG) House Assembly elections: an indication of both their frustration at, and as a creative way to shame, the Australian Government.[14] Secondly, Read's reading of the situation was a typical example of how colonial authorities explained away political and

---

13 Read to Director DDSNA, 20 September 1949, New Ireland District, Kavieng, 1948–1949, PNGA.
14 For more details on political development on New Hanover, see: Brad Underhill, 'Co-operatives and political development in PNG: Colonial failure or unrecognized success?', *Journal of Pacific History* 55, no. 3 (2019): 360–82, doi.org/10.1080/00223344.2019.1665461.

economic dissatisfaction as the 'confusion of the primitive mind',[15] whereas, an innovative argument, well explained by Tracey Banivanua Mar, was to regard any such activity as examples of locally defined decolonisation, of 'people doing independence, rather than waiting for it to be granted'.[16] In this way, while Read was reading the activity of the Lavongai as one of a frustrated unsophisticated people warranting containment, their actions are best understood as local people demonstrating agency, and openly searching for socioeconomic autonomy. The Australian development strategy was premised on a controlled gradual introduction of new socioeconomic and political concepts; there was limited space for innovative or autonomous Indigenous activity. While in Milne Bay the actions of local people were a sophisticated adaption of colonial development ideas, the impetus came from the Kwato mission and not the Territory Administration. In Sepik, the ideas espoused by Pita Simogun, a well-regarded and conformist Indigenous leader, aligned with the colonial government's village-based agricultural development strategy. On New Hanover, the reaction of local people in the early postwar period did not accord with the government's expectations and were therefore dismissed as 'primitive'.

Clearly, if the government were to be successful in implementing postwar community development, they would need to enlist the support of local leaders. Fortunately for them, the recently installed luluai of Baikeb (south-east coastal village), Singerau, would become a marshalling point, an outspoken leader, in support of government-sponsored socioeconomic development. However, despite Singerau's undoubted passion and energy, he was also assertive, aggressive and entrepreneurial, and relations with the administration would often be strained during his period of dominance, which lasted through until the early 1960s.[17] These characteristics challenged the Australian Government. They demanded a very particular kind of 'native' on a very narrow band. They wanted passion and energy but only on their terms. They said they fostered business but struggled when entrepreneurs demanded their rights to do things their way and became angry when the Australians refused to help or recognise their superior knowledge of place and people. This dynamic is explored throughout

---

15 WJ Read (DO Kavieng) correspondence to JH Jones (Director DDSNA), 26 February 1947, New Ireland District, Kavieng, 1946–1948.
16 Tracey Banivanua Mar, *Decolonisation and the Pacific: Indigenous globalisation and the ends of empire* (Cambridge, New York: Cambridge University Press, 2016), 134–40, doi.org/10.1017/CBO97811 39794688.
17 'Deaths of Islands People', *Pacific Islands Monthly* 33, no. 6 (January 1963): 137.

this case study and provides an important example of why the Australian plans, formed in Canberra and Port Moresby, too often did not meet their expectations for postwar development.

In the postwar period, New Hanover encompassed 62 villages, each of which was regarded by the administration as a central unit for socioeconomic and political leadership.[18] In terms of land tenure and economic utility, land remained the property of the clan (although clan members were linked with other villages across the island); descent was matrilineal, but under threat as the economic value of land became known, and government postwar policy was to prioritise household/smallholder farmer as the pre-eminent singular economic unit.[19] While there was not a centralised authority, the prewar colonial administration had instituted a classic system of indirect rule by installing a paramount luluai, a version of area leadership, who were expected to support village leaders (luluai) and help introduce government initiatives. These leaders extended a temporary form of unity and influence over several neighbouring settlements, although at the time of a paramount's death, individual leaders would reassert their autonomy. The first, and most significant, was Igua, a German-appointed paramount who was most responsible for settling the inland people on the coast. Later paramounts encouraged the pooling of plantation labour on recently alienated land.[20] The paramounts had a reputation among the Australians as despotic leaders; the last of these, Gapi of Umbukul, died in February 1948.[21] The attitude of the administration was to control and manage by channelling the paramount's efforts in the direction they wanted.[22]

Following the death of Gapi, the most influential leader on the island was Singerau.[23] Like Pita Simogun and Augen of the Sepik district, Singerau had been a long-term police officer, attaining the rank of sergeant-major first class.[24] He was regarded by the administration as the natural successor of Gapi, although patrol reports of the time equivocate over whether he was offered the position of paramount and rejected it or, what is more

---

18   Bloomfield, Report 7 of 1959/60, p. 3; Billings, *Cargo cult as theater*, 25.
19   Longgar, 'Towards a theology of land', 87–88; Billings, *Cargo cult as theater*, 17.
20   Bloomfield, Report 7 of 1959/60, pp. 7–9.
21   Kimmorley, Report 4 of 1947/48, p. 7; KW Jones, Report 3 of 1946/47, p. 6, New Ireland District, Kavieng, 1946–1948, PNGA.
22   Handwritten department minute, 20 April 1960, Bloomfield, Report 7 of 1959/60.
23   Bloomfield, Report No. 7 of 1957/58, p. 17, New Ireland District, Taskul, 1957–1958, PNGA; Bloomfield, Report No. 4 of 1958/59, p. 2, New Ireland District, Taskul, 1958–1959, PNGA.
24   Singerau commenced his police career in 1921 and retired in 1947. In 1950 he was awarded a Loyal Service Medal. 'Deaths of Islands People', *Pacific Islands Monthly*, January 1963, 137.

likely, aspired to the position but was not offered it because the system was being phased out in favour of village councils.[25] Regardless, Singerau was never officially appointed a paramount. He returned to his village in 1947 but found to his dismay that while most of the community were coconut owners he was not, and therefore not a money earner in the community.[26] In reaction to this situation, Singerau established a copra scheme which employed local people to cut and dry copra, similar to the scheme in Dagua (Sepik). Villagers worked one week on copra and three weeks on subsistence gardening.[27]

With the copra proceeds, Singerau purchased laplaps, blouses and tobacco and distributed them among the people of Baikeb. This village had a good anchorage for all ships, and he was able to charter vessels to transport the copra and purchase bags, twine and paint.[28] Later, he bought a piece of ground in Bagail village and built a house. The materials for this house were contributed by Baikeb and the surrounding villages, engaged to build at £2 per month.[29] Within two years, Singerau had established an organisation which included a fleet of canoes, a clerk, copra stores and labour for discharging and loading canoes and launches.[30] Aside from their shared heritage of police duties, Singerau's organisation had similar characteristics to those of Simogun's Dagua venture—an Indigenous agricultural economic organisation aligned across multiple villages (almost certainly through the clan alliances), which encouraged a mix of cash cropping and subsistence farming. However, whereas Simogun advocated a communal organisation with a board of leaders in control, in the case of Singerau, the organisation was controlled by, and appeared to reward, himself.[31] What is most interesting to note is how the village as an atomised unit was challenged by the work of people like Singerau and Simogun. An alternative reading suggests the village was never really an atomised unit and instead activities such as these were examples of a reactivation of clan networks over a broader area.

---

25   Kimmorley, Report 4 of 1947/48, pp. 12–16; B Hayes to New Ireland (Keenan) District Commissioner (DC), 14 December 1953, New Ireland District, Taskul, 1953–1954, PNGA.
26   JR Keenan to DDSNA Director, 12 August 1952, New Ireland District, Taskul, 1950–1953, PNGA.
27   WW Stokes, Report No. 1 of 1952/53, pp. 3–4, New Ireland District, Taskul, 1953–1954, PNGA.
28   BB Butcher, Report 2 of 1953/54, p. 1, New Ireland District, Taskul, 1953–1954, PNGA; Stokes, Report No. 1 of 1952/53, pp. 3–4.
29   Stokes, Report No. 1 of 1952/53, pp. 3–4.
30   Kaad, Report 12 of 1949/50, pp. 4–5.
31   Stokes, Report No. 1 of 1952/53, pp. 3–4.

In what would become an ongoing problem for the administration, Singerau's activities in trading ventures and 'entrepreneurial inventiveness' were often the source of investigation, or as District Commissioner (DC) Jack Keenan noted, 'could not stand too close an investigation'.[32] For instance, William Stokes claimed Singerau only paid labourers once in a 20-month period and explained:

> many had given copra to Singerau to sell. All this copra was entered in Singerau's name. Unfortunately, no record was kept, and no one remembers the natives' names or the individual amounts of copra.[33]

While Singerau denied the charges, by 1949, just before his organisation was taken over by the cooperative movement, Singerau had received £875 ($4,108 in 1969 Australian dollars) from the Production Copra Board.[34] The administration acknowledged Singerau was working hard to improve the conditions of his people, but as James Rogers explained, his experience in the police had alerted him to the potential for economic advancement, and he was determined his people would advance. Again, Singerau's attitude points to the fine line that colonised people must tread to stay within the boundaries of proper behaviour. Therefore, it was hardly surprising that Rogers stated his intentions were good but criticised his methods as 'on the fringe of the law'. Regardless, Rogers acknowledged that Singerau was 'a force that must be reckoned with [regarding] any plans for native development of the New Hanover area'.[35] Keenan succinctly explained the government's pragmatic, but controlling position, 'if he is guided and advised he can become a very useful leader and member of his community'.[36]

Non-statutory village councils

Prior to the war, the New Guinea administration had established non-statutory village councils (Kivungs), primarily as a function to hear local disputes and provide a modicum of Indigenous autonomy.[37] During the war, a number of discussion papers by Australian New Guinea Administrative

---

32 Keenan to JH Jones (DDSNA Director), 12 August 1952.
33 Stokes, Report No. 1 of 1952/53, pp. 3–4.
34 Stokes, Report No. 1 of 1952/53, pp. 3–4.
35 JM Rogers, Report 5 of 1950/51, pp. 8–9, New Ireland District, Taskul, 1950–1953, PNGA.
36 Keenan to Jones, 12 August 1952.
37 Primarily in New Britain. David M Fenbury, *Practice without policy: Genesis of local government in Papua New Guinea* (Canberra: The Australian National University, 1978), 12–13.

Unit (ANGAU) officers examined the structure of village leadership and argued in favour of councils as a more suitable village authority than the luluai system.[38] On 26 January 1945, Bert Jones issued a circular which outlined Australia's purpose as fostering communal interest and Indigenous responsibility, to act as a learning tool which would assist the current luluai in controlling village affairs.[39] Eighteen months later, Jones, now in his role as Department of District Services and Native Affairs (DDSNA) Acting Director, informed all officers of the administration's intention to introduce an ordinance to formalise village councils.[40] This would eventually lead to the introduction of local government councils (LGCs) in 1950 to New Britain, Milne Bay and Port Moresby. Whereas the original idea of informal village Kivungs would become a short-lived, but intensive, community development program on New Hanover, informal councils appealed to the administration as both a control measure and a simplified introduction to Western political concepts. Furthermore, in comparison to the introduction of LGCs, where a new division had to be established, the government did not consider the program required extra staffing, a significant appeal to the chronically short-staffed administration.[41]

Coincidentally, it was Bert Jones's son, Ken, an officer on New Hanover, who introduced the concept of village councils in late 1946 to the villages of Kulpetau (No. 1 and 2), located in the south-east of the island. He chose these villages specifically because they did not have any village officials.[42] Jones's role was to have casual informal talks with villagers around the island explaining the virtues of the concept and encouraging participation. Officers were warned most Territorial communities had 'grown restless under what they felt was static administration'. Despite this frustration, the administration viewed the war as an opportunity to enlist villager interest in material and social progress. The informal council system was the first tranche of community development to be introduced to Lavongai: it would provide a test of the 'expected enthusiastic support' for future government programs.[43]

---

38 JR Black to Director DDSNA, 'Village councils', 28 October 1946, Papers of John Black, MS8346/11/5, National Library of Australia (NLA).
39 JH Jones, District Services Instruction No. 17, 'Village councils', HQ Australian New Guinea Administrative Unit (ANGAU), 26 January 1945, Papers of John Black, MS8346/11/6, NLA.
40 This memorandum specifically referred to Circular 17 of January 1945. JH Jones, Circular instruction 23-46/47, 'Village councils', 7 October 1946, Papers of John Black, MS8346/11/6, NLA.
41 Fenbury, *Practice without policy*, 21–22.
42 Kimmorley, Report 4 of 1947/48, p. 9.
43 KW Jones to Read, 11 February 1947, New Ireland District, Kavieng, 1946–1948, PNGA.

Bert Jones, in communication with Jack Read, referred to an article by anthropologist Ian Hogbin, a widely read piece, which outlined a similar experience on nearby Solomon Islands in the 1930s, and the potential for replication in the Territory of Papua New Guinea (TPNG).[44] The administration regarded village councils as an early forerunner for the development of effective local government which envisaged a revival of the 'Indigenous native authority'. Moreover, Bert Jones observed the program was a perfect opportunity for:

> men as ex NGPF, AIB and those with more experience of the world will be possible in view of the democratic nature of the village councils and they must be encouraged to play their part in reviving village life. They must not be allowed to develop into a junta of the young opposed to old men.[45]

In other words, it was a control measure to enlist the support of the newly engaged, and potentially dangerous, young men in a government-sponsored program. Furthermore, as previously described, a revival of Indigenous native authority was already occurring with people like Singerau. The problem was that it was not what the Australian Administration had in mind. By March 1948, Kim Kimmorley had replaced Jones on New Hanover and reported that the Kulpetau councils were progressing quite well in managing the affairs of the village. Kimmorley was confident the program could be expanded quickly, considering the widespread interest across the island.[46]

The government acted on this suggestion and in early 1949 each of the 16 villages in the south-east held a meeting to inaugurate a village council. Each council comprised at least one representative of each clan residing in the village.[47] Graham Taylor patrolled the south-east in September 1949, noting there were now 55 councillors in the area, with villagers bringing concerns of welfare and conduct to them. From Taylor's perspective, he felt they were making every effort to be both fair and honest, and given the obvious 'sincerity and willingness observed', he was confident the scheme would be a success.[48] Councils continued to spread, and by the end of 1949 Fred Kaad reported almost every village had at least two councillors,

---

44   Herbert Ian Hogbin, 'Local government for New Guinea', *Oceania* 17 (1946): 44, doi.org/10.1002/ j.1834-4461.1946.tb00142.x; JH Jones to New Ireland District Officer (DO), 11 February 1947, New Ireland District, Kavieng, 1946–1948, PNGA; Fenbury, *Practice without policy*, 22.
45   JH Jones to New Ireland DO, 11 February 1947.
46   Kimmorley, Report 4 of 1947/48, p. 9.
47   BA McCabe, Report No. 6 of 1949/50, p. 5, New Ireland District, Kavieng, 1949–1951, PNGA.
48   GP Taylor, Report 4 of 1949/50, pp. 3, 6, New Ireland District, Kavieng, 1949–1951, PNGA.

each 'anxious to know more about their work and responsibilities'.[49] In the Australian Government's 1949 report to the United Nations (UN), the enthusiasm and confidence for the scheme was obvious. It described how councillors 'attend to matters of welfare, development and that portion of law and order limited by Native custom'.[50] For all intents and purposes, the scheme was meeting the goals set by the administration. For example, Kaad explained how the councils of Patiagaga and Narimlaua (inland eastern villages) had resolved a longstanding dispute over sago areas due to the activity of the councillors.[51] At another council meeting, this time held at Taskul in January 1950, councillors guaranteed the erection of necessary school buildings as soon as a teacher was made available.[52] The Paterina village council utilised excitement over cash cropping to build a communally owned canoe large enough to transport goods to Taskul for sale to the administration.[53]

Despite these examples, during 1951 the NID administration and officers were clearly losing patience with the scheme. The administration had introduced a second strand of leadership and while the plan was for councillors to act in an advisory capacity to the luluai, many began acting as pseudo-luluais and attempting to assert executive control.[54] This activity or effort to assert control was regarded as a challenge to the Australian Administration, but in reality it was an inevitable consequence of such a program.[55] Ian Downs, the recently installed DO in Kavieng, picked up on this concern, pointing out 'the Luluai system is supported by the Native Administration Regulations and the [unofficial] council system is not supported by any Ordinance'. In this sense, the NID Administration were embarking on the introduction of an unofficial leadership scheme when an official one already existed.[56]

---

49 FP Kaad, Report 8 of 1948/49, p. 13, New Ireland District, Kavieng, 1949–1951, PNGA.
50 Department of External Territories (DET), *Report to the General Assembly of the United Nations on the administration of the Territory of New Guinea: From 1st of July, 1948 to 30th June, 1949* (Canberra: Government Printer, 1949), 22.
51 Kaad, Report 12 of 1949/50, pp. 11–12.
52 FP Kaad, Report 16 of 1949/50, p. 4, New Ireland District, Kavieng, 1949–1951, PNGA.
53 KJ Lang, Report 2 of 1951/52, p. 10, New Ireland District, Taskul, 1950–1953, PNGA.
54 Kaad, Report 8 of 1948/49, p. 13.
55 GP Taylor, Report 4 of 1950/51, p. 7, New Ireland District, Taskul, 1950–1953, PNGA.
56 IFG Downs, Report 5 of 1948/49, pp. 1–2, New Ireland District, Kavieng, 1948–1949, PNGA.

While officers were worried and frustrated by the active dissonance between luluai and councillors on New Hanover, the recently inaugurated official council system on nearby New Britain was attaining what appeared a broader consensus between local people and the administration.[57] This comparison, so close to New Hanover, underlined the obvious defects in a community development scheme which was unofficial and under-resourced. Kenneth Lang's July 1951 report was an effective death knell for the scheme, for he pointed out how the program had been in operation for almost five years, and despite continued efforts by officers to instruct villagers on the basic principles and functions of the council system there had been very little progress.[58] It was clear the government misjudged how ingrained the luluai system had become; this loyalty emphasised divisions and inflamed antipathy. It resulted in these councillors taking control and interrupting the power of the administration through the luluai.[59] Another problem with the 'unofficial' council, one which hampered most community development schemes of the postwar period, was the constant demand for guidance coupled with continual staff changes and shortages.[60] And finally, the introduction of 'unofficial' village councils coincided with another community development scheme, cooperative societies which, without exception, preoccupied villagers across New Hanover during the 1950s.[61] Therefore, while the council program would meander on for another couple of years, it was decided the time was not ripe to foster such a movement, preferring to let the matter rest until such a time as local people themselves advocated for such a scheme, or the official version was inaugurated on the island.[62] The 'unofficial' council scheme is an example of how the provisional administration operated as a distinct entity from Canberra. While the Commonwealth had outlined development plans with the 'New Deal', the impetus for development moved to the Territory in the early postwar period. In this case, the lack of support and planning resulted in the administration instigating an alternative strand of authority to the luluai and then discovering it could not control it.

---

57 Taylor, Report No. 4 of 1950/51, p. 7; KJ Lang, Report No. 1 of 1951/52, p. 4, New Ireland District, Taskul, 1950–1953, PNGA.
58 KJ Lang, Report 2 of 1951/52, p. 4.
59 Lang, Report No. 1 of 1951/52, p. 4.
60 GP Hardy, Report 3 of 1952/53, pp. 4–5, New Ireland District, Taskul, 1950–1953, PNGA.
61 KJ Lang, Report 4 of 1951/52, p. 4, New Ireland District, Taskul, 1950–1953, PNGA.
62 KJ Lang, Report 3 of 1951/52, p. 3, New Ireland District, Taskul, 1950–1953, PNGA.

Copra: An export priority

Figure 11.4: Weighing and selling copra, 1948.
Source: NAA, A1200, L9904, item 11861723.

Before the war, copra production had been the mainstay of the NID economy. However, the destruction of almost a quarter of a million palms during the war threatened the viability of this industry.[63] At the same time, the 'New Deal' explicitly shifted from an expatriate plantation economy to one based on smallholder cash cropping. There were several factors driving this change. Firstly, Indigenous labourers would no longer be available in prewar numbers; the 'New Deal' had introduced new labour laws, put an end to indentured labour, and encouraged village-based economic activity.[64] Secondly, a significant number of plantations remained unoccupied, effectively abandoned, as many expatriate planters chose not to return to

---

63   NID accounted for almost 30 per cent of Territory copra production. I McDonald (Deputy Chairman ANG Production Control Board) to Department Secretary, Department of Agriculture, Stock and Fisheries (DASF), 'Copra production and accumulations', 19 November 1949, Copra Production—General 1948–57, A518 [A813/1/4 Part 3], National Archives of Australia (NAA).
64   Edward Ward, 'The New Deal', 4 July 1945, Native Labour 1945–7, A452 [1959/5650], NAA.

TPNG after the war.[65] Finally, cooperatives were a community development model which the administration hoped could overcome labour shortages, encourage smallholder farming and increase Indigenous plantings of coconut palms.

Table 11.1: Price of copra: Papua–New Guinea, 1925–48.

Year	Price per ton	% fluctuation
1925/26	$148.09	–
1926/27	$122.91	–17.0%
1927/28	$122.40	–
1928/29	$102.05	–16.6%
1929/30	$93.55	–8.5%
1930/31	$88.62	–5.3%
1931/32	$84.57	–4.57%
1932/33	$77.99	–7.78%
1933/34	$37.57	–51.83%
1934/35	$52.19	14.62
1935/36	$89.96	72.37%
1936/37	$124.19	38.1%
1937/38	$86.40	–30.4%
1938/39	$72.75	–15.8%
1939/1940	$60.10	–17.4%
1940/41	$36.13	–39.9%
1946/47	$181.45	402.2%
1947/48	$256.86	41.6%
Average	**$102.10**	**35.64%**

Note: Figures in 1969 Australian dollars, as per Statistics Section (Department of External Territories), *Compendium of Statistics for Papua New Guinea* (Canberra: Government Printer, 1969). Average per cent fluctuation calculated on 22 years.

Source: Report on visit to Papua–New Guinea by Acting Minister for External Territories (The Honourable Cyril Chambers) 11th–22nd January, 1949, pp. 112–13, Copra Stabilisation fund 1949–56, A518 [D56/3/1 Part 2], NAA.

---

65   On New Hanover, most plantations remained abandoned. KW Dyer, Report 15 of 1949/50, pp. 2–3, New Ireland District, Kavieng, 1949–1951, PNGA; Kaad, Report 12 of 1949/50, pp. 4–5.

An important stimulant for coconut planting was the price of copra, a notoriously unstable commodity, which in the early postwar period was benefiting from worldwide edible oil shortages.[66] The 1948 price of $256.86 was an all-time record high price on the open world market, but as Table 11.1 highlights, price discrepancy averaged 35.64 per cent for the years 1926–48.[67] Price uncertainty threatened the long-term viability of the industry, a problem only magnified by the impending introduction of cash cropping to villagers unaccustomed to global commodity markets.

The Australian Government made three important decisions in the early years after the war to provide equilibrium to the industry. Firstly, a copra stabilisation reserve fund was approved in February 1947. Contributions were collected from growers on a sliding scale and deposited in a fund provisioned against the exigencies of future price fluctuations.[68] Secondly, in March 1949 the Australian Government entered a nine-year agreement with the United Kingdom (UK) for the sale of copra.[69] This program proved a success: growth in copra exports to the UK increased threefold; for the year 1948/49 sales totalled 26,981 tons and by 1957/58 had risen to 92,298 tons.[70] The UK agreement limited price variation at 10 per cent. Planters were frustrated at the low prices paid, attributable to some extent to the devalued sterling.[71] For example, in July 1951 world copra prices reached a high of $560.67 per ton, whereas the UK price was $343.64.[72] Paul Hasluck negotiated a substantial increase in 1952. These two measures, which frustrated expatriate planters because they reduced profits, were expected to minimise price fluctuations, and provide certainty to Indigenous growers new to cash cropping and global export markets.[73] The third decision was the establishment of the Copra Marketing Board (CMB) in 1952 to replace the Production Board. The CMB was a statutory institution

---

66 Coconut oil per metric tonne: 1938 US$78; 1948 US$421. The price remained above US$300 per tonne until the middle of 1950s. Prices began to fall as substitutes such as soya bean oil began to be used. Coconut Research Institute, 'The long-term causes for the decline in the prices of coconut oil', *Ceylon Coconut Quarterly* 12, no. 3–4 (1961): 130.
67 Report on visit to Papua–New Guinea by Acting Minister for External Territories (Cyril Chambers) 11th–22nd January 1949, Copra Stabilisation fund 1949–56, A518 [D56/3/1 Part 2], NAA.
68 Draft paper, 'Copra: A well-established primary product', Copra 51–53, M331 [191], NAA.
69 Subject to Australian home consumption requirements (estimated 25,000 tons). Hasluck, 'Export marketing of copra to cabinet', draft paper 16 July 1951, Copra 51–53, M331 [191], NAA.
70 File papers, Copra 51–53, M331 [191], NAA.
71 Planters had suffered with the low prices during the depression; the stabilisation and UK contract provided certainty which was not acknowledged by planters.
72 Figures in 1969 Australian dollars.
73 Extract from *Pacific Islands Monthly* (September 1951), 'British MOF price of copra', Copra 51–53, M331 [191], NAA.

responsible for selling all copra produced in TPNG and, as such, was focussed on improving copra to enable farmers to receive the best possible return for their output.[74] The CMB acted as a liaison between growers and global markets.[75] Nonetheless, the CMB would also play a crucial role in the eventual downfall of many cooperatives who would struggle to meet its strict quality controls.

Conclusion

The introduction of socioeconomic and political development in the postwar period to New Hanover reflected a contrasting vision of control and ambition for improved living standards for Lavongai. The origins of this tension were a lack of government resources, primarily inexperienced and undermanned staff, and anxiety over the autonomous actions of local people. On the ground, as this chapter has highlighted, patrol reports interpreted the actions and behaviours of these Islanders on a Eurocentric scale of the compliant 'native'. Invariably this meant the patrol officer could explain away political and economic dissatisfaction as the 'confusion of the primitive mind', or the innovative actions of an Indigenous leader by referring to noncompliant behaviour. It fitted with the government's demand-driven evolutionary development strategy which assumed Papuans and New Guineans would accept 'advancement' on the colonialist's terms. In other words, there was limited space for innovative or autonomous Indigenous activity.

The introduction of 'unofficial' councils on New Hanover was an early example of a containment strategy disguised as political development. Patrol reports of the early postwar period express the level of concern the administration had for maintaining control. By enlisting the support of energetic, but potentially dangerous, leaders within a government-sponsored community development scheme, the administration was actively attempting to revive Indigenous authority while simultaneously limiting potential civil unrest. This strategy further isolated Indigenous leaders who were more inclined to act autonomously because they did not fit within the narrow parameters of what the government deemed as acceptable.

---

74 1952 Copra Marketing Board: 'Copra—agricultural production and marketing', 19 March 1952, Copra 51–53, M331 [191], NAA.
75 W Cottrell-Dormer, 'The implementation of agricultural policy', 25 November 1947, Papers of Sir Donald Cleland, MS9600/9/5/9, NLA.

The introduction of 'unofficial' councils also highlighted the disconnect between the provisional administration and the Canberra department. Not only was the scheme poorly planned and supported, but it resulted in promoting an alternative strand of authority to the indirect rule already in place, one it discovered it could not control. This narrative of development and containment is further explored in the following chapter. While the introduction of cooperatives would bring immediate financial benefit to the Islanders, once it began to falter in the second half of the 1950s, it exacerbated existing mistrust between local people and the Territory Administration.

12

Cooperatives and the Hasluck Pyramid at Work in the Villages of New Hanover

The introduction of cooperatives provided the people of New Hanover with an opportunity to transfer from subsistence production to a cash economy. The Lavongai invested their savings and, more importantly, their faith in cooperatives. From their inception in the early 1950s, and largely supported by high world copra prices, cooperatives rewarded them with a significant lift to their financial wellbeing. However, as this chapter explains, the collapse in copra prices coupled with waning passion, unskilled management and a lack of government support led to widespread failure and a disillusioned local population. As the cooperative movement stalled and tensions rose around the island, the administration made a concerted effort to find a more amenable leadership than that offered by Singerau.

This chapter provides a case study of the Hasluck Development Pyramid at work in the villages. Cooperative societies were a community development program expected to introduce new economic, social and political concepts while maintaining people in their villages. The assumption was that financial success would increase demand for 'needs and wants', stimulating economic activity and interest in more political responsibility. The results were somewhat mixed. On the one hand, cooperatives did incite enthusiasm for cash cropping and the successful introduction of a cash economy. They also provided an excellent opportunity to train Papuans and New Guineans in Western business management practices. While cooperatives enticed Indigenous leaders to engage with a colonial development program, leaders such as Singerau reinterpreted government programs to best suit themselves and their communities. This did not fit within Australian development parameters. The 'New Deal' and later Hasluck-inspired programs prioritised a particular version of Indigenous advancement premised on a gradual stepped approach to development on the ground in the villages. In this way, policy was consistently shaped within a containment strategy of minimising disruptive elements within the Indigenous community that did not align with the overall gradualist approach of the Australian Government.

Cooperatives: The Hasluck Development Pyramid at work

During 1949–50 there was a concerted effort by the administration to rapidly establish cooperatives in the Kavieng subdistrict. During this period, officers were expected 'to induce the natives in the various villages to become interested in cash crops' and encourage locals that 'the best way of disposing of their copra at the most favourable terms would be through the cooperative societies'.[1] By late 1949, a cooperative trade store and copra storage shed were constructed at Taskul in preparation for the first visit of the district cooperative officer, Reg Boyan.[2] The cooperative movement officially commenced on New Hanover in February 1950 with the formation of the New Hanover Native Society. This was followed by a secondary association—the New Ireland Natives' Societies Association (NINSA)—in 1951 to supply primary societies in the Kavieng subdistrict with external services: bookkeeping, banking, transport and marketing.[3]

Fred Kaad visited Baikeb on 17 January 1950 to follow up vague allegations Singerau was abusing his power, but instead, found a willing partner who was 'a great help to me in official matters and so far, I have had no reason to mistrust him'. He went on to explain how Singerau's copra trade scheme was frustrating planters, traders and recruiters. By selling their copra to the Production Board at Kavieng he was earning a 50 per cent premium for

---

1   JM Rogers, Report 1 of 1950/51, p. 6, New Ireland District, Kavieng, 1949–1951, National Archives of Papua New Guinea (PNGA).
2   IFG Downs to Director Department of District Services and Native Affairs (DDSNA), 14 December 1949, New Ireland District, Kavieng, 1949–1951, PNGA.
3   The New Hanover Native Society was soon broken into four smaller societies: Pelmatias, Tingwon, Matbung and Matas. Sumer Singh, *Co-operatives in Papua New Guinea* (Port Moresby: New Guinea Research Unit, The Australian National University, 1974), 51.

12. COOPERATIVES AND THE HASLUCK PYRAMID AT WORK IN THE VILLAGES OF NEW HANOVER

villagers, while actively undermining the allure of working on a plantation for young men. Cooperatives provided both Kaad and Singerau with a unique opportunity: Kaad to introduce centrally controlled communal development, and Singerau economic opportunity for himself and his people. Kaad envisioned 'when the cooperative begins functioning' Singerau should be acknowledged because:

> he has done a great deal for the progress of his people, i.e. the copra scheme is almost entirely due to his initiative and he is [will be] a prime mover in the cooperative venture.[4]

Kaad's prediction proved correct with the establishment of the Pelmatias Co-operative Society in south-east New Hanover in mid-1950. Singerau was named chairman and successfully negotiated the amalgamation of his copra and transport organisation within the cooperative society.[5] Singerau was quickly on the front foot, swept up in the enthusiasm for the project, 'point[ing] out in public, and quite strongly too, the advisability of everyone supporting the society's activities, particularly the marketing of copra'.[6] He freely admitted to Kaad he discouraged people leaving the village to work on plantations arguing it was vital that sufficient men were left to attend to community matters.[7] This was a common complaint from village leaders in each of the four case studies of this book; however, in Singerau's case, his forceful personality ensured his edicts were followed. His sphere of activity moved increasingly into surrounding villages. He ordered copra dryers to be built, and commenced working the abandoned Metewoi Plantation (west of Baikeb) with a line of villagers. Singerau enforced loyalty to the cooperative society, giving the impression it was compulsory to sell to it. He appears to have established a system of 'spies' to maintain control, threatening court action to anyone disobeying his orders. For instance, one Metewoi villager complained to Kaad 'three Baikeb natives had reported him to Singerau because he had sold some of his own copra to a Chinese trader'. The matter was investigated and Singerau was found guilty of the charge.[8]

---

4   Kaad reported Singerau was receiving '£3 per bag instead of selling it to traders at £2'. FP Kaad, Report 12 of 1949/50, pp. 8–9, New Ireland District, Kavieng, 1949–1951, PNGA.
5   Kaad, Report 12 of 1949/50, p. 4.
6   KW Dyer, Report 2 of 1950/51, p. 7, New Ireland District, Taskul, 1950–1953, PNGA.
7   Kaad, Report 12 of 1949/50, p. 9; BB Butcher, Report 2 of 1953/54, p. 3, New Ireland District, Taskul, 1953–1954, PNGA.
8   WW Stokes, Report 1 of 1952/53, pp. 3–4, New Ireland District, Taskul, 1953–1954, PNGA.

Figure 12.1: Husking coconuts for copra.
Source: National Archives of Australia (NAA), A1200, L9765, item 11861747.

Officers feared that an obsession with copra, a 'copra age', was distorting the incentive to work hard. Kenneth Lang reasoned that because villagers, with little apparent effort, could afford the 'dazzling array of articles so enticingly displayed in the trade stores', they would grow used to high prices and easy work.[9] The early 1950s were a period of high wages for casual labour and high prices for copra: 'a boom time which the native has not recognised and hence is failing to exploit'.[10] Officers encouraged investment in community development, but frustrated, made disparaging comments such as farmers preferring 'hair dye, scent and firecrackers' to 'saving for old age'.[11] Supply of labour dried up on the plantations managed by Europeans and Chinese, who instead had to rely on imported labour.[12] Michael Cockburn described the Lavongai as 'most uncooperative', as a people 'too wrapped up in their economic activities and now consider village work as an irksome drudge

---

9   KJ Lang, Report 1 of 1951/52, p. 4, New Ireland District, Taskul, 1950–1953.
10 Stokes, Report 1 of 1952/53, p. 4.
11 Stokes, Report 1 of 1952/53, p. 4; B Hayes, Report 1 of 1956/57, p. 5, New Ireland District, Kavieng, 1956–1957, PNGA.
12 BB Butcher, Report 1 of 1953/54, p. 4, New Ireland District, Taskul, 1955–1956, PNGA.

that must be avoided if possible'.[13] In short, officers were concerned the early success of copra production would create a dynamic whereby villagers would not understand the connection between hard work and financial reward. The Department of District Services and Native Affairs (DDSNA) Director Bert Jones responded to these fears by reminding officers the 'over-emphasis on copra as a cash crop is not unique', and warning under no circumstances should restrictions be imposed because he feared 'unfounded suspicion that the administration is against copra production'.[14]

By October 1951, the cooperative trade store at Taskul was operating efficiently, trading in copra and well supplied with items for sale.[15] Although collection of copra was limited to villages close to Taskul and the adjacent Tsoi Island, prevailing winds and rough seas made transportation by canoe exceptionally difficult.[16] This meant villagers from the west of New Hanover had little choice but to sell their copra to Chinese traders who bought it at substantially lower prices than the Taskul cooperative.[17] Transport would remain a problem for many years. In 1954 NINSA began to operate several motorised vessels but had problems with reliability. Inevitably this led to large amounts of copra deteriorating in storage facilities, sometimes waiting up to six months for transportation to the Copra Marketing Board (CMB) depot. Another consequence was poor cashflow because finance was tied up in copra stock.[18] This lack of cash in the community not only frustrated farmers but trade stores suffered a double blow: no replacement stock depleted stores of goods to sell and the reduced amount of cash in the economy meant businesses would practically cease for weeks, even months, until shipping became available.[19]

---

13   MJ Cockburn, Report 3 of 1955/56, p. 3, New Ireland District, Taskul, 1955–1956, PNGA.
14   JH Jones to New Ireland District Commissioner (DC), 22 April 1952, New Ireland District, Taskul, 1950–1953, PNGA.
15   J Young-Whitforde to New Ireland DC, 26 October 1951, New Ireland District, Taskul, 1950–1953, PNGA.
16   Dyer to New Ireland DC, 26 October 1951, New Ireland District, Taskul, 1950–1953, PNGA; KJ Lang, Report 4 of 1951/52, p. 4, New Ireland District, Taskul, 1950–1953, PNGA.
17   CJ Millar (Registrar) to Director DDSNA, 5 October 1951, New Ireland District, Taskul, 1950–1953, PNGA.
18   Singh, *Co-operatives*, 46, 53; G Neilsen to New Ireland DO, 12 March 1959, New Ireland District, Kavieng, 1958–1959, PNGA.
19   Singh *Co-operatives*, 50.

Figure 12.2: CJ Miller, Registrar of Co-operative Societies, Territory of Papua New Guinea (TPNG), speaking at the 1951 Congress of Queensland Co-operatives.
Source: NAA, A6510, 2399, item 7649618.

A cooperative school was built with volunteer labour at Kavieng to improve literacy and provide training in clerical and trade store management.[20] The Co-operative Section hoped this school would provide the skills to compete with the Chinese traders.[21] Whether or not the training proved sufficient is open to conjecture. However, within a short period of the school's opening there were 16 cooperatives within the Kavieng subdistrict, each operating trade stores in addition to their function of buying and marketing copra.[22] During this period, patrol, cooperative and agricultural extension officers worked closely together gathering the personal details of subscribers, explaining the concept of cooperatives, establishing

---

20   Department of Territories (DOT), *Report to the General Assembly of the United Nations on the administration of the Territory of New Guinea: From 1st of July, 1950 to June 30th, 1951* (Port Moresby: Government Printer, 1951), 54.
21   E Graham to J Jordan, Report 13 of 1956/57, New Ireland District, Kavieng, 1956–1957, PNGA.
22   The combined capital of the 16 societies was £5,962 ($21,565 1969 AUD), contributed by 13,891 residents in 169 separate villages. Department of External Territories (DET), *Report to the General Assembly of the United Nations on the administration of the Territory of New Guinea: From 1st of July, 1949 to 30th June, 1950* (Canberra: Government Printer, 1950), 54.

organisational structures and improving farming techniques. The workload was voluminous; Keith Dyer reported a process of widespread confusion, of villagers 'collect[ing] most of the money' and not documenting 'receipts or records of these transactions'.[23] Dyer explained how 'at every village visited names were obtained of the shareholders in the New Hanover Society'.[24] Despite efforts to the contrary, many villagers remained convinced the venture was a government-controlled one, primarily due to the cooperative store's location alongside that of the resident officer at Taskul.[25]

The concept of cooperatives was explained to local farmers in a paternalistic manner. For example, Basil Hayes explained:

> we have these things [European goods] because we have knowledge. You have not got many of them because of the simple reason that you have not studied these things as we have, but it is not the intention of the government that you remain ignorant.[26]

The government was portrayed as the font of all knowledge, of 'setting up schools so that you can learn to read and write' and 'your cooperative societies which are another type of school so that you can learn to make good copra, and practice selling your copra to world markets'. Officers would provide a general description of cooperatives, their purpose and activities, and how this form of organisation would benefit them as they 'learnt about better ways of living'.[27]

By late 1956, cooperatives were performing strongly with a large number of trade stores across the island, each with good turnover in proportion to the stocks held in a particular store.[28] The three New Hanover societies were marketing almost as much copra as the combined Kavieng subdistrict; officer Dickson attributed this success to the support and activity of 'the men of power' such as Singerau.[29] Villagers were now well aware of the economic potential of the coconut palm, and new plantings were a high priority.[30] While in the early days of Indigenous cash cropping

---

23 Payment by either cash or bags of copra. KW Dyer, Report 1 of 1950/51, p. 7, New Ireland District, Taskul, 1950–1953, PNGA.
24 KW Dyer, Report 2 of 1950/51, p. 7.
25 GP Taylor, Report 4 of 1950/51, p. 4, New Ireland District, Taskul, 1950–1953, PNGA.
26 B Hayes addressing West Coast villagers October 1957, Report 1 of 1956/57, p. 9, New Ireland District, Kavieng, 1956–1957, PNGA.
27 B Hayes addressing West Coast villagers October 1957, Report 1 of 1956/57, p. 9.
28 J Cochrane, Report 4 of 1956/57, p. 11, New Ireland District, Kavieng, 1956–1957, PNGA.
29 EE Dickson, Report 8 of 1956/57, p. 10, New Ireland District, Kavieng, 1956–1957, PNGA.
30 Cochrane, Report 4 of 1956/57, p. 20.

villagers had squandered new-found wealth in the trade stores, five years on an entrepreneurial fervour had seized the people. John Jordan explained how 'people stated that they desired to attain a sizeable bank account that might leave legacies for their children' and were 'endeavouring to form theories of certain communal enterprises which they could commence, and which would pay back dividends'.[31] During this period Singerau was busy expanding operations of the Pelmatias Society. This included construction of a road capable of taking vehicular traffic along the south-east coast between Meteran and Ungat. The society planned to purchase a truck which could collect and transport copra among the southern villages and back to Baikeb village, the point of concentration for collection by NINSA boats. The village itself was shifted a few hundred metres inland due to soil erosion by the sea, and a wharf built out to the passage offshore.[32]

Despite the early success of cooperatives, by the end of 1952 there were already many warning signs of impending problems that would eventually overwhelm the cooperative movement. Firstly, misunderstandings between administrative officers and colonised people contributed to a pattern of mixed messaging, magnified by the constant churn of new officers. For instance, officers spent significant time promoting and encouraging the voluntary uptake of cooperatives, and yet they would eventually hear rumours 'cooperatives were compulsory' and those 'disobeying will be gaoled'.[33] A likely source of many of these declarations would be Singerau, who was renowned for exaggerating government demands to garner greater effort from fellow farmers.[34] More concerning was the economic reliance on one cash crop, reducing the resilience of the economy to external price shocks. While the administration recognised the problem, Lang wrote, somewhat cryptically, 'it seems of little value to warn them that the price of copra is liable to fluctuate greatly within the next few years'.[35] Obviously there were communication problems, and villagers were already dealing with many new ideas within their control, so perhaps officers felt that to burden them with concerns outside their control was not worth the effort. Whether a warning would have been effective is a reasonable question. However, without doubt one of the chief concerns of local farmers, in the aftermath

---

31   J Jordan, Report 11 of 1956/57, p. 2, New Ireland District, Kavieng, 1956–1957, PNGA.
32   Cochrane, Report 4 of 1956/57, p. 4; EE Dickson, Report 8 of 1956/57.
33   Stokes, Report 1 of 1952/53, p. 1.
34   Butcher, Report 2 of 1953/54, p. 9.
35   Lang, Report 4 of 1951/52, p. 4. Catherine Snowden, 'Copra co-operatives', in *A time to plant and a time to uproot: A history of agriculture in Papua New Guinea*, ed. Donald Denoon and Catherine Snowden, (Port Moresby: Department of Primary Industry, 1979), 201.

12. COOPERATIVES AND THE HASLUCK PYRAMID AT WORK IN THE VILLAGES OF NEW HANOVER

of the breakdown of cooperatives, was the lack of transparency and full disclosure of potential problems such as a collapse in world copra prices.[36] Finally, officers reported many entrepreneurial villagers who, motivated by potential higher financial returns, had begun shipping directly to the CMB depot at Rabaul, New Britain.[37] While on the surface this could be viewed as a positive development of entrepreneurial skills, and indeed in many ways it was a clever use of resources, in the long run, the lack of loyalty to their cooperatives was fatal to the movement.

During the mid-1950s, enthusiasm for the New Ireland District (NID) cooperative movement began to wane, the high hopes held for the societies having not materialised. In the period 1955–61 membership dropped by 22 per cent and turnover by 31 per cent, and while trade store operations grew by 45 per cent, it could not make up for the 46 per cent fall in copra turnover.

Table 12.1: New Ireland cooperative societies, 1955–61.

Year	Society	Member	Member change	Average change	Store T/O	Copra T/O	Other T/O	Total	% change
1955	21	10,652	–	507	$109,992	$355,944	$58,183	$524,199	–
1958	25	10,081	-5.4%	403	$80,219	$213,076	$20,388	$313,683	-40.2%
1960	24	8,603	-14.7%	358	$125,174	$298,748	$6,090	$430,012	+37.1%
1961	21	8,292	-3.6%	394	$160,542	$191,352	$9,197	$361,091	-16.0%
Change	–	-2,360	-22.2%	-113	+$50,550	-$164,592	-$48,986	-$163,108	-31.1%

Note: Figures adjusted to 1969 Australian dollars.
Source: Territory of Papua and New Guinea, Annual Reports of the Co-operative Section from 1955–57, 1960, 1961, Co-operative Annual Reports 1955–61, A518 [EL840/1/4], NAA.

36 John Mugambwa, 'The saga of the co-operative movement in Papua New Guinea', *Journal of South Pacific Law* 9, no. 1 (2005).
37 BA McCabe, Report 9 of 1954/55, pp. 7–8, Bougainville District, Sohano, 1954–1955, PNGA.

Table 12.2: 1960 New Hanover cooperative societies.

Society	Members	Rebates	Rebate/member
Pelmatias	573	$3,640	$6.35
Tingwon	93	$2,219	$23.86
Matbung	185	$1,605	$8.67
Matas	479	$3,006	$6.28
Total	**1,330**	**$10,470**	–
Average	333	$2,618	$7.86

Notes: The first society on New Hanover was formed in February 1950 (New Hanover Native Society Ltd), by 1960 there were four societies. Figures adjusted to 1969 Australian dollars.

Source: P Bloomfield, Report 7 of 1959/60, p. 10, New Ireland District, Kavieng, 1959–1960, PNGA.

Table 12.3: World copra price (Pacific Coast), 1948–59.

Year	Price	Fluctuation
1948	$256.86	–
1949	$156.43	–39.1%
1950	$179.65	+14.8%
1951	$185.90	+3.5%
1952	$134.72	–27.5%
1953	$188.60	+40%
1954	$158.21	–16.1%
1955	$142.12	–10.2%
1956	$137.65	–3.2%
1957	$141.22	+2.6%
1958	$203.76	+44.3%
1959	$230.57	+13.2%
Average	$176.31	17.9%

Source: US Department of Agriculture, 'The fats and oils situation', *Agricultural Marketing Service*, 20 August 1959, p. 32.

On New Hanover, by 1960, there were four societies. The Tingwon Society was a former breakaway from Pelmatias Society: with only 93 members it relied on a rich trade in both shell and copra. The Pelmatias Society under the supervision of Singerau had always been a strong society. However, by 1960 there was dissension among the members, and Paul Bloomfield reported the Umbukul group had left the Pelmatias Society. Bloomfield felt the discord could well be due to the waning influence of Singerau, especially

12. COOPERATIVES AND THE HASLUCK PYRAMID AT WORK IN THE VILLAGES OF NEW HANOVER

regarding local government councils, which were becoming active during this period.[38] Posikei, the luluai of Noipuos, was the Chairman of the Matbung Co-operative Society and alongside Boski Tom was, by the late 1950s, regarded to have supplanted Singerau as the most influential leaders on the island. The Matas and Matbung societies had the disadvantage of having to compete with Chinese traders who enjoyed a virtual monopoly of trade in the north of the island.[39]

Copra prices continued to fluctuate throughout the 1950s (17.9 per cent average variance), and although somewhat protected by the copra stabilisation reserve fund (see Chapter 11), by 1956 the rate was 46 per cent below 1948 prices. What became increasingly evident was, because of the little skill or capital required, how vulnerable copra farmers were to additional competition. This created a crisis of confidence in a fragile one-dimensional economy, and across the Territory of Papua New Guinea (TPNG), copra turnover fell by 36 per cent and trade store sales by 72 per cent.[40]

The presence of Chinese traders was a constant source of irritation for administration officers who regarded their actions as efficient, but immoral. Whether the criticism was xenophobic is difficult to assess because of the limited number of European traders active on New Hanover, but the general description of 'the Chinese' suggested illegal and nefarious practices. Ironically, while officers regarded trading licences as undermining the financial viability of cooperatives, in 1956, at the low point for world copra prices, the government issued additional peddling licences.[41] Patrol reports are filled with criticism of Chinese activity; for example, Lang pondered how 'Asiatics who are married to native women and reside in the wife's village' were able to operate trade stores built on the village ground.[42] This, of course, was an example of how matrilineal societies work and show that Papuan and New Guineans had ways of incorporating outsiders into their societies.

---

38 P Bloomfield, Report 7 of 1959/60, pp. 10–11, New Ireland District, Kavieng, 1959–1960, PNGA.
39 P Bloomfield, Report 11 of 1957/58, p. 8, New Ireland District, Taskul, 1957–1958, PNGA.
40 Compared to cocoa, which required capital and technical skill to operate a fermentary. Singh, *Co-operatives*, 47, 61.
41 Singh, *Co-operatives*, 47.
42 Lang, Report 4 of 1951/52, p. 5.

Cooperative officer Harry Jackman described the situation as a 'copra war', threatening action against illegal trading.[43] In answer to these concerns, Bert Jones pointed out that in extreme cases, control of Asiatic traders could be exercised when the annual licences were renewed. However, this does not seem to have been accepted practice, and instead it was suggested as a 'general rule' officers should insist they 'obey local native custom': they could not have it both ways by attempting 'to exploit their alien descent as well as native inheritance and rights'.[44]

Concern over copra prices offered by the traders suggested both price gouging by the Chinese and laziness by the Lavongai. In areas where cooperatives were not easily reached and traders held almost monopolistic dominance, villagers would often ask officers if the government had the ability to control prices.[45] Alternatively, in areas where the cooperatives did operate, villagers would sometimes still prefer to sell to a trader despite the obvious socioeconomic benefit of the trade store. There were four main reasons for this decision: traditional matrilineal ownership systems; physical obstacles to transportation; rejection rates from the CMB; and the proficiency of traders at using whatever methods necessary to take advantage of circumstances.

Introduction of perennial crops complicated traditional matrilineal land management systems.[46] Once a farmer registered to sell their produce with the cooperative it would come to the notice of matrilineal elders who legally had the right to take over ownership on the death of the father. The children who helped establish cash cropping were predisposed to challenge the matrilineal system on the grounds of their labour in the crop. The dilemma of the father often meant that instead of selling through the local cooperative society they would take produce directly to Chinese traders and avoid needing to register activity.[47]

---

43   JR Keenan to Director DDSNA, 9 April 1952, New Ireland District, Taskul, 1950–1953, PNGA.
44   Anyone trading with Indigenous Papuans and New Guineans required a licence. Only children of mixed marriages had land tenure rights. JH Jones to New Ireland DC, 22 April 1952.
45   KJ Lang, Report 3 of 1951/52, pp. 3, 4, 6, 8, New Ireland District, Taskul, 1950–1953, PNGA; Report 1 of 1951/52, pp. 4–5.
46   Peter G Sack, 'Land in PNG future', in *Problem of choice: Land in Papua New Guinea's future*, ed. Peter G Sack (Canberra: Australian National University Press, 1974), 6–10.
47   Scarlett Epstein, *Capitalism, primitive and modern* (Manchester: Manchester University Press, 1968), 111, 126. See also: Michael French Smith, *Village on the edge* (Honolulu: University of Hawai'i Press, 2002), 34–38.

Often cooperative members lived in villages several kilometres away from trade or branch stores. Initial enthusiasm for the cooperative society often overcame such inconveniences, but over time, with declining loyalty, villagers tended to engage in private trading outside the cooperative framework. Assistant District Officer (ADO) Bob Bell disparagingly reasoned it was because they are 'too lazy to be bothered making copra when he can get a good return from a trader'.[48]

Chinese traders understood the difficulties these farmers faced transporting their produce and would use their own vehicles to collect produce. So determined were they to conduct business they would even offer to purchase whole nuts and then convert it themselves to copra.[49] Frustration bubbled over as officers accused these 'traders of supplying credit freely in the hope of encouraging native patronage, and bribing individuals to act as "dummies" so they could expand to multiple sites'.[50] Despite a strong correlation between the existence of a trade store and competitive prices from European and Chinese traders, most society members regarded their trade stores as merely a means for the sale of their cash crops or the purchase of household goods.[51]

In 1947 an informal program to train Indigenous cooperative staff in clerical and storeman activities commenced. Although this became a formalised education program in 1949, there was difficulty sourcing pupils of a sufficiently high basic standard to complete the course.[52] Consequently, there was a dearth of properly trained storeman to manage the society stores during the 1950s; this left them more or less entirely dependent on an already depleted European staff.[53] A major problem in recruiting trade store staff was wage rates for cooperative clerical and storemen, which were markedly lower than those paid for similar skilled employment.[54] This had two effects. Firstly, cooperatives could not attract suitable talent, and secondly, trained and competent personnel were attracted to the higher

---

48   RS Bell to J Jordan, 31 July 1957, New Ireland District, Kavieng, 1956–1957, PNGA.
49   Maxwell Rimoldi, 'The Hahalis Welfare Society of Buka' (PhD thesis, The Australian National University, 1971), p. 126, available at: openresearch-repository.anu.edu.au/items/3f163ed0-480f-4686-8af1-4020c761ecec.
50   RW Hallahan, Report 4 of 1959/60, p. 8, New Ireland District, Kavieng, 1959–1960, PNGA.
51   Singh, *Co-operatives*, 48.
52   'Native agricultural extension, training and education', May 1955, pp. 3–4, Advancement of native agriculture 1954–56, A518 [C2/1/1], National Archives of Australia (NAA).
53   Department of Native Affairs (DNA), 'Annual Report Co-operative Section 1955/56', p. 4, Co-operative reports 1955–7, A518 [EL840/1/4], NAA.
54   Singh, *Co-operatives*, 56.

wages available in private industry. This resulted in inadequate office records and stock control, a contributing factor in the failure of societies to make the progress anticipated by the administration.[55] Furthermore, familial (*Wontok*) pressure, and frustration with, or misunderstanding of, the cooperative movement resulted in widespread theft from the trade stores by clerks and storemen.[56] Cooperative Registrar Grainger Morris blamed the poor results on dishonesty, suggesting 'the irregularities probably stemmed from a grafting of traditional native behaviour patterns on to cooperative technique'.[57]

One person accused of theft was Walla Gukguk, a future Lavongai leader of national renown, who worked as a NINSA storekeeper from 1952 to 1957. He was jailed for distributing goods freely to his relatives, and later blamed his actions on dissatisfaction with the cooperative concept.[58] Another example was Kaleman, a villager from Metamona (west coast, slightly inland), and a close collaborator of Singerau. From 1952 to 1955 he was the clerk of the Neimal Co-operative store but was dismissed for theft. Kaleman returned to his village and bought two trading licences and materials for a hot-air dryer. He acquired coconuts from the Metamona people, and instead of paying them for their labour, lent Singerau £10 to help pay the shipping costs of his pinnace and repaid £50 to cover the deficit in society funds. With no money forthcoming, the villagers complained to Bloomfield, and Kaleman was sentenced to six months in jail.[59]

International marketing agreements pressured agricultural officers to focus on quality, on 'the need for better copra'.[60] Rejection rates for copra increased rapidly, often because of poor husbandry practices; however, regularly, it was no fault of the farmer as produce would deteriorate in storage waiting for transport. Initially, copra products had been almost exclusively of poor-quality smoke grade. This fetched lower prices and did not satisfy the

---

55   DNA, 'Annual Report Co-operative Section 1955/56', 4.
56   JN Dunkerley, Report 2 of 1959/60, p. 6, New Ireland District, Kavieng, 1959–1960, PNGA.
57   'N.G. co-operatives endangered', *Sydney Morning Herald*, 1 August 1957, Co-operative reports 1955–7, A518 [EL840/1/4], NAA.
58   Walla Gukguk was a leader in the Johnson Cult (1964–66), 1968 elected President of the Tutukuvul Isukal Association and local council, and 1977 elected to National Parliament. T Kanku, 'Wartime experience of Walla Gukguk, Lavongai, New Ireland Province', *Oral History: Institute of Papua New Guinea Studies* 10 (1982): 40; Dorothy Billings, *Cargo cult as theater: political performance in the Pacific* (Lanham: Lexington, 2002), 141.
59   Bloomfield, Report 11 of 1957/58, pp. 11–12.
60   P Bloomfield, Report 12 of 1956/57, p. 2, New Ireland District, Kavieng, 1956–1957, PNGA.

export market. After meetings with the expatriate Planters' Association in November 1952, Paul Hasluck announced an official copra inspection and grading system would be introduced.[61]

Table 12.4: New Ireland District copra rejection rates, October 1954–57.

Year	Bags produced	Bags rejected	Per cent
1954	2,265	500	22.08%
1955	1,903	280	14.71%
1956	1,988	67	3.4%
1957	2,079	0	0%

Source: EO Graham to ADO Kavieng, 14 November 1957, New Ireland District, Kavieng, 1956–1957.

With the appointment of a copra inspector at Kavieng, there was an immediate setback to the cooperatives due to heavy rejections of badly dried copra (1 in 5 bags in 1954).[62] This only stirred resentment among local farmers who believed copra inspectors were discriminating against them and having a 'marked effect on the amount of copra marketed through the Societies'. Don Barrett (New Guinea Islands) warned the Legislative Council that 'natives' regarded the downgrading or rejection of the copra as a signal it was not worth producing it, and 'they would just let the coconuts rot'.[63] As ADO Bell noted, 'a person who has had his copra rejected by cooperatives a number of times becomes discouraged and to ensure payment sells the primary product to the trader'.[64]

Despite a recommendation from the Department of Agriculture, Stock and Fisheries (DASF) in March 1951 for the introduction of hot-air dryers, in the intervening five years very few were built.[65] A NID heads of department meeting in December 1955 praised the planting program, which had yielded 180,000 new coconut palms, but raised concerns over the poor quality of copra produced.[66] There were just 65 hot-air dryers in

---

61 Hasluck, 'The copra industry', 21 November 1952, Copra 51–53, M331 [191], NAA.
62 'Agricultural extension work report for the six months ending 30th June 1955', p. 29, Advancement of Native Agriculture 1954–6, A518 [C2/1/1], NAA.
63 'Discrimination belief by natives reduced copra production—Barrett', *South Pacific Post*, 24 November 1954, Copra production—General 1948–57, A518 [A813/1/4 Part 3], NAA.
64 RS Bell to J Jordan, Report 13, New Ireland District, Kavieng, 1956–1957.
65 REP Dwyer and DH Urquhart, 'Report on the Prospects of cocoa extending the growing of cocoa in the Territory on New Guinea', March 1951, p. 9, Commodities cocoa—Research 1951–54, A518 [B58/3/1], NAA.
66 District of New Ireland, 'Minutes of meeting of heads of department', pp. 2, 22–24, Advancement of Native Agriculture 1954–6, A518 [C2/1/1], NAA.

the district, a manifestly insufficient number. To address this problem, in 1956 the Co-operative Section procured 400 drums and wire and instructed villagers to construct hot-air dryers. Twenty-five were immediately built but 18 months later Greg Collins reported there remained large stocks of drums uncompleted.[67] The lift in quality, at least in the immediate short term, was substantial. Co-operative Officer Ernest Graham was able to report:

> for the first time in the existence of NINSA, the month of October saw a total of 2079 bags of all grades produced of which 446 bags were downgraded and no rejections whatever recorded.[68]

Figure 12.3: United Nations Mission members with Mr Henry Ramon, Secretary of the New Ireland Native Societies Association, at the cooperative headquarters in Kavieng, 1959.
Source: NAA, A1200, L31383, item 7803978.

---

67 'Report for the six months ending 31st December 1958', p. 23, Advancement in Native Agriculture 1950–9, A452 [1960/8266], NAA; EO Graham to Assistant District Officer (ADO) Kavieng, 14 November 1957, New Ireland District, Kavieng, 1956–1957.
68 EO Graham (Co-operative Officer) correspondence to ADO Kavieng, 14 November 1957, New Ireland District, Taskul, 1956–1957.

Field, cooperative and agricultural extension support

The introduction of cooperatives in the 1950s to New Hanover was reliant on adequate staffing from three key areas of the administration: Agricultural Extension, the Co-operative Section and Native Affairs. There was a strong correlation between the amount of time an officer spent on supervision and the success of a society due to better stock control, a reduction in credit and theft, improved agricultural techniques and overall operational efficiency.

From 1947 officers were stationed at Taskul and in the early postwar years would patrol each of the three census divisions at least once a year.[69] However, by the early 1950s, the Taskul post was suffering a very high turnover of field staff, at one stage averaging almost three new officers per year.[70] Reasons for this included an inability to recruit sufficient staff, generous leave entitlements and study commitments at ASOPA.[71] The situation only worsened in July 1956 when the Taskul patrol post closed for over a year due to staff shortages.[72] It took until 1958 for the government to finally provide a significant boost to personnel on the ground in New Hanover.[73]

Table 12.5: Whole-of-government effort on New Hanover, 1958.

Department	Officer/s	Days patrolling
Native Affairs	P Bloomfield	99
Public Health	V Kohout; A Dash	105
Education	J McNewman	25
Agriculture	J Carey	25
Agriculture	Filed workers and trainees	267
Total		521

Source: P Bloomfield, Report 4 of 1958/59, p. 1, NID, Taskul, 1958–1959, PNGA.

---

69   The three census divisions were south/east, west coast, north/east. Bloomfield, Report 7 of 1957/58, pp. 3, 15, New Ireland District, Taskul, 1957–1958, PNGA.
70   Dyer to New Ireland DC, 12 September 1951, New Ireland District, Taskul, 1950–1953, PNGA.
71   James Sinclair, *Kiap: Australia's patrol officers in Papua New Guinea* (Sydney: Pacific Publications, 1981), 45, 150.
72   Cochrane, Report 4 of 1956/57, p. 1; AF Gow to DNA Director, 22 July 1957, New Ireland District, Kavieng, 1956–1957, PNGA.
73   Bloomfield, Report 4 of 1958/59, p. 1, New Ireland District, Taskul, 1958–1959, PNGA.

The relative status of the registrar as a mere section head directly affected the rate of pay and opportunities for promotion afforded to registry staff. Cooperative personnel came under the Department of Native Affairs (DNA), which had two other branches: magisterial and local council.[74] The personnel from these two branches were interchangeable, while cooperatives were regarded as the 'third branch' and officers had little chance of moving out of this section.[75] This led to serious staff losses through resignations and had an important bearing on the quality of the supervision available to cooperatives.[76] Furthermore, there was a constant struggle to recruit new officers with suitable training and experience; unfilled vacancies usually ran very high (see Table 12.6) and left an insufficient level of staff to properly manage complex and diverse conditions.[77]

Table 12.6: Percentage of cooperative staff positions filled, 1955–61.

Year	1955	1956	1957	1958	1959	1960	1961
Establishment	59	99	99	101	96	96	129
Appointed	52	60	54	41	59	69	83
Percentage	88.1%[a]	60.6%	54.5%	40.6%	61.4%	71.9%	64.3%

Note: [a] Denotes percentage inflated due to all Indigenous positions having been filled (34).
Source: Department of Native Affairs, 'Annual Report of the Co-operative Section' [reports from 1955–61], Co-operative Reports 1955–7, A518 [EL840/1/4], NAA.

Expatriate cooperative staff numbers were stagnant for much of the 1950s despite the ever-increasing number of cooperatives. For instance, in 1955 there were 18 officers, and four years later there were 19. The improvement (in percentage terms) for 1959–61 of cooperative staff was solely due to the increase in the strength of trainee (Indigenous) officers; an indication of a new policy to 'Indigenise' the public service. The overall administration and Co-operative Section staffing difficulties, as indicated in Tables 12.6 and 12.7, suggest cooperative activity may have expanded beyond its resources. Moreover, the administration was facing increasing pressure from local people to keep pace with spontaneous Indigenous development yet, due to limitation of financial and personnel resources, were powerless to address

---

74 Patrol officers focussed on control and magisterial powers, Native Authorities on the introduction of local government councils.
75 For instance, one registrar but 14 District Commissioners. 'Soul-searching for higher-ups PNG REGISTRAR HAS CO-OPERATIVES', *Pacific Islands Monthly* 28, no. 1 (August 1957): 147–48.
76 In November 1955, the DDSNA was abolished and reorganised as the DNA.
77 In 1947 there were six officers; by 1953 there were 28 officers. Sinclair, *Kiap*, 45.

the problem.[78] Officers faced an ever more difficult situation: not only were they manifestly understaffed, but the continuous expansion of cooperatives and difficulties of transport and communication meant the registry was never likely to prove adequate.

Table 12.7: Cooperative staff, 1955–61.

Position	1955	1956	1957	1958	1959	1960	1961
Registrar	1	1	1	1	1	1	1
Assistant registrar	2	1	1	1	2	2	3
Chief inspector	–	1	1	1	1	1	1
Cooperative officers	15	13	13	18	15	21[a]	30[b]
Cooperative Indigenous inspectors	34	44	38	33	40[a]	44[a]	48
Total	52	60	54	54	59	69	83

Note: [a] Includes a substantial increase in training positions; [b] Denotes the inclusion of Third Division Indigenous Co-operative Officers.
Source: Department of Native Affairs, 'Annual Report of the Co-operative Section' [reports from 1955–61], Co-operative Reports 1955–7, A518 [EL840/1/4], NAA.

Table 12.8: New Ireland District extension staff: 1954–58.

Staff	June 1954	June 1955	June 1956	June 1957	June 1958
Agricultural officer/s	3	–	1	1	1
Assistant agricultural officer	2	–	–	1	1
Agricultural assistant (Auxiliary Division)	–	–	–	1	1
Indigenous assistants	–	–	3	5	7
Indigenous trainees	–	–	1	5	15
Total	5	–	5	13	25

Sources: Advancement of Native Agriculture 1954–6; 1957 Appendix A, p. 2; 1958 Appendix A, p. 2, A518 [C2/1/1], NAA.

Despite approval for an increase in strength for agricultural officers in late 1951, it had little effect on New Ireland.[79] Table 12.8 indicates that at no stage did the administration source enough expatriate officers, although the

---

78 Cleland to Lambert, '1957 Annual Report of the Co-operative Section', p. 2, Co-operative reports 1955–7, A518 [EL840/1/4], NAA.
79 Hasluck to Ward, 7 December 1951, Co-operative societies, M331 [190], NAA.

introduction of the Auxiliary Division gradually improved staffing ratios. The district lacked a proper extension centre, a hub to grow and test new plant varieties, and in 1955, was unable to supply any agricultural staff.[80]

Cooperatives transformed village subsistence to communal cash cropping, encouraged efficient farming practices and introduced new business concepts. In the first years of the 1950s, they were rewarded with remarkable growth and, on the back of high world copra prices, a significant lift in their financial wellbeing. However, cooperatives had limited success due to several factors: reliance on a volatile cash crop commodity, poor management and supervision by an under-resourced administration, rejection rates from the CMB, losses through credit sales, theft by employees and considerable competition from Chinese traders. Once the global copra price had reached its low point (1956), difficult trading conditions exposed how little the Lavongai understood the aims and methods of the cooperative movement: community benefit, competitive prices and future disbursements. The failure of cooperatives following the conceptual misadventure of village councils tested the credibility of colonial development programs for the New Hanover people.

Indigenous leadership and colonial control

As the cooperative movement stalled, the administration made a concerted effort to find a more amenable leadership than offered by Singerau. Reports from the late 1950s indicate growing uneasiness at the methods employed by Singerau and his manipulation of government programs to suit both himself and his local community. During the 1950s the administration had chosen a pragmatic path when enlisting his support for economic development schemes, arguing it was better 'to channel their efforts in the direction we want to go'.[81] Although comments such as those from Native Affairs Director Allan Roberts suggest this endeavour failed. He wrote in 1957 that the New Hanover ventures had been 'hampered by lack of any suitable [underlined in the document] outstanding personalities within their group to whom they could look for guidance and direction'.[82] Furthermore,

---

80   REP Dwyer, 'July–December 1954 Native Agricultural Extension Work', Advancement of native agriculture 1954–6, A518 [C2/1/1], NAA.
81   Bloomfield, Report 7 of 1959/60, p. 2.
82   Roberts to Assistant Administrator, 21 October 1957, New Ireland District, Kavieng, 1957–1958, PNGA.

Singerau's fractious relations with missions, traders, some villagers and officers had gradually undermined his standing within the administration. The south coast of New Hanover was regarded as the political hub of the island; there was a larger local population, and more Europeans and missionaries. This was also where Singerau lived and enforced his sphere of influence. However, by 1957 the region was enveloped in an atmosphere of high political tension, Bloomfield reported there were 'transition forces at work and breaking up of Singerau's influence'.[83]

Table 12.9: 1959 estimated religious breakdown of New Hanover population.

Religion	Followers	Per cent
Methodist	3,500	50%
Catholic	3,220	46%
Seventh-day Adventist	280	4%
Total	7,000	100%

Source: P Bloomfield, Report 4 of 1958/59, p. 9, New Ireland District, Taskul, 1958–1959.

In late 1957, Rev. B Otto (Missionaries of the Sacred Heart of Jesus) accused Singerau of illegal activity. This allegation was tempered by the widely known, and longstanding, feud between these two parties.[84] In 1950, Father Stamm condemned Singerau's polygamy. Singerau responded in typically aggressive manner to this criticism by, first, inviting the Seventh-day Adventist (SDA) Mission into the village of Baikeb, second, preventing Rev. Otto from entering the village, and finally, maintaining a rage at the church and undermining it at any opportunity.[85]

As for undermining the church, one example reported was of a gathering Singerau attended with some Catholic luluais on the Lavongai beach to welcome the Bishop of the New Ireland and District Education Officer J McNewman. In front of both Bloomfield and the Bishop, Singerau requested an administration school, knowing full well Catholic children would be forbidden to attend. Bloomfield argued this was an example of his 'two facedness', tantamount to a request for the administration to supply a school for Singerau's own children despite a readily accessible SDA school at nearby Konkavul.[86] Bloomfield was understandably concerned,

---

83 P Bloomfield, Report 1 of 1957/58, p. 19, New Ireland District, Taskul, 1957–1958, PNGA.
84 Bloomfield, Report 1 of 1957/58, p. 16; KW Dyer, Report 1 of 1950/51, pp. 5–6.
85 Stokes, Report 1 of 1952/53, pp. 3–4.
86 Bloomfield, Report 4 of 1958/59, p. 6.

from an administration perspective, that if McNewman had agreed to Singerau's request, tensions would have further inflamed in the south-east. An alternative reading of this situation emphasises Singerau's extraordinary capacity for independent, calculating and entrepreneurial action. Clearly, if Singerau had managed to have an administration school built locally then it would be a fillip politically, but just as importantly, it was congruent with his ability (and desire) to claim government services and programs to improve the lives of his people.

The government had, since 1955, been laying the groundwork for the introduction of (official) government councils.[87] This new scheme provided an opportunity for the government to encourage more amenable (Westernised) leaders to enter council elections and actively undermine Singerau's 'sphere of influence'. In the south of the island, Iguaravis, the recently installed luluai of Ungat (nearby to Baikeb) indicated interest in the council movement. As a result, a political duel between them led to 17 Iguaravis sympathisers migrating to Ungat from Baikeb. Bloomfield gleefully pointed out Iguaravis was not a protégé of the Catholic Mission, but a leader in his own right, one perhaps more amenable to work with, and an example of how the council movement was sponsoring the 'emergence of other leaders which should be encouraged'.[88]

In the north, Boski Tom was also interested in the council system, and more importantly, was a longstanding rival to Singerau.[89] From the village of Meterankan, although with close affiliations to Umbukul, Boski Tom could speak, read and write English fluently.[90] Bloomfield regarded him as 'the only native leader among the Lavongai for whom I have any regard', a member of the 'new educated elite' with great standing among villagers and expatriates. Boski Tom was an administration teacher, a role which took him away to Kavieng for long periods and thus, had not been a suitable foil to Singerau.[91] This situation was untenable according to Bloomfield, who believed it 'would prove more useful to the Administration and to his department if he returned to Lavongai' and acted as 'an effective buffer to Singerau's influence'.[92] Kavieng ADO Gregory Collins agreed Tom had a great deal of influence which 'could be fostered were it not for the fact that

---

87 District of New Ireland, 'Minutes of meeting of heads of department', p. 7.
88 Bloomfield, Report 7 of 1959/60, pp. 8–9.
89 Bloomfield, Report 7 of 1957/58, p. 17.
90 'What manner of men are they?', *Pacific Islands Monthly* 31, no. 8 (March 1961): 23, 141.
91 'People', *Pacific Islands Monthly* 31, no. 1 (August 1960): 5–6.
92 Bloomfield, Report 4 of 1958/59, p. 2.

12. COOPERATIVES AND THE HASLUCK PYRAMID AT WORK IN THE VILLAGES OF NEW HANOVER

he is frequently absent in his work as a teacher on the mainland'.[93] Boski Tom was regarded as an ideal leader, in the mould of Pita Simogun of Sepik with whom he served as a delegate at the 1956 South Pacific Conference, someone interested in development and advancement, but in a manner more agreeable to the administration than Singerau's unorthodox and confrontational methods.[94]

The relationship between the administration and Singerau was dynamic, fractious, but equally pragmatic. Even after the criticisms of late 1957, the Australians were willing, if somewhat grudgingly, to work with him. Although not as powerful as he once was, Collins warned it would be a grave mistake to underestimate his influence, particularly regarding economic development.[95] This proved the case when the government introduced coffee as a complementary perennial crop during this period. Singerau displayed his typical enthusiasm for agroeconomic development, taking responsibility and influencing villagers to plant in the communal Dinarigal coffee garden.[96] Bloomfield, relieved, noted the coffee project was fully occupying him, so much so he had 'ceased baiting the Catholic Mission, and dabbling in other matters that do not concern him'.[97] The administration was again forced to act in a pragmatic manner. That is, utilise Singerau's undoubted energy and passion for economic development but accept that its other priority, maintenance of colonial control, would be undermined by Singerau.

Another example of the administration trying to balance Indigenous autonomy and maintain control was the introduction of coffee as a cash crop to inland New Hanover. This constant need for the administration to frequently change direction in their hunt for guided development is something of a theme throughout the postwar period. First this crop then that. First this policy then that. First support one leader then another. So, it comes as no surprise that the new coffee program was, to a large extent, expected to rectify an earlier prewar directive to mobilise people on the coast as a centralisation and control measure. This decision had created a

---

93 GD Collins to New Ireland DC, 20 January 1958, New Ireland District, Kavieng, 1957–1958, PNGA.
94 'Pacific Islands affairs for review at SPC's Third South Pacific Conference', *Pacific Islands Monthly* 26, no. 9 (April 1956): 41.
95 EE Collins to New Ireland DC, 5 March 1959, New Ireland District, Kavieng, 1959–1960, PNGA.
96 Bloomfield, Report 2 of 1959/60, p. 4, New Ireland District, Kavieng, 1959–1960, PNGA; Bloomfield, Report 4 of 1958/59, p. 6.
97 Bloomfield, Report 11 of 1957/58, p. 6.

certain artificiality to sociopolitical cohesiveness and removed traditional usufruct rights over land use. For many villages, the garden land proved unsuitable or was inconveniently located. The tenability of their residence on the coast depended on the disposition and the charity of the members of the land-owning coastal clans. In effect, it made these people poor relations and created friction between them and the members of the land-owning clan.[98] As a result, for many villages, there was constant friction and bickering among themselves as to whether they would return to their old sites or not.[99] They were torn between a desire for inland living (and land tenure) and the opposing necessity for coastal residence on the score of cash cropping.[100] The allure of ancestral land was tempered by the realisation, after a generation or more of coastal life, that it entailed much inconvenience: long distances to obtain religious and medical benefits, to patronise coastal trade stores, and collect salt water and catch fish.[101]

The introduction of lowland coffee as a new cash crop was expected to be the solution to this problem. Firstly, it made sense economically to ameliorate the instability of relying on copra as the sole cash crop of consequence and secondly, provided the economic incentive to return to their ancestral ground. During November–December 1957, the district agricultural officer introduced the idea of coffee planting to Lavongai. He reported the island, especially the inland areas, was particularly suitable for the growing of coffee, and thus, an ideal crop to encourage migration inland and provide an adequate income in the long term.[102]

Min and Potpotingan villages

Most inland villages relied upon the sale of foodstuffs to coastal people for a small cash income; if larger amounts were required, they would work at a plantation. Therefore, the addition of coffee blocks would be an income enticement to inland villagers. The program quickly ran into problems: communication difficulties, the disruptive impact of moving inland, delayed financial returns and inability of administration staff to easily reach

---

98   Bloomfield, Report 7 of 1959/60, p. 6.
99   Cochrane, Report 4 of 1956/57, p. 9.
100 New Ireland ADO to J Cochrane, December 1956, New Ireland District, Kavieng, 1956–1957, PNGA.
101 Bloomfield, Report 7 of 1959/60, pp. 6–7.
102 Bloomfield, Report 7 of 1957/58, pp. 18–21.

new gardens.[103] The situation around Potpotingan and Min is an interesting example of how these problems manifested themselves during this period. Potpotingan is approximately 30 kilometres inland from the north-east passage, and in the early postwar period, people had begun moving back to their ancestral lands. In 1957, many of these villagers migrated a further 12 kilometres inland to Min, the site of their coffee gardens. This decision effectively divided the village again, making it more difficult for officers to monitor crop development, dividing labour and attention among villagers, and further isolating the people from the coast.[104]

Table 12.10: Inland vs coastal income, Lavongai census division, 1961.

Village	Pop.	Cash crop ($)	Labour ($)	Trading profit ($)	Livestock ($)	Garden ($)	Total income ($)	$ per capita
Narimlaua (I)	181	–	576	96	–	227	899	4.97
Potpotingan (I)	120	–	460	–	–	189	649	5.41
Kulungat (I)	132	–	666	–	–	157	823	6.23
Min (I)	99	–	702	–	–	135	837	8.45
Baue (I)	124	155	869	–	–	87	1,111	8.96
Umbukul (C)	243	1,831	2,389	–	–	249	4,469	18.39
Ungat (C)	114	2,040	–	164	–	77	2,281	20.01
Baikeb (C)	149	2,355	809	215	–	48	3,427	23.00
Ungalabu (C)	49	605	678	109	–	–	1,392	28.41
Lukus Is. (C)	78	2,534	290	315	–	–	3,139	40.24
Tingwon Is. (C)	110	10,542	–	–	–	–	10,542	95.84

Notes: (I) denotes inland village; (C) denotes coastal village. Figures adjusted to 1969 Australian dollars as per Reserve Bank of Australia (RBA) pre-decimal inflation calculator, available at: www.rba.gov.au/calculator/annualPreDecimal.html.
Source: R Willard, Report 4 of 1962/63, p. 3, New Ireland District, Kavieng, 1962–1963.

Migration from Potpotingan continued over the next few years; in August 1960 the population reduced to 200, and 120 in 1961. Min increased from 80 (1960) to 99 in 1961. Bob Hallahan described them as 'amongst the poorest in the district', which, as Table 12.10 indicates, is an accurate summation.[105] There is a clear disparity of income between inland and coastal villagers. On the coast, many were successfully operating trade

---

103 RW Hallahan, Report 7 of 1960/61, New Ireland District, Kavieng, 1960–1961, PNGA.
104 Bloomfield, Report 4 of 1958/59, pp. 4–5.
105 RW Hallahan, Report 4 of 1960/61, p. 3, New Ireland District, Kavieng, 1960–1961, PNGA.

stores at small profits, while making substantial income from copra sales. This was unavailable to inland villagers, as demonstrated by Potpotingan, which had the second lowest income on the island at $5.41 per capita, Min only slightly higher at $8.45. Their earning capacity reflected their limited money-making opportunities.

Table 12.11: 1961 Lavongai census division.

	Pop.	Cash crop	Labour	Trading profit	Livestock sales	Garden sales	Total income	$ per capita
Total	7,269	$69,284	$46,277	$1,653	$196	$6,663	$124,073	$17.07

Note: Figures adjusted to 1969 Australian dollars as per RBA pre-decimal calculator.
Source: R Willard, Report 4 of 1962/63, p. 3, New Ireland District, Kavieng, 1962–1963.

Table 12.11 is a summary of a comprehensive 1961 income survey of Lavongai. Average per capita per annum income was $17.07 (median $17.45). Inland income was substantially below this average, and with a wait of up to five years for the first coffee harvest, circumstances would prove insurmountable for most newly arrived inland migrants. The resultant disappointment of inland coffee crops was widespread across the island.[106] At Min and Potpotingan the experience was 'typical' according to Ron Willard, for within two years enthusiasm for the project had begun to wane. Disinterest in maintenance led to failing crops, frustration and disinterest 'in any form of development'.[107] Administration officers blamed the economic failure on inland villagers, particularly those like Potpotingan, who had moved further into the bush. Bloomfield accused them of 'escapism', of trying to 'avoid the watchful eye of the administration', clearly there were insufficient officers to maintain 'control'.[108] An alternative, and ironic, explanation is the government had initiated another community development plan without providing adequate resources to support a disparate group, a people attempting to reconnect with ancestral land, land which they had been forced off by the very same colonial authorities.

---

106 RW Hallahan, Report 4 of 1960/61, p. 3.
107 R Willard, Report 4 of 1962/63, pp. 2, 4, New Ireland District, Kavieng, 1962–1963, PNGA.
108 Bloomfield, Report 4 of 1958/59.

Conclusion

The introduction of cooperative societies proved very popular; the quick uptake aided by the simultaneous payment of war damage compensation for merchant capital. Throughout the 1950s, despite some success, there remained a fractious relationship, almost a distrust, between the government and the people of New Hanover. During this period, communication, transport and tensions arising from inland migration resulted in an independent and internally focussed community. This further hampered relations and socioeconomic and political development. In something of an irony, given the government's stated goal to maintain control, their primary Indigenous agent on the island was Luluai Singerau, a dynamic, forceful and entrepreneurial person who skilfully manipulated government programs to benefit himself and his community. Despite repeated complaints from various quarters about Singerau's penchant for cutting corners or perhaps partake in illegal activities, the administration accepted this as the cost of Singerau's ability to inspire and coordinate local socioeconomic activity. In later years, as the economic performance of colonial development failed, the administration became less receptive to Singerau's behaviour. Instead, they favoured a more Westernised style of 'native' leader, more amenable to colonial demands, and actively searched for ways to remove Singerau from leadership positions. Postwar New Hanover encapsulates much of the 'on the ground' experience for local people and administration officers: a tension between a lack of resources and an administration determined to maintain control while, when Papua and New Guineans acted autonomously in a manner not befitting a 'native', they brought upon themselves the ire of the coloniser.

On the ground, local people were expected to remain in their villages where the government targeted policy at improving socioeconomic, political and health outcomes. The New Hanover case study has exposed how constant shortages of staff, particularly in agriculture and education, and poor planning undermined the implementation of development programs as outlined in the 'New Deal'. This was exacerbated by the government's penchant to prioritise control over Indigenous autonomy in circumstances where subjugated people objected to or resisted the expected narrative of the compliant or Westernised 'native'. An alternative reading of the autonomous activity of Singerau and the people of New Hanover during the 1950s was for a remarkable gift for creativity, innovation and belief in their own sociopolitical agency. Therefore, despite the appearance of positive and liberal development, the lived reality for most local people was that the Australian Government did not deliver on their aspirations. The 'New Deal' and Hasluck's program of gradualism and universal development were rendered impossible by the failure to account for the autonomous reinterpretation of government programs by leaders such as Singerau.

CONCLUSION

13

The 'New Deal' Assessed: Just Rhetoric or the Basis for Independence?

> We recognise the magnitude of the undertaking in New Guinea which faced Australia when the Japanese surrendered. It presented a challenge and opportunity with few parallels in the history of under-developed areas. Australia tackled this new task with courage and enterprise and drive, and soon produced remarkable results. It went to work with a will. Perhaps the finest examples of Australian effort were in the patrol posts, where young men created order and carried a message of progress and new hope to people living in the most undeveloped conditions in the world.
>
> 1962 UN Visiting Mission, 15[1]

This book has addressed the crucial question of Australian colonialism in the Territory of Papua New Guinea (TPNG): To what extent did Australia prepare TPNG for independence? And further, it considered what were the policies and the ideologies behind colonial development implemented after World War II. While other scholars have addressed these issues, the innovation of this book was to take these questions from the policy desks in Canberra and Port Moresby to the villages of four administrative districts in TPNG. It has explored the implementation of postwar development through patrol officer reports and assessed their success or failure on the ground by analysing Indigenous responses to policy directives. This research project spans the period 1945–63, one which encompassed both

---

1   United Nations Visiting Mission to Trust Territories in the Pacific, *Report on New Guinea* (New York: UN Trusteeship Council, 1962), 15.

the Australian Labor and Liberal/Country governments. This time frame provides an opportunity to assess how successful, or not, Australia was in meeting the development goals outlined in Eddie Ward's 'New Deal' speech and preparing the Territory for its eventual independence. On the question of whether there was continuity of policy between the Chifley Labor Government and the Menzies Liberal/Country Party Government, this work has strengthened the position of the school of historians who depict the postwar era as one of bipartisan approach as against those who argue for a significant break after the 1949 election. This continuity can be seen in high-level policy, the motivation for policy and the implementation of policy on the ground.

On a macro level, a comparison can be made on the physical, civic, economic, political and health conditions in 1946–47 and at the end of the Hasluck period in 1963. Additionally, by undertaking extensive research of the colonial archives, this book has identified the 'real' impact of Australian colonial development on the ground in the villages of TPNG. It has made a special focus on the Indigenous reaction to Australian development, and how the colonial state, guided by trusteeship and security concerns, struggled to accommodate the emergence of Papuan and New Guinean agency and autonomy. This book has primarily relied on colonial archives to explore the contested space in the villages. Patrol reports provided many examples of how the administration expected the local population to behave. Patrol officers would complain and directly address any autonomous actions which did not conform with their expectation of the 'compliant native'. The report entries were framed to suggest the individuals were a destabilising element in the community, incapable of understanding government directives. This dynamic speaks much to the slow devolution of power, of the Australian fears of a future failed state and how this motivated government action to limit Indigenous autonomy to a certain point.

1963: A change of strategy

As this book has demonstrated, the long-term Territories Minister, Paul Hasluck, argued his administration had always shaped government policy towards the goal of Indigenous self-government.[2] To meet this objective,

---

2   Paul Hasluck, 'The legend of remote control', 12 May 1958, cited in Paul Hasluck, *A time for building: Australian administration in Papua and New Guinea, 1951–1963* (Carlton: Melbourne University Press, 1976), 210.

13. THE 'NEW DEAL' ASSESSED

a nation-building strategy of universal development was employed, one which prioritised Indigenous socioeconomic welfare, but contained a control measure to limit the emergence of one Indigenous group at the expense of another. It was a policy which aimed to accelerate development in areas so they could catch up, while not restricting the continued progress of the more 'advanced' groups.[3] The assumption was that as new skills were learnt, from first contact and pacification through to working in the public service or in their own business, local people would be empowered to demand self-government.[4] This strategy was replaced in the mid-1960s with an ambition for faster economic growth and political enfranchisement. The impetus for this new approach was threefold: the 1962 United Nations (UN) Visiting Mission; the 1963 World Bank economic mission; and finally, the promotion of Hasluck to the Defence portfolio in December 1963.

During April and May 1962, a UN Visiting Mission led by British representative Sir Hugh Foot made a series of recommendations that would have a profound impact on the future direction of TPNG. Foot realised the task of heading the Visiting Mission would be a delicate one, reconciling the UN's anxiety to see rapid steps to end colonialism with Australian insistence on solid preparation for self-government. In his autobiography, *A Start in Freedom*, he considered the ramifications if the mission failed:

> Australia would become vulnerable to anti-colonial attack and, at the same time, those who wished to discredit the UN would be encouraged in their contention that the UN is unrealistic, unpractical and unreasonable.[5]

During his tour, Foot noted widespread Indigenous admiration for what had been achieved by Australia and a noticeable lack of local political consciousness.[6] Dudley McCarthy, the Australian representative who chaperoned the Visiting Mission, maintained that this was proof of Australia

---

3   Hasluck, *A time for building*, 164–65; Huntley Wright, 'State practice and rural smallholder production: Late-colonialism and the agrarian doctrine in Papua New Guinea, 1942–1969' (PhD thesis, Massey University, 1999), 219; Scott MacWilliam, *Securing village life: Development in late colonial Papua New Guinea* (Canberra: ANU Press, 2013), 77, doi.org/10.22459/SVL.05.2013; Brian Jinks, 'Policy, planning and administration in Papua New Guinea, 1942–1952: With special reference to the role of Colonel J.K. Murray' (PhD thesis, University of Sydney, 1975), 642; Ian Downs, *The Australian trusteeship: Papua New Guinea 1945–75* (Canberra: Australian Government Publishing Service, 1980), 126–28.
4   Hasluck, *A time for building*, 76, 78.
5   Hugh Foot, *A start in freedom* (London: Hodder and Stoughton, 1964), 214.
6   Foot, *A start in freedom*, 206.

offering a different colonial experience compared to elsewhere.[7] On this point, there is evidence the mission did meet some anti-colonial groups but chose to ignore, minimise or not recognise such elements. For instance, there were repeated demands from local people for the Americans or British to replace the Australians, most noticeably on New Hanover and in the Sepik subdistrict.[8] In addition, Foot acknowledged that in the townships there were 'indications of some restlessness and dissatisfaction with anything which discriminated against the "natives"',[9] a clear sign of growing frustration at the slow change in political infrastructure.

An alternative reading points to the success of the Australian containment strategy in limiting the emergence of an Indigenous elite capable of leading and organising a widespread independence movement. In a meeting with Hugh Foot at the conclusion of the mission's tour, Hasluck was explicit in his contempt for education as a precursor for successful leadership, arguing:

> the people produce their own leaders—merely selecting bright boys and giving them academic training did not mean they would be the leaders, for the people might choose and trust someone else.[10]

His attitude is in keeping with a primary argument of this book, that the administration utilised universal primary education and obstructive or officious tactics on the ground as a deliberate suppression strategy. Even at such a late stage in the colonial age, Hasluck continued to justify or link universal development with political autonomy and advancement. The result was a complete disconnect between personal autonomy or ambition of Papuans and New Guineans as individuals (a key tenet of a liberal democracy) and an independent and self-governing TPNG.

Ironically, the success of the containment strategy encouraged the Visiting Mission to advocate for a freeing up of political freedoms, and in doing so, provide an effective outlet 'while there was still time'. Foot warned:

---

7   Australian Mission to the United Nations, 'Opening statement of the Trust Territory of New Guinea by the Special Representative, Mr Dudley McCarthy', 10 July 1962, p. 5, Personal papers of Dudley McCarthy, A2127 [1/1], National Archives of Australia (NAA).
8   United Nations Visiting Mission, *Report on New Guinea* (1962), 3, 5, 7.
9   Foot, *A start in freedom*, 206, 214.
10 Department of Territories (DOT), 'United Nations Visiting Mission: Summary record of discussions with Minister for Territories', 16 May 1962, p. 5, Copra Production 1958, A452 [1958/2917], NAA.

13. THE 'NEW DEAL' ASSESSED

elsewhere colonialism in its old form will probably not outlast the present decade. The danger is that Australia as perhaps the last colonial power will become the butt of intense anti-colonial feeling.[11]

On the back of this attitude, the Visiting Mission put forward three principal propositions: a full economic survey by the World Bank; a new program of university and higher education to train and guide potential leaders; and the development of a representative democratic government at the centre 'to overcome the divisions which have so far bedevilled the Territory'.[12] Subsequently, the Legislative Council was replaced with a House of Assembly of 64 members, 54 elected on a common roll by adult suffrage.

Hasluck's acceptance of most of the Visiting Mission's recommendations, including the proposition for a World Bank economic survey, represented a significant change in attitude and policy direction.[13] Firstly, Foot noted that the Australian Government had a reputation for eschewing accumulated knowledge from external sources.[14] Even on this point, the government actively discredited the influence of the Foot Report, pointing to decisions made by the administration prior to the UN visit.[15] Secondly, the World Bank's economic mission rejected the principle of universal development in favour of accelerated or concentrated effort. It strongly recommended against 'an across-the-board policy which distributes scarce manpower and finance throughout the Territory without due regard to the benefits to be derived in comparison with those realizable elsewhere'. Instead, to obtain maximum benefit from the development effort, expenditure and manpower would be concentrated in areas and on activities where the prospective return was highest.[16]

---

11 Foot, *A start in freedom*, 206, 214.
12 United Nations Visiting Mission, *Report on New Guinea* (1962), 15.
13 DOT, 'United Nations Visiting Mission discussions', 16 May 1962, p. 2.
14 Foot, *A start in freedom*, 212.
15 DOT, *Annual Report of the Territory of Papua for the period, 1st July 1962 to 30th June 1963* (Canberra: Government Printer, 1963), 23.
16 International Bank for Reconstruction and Investment (World Bank), *The economic development of the Territory of Papua and New Guinea* (Canberra: Department of Territories, 1964), 20–22.

PREPARING A NATION?

Assessing the 'New Deal' development strategy

This new approach recommended by the World Bank ended the Ward–Hasluck era of universal and gradualist development and provided an opportunity to assess how successful the Australian Government was in preparing TPNG for independence.

Table 13.1: Comparison of postwar development: 1946/47–1963/64.

Postwar development	1946/47	1963/64	Change
Commonwealth grants	$505,000	$40,000,000	+$39,495,000
Internal revenue (duties/licences/taxes)	$4,781,754[a]	$18,048,922	+$13,267,168
Gross domestic product (GDP)	$15,350,352[a]	$59,845,930	+$44,495,578
Internal revenue % of GDP	31.15%	30.16%	–
Indigenous copra production	19,800[b] tons	30,157 tons	+10,357 tons
Indigenous coconut holdings	77,954[b] acres	232,879 acres	+154,925 acres
Indigenous coffee production	18[b] tons	2,390 tons	+2,372 tons
Indigenous coffee holdings	516 acres	15,985 acres	+15,649 acres
Administration school pupils	3,375	49,947	+46,572
Administration schools	61	450	+389
Local government councils (LGC)	5[a]	142	+137
LGC population covered	18,982[a]	1,858,564	+1,839,582
Cooperative societies	109[a]	270	+161
Members of cooperatives	22,172[a]	85,451	+63,279
Cooperative turnover	$379,100[a]	$2,287,774	+$1,908,674
Kilometres of vehicular roads	5,140[a]	11,346	+6,206

Notes: [a] No figures available prior to 1952; [b] No figures available prior to 1955. Amounts in 1969 Australian dollars, as per Reserve Bank of Australia (RBA) pre-decimal inflation calculator, available at: www.rba.gov.au/calculator/annualPreDecimal.html.

Source: Statistics Section (Department of External Territories) (DET), *Compendium of Statistics for Papua New Guinea* (Canberra: Government Printer, 1969).

As discussed in Chapter 2, the chaotic state of prewar infrastructure and the loss of personnel during the war hampered reconstruction and development. This could not be remedied overnight. It is clear that the economy grew significantly, largely because of greater government spending and revenue raised by the administration. However, as Table 13.1 indicates, the proportion of administration receipts raised in the Territory did not increase, and the absolute gap between expenditures and local revenues steadily widened. In other words, the Territory became increasingly dependent on external aid. A direct effect of the growth in spending was a sharp rise in employment and income; the administration increased staffing from 1,400 in 1950 to more than 6,000 in 1963. Perversely, only 125 permanent and temporary higher-level posts were allocated to Papuans and New Guineans, the balance, filled by expatriates, illustrating how government policy of universal primary education inhibited Indigenous opportunity outside the village economy. Furthermore, while Commonwealth grants grew exponentially, much of this expenditure was soaked up by salary and conditions high enough to attract Australians. It also encouraged a dependence on imports and the adoption of standards of new facilities which equated with those of Australia, not that 'of one [a country] in the very early stages of economic development'.[17]

This book has introduced a new pyramid analytical framework to understand and assess Paul Hasluck's thinking, actions and policy instructions. The Hasluck Development Pyramid outlines how community development schemes such as rural progress societies, cooperatives and local government councils placed the village at the centre of development policy. This fitted with the government's overall economic strategy for the Territory based around household agricultural production. Table 13.1 provides a snapshot of growth in Indigenous agricultural production and community development groups. In terms of copra and coffee, both acreage holdings and production increased significantly off a low base for the period 1955–1963 (no figures available prior to 1955). Although not indicated in Table 13.1, expatriate holdings for copra remained almost unchanged over this period (1955: 245,430; 1963: 262,078 acres), and by 1965 had been surpassed by Indigenous acreage (287,977). While expatriate holdings in coffee increased substantially (1955: 1,807; 1963: 10,305 acres), it was outstripped by Papuans and New Guineans in both acreage and production. By 1967 Indigenous production (10,566 tons) had doubled expatriate output (4,910 tons), these results emphasise the success of the Australian strategy of prioritising community development and household production.[18]

---

17 World Bank, *The economic development of the Territory*, 16–19.
18 Statistics Section (Department of External Territories) (DET), *Compendium of statistics for Papua New Guinea* (Canberra: Government Printer, 1969), 8–10.

Placing rural households at the forefront of economic plans minimised the destructive capacity of commercial operations to village social structures, brought development to the village, dissuaded a landless proletariat and, as explained by the Hasluck Development Pyramid, enabled a first step (a strong local economy) towards creating the political infrastructure for eventual self-government. The Hasluck pyramid assumed targeted policies would stimulate needs and wants, and as demonstrated in Table 13.1, the village-based strategy was effective in harnessing compliant Papuans and New Guineans in favourable agroeconomic circumstances (for instance: climate, topography, transport, available land). In terms of political development, the assumption was that as people became increasingly aware of the opportunities available, they would demand education in social and political affairs. However, as this book has exposed, this approach was undermined by an administration-wide approach to quash Indigenous autonomy where a person or group did not act in accordance with government expectations. Furthermore, government policy of universal primary education inhibited the opportunity or capacity of Papuans and New Guineans to participate at the centre of socioeconomic and political activity. Therefore, while government agroeconomic policy did expose local people in the villages to new agricultural practices, new crops, a money economy and globalised trade, the actions on the ground and education policy diminished the effectiveness of such an approach, or cynically, manipulated circumstances to best suit the coloniser.

Table 13.2: Comparison of education facilities for the year 1963.

Schools	Eastern Highlands District	Sepik	New Ireland	Milne Bay
Administration primary	41	41	26	22
Mission primary	301	413	111	191
Junior high	1	1	1	1
Secondary	1	-	-	-
Technical	2	2	-	1

Sources: Department of Territories (DOT), *Report to the General Assembly of the United Nations on the administration of the Territory of New Guinea for Year 1962-63* (Canberra: Government Printer, 1963), 288–90; DOT, *Annual Report of the Territory of Papua for the period, 1st July 1962 to 30th June 1963*, (Canberra: Government Printer, 1963), 256–57.

Hasluck regarded education policy as essential to nation-building; the policy of universal primary education and English language designed to ensure people from as wide a range of areas as possible had an equality of opportunity in eventual self-government. It was also part of a concerted containment strategy to ensure the problems of Africa introduced by a small, educated elite were not replicated in TPNG. In 1946–47, a consequence of the war and prewar inattention meant there were minimal opportunities for local children to attend government schools. For instance, in the Territory of New Guinea in 1947 there were only 975 students at school, the majority living in the Rabaul area.[19] By 1963, despite expenditure in education rising sharply to $6 million (14 per cent of budget)[20] and a significant increase in the number of students attending government schools, almost four in five students continued to attend mission schools.[21] Table 13.2 highlights the education options available to the students in Chimbu (Eastern Highlands District, or EHD), Maprik (Sepik), New Hanover (New Ireland) and Milne Bay. The prioritisation of primary school education at the expense of an expanded secondary education resulted in only one district providing a secondary school option (EHD). Government policy of universal primary education came at the expense of higher education and directly affected Indigenous opportunity to advance within the administrative or private sector. It was designed to limit the potential creation of a class of 'educated unemployables' which, in other colonial territories, had led to the more intelligent and ambitious leaving the village but facing a scenario of few suitable employment prospects. Education was expected to bind Papua New Guinean villages and subdistricts in a nation-building project, of achieving a sense of unity without doing damage to Australia; it was a strategy on the terms of the coloniser, not the colonised.

Table 13.3: Comparative change in public health facilities, 1947–63.

Medical service	1947	% 1947	1963	% 1963
Administration hospitals	55	82%	102	52%
Mission hospitals	12	18%	93	48%
Administration welfare centres	1	3.7%	562	85.8%
Mission welfare centres	26	96.3%	97	14.2%
Administration aid posts	7	7.7%	1,559	82.2%
Mission aid posts	84	92.3%	338	17.8%

Source: Statistics Section (DET), *Compendium of Statistics for Papua New Guinea* (Canberra: Government Printer, 1969).

---

19   DET, *Report to the General Assembly of the United Nations on the administration of the Territory of New Guinea: From 1st July 1946 to 30th June, 1947* (Canberra: Government Printer, 1947), 45.
20   Figure in 1969 Australian dollars.
21   Statistics Section (DET), *Compendium of statistics*, 65.

Public health was the most immediate priority for the provisional administration in the early postwar years: access to health facilities was regarded as an essential first step in improving Indigenous welfare. The administration spent almost 40 per cent of its budget in the first five years postwar on public health and, while tapering in later years (compared to education), expenditure still averaged 20 per cent for the entire Ward–Hasluck period.[22] The size of the Public Health Department grew exponentially in the Ward–Hasluck era: in June 1946, the department employed 91 staff and by 1963 it had exceeded 1,000 (including a threefold increase 1955–63).[23] Unlike education, by 1963 the administration was providing the majority of medical services, much of this based on a massive expansion in medical aid posts and welfare centres, which provided direct medical assistance on the ground in the villages. In crude terms, the Australian success in improving the health outcomes for Papua and New Guineans is clear from the increase in population size. In 1950, the Indigenous population was 1,439,664 persons and by 1963 had increased by approximately 40 per cent to 2,031,797.[24]

A contested space: The 'New Deal' on the ground in the villages

Despite the appearance of positive and progressive development plans outlined in the 'New Deal' and by the Hasluck Administration, the lived reality for most local people was that the Australian Government often did not deliver on their aspirations. This was primarily due to inadequate staff and resources and poor planning on the ground, but also the government's inclination to prioritise control over Indigenous autonomy in circumstances where subjugated people objected to or resisted the expected narrative of the compliant or Westernised 'native'. At the heart of this research project has been the dichotomy of these positions, of liberal ambition versus colonial control, and how this fundamentally influenced both the effectiveness of government programs and the lived experience of Papua and New Guineans.

---

22   World Bank, *The economic development of the Territory,* 17.
23   World Bank, *The economic development of the Territory,* 16; DET, *Territory of Papua Annual Report for the Period 30th October, 1945 to 30th June, 1946* (Canberra: Government Printer, 1946), 22.
24   Statistics Section (DET), *Compendium of statistics,* 1.

13. THE 'NEW DEAL' ASSESSED

This book has argued that a liberal 'extreme centre' as outlined by Alexander Zevin is one way to understand how moderates such as Percy Spender and Paul Hasluck were able to align classical liberal imperatives of individualism with the Fabian intent of the original architects of Ward's 'New Deal'. On this point, it is worth speculating whether, if the Chifley Labor Government had been returned in December 1949, there would have been a different outcome or approach to Australia's development of TPNG. Would the influence of External Affairs Minister, HV Evatt, and his lieutenants such as John Burton and Bill Forsyth moved Australia towards a more internationalist agenda than Hasluck? Clearly, Hasluck was uninterested in the learnings of other colonial regimes, and his rigidity on this point had a significant influence over the policy direction in the 1950s. Given Forsyth's later career as a significant figure in the South Pacific Commission, it is possible the Chifley Labor Government would have moved more quickly to address the UN concerns over the slow transfer of political and economic power to Papua and New Guineans. Alternatively, it is difficult to imagine how another individual, one as capable and energetic as Paul Hasluck, would have been appointed to the lowly Territory Ministerial position.

Regardless of speculation, there was a consistent approach to prioritising Indigenous welfare by Australian political parties of both persuasions during the Ward–Hasluck era. The 'New Deal' planners had recognised the end of the Pacific War was a unique opportunity to generate change, reflective of new attitudes around the world to imperialism and an awakening of interest by the Australian public to the plight of the Territory. Instead, it was the European community who became an effective opposition to postwar planning, hampering efforts while instigating political unrest in Canberra. Whether this had any effect on policymakers is hard to evaluate, except to note that personal papers and correspondence of these officials were often derogatory of the attitudes of the expatriate community. What is clear from the government archives of the 1940s and 50s was that government policy was never formed purely on humanitarian or even geopolitical grounds. Rather, policy was framed around practical benefits to Australia: maintain a security land barrier and a stable, non-threatening people to the north. In other words, a containment strategy, one premised on limiting potential civil unrest. This was evident in the February 1944 letter from General Thomas Blamey (written by 'New Deal' planners) to Prime Minister Curtin outlining the situation in the Australian colonies, in the papers and correspondence of senior Territory officials such as John Black, David Fenbury and Keith McCarthy, and the speeches and ministerial directives of Paul Hasluck. Furthermore, planning until the 1960s presumed Australia was committed to TPNG indefinitely unless forced out by superior foreign armed forces or by internal unrest. The strategy was for a gradual move towards self-rule, and therefore the priority of the Australian Government had to be the satisfaction of the Indigenous population: an aspiration to manage affairs so that its continuing presence was regarded as essential by Papuans and New Guineans.

However, on the ground, patrol and other government officials were overwhelmed with bureaucracy, postwar reconstruction, pacification, census taking and war damage compensation. There were constant shortages of staff, particularly in agriculture and education. Exacerbating this tension, the case studies have exposed examples of poor or rushed planning by head office in Port Moresby. For instance, the village rice scheme in the Sepik District, or in Milne Bay when the administration perceived the threat of an energetic Indigenous enterprise to such an extent it bypassed its own specialty section and introduced a local council with almost no planning, or the confusing decision to introduce unofficial councils on New Hanover when there already existed an official system of indirect rule by village headman.

The four case studies of this book provided an opportunity to contrast colonial intention with Indigenous experience. The individual experience of each subdistrict was influenced by regional characteristics such as the landform geography, road and transport access, population levels, Indigenous leadership style, previous and ongoing contact with Westerners by local communities, war damage, relationship with missionaries and available administrative resources. On the other hand, implementation of the 'New Deal' was the first time most Papuans and New Guineans had been exposed to a concerted whole-of-government effort to transform their local communities to align with Western concepts of civic, religious, political, economic and social ideas. In this way, the case studies explicitly focussed on the contested colonial space between the local population and government officials, on the expectation and implementation of government programs, and the reaction of Papuans and New Guineans.

What became apparent was the immediate enthusiasm for and adoption by local people of the new socioeconomic development ideas. In some cases, community enthusiasm for economic advancement meant local people were ahead of the Australian Government in introducing these new concepts. This research project has documented how local people in Chimbu, Maprik,

New Hanover and Milne Bay utilised the proceeds from war compensation or proceeds of plantation labour to establish socioeconomic enterprises of dynamism and vision. In each case study there were examples of the Territory Administration actively undermining leaders and community ventures which did not align with government strategy. Justification for such an attitude, as described in the patrol reports, portray the 'native' as helpless and promote Australia as a benevolent coloniser or neighbour, one steeped in an evolutionary appeal to colonial wisdom. The result increased tension on the ground, undermined government messaging and hampered efforts at improving the lived experience of local people.

One example: the Chimbu returnees from the government-sponsored Highland Labour Scheme who, as the first generation of Chimbu to travel to the coast and get to know white men and experience plantation working conditions, exhibited a desire to initiate change within their community. The administration frowned on and attempted to contain this activity where it actively undermined traditional social structures, fearing a challenge to indirect rule in a densely populated area where government resources were inadequate to control the local population. Whereas, when these returnees displayed an urgency in the direction of approved economic development, patrol reports were effusive in their praise as they were moving towards a sustainable village economy, introducing new agricultural techniques and the cash economy to their local communities.

While many new Indigenous economic organisations failed within the first 10 years of establishment, they did provide some economic literacy and opportunity for a nascent Indigenous elite. For instance, on New Hanover the introduction of cooperative societies proved very popular, the quick uptake aided by the simultaneous payment of war damage compensation for merchant capital. Within five years an entrepreneurial fervour had seized the island—a 'copra age'—and yet, by the early 1960s, many cooperative societies on the island had failed due to poor management and supervision by the Registrar, losses through credit sales, theft by employees and considerable competition from Chinese traders. However, cooperatives also provided the people of New Hanover with experience in the cash economy, a measure of business proficiency, and an understanding of one form of organisational structure capable of harnessing village resources for singular socioeconomic action. On New Hanover, the failure of the cooperatives fuelled anti-Australian sentiment, and provided the stimulus for an emerging protest movement. This local organisation, the Tutukuvul Isukal Association adopted many of the positive practices learnt during the cooperative period;

it was an independent, economically focussed, communal-based and firmly anti-Australian organisation. It not only provided material and cultural independence but proved to be an agrarian protest or micro-nationalist movement with a power base capable, for a short while, of challenging the power of the state.[25]

The Australian postwar ambition for TPNG was an amalgamation of humanitarian intent, security for Australia and ensuring a stable, non-threatening colony to the north. This book has explored the broad outline of Australian colonial ambition, one which espoused political and economic autonomy for the Indigenous population but was undermined by a lack of resources on the ground and anxiety over the independent actions of local people. Papua and New Guineans during the Ward–Hasluck era played no part in the development of policy. Furthermore, during the 1950s, Australia largely ignored accumulated colonial experience from other parts of the world and pressed forward with a gradualist program of progressive change. Instead, the Hasluck Administration instituted a 'demand-driven' development policy for TPNG, a form of hierarchical pyramid which was expected to develop the needs and wants of local people and progressively prepare them for the ultimate attainment of self-government. On the ground, local people were expected to remain in their villages where the government targeted policy at improving socioeconomic, political and health outcomes. This policy, in conjunction with limited education opportunities, meant that by 1963 (just 12 years before independence), there were very few Papuans or New Guineans working in responsible positions in the Territory Administration. Australia feared an Indigenous elite and actively worked against the potential for a disruptive element; policy was consistently shaped by this containment strategy, resulting in a lack of input from Papuans or New Guineans in their own territory's future. Nevertheless, in 2024, these two factors, security for Australia and encouraging stable governance in Papua New Guinea (PNG), remain the most influential elements in Australia's relationship with PNG. These two conditions are interrelated: Australia's current aid, like the basis for the 1945 'New Deal for PNG', are premised on maintaining a strong influence over PNG society and thus, control of unstable elements to its north.

---

25   For more details see: Dorothy Billings, *Cargo cult as theater: political performance in the Pacific* (Lanham: Lexington, 2002); Brad Underhill, 'Co-operatives in Papua New Guinea' (Honours thesis, Deakin University, 2017).

Bibliography

Primary sources

National Archives of Australia

A1361 [45/2/1 Part 3]: Native Education.
A2127 [1/1]: Papers of Dudley McCarthy—Miscellaneous papers UN Council.
A452 [1957/2748]: Native labour from Highlands.
A452 [1958/2917]: Copra Production 1958.
A452 [1959/5650]: Native Labour 1945–7.
A452 [1959/5851]: Native labour policy 1945–56.
A452 [1959/5852]: Native labour 1955–60.
A452 [1961/25]: Native labour 1960–61.
A452 [1960/8266]: Advancement in Native Agriculture 1950–9.
A452 [1960/8272]: Education and advancement of Native women.
A518 [A813/1/4 Part 3]: Copra Production-General 1948–57.
A518 [AM927/4]: Agricultural village-rice production 1952–7.
A518 [B58/3/1]: Commodities Cocoa–Research 1951–54.
A518 [C2/1/1]: Advancement of native agriculture 1954–6.
A518 [D56/3/1 Part 2]: Copra Stabilisation fund 1949–56.
A518 [EL840/1/4]: Co-operative reports 1955–7.
A518 [E840/1/4 Part 1]: Native Cooperative movement 1945–50.
A518 [E840/1/4/ Part 2]: Native Cooperative movement 1951–55.
A518 [V840/1/4 Part 1]: Establishment cooperatives 1950–1.
A52/7 [349/95]: Survey of Legal systems of TPNG.
A5954 [603/4]: Civil Administration of Papua and New Guinea.
A989 [1943/735/144/3]: Australia- Internal External Territories-General.
A989 [1944/655/22]: Pacific—Australian Territories—ANGAU.

A989 [1944/735/144/6]: Civil Administration 1944.
B213 [3/2]: Native Labour: 1945–51.
CP637/1 [21]: Information for Minister for External Territories.
CP637/1 [30]: Director DASF to Conference of District Offices.
CP637/1 [44]: Reconstruction Policy and Post-War Planning.
M1775 [2]: New Guinea Speeches, articles and notes.
M1776 [Volume 1]: Instructions to Department 4/6/51 to 30/6/52.
M2101 [1]: Mandated Territory of New Guinea, *Report of a Commission appointed to inquire into the matter of native labour in the Territory, Majority Report*.
M331 [73]: Native Economic Development, June 1956.
M331 [190]: Cooperative societies.
M331 [191]: Copra 51–53.
M335 [3]: Agriculture and Land January 1954.

National Library of Australia

MS2396: Papers of Edward John Ward.
MS3762: Papers of William Cottrell-Dormer.
MS5581: Papers of J.K. McCarthy.
MS5700: Papers of William Douglass Forsyth.
MS6747: Papers of David Maxwell Fenbury.
MS8254: Papers of Ian Downs.
MS8346: Papers of John Black.
MS9600: Papers of Sir Donald Cleland.

Historic Hansard

Commonwealth (Australia), House of Representatives, *Parliamentary debates*, 1945–1959. Accessed at: historichansard.net/.

National Archives of Papua New Guinea

Accession 496: Patrol Reports. National Archives of Papua New Guinea. Accessed at: library.ucsd.edu/dc/collection/bb30391860.
Box 869: Monthly Reports 1946–1953.
Bougainville District, Sohano, 1954–1955.
Chimbu District, Chimbu, 1954–1955 (Volumes 1–3); 1956–1957; 1957–1958.
Chimbu District, Chuave, 1953–1954.

Chimbu District, Gembogl, 1960–1961; 1963–1964.

Chimbu District, Gumine, 1962–1963; 1964–1965.

Chimbu District, Kundiawa, 1940–1950; 1950–1952; 1952–53; 1953–1954.

Milne Bay District, Gehua, 1945–1950; 1950–1953; 1953–1955 (Volume 1–3).

Milne Bay District, Milne Bay, 1956–1957.

Milne Bay District, Samarai, 1949–1953.

East Sepik District, Maprik, 1945–1953; 1953–1956; 1956–1957; 1958–1959; 1959–1960; 1960–1961; 1961–1962.

East Sepik District, Wewak, 1949–1953; 1953–1956; 1958–1959.

East Sepik District, Yangoru, 1949–1953; 1961–1962.

New Ireland District, Kavieng, 1946–1948; 1948–1949; 1949–1951; 1956–1957; 1957–1958; 1958–1959; 1959–1960; 1960–1961; 1962–1963.

New Ireland District, Taskul, 1950–1953; 1953–1954; 1955–1956; 1957–1958; 1958–1959;

Newspapers and magazines

The Courier-Mail: 1954. Accessed at: trove.nla.gov.au/search/advanced/category/newspapers?keyword=The%20Courier-Mail&date.from=1954-01-01&date.to=1955-12-31.

The Daily Telegraph: 1952. Accessed at: trove.nla.gov.au/search/advanced/category/newspapers?keyword=the%20daily%20telegraph&date.from=1952-01-01&date.to=1953-12-31.

The Herald (Melbourne): 1945. Accessed at: trove.nla.gov.au/search/advanced/category/newspapers?keyword=The%20%28Melbourne%29%20Herald&date.from=1945-01-01&date.to=1946-12-31.

The Methodist: 1947–1949. Accessed at: trove.nla.gov.au/search/advanced/category/newspapers?keyword=the%20methodist&date.from=1947-01-01&date.to=1949-12-31.

Pacific Islands Monthly: 1950–1963. Accessed at: trove.nla.gov.au/search/advanced/category/newspapers?keyword=pacific%20islands%20monthly.

Papuan Times: 1951–1954. Accessed at: trove.nla.gov.au/search/advanced/category/newspapers?keyword=papuan%20times.

Papua New Guinea Post-Courier: 1969–1982. Accessed at: trove.nla.gov.au/search/category/newspapers?keyword=Papua%20New%20Guinea%20Post-Courier.

The Sun (Sydney): 1950. Accessed at: trove.nla.gov.au/search/advanced/category/newspapers?keyword=The%20Sun%20%28Sydney%29&date.from=1950-01-01&date.to=1951-12-31.

The Sydney Morning Herald: 1952. Accessed at: trove.nla.gov.au/search/advanced/category/newspapers?keyword=Sydney%20Morning%20Herald&date.from=1952-01-01&date.to=1953-12-31.

Government publications and political speeches

'Administration of the Territory of New Guinea'. *South Pacific* 3, 2 (1948): 30–35.

Australian Government. 'Cocoa in PNG climbing to new heights'. *Australian Centre for International Agricultural Research*. Accessed 20 June 2020 at: www.aciar.gov.au/media-search/blogs/cocoa-png-climbing-new-heights.

Belshaw, Cyril S. *Economic development in South East Papua*. Port Moresby: Government Printer, 1950.

Commonwealth Department of Health. *The New Guinea nutrition survey expedition*. Sydney, 1947.

Commonwealth of Australia. 'Budget' for years 1951/52 and 1962/63, *Archive of Budgets*. Accessed 24 September 2020 at: archive.budget.gov.au/.

Department of District Services and Native Affairs. *Annual Report for the year ending June 1954*. Port Moresby: Government Printer, 1954.

——. *Milne Bay District Annual Report 1956/57*. Port Moresby: Government Printer, 1957.

Department of External Territories. *Report to the General Assembly of the United Nations on the administration of the Territory of New Guinea: From 1st July 1946, to 30th June, 1947*. Canberra: Government Printer, 1947.

——. *Report to the General Assembly of the United Nations on the administration of the Territory of New Guinea: From 1st of July, 1948 to 30th June, 1949*. Canberra: Government Printer, 1949.

——. *Report to the General Assembly of the United Nations on the administration of the Territory of New Guinea: From 1st of July, 1949 to 30th June, 1950*. Canberra: Government Printer, 1950.

——. *Territory of Papua, Annual Report for the year, 1940–41*. Canberra: Government Printer, 1941.

——. *Territory of Papua Annual Report for the period 30th October, 1945 to 30th June, 1946*. Canberra: Government Printer, 1946.

——. *Territory of Papua. Annual Report for the period 1st July, 1947 to 30th June, 1948*. Canberra: Government Printer, 1948.

Department of Native Affairs. *Annual Report of the Co-operative Section, 1st April 1959 to March 1960*. Port Moresby: Government Printer, 1961.

——. *Annual Report of the Co-operative Section, 1st April 1960 to March 1961*. Port Moresby: Government Printer, 1961.

Department of Territories. *Report to the General Assembly of the United Nations on the administration of the Territory of New Guinea: From 1st of July, 1950, to June 30th, 1951*. Port Moresby: Government Printer, 1951.

——. *Report to the General Assembly of the United Nations: From 1st of July, 1953 to 30th June, 1954*. Canberra: Government Printer, 1954.

——. *Report to the General Assembly of the United Nations on the administration of the Territory of New Guinea for Year 1962–63*. Canberra: Government Printer, 1963.

——. *Territory of Papua Annual Report for the period 1st of July, 1951, to 30th June 1952*. Canberra: Government Printer, 1952.

——. *Territory of Papua Annual Report for the period 1st of July, 1955, to 30th June 1956*. Canberra: Government Printer, 1956.

——. *Annual Report of the Territory of Papua for the period, 1st July 1962 to 30th June 1963*. Canberra: Government Printer, 1963,

Derham, David. *Report on the system for the administration of justice in the Territory of Papua New Guinea*. Canberra: The Australian National University, 1961.

Evatt, Herbert. *Foreign policy of Australia: Speeches*. Sydney: Angus and Robertson, 1945.

Hasluck, Paul. *Australian policy in Papua and New Guinea: Statement in the House of Representatives*. Canberra: Government Printer, 1960.

Howlett, Diana, R Hide, and Elspeth Young, with J Arba, H Bi and B Kaman. *Chimbu: issues in development*. Canberra: Development Studies Centre, Monograph no. 4, The Australian National University, 1976.

Poggendorff, Walter. *Visit to Papua and New Guinea: Rice production*. Canberra: Department of Territories, 1953.

Powell, Alan. *The third force: ANGUA's New Guinea War, 1942–46*. Melbourne: Oxford University Press, 2003.

Reserve Bank of Australia. Pre-decimal inflation calculator. Accessed 22 January 2020 at: www.rba.gov.au/calculator/annualPreDecimal.html.

Shand, Richard T, and W Straatmans. *Transition from subsistence: Cash crop development in Papua New Guinea*. Port Moresby: The Australian National University, 1974.

Singh, Sumar. *Cooperatives in Papua New Guinea*. Canberra: The Australian National University, 1974.

——. *A cost analysis of resettlement in the Gazelle Peninsula*. Canberra: The Australian National University, 1967.

Spate, Oskar, Cyril Belshaw, and T Swan. *Some problems of development in New Guinea* [the *Spate report*]. Canberra: The Australian National University, 1953.

Statistics Section (Department of External Territories). *Compendium of statistics for Papua New Guinea*. Canberra: Government Printer, 1969.

Territory of Papua New Guinea. *The members of the House Assembly, 1964*. Port Moresby: Department of Information and Extension Services, 1964.

Secondary sources

Books

Anderson, Benedict. *Imagined communities: reflections on the origin and spread of nationalism*. London: Verso, 2006.

Banivanua Mar, Tracey. *Decolonisation and the Pacific: Indigenous globalisation and the ends of empire*. New York: Cambridge University Press, 2016. doi.org/10.1017/cbo9781139794688.

Billings, Dorothy. *Cargo cult as theater: Political performance in the Pacific*. Lanham: Lexington, 2002.

Bolton, Geoffrey. *Paul Hasluck: A life*. Crawley: University of Western Australia Press, 2014.

Brown, Paula. *Beyond a mountain valley: The Simbu of Papua New Guinea*. Honolulu: University of Hawai'i Press, 1995. doi.org/10.1515/9780824840761.

———. *The Chimbu: A study of change in the New Guinea Highlands.* London: Routledge, 1972.

Brown, Paula, and Harold C Brookfield. *Struggle for land.* Melbourne: Oxford University Press, 1963.

Cleland, Rachel. *Papua New Guinea: Pathways to independence.* Perth: Artlook books, 1983.

Connell, John. *Papua New Guinea: The struggle for development.* Sydney: Routledge, 1997.

Cowen, Michael, and Robert W Shenton. *Doctrines of development.* London: Taylor and Francis, 1996.

Downs, Ian. *The Australian trusteeship: Papua New Guinea 1945–75.* Canberra: Australian Government Publishing Service, 1980.

Epstein, AL. Matupit: *Land, politics and change among the Tolai of New Britain.* Canberra: Australian National Univeristy Press, 1968.

Epstein, Scarlett. *Capitalism, primitive and modern.* Manchester: Manchester University Press, 1968.

Ezard, Bryan. *A grammar of Tawala: An Austronesian language of the Milne Bay Area, Papua New Guinea.* Canberra: Pacific Linguistics, Research School of Pacific and Asian Studies, The Australian National University, 1997.

Fenbury, David M. *Practice without policy: Genesis of local government in Papua New Guinea.* Canberra: The Australian National University, 1978.

Ferns, Nicholas. *Australia in the age of international development, 1945–1975: Colonial and foreign aid policy in Papua New Guinea and Southeast Asia.* Cham: Palgrave Macmillan, 2020. doi.org/10.1007/978-3-030-50228-7.

Foot, Hugh. *A start in freedom.* London: Hodder and Stoughton, 1964.

Gammage, Bill. *The sky travellers: Journeys in New Guinea 1938–1939.* Carlton: Melbourne University Press, 1998.

Griffin, James, Hank Nelson, and Stewart Firth. *Papua New Guinea, a political history.* Richmond: Heinemann Educational Australia, 1979.

Hasluck, Paul. *Mucking about.* 2nd ed. Nedlands: University of Western Australia Press, 1994.

———. *Shades of darkness: Aboriginal Affairs, 1925–65.* Melbourne: Melbourne University Press, 1988.

———. *A time for building: Australian administration in Papua and New Guinea, 1951–1963*. Carlton: Melbourne University Press, 1976.

Hodge, Joseph Morgan. *Triumph of the expert: Agrarian doctrines of development and the legacies of British colonialism*. Athens: Ohio University Press, 2007.

Howlett, Diana. *Papua New Guinea: Geography and change*. Melbourne: Thomas Nelson, 1973.

Hudson, W. *Australia and the new world order: Evatt at San Francisco, 1945*. Canberra: Australia National University Press, 1993.

James, Walter. *What were they thinking: 150 years of political thinking in Australia*. Sydney: University of New South Wales Press, 2010.

Jinks, Brian. *New Guinea government: An introduction*. Sydney: Angus and Robertson, 1971.

Kituai, August Ibrum. *My gun, my brother: The world of the Papua New Guinea Colonial Police, 1920–1960*. Honolulu: University of Hawai'i Press, 1998. doi.org/10.1515/9780824863692.

Legge, John D. *Australian colonial policy: A survey of native administration and European development in Papua*. Sydney: Australian Institute of International Affairs, 1956.

Lowe, David. *Australian between empires: The life of Percy Spender*. London: Pickering and Chatto, 2010.

MacWilliam, Scott. *Securing village life: Development in late colonial Papua New Guinea*. Canberra: ANU Press, 2013. doi.org/10.22459/SVL.05.2013.

Mair, Lucy. *Australia in New Guinea*. London: Christophers, 1948.

May, Ron. *State and society in Papua New Guinea*. Canberra: ANU ePress, 2004.

Narokobi, Bernard. *Lo bilong yumi yet = law and custom in Melanesia*. Edited by Ron Crocombe, John May and Paul Roche. Goroka: University of the South Pacific, 1989.

Porter, Robert. *Paul Hasluck: A political biography*. Nedlands: University of Western Australia Press, 1993.

Robinson, Neville K. *Villagers at war: Some Papuan New Guineans in World War II*. Canberra: Australian National University Press, 1981.

Sinclair, James. *Kiap: Australia's patrol officers in Papua New Guinea*. Sydney: Pacific Publications, 1981.

Sligo, Graeme. *The backroom boys: Alfred Conlon and Army's Directorate of Research and Civil Affairs, 1942–1946*. Newport: Big Sky Publishing, 2013.

Smith, Michael French. *Village on the edge*. Honolulu: University of Hawai'i Press, 2002.

Somare, Michael. *Sana: An autobiography of Michael Somare*. Port Moresby: Niugini Press, 1975.

Spratt, Elwyn. *Eddie Ward: Firebrand of East Sydney*. Adelaide: Rigby, 1965.

Stanner, WEH. *The South Seas in transition*. Sydney: Australasian Publishing Company, 1953.

Tudor, Judy, ed. *Pacific Islands year book and who's who*. 9th ed. Sydney: Pacific Publications, 1967.

Wedega, Alice. *Listen my country*. Sydney: Pacific Publications, 1981.

Wetherell, David. *Charles Abel and the Kwato Mission of Papua New Guinea, 1891–1975*. Carlton: Melbourne University Press, 1996.

Zevin, Alexander. *Liberalism at large: The world according to the* Economist. London: Verso, 2019.

Book chapters

Brett, Judith. 'Limited politics'. In *Paul Hasluck in Australian history: Civic personality and public life*, edited by Tom Stannage, Kay Saunders, and Richard Nile, 183–95. St Lucia: University of Queensland Press, 1999.

Fisk, Ernest. 'The economic structure'. In *New Guinea on the threshold: Aspects of social, political and economic development*, edited by Ernest Fisk, 23–43. Canberra: Australian National University Press, 1966.

Godelier, Maurice. 'Is the West the model for humankind? The Baruya of New Guinea between change and decay'. In *Pacific Islands trajectories: Five personal views*, edited by Ton Otto, 56–82. Canberra: The Australian National University, 1993.

Gray, Geoffrey G. 'Introduction'. In *Scholars at war: Australasian social scientists*, edited by Geoffrey Gray, Doug Munro, and Catherine Winters, 2–34. Canberra: ANU Press, 2012.

Haebich, Anne. 'The formative years: Paul Hasluck and Aboriginal issues during the 1930s'. In *Paul Hasluck in Australian history: Civic personality and public life*, edited by Tom Stannage, Kay Saunders, and Richard Nile, 93–105. St Lucia: University of Queensland Press, 1999.

Healy, Allan M, 'Hasluck on himself'. In *The Hasluck years: Some observations. The administration of Papua New Guinea, 1952–63*, edited by Alan Ward, Tony Voutas and Brian Jinks, 31–48. Bundoora: Latrobe University, 1977.

Jinks, Brian. 'Hasluck's inheritance: Papua New Guinea in May 1951'. In *The Hasluck years: Some observations. The administration of Papua New Guinea, 1952–63*, edited by Alan Ward, Tony Voutas and Brian Jinks, 15–30. Bundoora: Latrobe University, 1977.

Keesing, Roger M. 'A tin with the meat taken out: A bleak anthropological view of unsustainable development in the Pacific'. In *Pacific Islands trajectories: Five personal views*, edited by Ton Otto, 29–55. Canberra: The Australian National University, 1993.

Lee, David. 'The Curtin and Chifley governments: Liberal internationalism and world organisation'. In *Evatt to Evans: The Labor tradition in Australian foreign policy*, edited by David Lee and Christopher Waters, 48–61. St Leonards: Allen and Unwin, 1997.

Nelson, Hank. 'Filling in some gaps and building for a nation'. In *The Hasluck years: Some observations. The administration of Papua New Guinea, 1952–63*, edited by Alan Ward, Tony Voutas and Brian Jinks, 64–77. Bundoora: Latrobe University, 1977.

Oram, Nigel. 'Administration, development and public order'. In *Alternative strategies for Papua New Guinea*, edited by Anthony Clunies Ross and John Langmore, 1–58. Melbourne: Oxford University Press, 1973.

——. 'Canberra and Konedobu under Hasluck and the Colonial Office—A comparison'. In *The Hasluck years: Some observations. The administration of Papua New Guinea, 1952–63*, edited by Alan Ward, Tony Voutas and Brian Jinks, 78–87. Bundoora: Latrobe University, 1977.

Sack, Peter G. 'Land in PNG future'. In *Problem of choice: Land in Papua New Guinea's future*, edited by Peter G Sack, 6–10. Canberra: Australian National University Press, 1974.

Sanders, Will. 'An abiding interest and a constant approach'. In *Paul Hasluck in Australian history: Civic personality and public life*, edited by Tom Stannage, Kay Saunders, and Richard Nile, 106–18. St Lucia: University of Queensland Press, 1999.

Sinclair, James. 'Australian colonial administration of Papua New Guinea—1951–1963: A field staff point of view'. In *The Hasluck years: Some observations. The administration of Papua New Guinea, 1952–63*, edited by Alan Ward, Tony Voutas and Brian Jinks, 49–63. Bundoora: Latrobe University, 1977.

Snowden, Catherine. 'Copra cooperatives'. In *A time to plant and a time to uproot: A history of agriculture in Papua New Guinea*, edited by Donald Denoon and Catherine Snowden, 185–204. Port Moresby: Department of Primary Industry, 1979.

Voutas, Tony. 'Preface'. In *The Hasluck years: Some observations. The administration of Papua New Guinea, 1952–63*, edited by Alan Ward, Tony Voutas and Brian Jinks, 2–11. Bundoora: Latrobe University, 1977.

Waters, Christopher. 'Creating a tradition: The foreign policy of the Curtin and Chifley Governments'. In *Evatt to Evans: The Labor tradition in Australian foreign policy*, edited by David Lee and Christopher Waters, 35–47. St Leonards: Allen and Unwin, 1997.

Journal articles

Barker, John. 'Village inventions: Historical variations upon a regional theme in Uiaku, Papua New Guinea'. *Oceania* 66 (1996): 211–29. doi.org/10.1002/j.1834-4461.1996.tb02552.x.

Bashkow, Ira. 'The cultural and historical openness of Bernard Narokobi's "Melanesian Way"'. *Journal of Pacific History* 55, no. 2 (2020): 187–219. doi.org/10.1080/00223344.2020.1759410.

Bastian, Jeanette Allis. 'Reading colonial records through an archival lens: The provenance of place, space and creation'. *Archival Science* 6 (2006): 267–84. doi.org/10.1007/s10502-006-9019-1.

Beckett, J and Geoffrey Gray. 'Hogbin, Herbert Ian Priestley (1904–1989)'. *Australian Dictionary of Biography*, National Centre of Biography, The Australian National University. Published first in hardcopy 2007. Accessed 21 December 2021 at: adb.anu.edu.au/biography/hogbin-herbert-ian-priestley-12644/text22783.

Belshaw, Cyril. 'Native administration in South-Eastern Papua'. *Australian Journal of International Affairs* 5 (1951): 106–115. doi.org/10.1080/10357715108443774.

——. 'In search of wealth: A study of the emergence of commercial operations in the Melanesian society of Southeastern Papua'. *American Anthropologist* 57 (1955): 1–84. doi.org/10.1525/aa.1956.58.2.02a00350.

Brison, Karen. 'Community and prosperity: Social movements among the Kwanga of Papua New Guinea'. *The Contemporary Pacific* 3 (1991): 325–55.

Brookfield, Harold C. 'Native employment within the New Guinea Highlands'. *The Journal of Polynesian Society* 70 (1961): 300–13.

——. 'Population distribution and labour migration in New Guinea'. *Australian Geographer* 7 (1960): 233–42. doi.org/10.1080/00049186008702352.

——. 'Two population problem areas in Papua–New Guinea'. *South Pacific* 9 (1959): 133–37.

Brown, Paula. 'Chimbu leadership before provincial government'. *Journal of Pacific History* 14 (1979): 100–17. doi.org/10.1080/00223347908572368.

Carnell, Ian. 'Fry, Thomas Penberthy (1904–1952)'. *Australian Dictionary of Biography*, National Centre of Biography, The Australian National University. Published first in hardcopy 1996. Accessed 21 December 2021 at: adb.anu.edu.au/biography/fry-thomas-penberthy-10257/text18141.

Cotton, James. 'The Institute's seventieth volume: The journal, its origins and its engagement with foreign policy debate'. *Australian Journal of International Affairs* 70, no. 5 (2016): 471–83. doi.org/10.1080/10357718.2016.1167836.

Dickson-Waiko, Anne. 'Women, nation and decolonisation in Papua New Guinea'. *Journal of Pacific History* 48 (2013): 177–93. doi.org/10.1080/00223344.2013.802844.

Douglas, Bronwen. 'Encounters with the enemy? Academic readings of missionary narratives on Melanesians'. *Comparative Studies in Society and History* 43 (2001): 37–64. doi.org/10.1017/s0010417501003577.

——. 'Introduction: Fracturing boundaries of time and place in Melanesian anthropology'. *Oceania* 66 (1996): 177–88. doi.org/10.1002/j.1834-4461.1996.tb02550.x.

Hasluck, Paul. 'The economic development of Papua and New Guinea'. *Australian Outlook: The Australian Journal of International Affairs* 16 (1962): 5–18. doi.org/10.1080/10357716208444101.

——. 'A policy for New Guinea'. *South Pacific* 5, no. 11 (January 1952): 225–27.

Hawksley, Charles. 'Constructing hegemony: Colonial rule and colonial legitimacy in the Eastern Highlands of Papua New Guinea'. *ReThinking Marxism* 19 (2007): 195–207. doi.org/10.1080/08935690701219025.

Hogbin, Herbert Ian. 'Local government for New Guinea'. *Oceania* 17 (1946): 38–65. doi.org/10.1002/j.1834-4461.1946.tb00142.x.

Holland, EM. 'Leprosy in New Guinea'. *International Journal of Leprosy* 4 (1936): 171–76.

Leifer, Michael. 'Australia, trusteeship and New Guinea'. *Pacific Affairs* 36, no. 3 (1963): 250–64. doi.org/10.2307/2754350.

MacWilliam, Scott. 'Anti-conservatism: Paul Hasluck and liberal development in Papua New Guinea'. *Australian Journal of Politics and History* 65 (2019): 83–99. doi.org/10.1111/ajph.12535.

McAuley, James. 'Defence and development in Australian New Guinea'. *Pacific Affairs* 23 (1950): 371–80. doi.org/10.2307/2752744.

——. 'Paradoxes of development in the South Pacific'. *Pacific Affairs* 27 (1954): 138–49. doi.org/10.2307/2753623.

Mugambwa, John. 'The saga of the co-operative movement in Papua New Guinea', *Journal of South Pacific Law* 9, no. 1 (2005).

Murray, JK, 'In Retrospect—Papua–New Guinea 1945–1949 and Territory of Papua and New Guinea 1949–1952'. *Australian Journal of Politics and History* 14 (1968): 320–41. doi.org/10.1111/j.1467-8497.1968.tb00711.x.

Nilles, John. 'The Kuman of the Chimbu Region, Central Highlands, New Guinea'. *Oceania* 21 (1950): 25–65. doi.org/10.1002/j.1834-4461.1950.tb00171.x.

Parker, RS, 'Economics before politics—A colonial phantasy'. *Australian Journal of Politics and History* 17 (1971): 202–14. doi.org/10.1111/j.1467-8497.1971.tb00837.x.

Schram, Ryan. 'The tribe next door: The New Guinea Highlands in a postwar Papuan newspaper'. *The Australian Journal of Anthropology* 30 (2019): 18–34. doi.org/10.1111/taja.12301.

Simpson, Gerry. 'The Great Powers, sovereign equality and the making of the United Nations Charter'. *Australian Year Book of International Law* 21: 133. doi.org/10.22145/aybil.21.8.

Spate, Oskar. 'The rice problem in New Guinea'. *South Pacific* 7 (1953): 731–36.

Stent, WR. 'An interpretation of a cargo cult'. *Oceania* 47 (1977): 187–219. doi.org/10.1002/j.1834-4461.1977.tb01287.x.

Stoler, Ann Laura. 'Colonial archives and the arts of governance'. *Archival Science* 2 (2002): 87–109. doi.org/10.1007/bf02435632.

Terrell, John Edward. 'Language, ethnicity, and historic material culture on the Sepik Coast'. *Fieldiana Anthropology* 42 (2011): 5–19. doi.org/10.3158/0071-4739-42.1.5.

Underhill, Brad. 'Cooperatives and political development in PNG: Colonial failure or unrecognized success?' *Journal of Pacific History* 55 (2019): 360–82. doi.org/10.1080/00223344.2019.1665461.

Ward, R Gerard. 'Contract labor recruitment from the Highlands of Papua New Guinea, 1950–1974'. *International Migration Review* 24 (1990): 273–96. doi.org/10.1177/019791839002400204.

Wetherell David, and Charlotte Carr-Gregg. 'Moral Re-armanent in Papua, 1931–42'. *Oceania* 54 (1984): 177–203. doi.org/10.1002/j.1834-4461.1984.tb02044.x.

Wright, Huntley. 'A liberal "respect for small property": Paul Hasluck and the "landless proletariat" in the Territory of Papua and New Guinea, 1951–63'. *Australian Historical Studies* 33 (2002): 55–72. doi.org/10.1080/10314610208596201.

Other published works

Coconut Research Institute. 'The long-term causes for the decline in the prices of coconut oil'. *Ceylon Coconut Quarterly* 12, no. 3–4 (1961).

Downs, Ian. 'Fenbury, David Maxwell (1916–1976)'. *Australian Dictionary of Biography*, 14th ed. Melbourne: Melbourne University Press, 1996.

Fox, Liam. 'Historical records of Australian patrol officers in Papua New Guinea documented online'. *ABCNews*, 25 August 2016. Accessed 14 August 2021 at: www.abc.net.au/news/2016-04-25/history-of-png-kiaps-documented-online/7356286.

Hassall, Graham. 'Religion and proto-nationalism: Apelis Mazakmat and "traces of mild sectarian strife" in New Ireland'. *Baha'i Library Online*, February 2001. Accessed 22 April 2019 at: bahai-library.com/hassell_apelis_majakmat_ireland.

Inglis, Ken S. *Papua New Guinea: Naming a nation*. The Academy of the Social Sciences in Australia: Annual lecture. Canberra: The Australian National University, 1974.

International Bank for Reconstruction and Investment (the World Bank). *The economic development of The Territory of Papua and New Guinea*. Canberra: Department of Territories, 1964.

Kanku, T. 'Wartime experience of Walla Gukguk, Lavongai, New Ireland Province'. In *Oral history: Institute of Papua New Guinea Studies* 10 (1982): 32–47.

Martin, Peter. 'The unemployment floor'. ABC local radio *AM* program, 23 July 1999. Accessed 1 February 2020 at: www.abc.net.au/am/stories/s38400.htm (site discontinued).

United Nations Visiting Mission to Trust Territories in the Pacific. *Report on New Guinea*. New York: UN Trusteeship Council, 1953.

United Nations Visiting Mission to Trust Territories in the Pacific. *Report on New Guinea*. New York: UN Trusteeship Council, 1956.

United Nations Visiting Mission to Trust Territories in the Pacific. *Report on New Guinea*. New York: UN Trusteeship Council, 1962.

United States Department of Agriculture. 'The fats and oils situation'. *Agricultural Marketing Service*, 20 August 1959. Accessed 1 December 2023 at: downloads.usda.library.cornell.edu/usda-esmis/files/3n203z084/g445ch260/cz30pw98t/FATSANDOILSSITUATION-05-09-1980.pdf.

United States Navy Department. *Building the Navy's bases in World War II*. Washington DC: US Government Printing Office, 1947.

Unpublished theses

Allen, Bryant James. 'Information flow and innovation diffusion in the East Sepik District, Papua New Guinea'. PhD thesis, The Australian National University, 1976.

Curtain, Richard. 'Dual dependence and Sepik labour migration'. PhD thesis, The Australian National University, 1980.

Godbold, Kim. 'Didiman: Australian Agricultural Extension Officers in the Territory of Papua and New Guinea, 1945–75'. PhD thesis, Queensland University of Technology, 2010.

Hassall, Graham. 'Religion and nation-state formation in Melanesia: 1945 to independence'. PhD thesis, The Australian National University, 1989.

Healy, Allan M. 'Native administration and local government in Papua, 1880–1960'. PhD thesis, The Australian National University, 1962.

Jinks, Brian. 'Policy, planning and administration in Papua New Guinea, 1942–1952: With special reference to the role of Colonel J.K. Murray'. PhD thesis, University of Sydney, 1975.

Longgar, William. 'Towards a theology of land for the New Guinea Islands'. PhD thesis, Asbury Theological Seminary, 2006.

Nason, Patrick. 'Sounding sovereignty: The politics of presence in the Bismarck Archipelago'. PhD thesis, Columbia University, 2018.

Reynolds, Wayne. 'H.V. Evatt: The imperial connection and the quest for Australian security, 1941–1945'. PhD thesis, Newcastle University, 1985.

Rimoldi, Maxwell. 'The Hahalis Welfare Society of Buka'. PhD thesis, The Australian National University, 1971. Available at: openresearch-repository.anu.edu.au/items/3f163ed0-480f-4686-8af1-4020c761ecec.

Standish, B, 'Simbu Paths to Power: political change and cultural continuity'. PhD thesis, The Australian National University, 1992.

Timms, Wendy. 'The post World War Two colonial project and Australian planters in Papua New Guinea: The search for relevance in the colonial twilight'. PhD thesis, The Australian National University, 1996.

Underhill, Brad. 'Co-operatives in Papua New Guinea'. Honours thesis, Deakin University, 2017.

Weir, Christine. 'Education for citizenship or tool of evangelism? All Saints Anglican School, Labasa, 1952–1970'. PhD thesis, The Australian National University, 2005.

Wright, Huntley. 'State practice and rural smallholder production: Late-colonialism and the agrarian doctrine in Papua New Guinea, 1942–1969'. PhD thesis, Massey University, 1999.

www.ingramcontent.com/pod-product-compliance
Lightning Source LLC
Chambersburg PA
CBHW051557230426
43668CB00013B/1879